A Practical Guide
to UNIX™ System V

A Practical Guide
to UNIX System V

Mark G. Sobell

The Benjamin/Cummings Publishing Company, Inc.
Menlo Park, California ● Reading, Massachusetts ● Don Mills,
Ontario ● Wokingham, U.K. ● Amsterdam ● Sydney ● Singapore ●
Tokyo ● Mexico City ● Bogota ● Santiago ● San Juan

Sponsoring Editor: Alan Apt
Production Supervisor: Larry Olsen
Copy Editor: Rhoda Simmons
Illustrator: David Fields

This book was typeset by the author using the tools of the UNIX System. Drafts were
printed on a Xerox 2700 laser printer using xroff, which is device independent troff plus
Image Network Inc.'s proprietary post-processor. Production simulation of typeset output
was generated by Image Network's simulation program and output on a 2700 laser printer.
The book was set using Century Schoolbook and Geneva font families on an Autologic
APS-5 phototypesetter using device independent troff and Image Network's device driver.

Library of Congress Cataloging in Publication Data

Sobell, Mark G.
      A practical guide to UNIX System V.

      Includes index.
        1. UNIX (Computer operating system)   I. Title.
QA76.76.063S6   1985   001.64'2   85-7698
ISBN 0-8053-8915-6

EFGHIJ-AL-8987

The Benjamin/Cummings Publishing Company, Inc.
2727 Sand Hill Road
Menlo Park, California 94025

for Laura

PREFACE

A Practical Guide to UNIX System V is intended for people with some computer experience but little or no experience with the UNIX system. However, more experienced UNIX system users will find the later chapters and Part II to be useful sources of information on such subjects as Shell programming and system administration. This book is *practical* because it uses tutorial examples that show you what you will see on your terminal screen each step of the way. It is a *guide* because it takes you from logging on your system (Chapter 2) through writing complex Shell programs (Chapters 8 and 9) to system administration (Chapter 10). Part II is a *reference guide* to 64 UNIX utilities.

This book is about UNIX System V, Release 2, and covers the important new features of System V, including:

at	new utility for delayed execution (page 328)
grep	new options (page 414)
lp	new printer spooler (pages 45 and 422)
mailx	Berkeley-like electronic mail (page 437)
passwd	new options and features (pages 23 and 296)
shl	job control (pages 238 and 491)
pg	new utility for viewing a file (page 465)
sort	new options (page 495)
vi	Berkeley UNIX editor (page 27 and Chapter 6)
who	new options (page 537)
file structure	changes to the file structure (page 304)
Shell functions	new Shell feature (page 240)
Shell variables	additional Shell variables (page 202)

A Practical Guide to UNIX System V shows you how to use your UNIX system from your terminal. Part I comprises the first ten chapters, which contain step-by-step tutorials covering the most important aspects of the UNIX operating system. (If you have used a UNIX system before, you may want to skim over Chapters 2 and 3.) Part II offers a comprehensive, detailed reference to the major UNIX utility programs, with numerous examples. If you are already familiar with the UNIX system, this part of the book will be a valuable, easy-to-use reference. If you are not an experienced user, you will find Part II a useful supplement while you are mastering the tutorials in Part I.

Organizing Information. In Chapters 2, 3, and 4 you will learn how to create, delete, copy, move, and search for information using your system. You will also learn how to use the UNIX system file structure to organize the information you store on your computer.

Electronic Mail and Telecommunications. Chapter 3 and Part II include information on how to use the UNIX system utility programs (mail, mailx, and write) to communicate with users on your system and other systems.

Using the Shell. In Chapter 5 you will learn how to send output from a program to the printer, to your terminal, or to a file—just by changing a command. You will also see how you can combine UNIX utility programs to solve problems right from the command line.

Word Processing. Chapters 6 and 7 show you how to use the word-processing tools that are a part of your UNIX system. Chapter 6 explains the vi editor, and Chapter 7 demonstrates the use of nroff with the **mm** macros. These chapters show you how to produce professional-looking documents, including manuscripts, letters, and reports.

Shell Programming. Once you have mastered the basics of the UNIX system, you can use your knowledge to build more complex and specialized programs using the Shell programming language. Chapter 8 shows you how to use the Bourne Shell to write your own programs composed of UNIX system commands. Chapter 9 covers the C Shell. The examples in Part II also demonstrate many features of the UNIX utilities that you can use in Shell programs.

System Administration. Chapter 10 explains the inner workings of UNIX System V, Release 2. It details the responsibilities of the Superuser and explains how to bring up and shut down a UNIX system, add users to your system, back up files, set up new devices, check the integrity of a file system, and more. This chapter goes into detail about the structure of a file system and explains what administrative information is kept in which files.

Using UNIX Tools.   The UNIX System includes a group of over 200 utility programs. Part II contains extensive examples of how to use many of these utilities to solve problems without resorting to time-consuming programming in C (or another language). The example sections of awk (over 30 pages starting on page 331) and sort (page 495) use real-life examples to demonstrate how to use these utilities alone and with other utilities to generate reports, summarize data, and extract information.

Regular Expressions.   Many UNIX system utilities allow you to use regular expressions to make your job easier. The Appendix explains how to use regular expressions so that you can take advantage of some of the hidden power of your UNIX system.

Acknowledgments

This book would not have been possible without the help and support of everyone at Relational Database Systems, Inc., the developers of INFORMIX-SQL. Special thanks to Roger Sippl, Laura King, and Roy Harrington for introducing me to the UNIX system. My mother, Dr. Helen Sobell, provided invaluable comments on the manuscript at several junctures. Isaac Rabinovitch of Convergent Technologies provided a very thorough review of the system administration chapter. Howard Ensler and everyone else at Image Network made it possible for me to typeset the book.

In addition, I want to thank the following people for their critical reviews and general helpfulness during the long haul: Mike Denny of Basis, Joe DiMartino of Hewlett-Packard, John Mashey of MIPs Computer, Diane Schulz and Robert Jung of UniSoft, Inc., and Charles Whitaker of Relational Database Systems, Inc.

Many people improved the accuracy and continuity of the original manuscript; the author accepts responsibility for any remaining errors.

Finally, I must also thank the black cat without a tail who harassed me during the preparation of the manuscript and who is now sitting upstairs somewhere laughing at us mortals who work all day in front of CRTs instead of stretching out in the sun. This book is for you too, Odie.

Mark G. Sobell

BRIEF CONTENTS

PART I
UNIX SYSTEM V

PART II
THE UNIX UTILITY PROGRAMS   323

CONTENTS

4 THE FILE STRUCTURE 51

5 THE SHELL 73

6 THE vi EDITOR   99

PART II
THE UNIX UTILITY PROGRAMS 323

A Practical Guide
to UNIX™ System V

Part I
UNIX SYSTEM V

THE UNIX
OPERATING
SYSTEM

UNIX is the name of a computer operating system and its family of related utility programs. Over the past few years, the UNIX operating system has matured and gained unprecedented popularity. This chapter starts with a definition of an operating system and a discussion of some of the features that are new in System V. It continues with a brief history and overview of the UNIX system that explains why it is becoming so popular.

WHAT IS AN OPERATING SYSTEM?

An operating system is a control program for a computer. It allocates computer resources and schedules tasks. Computer resources include all the hardware: the central processing unit, system memory, disk and tape storage, printers, terminals, modems, and anything else that is connected to or inside the computer.

An operating system performs many varied functions almost simultaneously. It keeps track of filenames and where each file is located on the disk, and it monitors every keystroke on each of the terminals. Memory must be allocated so that only one task uses a given area of memory at a time. Other operating system functions include fulfilling requests made by users, running accounting programs that keep track of the use of resources, and executing backup and other maintenance utilities. An operating system schedules tasks so that the central processor is only working on one task at a given moment, although the computer may appear to be running many programs at the same time.

UNIX SYSTEM V FEATURES

The UNIX operating system was developed at Bell Laboratories in Murray Hill, New Jersey—one of the largest research facilities in the world. Since the original design and implementation of the UNIX operating system by Ken Thompson in 1969, many people have contributed to it. The most recent release and the subject of this book is UNIX System V.

System V is the culmination of the effort of many people over many years and the consolidation of many different strains of UNIX, most notably AT&T Bell Labs UNIX and the Berkeley Software Distribution (BSD) UNIX. Following is a discussion of the most important new features that you will see when you use UNIX System V. The discussion only touches the surface of what is new in System V. Many features, such as shared memory and named pipes, are beyond the scope of this book. Many others are only significant if you are familiar with previous versions of the UNIX system—these features are discussed at the appropriate places throughout the book. If UNIX is new to you, you may just want to scan this list of features and come back to it after reading the first few chapters.

The AT&T 3B20 computer runs UNIX System V. It was originally developed for use in telephone switching applications and is now available as one of the AT&T 3B line of computers. (Photograph courtesy of AT&T.)

Shell Functions

One of the most important features of the Shell (the UNIX command interpreter) is that you can use it as a programming language. Because the Shell is an interpreter, it does not compile programs you write for it but interprets them each time you load them in from the disk. Interpreting and loading programs can be time-consuming.

You can now write Shell functions that the Shell will hold in main memory so it does not have to read them from the disk each time you want to execute them. The Shell also keeps functions in an internal format so it does not have to spend as much time interpreting them. Refer to page 240 for more information on Shell functions.

Job Control

Job control allows you to work on several jobs at once, switching back and forth between them as you desire. Normally, when you start a job, it is in the foreground, so it is connected to your terminal. Using job control, you can move the job you are working with into the background so you can work on another job while the first is running. If a background job needs your attention, you can move it into the foreground so it is once again attached to your terminal.

The concept of job control was borrowed from Berkeley UNIX, although the System V implementation differs from that of Berkeley. Under System V, job control is coordinated by the Shell layer manager (shl). The name is derived from the concept of Shell *layers*, each layer running a different one of your jobs. Refer to page 238 for an example of the use of job control and to shl in Part II for more information on the Shell layer manager.

Advanced Electronic Mail

Another feature System V borrowed from Berkeley UNIX is the mailx utility. This utility enhances the features of the mail utility. It

- allows you to use an editor (such as vi) to edit a piece of electronic mail while you are composing it
- presents you with a summary of all messages waiting for you when you call it up to read your mail
- can automatically keep a copy of all electronic mail you send
- allows you to create an Alias that makes it easier to send mail to a group of people
- allows you to customize its features to suit your needs

This book describes both conventional mail (see page 41 for a tutorial) and mailx (refer to Part II).

Screen-Oriented Editor

Although the vi (visual) editor from Berkeley has been widely available for several years, it became an official part of AT&T UNIX only with the introduction of System V.

The vi editor is an advance over its predecessor, ed, because it

The Hewlett-Packard Integral Personal Computer runs HP-UX, a UNIX-derived operating system. The Integral is portable, has a built-in printer, and provides windows. (Photograph courtesy of Hewlett-Packard.)

displays a context for your editing: Where ed displayed a line at a time, vi displays a screenful of text.

This book explains how to use vi in stages, from the introduction in Chapter 2 (page 27) through "Advanced Editing Techniques" (page 127). Most of the vi coverage is in Chapter 6, which is entirely dedicated to the use of this editor.

Delayed Execution of Jobs

The new at utility lets you schedule a job to run *at* a certain time. You can tell at you want to run the job in a few hours, next week, or even on a specific date in the future. This utility allows you to schedule jobs that slow the machine down or tie up the printer so they run when your machine is not normally used (e.g., at night or on weekends).

Scrolling Through a File

The pg (page) utility displays a file on your terminal, one screenful at a time. When you finish reading what is on the screen, you ask for another screenful by pressing the RETURN key. It also has the ability to scroll backward through a file. See pg in Part II for more information.

THE HISTORY OF THE UNIX OPERATING SYSTEM

Since its inception sixteen years ago, the UNIX operating system has gone through a maturing process, bringing it to its current state, System V. When the UNIX operating system was developed, many computers still ran single jobs in a *batch* mode. Programmers fed these computers input in the form of punch (IBM) cards and didn't see the program again until the printer produced the output. Because these systems served only one user at a time, they did not take full advantage of the power and speed of the computers. Further, this work environment isolated programmers from each other. It did not make it easy to share data and programs, and it did not promote cooperation among people working on the same project.

The UNIX time-sharing system provided two major improvements over single-user, batch systems. It allowed more than one person to use the computer at the same time (the UNIX operating system is a *multiuser* operating system), and it allowed a person to communicate directly with the computer via a terminal (it is *interactive*).

The UNIX system was not the first interactive, multiuser operating system. An operating system named Multics was in use briefly at Bell Labs before the UNIX operating system was created. The Cambridge Multiple Access System had been developed in Europe, and the Compatible Time Sharing System (CTSS) had also been used for several years. The designers of the UNIX operating system took advantage of the work that had gone into these and other operating systems by combining the most desirable aspects of each of them.

The UNIX system was developed by researchers who needed a set of modern computing tools to help them with their projects. It allowed a group of people working together on a project to share selected data and programs, while keeping other information private.

This terminal screen shows a relational database management system (DBMS) displaying information about a customer and the customer's order. This DBMS was written in C for the UNIX system, enabling it to run on many different machines. A DBMS is a necessary component of a wide range of application programs. (INFORMIX screen courtesy of Relational Database Systems, Inc.)

Universities and colleges have played a major role in furthering the popularity of the UNIX operating system through the "four year effect." When the UNIX operating system became widely available in 1975, Bell Labs offered it to educational institutions at minimal cost. The schools, in turn, used it in their computer science programs, ensuring that all computer science students became familiar with it. Because the UNIX system is such an advanced development system, the students became acclimated to an optimum programming environment. As these students graduated and went into industry, they expected to work in a similarly advanced environment. As more of these students worked their way up in the commercial world, the UNIX operating system found its way into industry.

In addition to introducing its students to the UNIX operating system, the Computer Science Department of the University of California at Berkeley made significant additions and changes to it. They made so many popular changes that one version is called the Berkeley Software Distribution (BSD) of the UNIX system. System V from AT&T has adopted many of the features developed at Berkeley. In addition, many BSD features appear in UNIX systems produced by software companies that specialize in adapting the UNIX system to different computers.

It is this heritage—development in a research environment and enhancement in a university setting—that has made the UNIX operating system such a powerful software development tool.

THE UNIX SYSTEM ON MICROCOMPUTERS

In the mid-1970s minicomputers began challenging the large mainframe computers. Minicomputer manufacturers demonstrated that in many applications their products could perform the same functions as mainframe machines for much less money. Today microcomputers are challenging the minis in much the same way. Powerful 16-bit processor chips, plentiful, inexpensive memory, and lower-priced hard-disk storage have allowed manufacturers to install multiuser operating systems on microcomputers. The cost and performance of these systems are rivaling those of the minis.

WHY IS THE UNIX SYSTEM POPULAR WITH MANUFACTURERS?

Advances in hardware technology are creating the need for an operating system that can take advantage of available hardware power. CP/M™, the standard for 8-bit microcomputers, does not fill the need. Among other reasons, CP/M and its multiuser derivative MP/M™ lack file structures that can reasonably support the large number of files normally stored on a hard-disk system.

With the cost of hardware dropping, hardware manufacturers cannot afford to develop and support proprietary operating systems. In a similar manner, application-software manufacturers

The heart of a computer system: the Central Processing Unit
(CPU). This CPU contains two microprocessor chips, an
MC68000 (the large rectangular gray object) and a Z80A (just
above the MC68000). (Photograph courtesy of Cromemco, Inc.)

cannot afford to convert their products to run under many
different proprietary operating systems. Software manufacturers
have to keep the price of their product down—in line with the
price of the hardware.

Hardware manufacturers need a generic operating system that
they can easily adapt to their machines. They want to provide a
hospitable environment for third-party software. Software manufacturers need a generic operating system as a common environment for their products.

The UNIX operating system satisfies both needs. Because it
was initially designed for minicomputers, the UNIX operating system file structure takes full advantage of large, fast hard disks.
Equally important, the UNIX operating system was intended to be
a multiuser operating system—it was not modified to serve several
users as an afterthought. Finally, because the UNIX system was
originally designed as a development system, it provides an ideal
working environment for a software company.

The advent of a standard operating system legitimized the
birth of the software industry. Now software manufacturers can
afford to make one version of one product available on many
different machines. No longer does one speak of "the company
that makes the MRP package for the IBM machine" but rather

"the company that makes the MRP package for the UNIX operating system." The hardware manufacturer who offers a UNIX-based system can count on third-party software being available to run on the new machine.

IS THE UNIX SYSTEM BEING ACCEPTED?

The UNIX operating system is gaining widespread commercial acceptance. UNIX system user groups are springing up, UNIX system magazines are starting to appear, and articles on the UNIX operating system are becoming more plentiful. The UNIX operating system is available on many machines, from smaller microcomputers and minicomputers to the largest mainframes. Even non-UNIX operating systems, such as MS-DOS™, are beginning to adopt some of the traits of the UNIX system. In addition, many companies are manufacturing operating systems, such as the Cromix® system, that are very similar to the UNIX system.

HOW CAN IT RUN ON SO MANY MACHINES?

An operating system that can run on many different machines is said to be portable. About 95 percent of the UNIX operating system is written in the C programming language, and C can be portable because it is written in a higher-level, machine-independent language. (The C compiler is actually written in itself, C.)

The C Programming Language

Ken Thompson originally wrote the UNIX operating system in PDP-7 assembly language. Assembly language is a machine-dependent language—programs written in assembly language work on only one machine or, at best, one family of machines. Therefore, the original UNIX operating system could not easily be transported to run on other machines.

In order to make the UNIX system portable, Thompson developed the B programming language, a machine-independent language. Dennis Ritchie developed the C programming language by modifying B and, with Thompson, rewrote the UNIX system in

C. After this rewrite, it could more easily be transported to run on other machines.

That was the start of C. You can see in its roots some of the reasons why it is such a powerful tool. C can be used to write machine-independent programs. A program that is designed to be portable, and is written in C, can be easily moved to any computer that has a C compiler. As C and the UNIX operating system have become more popular, more machines have C compilers.

C is a modern systems language. You can write a compiler or an operating system in C. It is highly structured, but it is not necessarily a high-level language. C allows a programmer to manipulate bits and bytes, as is necessary when writing an operating system. But it also has high-level constructs that allow efficient, modular programming.

C is becoming popular for the same reasons the UNIX operating system is successful. It is portable, standard, and powerful. It has high-level features for flexibility and can still be used for systems programming. These features make it both useful and usable.

OVERVIEW OF THE UNIX SYSTEM

The UNIX operating system has many unique features. Like other operating systems, the UNIX system is a control program for computers. But it is also a well-thought-out family of utility programs (see Figure 1-1) and a set of tools that allows you to connect and use these utilities to build systems and applications. This section discusses both the common and unique features of the UNIX operating system.

Utilities

The UNIX system includes a family of several hundred utility programs. These utilities perform functions that are universally required by users. An example is sort. The sort utility puts lists (or groups of lists) in order. It can put lists in alphabetical or numerical order, order by part number, author, last name, city, ZIP code, telephone number, age, size, cost, and so forth. The sort utility is an important programming tool and is part of the standard UNIX system. Other utilities allow you to display, print, copy, search, and delete files. There are also text editing, formatting, and typesetting utilities. The man (for manual) utility provides on-line documentation of the UNIX system itself. Because the UNIX system provides these frequently used utilities, you don't have to write them. You can incorporate them in your work, allowing you to spend more of your time working on the unique aspects of your project and less time on the aspects that are common to many other projects.

The UNIX System Can Support Many Users

The UNIX operating system is a multiuser operating system. Depending on the machine being used, a UNIX system can support from one to over one hundred users, each concurrently running a different set of programs. The cost of a computer that can be used by many people at the same time is less per user than that of a computer that can only be used by a single person at a time. The cost is less because one person cannot generally use all of the resources a computer has to offer. No one can keep the printer going 24 hours a day, keep all the system memory in use, keep the disk busy reading and writing, keep the tape drives spinning, and keep the terminals busy. A multiuser operating system allows many people to use the system resources almost simultaneously. Thus, resource utilization can approach 100 percent, and the cost per user can approach zero. These are the theoretical goals of a multiuser system.

The UNIX System Can Support Many Tasks

The UNIX operating system allows you to run more than one job at a time. You can run several jobs in the background while giving all your attention to the job being displayed on your terminal. With the advent of job control in System V, you can even switch back and forth between jobs. This *multitasking* capability allows you to be more productive.

The Shell

The Shell is the utility that processes your requests. When you enter a command at a terminal, the Shell interprets the command and calls the program you want. There are two popular shells in use today, the Bourne Shell (standard System V UNIX) and the C

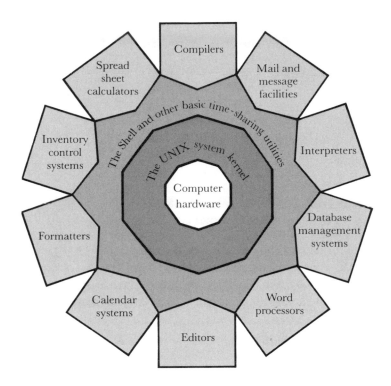

Figure 1-1
The UNIX System

Shell (BSD UNIX system). More shells are available, including menu shells that provide easy to use interfaces for computer-naive users. Because separate users can use different shells at the same time on one system, a system can appear different to different users. The choice of shells demonstrates one of the powers of the UNIX operating system: the ability to provide a customized user interface.

The Shell is also a high-level programming language. You can use this language to combine standard utility programs to build entire applications in minutes instead of weeks. Using the tools described in this book, you can even construct many useful applications right on the command line. A Shell program can, for example, allow an inexperienced user to perform a complex task easily. The Shell is one of the UNIX system tools that makes your job easier.

File Structure

A *file* is a set of data, such as a memo, report, or group of sales figures, that is stored under a name, frequently on a disk. The UNIX system file structure is designed to assist you in keeping track of large numbers of files. It uses a hierarchical or treelike data structure that allows each user to have one primary directory with as many subdirectories as required.

Directories are useful for collecting files pertaining to a particular project. In addition, the UNIX system allows users to share files by means of *links*, which can make files appear in more than one user's directory.

Security—Private and Shared Files

Like most multiuser operating systems, the UNIX system allows you to protect your data from access by other users. The UNIX system also allows you to share selected data and programs with certain users by means of a simple but effective protection scheme.

Filename Generation

Using special characters that the Shell command processor recognizes, you can construct patterns. These patterns can generate filenames that you can use to refer to one or more files whose names share a common characteristic. Commands can include a pattern when you do not know the exact filename you want to reference or when it is too tedious to specify it. You can also use a single pattern to reference many filenames.

Device-Independent Input and Output

Devices (such as a printer or terminal) and disk files all appear as files to UNIX programs. When you give the UNIX operating system a command, you can instruct it to send the output to any one of several devices or files. This diversion is called output *redirection*.

In a similar manner, a program's input that normally comes from a terminal can be redirected so that it comes from a disk file instead. Under the UNIX operating system, input and output are *device independent;* they can be redirected to or from any appropriate device.

As an example, the cat utility normally displays the contents of a file on the terminal screen. When you enter a cat command, you can cause its output to go to a disk file, or the printer, instead of the terminal.

Interprocess Communication

The UNIX system allows you to establish both pipes and filters on the command line. A *pipe* redirects the output of a program so that it becomes input to another program. A *filter* is a program designed to process a stream of input data and yield a stream of output data. Filters are often used between two pipes. A filter processes another program's output, altering it in some manner. The filter's output then becomes input to another program. Pipes and filters frequently join utilities to perform a specific task.

WHAT ARE THE LIMITATIONS OF THE UNIX SYSTEM?

The most commonly heard complaints about the UNIX operating system are that it has an unfriendly, terse, treacherous, unforgiving, and nonmnemonic user interface. These complaints are well founded, but many of the problems have been rectified by newer versions of the operating system and by some application programs. Those problems that haven't been addressed directly can usually be solved by writing a simple Shell program.

The UNIX system is called unfriendly and terse because it seems to follow the philosophy that "no news is good news." The ed editor does not prompt you for input or commands, the cp (copy) utility does not confirm that it has copied a file successfully, and the who utility does not display a banner before its list of users.

This terseness is useful because it facilitates *redirection*, allowing the output from one program to be fed into another program as its input. Thus, you can find out how many people are using the system by feeding the output of who into a utility that counts the number of lines in a file. If who displayed a banner before it displayed the list of users, you could not make this connection. (The latest version of who has an option that displays a banner and another that tells you how many people are using the system.)

In a similar manner, although it would be nice if **ed** prompted you when you were using it as an interactive editor, it would not be as useful when you wanted to feed it input from another program and have it automatically edit a group of files.

The UNIX system was designed for slow hard-copy terminals. The less a program printed out, the sooner it was done. With high-speed terminals, this is no longer true. Editors that display more information (e.g., **vi**) now run on the UNIX system with these newer high-speed terminals.

The Shell user interface can be treacherous, however. A typing mistake on a command line can easily destroy important files, and it is possible to inadvertently log off the system. You must use caution when working with a powerful operating system. If you want a foolproof system, you can use the tools the UNIX system provides to modify the Shell. Some manufacturers are producing menu-driven user interfaces that make it very difficult to make mistakes with such far-reaching consequences. The C Shell has optional built-in safeguards against many of these problems.

Due to its simplicity, the UNIX operating system has had, and still has, some limitations. In versions prior to System V, mechanisms to synchronize separate jobs were poorly implemented and there was no way to lock files—an important feature in a multiuser operating system. System V has rectified these problems. The objection that is perhaps the most serious and hard to overcome is that the UNIX operating system does not have a guaranteed hardware-interrupt response time. This prevents a standard UNIX system from being used in some real-time applications.

SUMMARY

Although the UNIX operating system has some shortcomings, most of them can be rectified using the tools that the UNIX system itself provides. The unique approach that the UNIX operating system takes to the problems of standardization and portability, its strong foothold in the professional community, its power as a development tool, and its chameleon-like user interface are causing it to emerge as the standard choice of users, hardware manufacturers, and software manufacturers.

2

GETTING STARTED

This chapter explains how to log on to, and use, your UNIX system. It discusses several important names and keyboard keys that are specific to you, your terminal, and your installation. Following a description of conventions used in this book, this chapter leads you through a brief session with your UNIX system. After showing you how to log on and off, it explains how to correct typing mistakes and abort program execution. Finally, it guides you through a short session with the vi editor and introduces other important utilities that manipulate files. With these utilities you can obtain lists of filenames, display the contents of files, and delete files.

BEFORE YOU START

The best way to learn is by doing. You can read and use Chapters 2 through 9 while you are sitting in front of a terminal. Learn about the UNIX system by running the examples in this book and by making up your own. Feel free to experiment with different commands and utilities. The worst thing that you can do is erase one of the files that you have created. Because these are only practice files, you can easily create another.

Before you log on to a UNIX system for the first time, take a couple of minutes to find out the answers to the following questions. Ask the system administrator, or someone else who is familiar with your installation.

What Is My Login Name?   This is the name that you use to identify yourself to the UNIX system. It is also the name that other users use to send you electronic mail and messages.

What Is My Password?   On systems with several users, passwords prevent others from gaining access to your files. To start with, the system administrator assigns you a password. You can change your password at any time.

Which Key Ends a Line?   Different terminals use different keys to move the cursor to the beginning of the next line. This book always refers to the key that ends a line as the **RETURN** key. Your terminal may have a **RET**, **NEWLINE**, **ENTER**, or other key. Some terminals use a key with a bent arrow on it. (The key with the bent arrow is not an **ARROW** key. **ARROW** keys have arrows on straight shafts—you will use them when you use the vi editor.) Each time this book asks you to "press the **RETURN** key" or "press **RETURN**," press the equivalent key on your terminal.

Which Is the Erase Key?   **CONTROL-H** (press **H** while holding the **CONTROL**, **CNTRL**, or **CTRL** key down) will often back up over and erase the characters you just entered, one at a time. There is usually another key, frequently #, that you can also use to erase characters. Ask your system administrator or refer to page 514 for examples of how to determine which key is your *erase* key and how to change it to one that is more convenient.

Which Is the Line Kill Key?   The standard key that deletes the entire line you are entering is **@**. This key is called the *line kill* or simply *kill* key. Refer to page 514 for examples of how to determine which key is your line kill key and how to change it.

Which Key Interrupts Execution?   There is one key that interrupts almost any program you are running. This book refers to this key as DEL. On most terminals it is labeled RUBOUT, DEL, or DELETE. You may have to hold the SHIFT key down while you press this key to make it work.

What Is the Terminfo Name for My Terminal?   A Terminfo name describes the functional characteristics of your terminal to any program that requires this information. You will need to know this name if you use vi (the visual editor). Some application programs also need this information.

Earlier versions of the UNIX system used Termcap names in place of Terminfo names. Although the two methods for specifying a terminal are different, the way you use the names is the same. If your system uses Termcap names, use the Termcap name for your terminal when this book calls for a Terminfo name.

Which Shell Will I Be Using?   The Shell interprets the commands you enter from the keyboard. You will probably be using either the Bourne Shell or the C Shell. They are similar in many respects. The Bourne Shell is part of UNIX System V, but many manufacturers also provide the C Shell. The examples in this book show the Bourne Shell but are generally applicable to both shells. Chapter 9 describes differences between the shells.

Conventions

This book uses conventions to make its explanations shorter and clearer. The following paragraphs describe these conventions.

Keys and Characters.   This book uses SMALL CAPS to show three different items.

➡ Important terminal keys, such as the SPACE bar and the RETURN, ESCAPE, and TAB keys.

▶ The characters that keys generate, such as the SPACEs generated by the SPACE bar.

▶ Terminal keys that you press with the CONTROL key, such as CONTROL-D. (Even though **D** is shown as an uppercase letter, you do not have to press the SHIFT key; enter CONTROL-D by holding the CONTROL key down and pressing **d**.)

Utility Names.   Within the text, names of utilities and common programs are printed in this typeface. Thus you will see references to the sort utility and the vi editor.

Filenames.   Within the text, all filenames appear in lowercase letters in a **bold** typeface. Examples of files that appear in the text are: **memo5**, **letter.1283**, and **reports**. Filenames can include uppercase letters, but this book avoids such filenames for clarity.

Commands.   Within the text, all commands that you can enter at the terminal are printed in a **bold** typeface. This book refers to the ls utility, or just ls, but instructs you to enter **ls −a** on the terminal.

Screens and Examples.   In the screens and examples shown throughout this book, the items that you would enter are printed in **boldface** type. In the first line of Figure 2-1, for example, the word login: is printed in a regular typeface because the UNIX system displayed it. The word **jenny** is in boldface to show that the user entered it.

Prompts and RETURNS.   All examples include the Shell prompt—the signal that the UNIX system is waiting for a command—as a dollar sign (**$**). Your prompt may differ—another common prompt is a percent sign (%). The prompt is printed in a regular typeface because you do not enter it. Do not enter the prompt on the terminal when you are experimenting with examples from this book. If you do, the examples will not work.

Examples *omit* the RETURN keystroke that you must use to execute them. An example of a command line follows.

```
$ vi memo.1204
```

To use the previous example as a model for calling the vi editor, enter **vi memo.1204** and then press the RETURN key. This method of giving examples makes the example in the book and what appears on your terminal screen the same—see the next section for a complete example.

USING THE UNIX SYSTEM

Now that you are acquainted with some of the special characters on the keyboard and the conventions this book uses, it will be easier to start using the UNIX system. This section leads you through a brief session, explaining how to log on, change your password, and log off.

Logging On

Since many people can use the UNIX operating system at the same time, it must be able to differentiate between you and other users. You must identify yourself before the UNIX system will process your requests.

```
login: jenny
password:

Welcome to UNIX!

$
```

Figure 2-1
Logging On

Figure 2-1 shows how a typical login procedure appears on a terminal screen. Your login procedure may look different. If your terminal does not have the word login: on it, check to see that the terminal is turned on, then press the RETURN key a few times. If login: still does not appear, try pressing CONTROL-Q. You can also try pressing the BREAK key and the RETURN key alternately. If these procedures don't work, check with the system administrator. (If LOGIN: appears in uppercase letters, proceed. This situation is covered shortly.)

You must end every message or command to the UNIX system by pressing the RETURN key. Pressing RETURN signals that you have completed giving an instruction and that you are ready for the operating system to execute the command or respond to the message.

The first line of Figure 2-1 shows the UNIX system login: prompt followed by the user's response. The user entered **jenny**, her login name, followed by a RETURN. Try logging on, making sure that you enter your login name exactly as it was given to you. The routine that verifies the login name and password is *case-sensitive*—it differentiates between uppercase and lowercase letters.

The second line of Figure 2-1 shows the password: prompt. If your account does not require a password, you will not see this prompt. In the example, the user *did* respond to the prompt with a password followed by a RETURN. For security, the UNIX operating system never displays a password. Enter your password in response to the password: prompt, then press RETURN. The characters you enter will not appear on the terminal screen.

You will see a message and a prompt when you successfully log on. The message, called the *message of the day*, is generally something like Welcome to UNIX! and, if you are using the Bourne Shell, the prompt is usually a dollar sign ($). The C Shell generally prompts you with a percent sign (%) or a number followed by a percent sign. Either of these prompts indicates that the system is waiting for you to give it a command.

The Uppercase LOGIN Prompt. If the login prompt appears in all uppercase letters (LOGIN:), everything you enter will also appear in uppercase letters. The UNIX system thinks you have a terminal that can only display uppercase characters. It sends uppercase characters to the terminal and translates everything you enter to lowercase for its internal use. If you are having this problem and your terminal is capable of displaying both uppercase and lowercase characters, give the following command *after you log on*. Press RETURN after you enter the command.

```
$ STTY —LCASE
$
```

Incorrect Login.   If you enter an invalid login name or password, the login utility displays the following message, after you finish entering both your login name *and* password.

```
Login  incorrect
```

This message tells you that you have entered either the login name *or* password incorrectly or that they are not valid. The message does not differentiate between an unacceptable login name and an unacceptable password. This policy discourages unauthorized people from guessing at names and passwords to gain access to the system.

After You Log On.   Once you log on, you are communicating with the command interpreter known as the Shell. The Shell plays an important part in all your communication with the UNIX operating system. When you enter a command at the terminal (in response to the Shell prompt), the Shell interprets the command and initiates the appropriate action. This action may be executing your program, calling a standard program such as a compiler or a UNIX utility program, or giving you an error message telling you that you have entered a command incorrectly.

Changing Your Password

When you first log on to a UNIX system, you will either not have a password or have a password that the system administrator assigned. In either case, it is a good idea to give yourself a new password. An optimal password is seven or eight characters long and contains a combination of numbers, uppercase letters, and lowercase letters. Don't use names or other familiar words that someone can easily guess.

Figure 2-2 shows the process of changing a password using the passwd utility. For security reasons, none of the passwords that you enter are ever displayed by this or any other utility.

```
$ passwd
Changing password for jenny
Old password:
New password:
Re—enter new password:
$
```

Figure 2-2
The passwd **Utility**

Give the command **passwd** (followed by a RETURN) in response to the Shell prompt. This command causes the Shell to execute the passwd utility. The first item passwd asks you for is your *old* password (it skips this question if you do not yet have a password). The passwd utility verifies this password to ensure that an unauthorized user is not trying to alter your password. Next, passwd requests the new password. Your new password must meet the following criteria.

● It must be at least six characters long.

● It must contain at least two letters and one number.

● It cannot be your login name, the reverse of your login name, or your login name shifted by one or more characters.

● If you are changing your password, the new password must differ from the old one by at least three characters. Changing the case of a character doesn't make it count as a different character.

After you enter your new password, passwd asks you to retype it to make sure you did not make a mistake when you entered it. If the new password is the same both times you enter it, your password is changed. If the passwords differ, it means that you made an error in one of them; passwd displays the following message.

```
They don't match; try again.
New password:
```

After you enter the new password again, passwd will ask you to reenter it.

If your password does not meet the criteria listed above, passwd displays the following message.

```
Password is too short — must be at least 6 digits.
New password:
```

Enter a password that meets the criteria in response to the New password: prompt.

When you successfully change your password, you change the way you will log on. You must always enter your password *exactly* the way you created it. If you forget your password, the system administrator can help straighten things out. Although no one can determine what your password is, the administrator can change it and tell you your new password.

Logging Off

Once you have changed your password, log off and try logging back on using your new password. You can log off by pressing CONTROL-D in response to the Shell prompt. If CONTROL-D does not work, try giving the command **logout**.

CORRECTING MISTAKES

This section explains how to correct typing and other errors you may make while you are logged on. (The techniques covered here do not work to correct errors you make while entering your name and password.) Log on to your system and try making and correcting mistakes as you read this section.

Because the Shell and most other utilities do not interpret the command line (or other text) until after you press the RETURN key, you can correct typing mistakes before you press RETURN. There are two ways to correct typing mistakes. You can erase one character at a time, or you can back up to the beginning of the command line in one step. After you press the RETURN key, it is too late to correct a mistake; you can either wait for the command to run to completion or abort execution of the command. Refer to the subsequent section on "Aborting Program Execution."

Erasing Characters

While entering characters from the keyboard, you can backspace up to and over a mistake by pressing the erase key (#) one time for each character you want to delete. (Use the erase key you inquired about at the start of this chapter in place of # throughout this book.) As the cursor moves to the left, the characters it moves over are discounted, even if they still appear on the screen. A Teletype™ or other hard-copy terminal displays a # each time you press the erase key; this type of terminal cannot backspace. The erase key backs up over as many characters as you wish. It will not, however, back up past the beginning of the line.

Deleting an Entire Line

You can delete the entire line you are entering, any time before you press RETURN, by pressing the line kill key (@). (Use the line kill key you inquired about at the start of this chapter in place of @ throughout this book.)

When you press the @ key, the cursor moves down to the next line and all the way to the left. The Shell does not give you another prompt, but it is as though the cursor is sitting just following a Shell prompt. The operating system does not remove the line with the mistake on it but ignores it. Enter the command (or other text) again, from the start.

Aborting Program Execution

Sometimes you may want to terminate a running program. A UNIX program may be performing a task that takes a long time, such as displaying the contents of a file that is several hundred pages or copying a file that is not the file you meant to copy.

To terminate program execution, press the interrupt execution key (DEL). (Use the interrupt execution key you inquired about at the start of this chapter in place of DEL throughout this book.) When you press this key, the UNIX operating system sends a terminal interrupt signal to all of your programs, including the Shell. Exactly what effect this signal has depends on the program. Some programs stop execution immediately, while others ignore the signal. Some programs take other, appropriate actions. When the Shell receives a terminal interrupt signal, it displays a prompt and waits for another command.

CREATING AND EDITING A FILE USING vi

A *file* is a collection of information that you can refer to by a *filename*. It is stored on a disk. *Text* files typically contain memos, reports, messages, program source code, lists, or manuscripts. An *editor* is a utility program that allows you to create a new text file or change a text file that already exists. There are many editors in use on UNIX systems. This section shows you how to create a file using vi (visual), a powerful (although sometimes cryptic), interactive, visually oriented text editor. It also covers elementary vi editing commands. Chapter 6 goes into detail about using more advanced vi commands.

The vi editor is not a text formatting program. It does not justify margins, center titles, or provide the features of a word processing system. You can use nroff (Chapter 7) to format the text that you edit with vi.

Specifying a Terminal

Because vi takes advantage of features that are specific to various kinds of terminals, you must tell it what type of terminal you are using. The Terminfo name for your terminal that you inquired about at the beginning this chapter communicates this information to vi.

If you are using the Bourne Shell, follow the command formats below to identify the type of terminal you are using. You can also place these commands in your **.profile** file so that the UNIX system automatically executes them each time you log on (see Chapter 4). Replace **name** with the Terminfo name for your terminal.

> **TERM = name**
> **export TERM**

Following are the actual commands you would enter if you were using a vt100 terminal.

```
$ TERM=vt100
$ export TERM
```

The C Shell requires the following command format.

setenv TERM name

You can place a command such as the one shown above in your
.login file for automatic execution (see Chapter 4). Again, replace
name with the Terminfo name for your terminal.

An Editing Session

This section describes how to call up vi, enter text, move the cursor, correct text, and exit from vi. Most vi commands take effect
immediately. Except as noted, you do not need to press RETURN
to end a vi command.

When giving vi a command, it is important that you distinguish between uppercase and lowercase letters. The vi editor
interprets the same letter as two different commands, depending
on whether you enter an uppercase or lowercase character.

Calling vi. Call vi with the following command line to create a
file named **practice**. Terminate the command line with RETURN.

```
$ vi practice
```

```
~
~
~
~
~
~
~
~
"practice" [New file]
```

Figure 2-3
Calling vi

The terminal screen will look similar to the one shown in Figure 2-3. If it doesn't, your terminal type is probably not set correctly.

If you need to set your terminal type correctly, press ESCAPE and then give the following command to get the Shell prompt back.

```
:q!
```

When you enter the colon, vi will move the cursor to the bottom line of the screen. You must press RETURN after you give this command.

Once you get the Shell prompt back, refer to the preceding section, "Specifying a Terminal."

The **practice** file is new; there is no text in it yet. The vi editor displays the following message on the status (bottom) line of the terminal to show that you are creating and editing a new file. Your system may display a different message.

```
"practice" [New file]
```

When you edit an existing file, vi displays the first few lines of the file and gives status information about the file on the status line.

Command and Input Modes.   The vi editor has two modes of operation: *Command Mode* and *Input Mode*. While vi is in Command Mode, you can give vi commands. For example, in Command Mode you can delete text or exit from vi. You can also command vi to enter the Input Mode. While in the Input Mode, vi accepts anything you enter as text and displays it on the terminal screen. You can press ESCAPE to return vi to Command Mode.

The vi editor does not normally keep you informed about which mode it is in. If you give the following command, vi will display INPUT MODE at the lower right of the screen while it is in Input Mode. (Only newer releases of System V have this feature.)

```
:set showmode
```

When you enter the colon, vi will move the cursor to the status line. Enter the command and press RETURN. Refer to page 126 for more information on **showmode**.

Entering Text. Once you have called up vi, you have to put it in Input Mode before you can enter text. Put vi in Input Mode by pressing the **i** key. If you have not set **showmode**, vi will not respond to let you know that it is in Input Mode.

If you are not sure if vi is in Input Mode, press the ESCAPE key; vi will return to Command Mode if it was in Input Mode or beep (some terminals flash) if it was already in Command Mode. You can put vi back in Input Mode by pressing the **i** key again.

While vi is in Input Mode, you can enter text by typing on the terminal. If the text does not appear on the screen as you type it, you are not in Input Mode.

Enter the sample paragraph shown in Figure 2-4, pressing the RETURN key to end each line. As you are entering text, you should prevent lines of text from wrapping around from the right side of the screen to the left by pressing the RETURN key before the cursor reaches the far right side of the screen. Also, make sure that you do not end a line with a SPACE. Some vi commands will not behave properly when they encounter a line that ends with a SPACE.

While you are using vi, you can always correct any typing mistakes you make. If you notice a mistake on the line you are entering, you can correct it before you continue. Refer to the next paragraph. You can correct other mistakes later. When you finish entering the paragraph, press the ESCAPE key to return vi to Command Mode.

Correcting Text as You Insert It. The keys that allow you to back up and correct a Shell command line (the erase and line kill keys you inquired about earlier—usually # and @) serve the same functions when vi is in Input Mode. Although vi may not remove deleted text from the screen as you back up over it, vi will remove it when you type over it or press ESCAPE.

There are two restrictions on the use of these correction keys. They will only allow you to back up over text on the line you are entering (you cannot back up to a previous line), and they will only back up over text that you just entered. As an example, assume that vi is in Input Mode—you are entering text and press the ESCAPE key to return vi to Command Mode. Then you give the **i** command to put vi back in Input Mode. Now you cannot back up over text you entered the first time you were in the Input Mode, even if the text is part of the line you are working on.

```
vi (visual) is a powerful,
interactive, visually oriented
text editor.
This section shows you how to create a
file using vi.
It also covers beginning editing commands.
Chapter 6 goes into detail about using
more advanced vi commands.
~
~
~
~
~
~
~
~
~
~
~
~
~
~                                    INPUT MODE
"practice" New file
```

Figure 2-4
Entering Text with vi

Moving the Cursor. When you are using vi, you will need to move the cursor on the screen so you can delete text, insert new text, and correct text. While vi is in Command Mode, you can use the RETURN key, the SPACE bar, and the ARROW keys to move the cursor.

Deleting Text. You can delete a single character by moving the cursor until it is over the character you want to delete and then giving the command **x**. You can delete a word by positioning the cursor on the first letter of the word and giving the command **dw** (delete word). You can delete a line of text by moving the cursor until it is anywhere on the line you want to delete and then giving the command **dd**.

The Undo Command.   If you delete a character, line, or word by mistake, give the command **u** (undo) immediately after you give the Delete command, and vi will restore the deleted text.

Inserting Additional Text.   When you want to insert new text within text that you have already entered, move the cursor so that it is on the character that will follow the new text you enter. Then give the **i** command to put vi in Input Mode, enter the new text, and press ESCAPE to return vi to Command Mode.

To enter one or more lines, position the cursor on the line above where you want the new text to go. Give the command **o** (open). The vi editor will open a blank line, put the cursor on it, and be in Input Mode. Enter the new text, ending each line with a RETURN. When you are finished entering text, press ESCAPE to return vi to Command Mode.

Correcting Text.   To correct text, use **dd**, **dw**, or **x** to remove the incorrect text. Then use **i** or **o** to insert the correct text.

For example, one way to change the word *beginning* to *elementary* in Figure 2-4 is to use the ARROW keys to move the cursor until it is on top of the *b* in *beginning.* Then give the command **dw** to delete the word *beginning.* Finally, put vi in Input Mode by giving an **i** command, enter the word *elementary* followed by a SPACE, and press ESCAPE. The word is changed and vi is in Command Mode, waiting for another command.

Ending the Editing Session.   While you are editing, vi keeps the edited text in an area called the *Work Buffer.* When you finish editing, you must write out the contents of the Work Buffer to a disk file so that the edited text will be saved and available when you next want it.

Make sure vi is in Command Mode and use the **ZZ** command (you must use uppercase **Z**s) to write your newly entered text to the disk and end the editing session. After you give the **ZZ** command, vi displays the name of the file you are editing and the number of characters in the file; then it returns control to the Shell. See Figure 2-5.

```
vi (visual) is a powerful,
interactive, visually oriented
text editor.
This section shows you how to create a
file using vi.
It also covers elementary editing commands.
Chapter 6 goes into detail about using
more advanced vi commands.
~
~
~
~
~
~
~
~
~
"practice" [New file] 8 lines, 235 characters
$
```

Figure 2-5
Exiting from vi

LISTING THE CONTENTS
OF A DIRECTORY

If you followed the preceding example, you used vi to create a file
named **practice** in your directory. After exiting from vi, you can
use the ls (list) utility to display a list of the names of the files in
your directory. The first command in Figure 2-6 shows ls listing
the name of the **practice** file.

DISPLAYING THE CONTENTS
OF A TEXT FILE

The cat utility displays the contents of a text file. The name of
the command is derived from *catenate*, which means to join
together one after another. As Chapter 5 explains, one of cat's
functions is to join files together in this manner. Use cat by

```
$ ls
practice

$ cat practice
vi (visual) is a powerful,
interactive, visually oriented
text editor.
This section shows you how to create a
file using vi.
It also covers elementary editing commands.
Chapter 6 goes into detail about using
more advanced vi commands.

$ rm practice

$ ls

$ cat practice
cat: cannot open practice
$
```

Figure 2-6
Using ls, cat, **and** rm

entering **cat** followed by a SPACE and the name of the file that you want to display.

Figure 2-6 shows cat displaying the contents of **practice**. This figure shows the difference between the ls and cat utilities. The ls utility displays the *names* of the files in a directory, while cat displays the *contents* of a file.

If you want to view a file that is longer than one screenful, you can use the pg (page) utility in place of cat. The pg utility will stop after it displays a screenful. It waits for you to press RETURN before it displays another screenful. When pg gets to the end of the file, it displays an EOF (end of file) message and waits for you to press RETURN before returning you to the Shell. Give the command **pg practice** in place of the **cat** command in Figure 2-6 to see how pg works. (If your system doesn't have pg, see if it has more, which works similarly to the way pg works. When using more you must press the SPACE bar to view each new screenful of text. Part II describes both utilities more fully.)

DELETING A FILE

The rm (remove) utility deletes a file. Figure 2-6 shows rm deleting the **practice** file. After rm deletes the file, ls and cat show that **practice** is no longer in the directory: ls does not list its filename, and cat says it cannot open the file.

SPECIAL CHARACTERS

Special characters—those that have a special meaning to the Shell—are discussed in Chapter 5. These characters are mentioned here so that you can avoid accidentally using them as regular characters until you understand how the Shell interprets them. A list of the standard special characters follows.

>   & ; | * ? ´ " ` [ ] ( ) $ < >

In addition, {, }, %, and ! are special characters to the C Shell.

Although not considered special characters, RETURN, SPACE, and TAB also have a special meaning to the Shell. RETURN usually ends a command line and initiates execution of a command. The SPACE and TAB characters separate elements on the command line and are collectively known as *white space*.

Quoting Characters

If you need to use one of the characters that has a special meaning to the Shell as a regular character, you can *quote* it. When you quote a special character, you keep the Shell from giving it special meaning. The Shell treats a quoted special character as a regular character.

To quote a character, precede it with a backslash (\). One backslash must precede each character that you are quoting. If you are using two or more special characters, you must precede each with a backslash (e.g., ** must be entered as **). You can quote a backslash just as you would quote any other special character—by preceding it with a backslash (\\).

Another way of quoting special characters is to enclose them between single quotation marks (e.g., ´**´). You can quote many special and regular characters between a pair of single quotation

marks (e.g., ′This is a special character: >′). The regular characters remain regular, and the special characters are also interpreted
as regular characters.

You can quote the erase character (#) and the line kill character (@) (and the exclamation point in the C Shell) by preceding
any one with a backslash. Single quotation marks will not work.

SUMMARY

After reading this chapter and experimenting on your system, you
should be able to log on and use the utilities and special keys
listed below. Chapter 6 explains more about vi, and Part II has
more information on ls, rm, and cat.

- passwd changes your password.
- CONTROL-D or **logout** logs you off the system.
- The # (or another) key is the erase key. It erases a character
  on the command line.
- The @ (or another) key is the line kill key. It deletes the
  entire command line.
- The DEL (or another) key interrupts execution of the program
  you are running.
- vi creates and edits a text file.
- ls displays a list of files.
- cat displays the contents of a file.
- rm deletes a file.

3

AN INTRODUCTION
TO THE UTILITIES

UNIX utility programs allow you to work with the UNIX system and manipulate the files you create. Chapter 2 introduced the Shell, the most important UNIX utility program, and passwd, the utility that allows you to change your password. It also introduced some of the utilities that you can use to create and manipulate files: vi, ls, cat, and rm. This chapter describes utilities that allow you to find out who's logged on, communicate with other users, display system documentation, print files, and perform other useful functions.

Some of the utilities included in this chapter were chosen because you can learn to use them easily and they allow you to communicate with other people using the system. Others were chosen because they form the bases for examples in later chapters. Part II of this book covers these and other utilities more concisely and completely.

USING who TO FIND OUT WHO IS USING THE SYSTEM

The who utility displays a list of the users currently logged on. In Figure 3-1, the first column who displays shows that hls, scott, barbara, and chas are logged on. The second column shows the designation of the terminal that each person is using. The third column shows the date and time that the person logged on. To find out which terminal you are using, or to see what time you logged on, give the command **who am i**.

```
$ who
hls            console        May 22  12:48
scott          tty2           May 21  09:07
barbara        tty3           May 22  12:53
chas           tty6           May 22  10:31
$
```

Figure 3-1
The who **Utility**

The information that who displays is useful if you want to communicate with someone at your installation. If who does not show that the person is logged on, you can send that person UNIX system mail (page 41). If the person is logged on, you can also use the write utility (below) to establish communication immediately.

USING write TO SEND A MESSAGE

You can use the write utility to send a message to another user who is logged on. When the other user also uses write to send you a message, you establish two-way communication.

When you give a **write** command, it displays a banner on the other user's terminal saying that you are about to send a message. The format of a write command line is shown below.

write destination-user [terminal]

The **destination-user** is the login name of the user you want to communicate with. You can find out the login name of the users who are logged on by using the who utility (above).

If the person you want to write to is logged in on more than one terminal, you can direct write to send your message to a specific terminal by including the **terminal** designation. Replace **terminal** on your command line with the terminal designation that who displays. Do not enter the square brackets ([ ])—they just indicate that the **terminal** part of the command is optional.

To establish two-way communication with another user, you and the other user must each execute write, each specifying the other's login name as the **destination-user**. The write utility then copies text, line-by-line, from one terminal to the other. When you want to stop communicating with the other user, press CONTROL-D at the beginning of a line. CONTROL-D tells write to quit, displays EOT (end of transmission) on the other user's terminal, and returns you to the Shell. The other user must do the same.

It is helpful to establish a protocol for carrying on communication using write. Try ending each message with **o** (for *over*) and ending the transmission with **oo** (for *over and out*). This protocol gives each user time to think, and to enter a complete message, without the other user wondering if the first user is finished. Because write copies one line at a time, if you write several short lines of text rather than one long line, the other user will frequently be reassured that you're still there.

The following example shows how one side of a two-way communication using write appears to Jenny. Figure 3-2 shows Jenny initiating communication by calling the write utility and specifying alex as the **destination-user**. She enters a message, terminated by **o**, and waits for a reply.

```
$ write alex
Hi Alex, are you there? o
```

Figure 3-2
The write Utility

As soon as Alex has a chance to respond and execute write, write sends a banner to Jenny's terminal. Then, Alex sends a message indicating that he is ready to receive Jenny's message (Figure 3-3). Following the protocol that he and Jenny have established, Alex terminates his message with **o**.

```
$ write alex
Hi Alex, are you there? o
Message from alex (tty11) [Sat Jan 5 15:08]...
Yes Jenny, I'm here. o
```

Figure 3-3
The write **Utility**

At this point, Jenny and Alex can communicate back and forth. Each time one of them types a line and presses RETURN, the line appears on the other's terminal. When they are done, Jenny enters a final message terminated by **oo** and then presses CONTROL-D (as the first and only thing on a line) to sign off (see Figure 3-4). The Shell prompt appears. Then Alex signs off, and Jenny sees the EOT that results from Alex pressing CONTROL-D. Alex's final message appears after Jenny's Shell prompt. Because Jenny did not give any commands, she can display another Shell prompt by simply pressing the RETURN key.

```
$ write alex
Hi Alex, are you there? o
Message from alex (tty11) [Sat Jan 5 15:08]...
Yes Jenny, I'm here. o
.
.
Thank you, Alex — bye oo
CONTROL-D
$ Bye, Jenny oo
<EOT>
```

Figure 3-4
The write **Utility**

Throughout this communication, Alex and Jenny followed the convention of using **o** after each message. This is just a convention and is not recognized by write. You can use any convention you please, or none at all.

USING mesg TO DENY OR ACCEPT MESSAGES

If you do not want to receive messages, you can give the following command.

```
$ mesg n
$
```

After giving this command, another user cannot send you messages using write.

If Alex had given the preceding command before Jenny tried to send him a message, she would have seen the following.

```
$ write alex
Permission denied.
$
```

You can allow messages again by entering **mesg y**.

If you want to know if someone can write to you, give the command **mesg** by itself. The mesg utility will respond with a y (for yes, messages are allowed) or n (for no, messages are *not* allowed).

USING mail TO SEND AND RECEIVE ELECTRONIC MAIL

The mail utility program allows you to send and receive electronic mail. Electronic mail (or *e-mail* as it is sometimes called) is similar to post office mail except it is quicker and does not physically move your piece of correspondence from one place to another. You can use it to send and receive letters, memos, reminders, invitations, and even junk mail. It differs from post office mail in that mail only delivers mail addressed to you when you request it. Until then, the UNIX operating system keeps your mail for you and reminds you that you have mail waiting each time you log on to the system.

You can use mail to communicate with users on your system and, if your installation is part of a uucp network, with other users on a the network. (The uucp utility uses a communications network to link UNIX systems together.)

The mail utility differs from write, described on page 38. While mail allows you to send a message to a user whether or not that user is logged on to the system, write only allows you to send messages if the user is logged on and willing to receive messages.

UNIX System V, Release 2, introduced a new electronic mail utility, mailx. The mailx utility is patterned after the Berkeley UNIX electronic mail program. It is more complex than the mail utility that this section describes because it gives you more options. Refer to mailx in Part II for more information.

The UNIX operating system mail utility has two distinct functions: sending electronic mail and receiving it. The following example demonstrates these two functions. Try it on your system, replacing **alex** with your login name.

First, Alex uses mail to send himself a message.

```
$ mail alex
This is a test message that I am sending myself.
.
$
```

After he calls up mail (**mail alex**), Alex types his message. He ends each line with a RETURN and, when he is finished, enters a period on a line by itself. (Some versions of mail require a CONTROL-D at the beginning of a line to terminate the message.) The mail utility sends the mail and returns Alex to the Shell.

After a while, the UNIX operating system sends Alex a message telling him he has mail.

```
You have mail.
```

Your system may send you a similar message while you are logged on, or it may only tell you that you have mail when you first log on to the system. Whether your system displays the above message or not, your mail will be waiting for you after a few moments.

Alex uses mail to display the message he sent himself. When you call up mail without a name (just **mail**, not **mail alex**), the mail utility displays any mail that is waiting for you. After viewing his message, Alex uses a **d** command (followed by a RETURN) to delete the message. He could have just pressed RETURN without entering an explicit command, and mail would have left his mail for him to read the next time he read his mail.

```
$ mail
From alex Wed Dec 19 09:23:15 1984
This is a test message that I am sending myself.
? d
$
```

If Alex had had more mail waiting for him, mail would have displayed it after he disposed of the first piece of mail. Because he has no more mail, the mail utility returns him to the Shell. (On some systems you have to give a **q** command or press CONTROL-D to exit from mail.)

The mail utility has a built-in help feature. Enter * in response to the mail prompt (?) to get a list of other commands you can use. Also see Part II of this book for more information on mail commands.

The mail utility will tell you if you do not have any mail. If Alex checks his mail after deleting his only message, he will see the following.

```
$ mail
No mail.
$
```

You can send mail to more than one person at a time. Below, Jenny sends a reminder to alex, barbara, and hls (Helen's login name).

```
$ mail alex barbara hls
Please remember to bring your notes from our
last meeting to the meeting on 11/28 at 3:00pm
in my office.

Jenny
.
$
```

When alex, barbara, and hls each log on, the system will tell them they have mail.

If your system is part of a uucp network, you can send mail to and receive mail from users on other systems. If you have this facility, you can use it by preceding the user's name with the name of a remote system and an exclamation point. The following command line sends mail to bill on the system named bravo.

```
$ mail bravo!bill
.
.
.
```

You can mix the names of users on your system and on other systems on one command line.

```
$ mail alex bravo!bill hls
.
.
.
```

If you are using the C Shell, you must quote the exclamation point by preceding it with a backslash.

```
$ mail bravo\!bill
.
.
.
```

You can obtain a list of machine names and users that are part of your network from the system administrator.

USING cp TO COPY A FILE

The cp utility makes a copy of a file. It can copy any file, including text and executable program files. Among other uses, you can use cp to make a backup copy of a file or a copy for experimentation.

A cp command line specifies a source and destination file. The format is shown below.

cp source-file destination-file

The **source-file** is the name of the file that cp is going to copy. The **destination-file** is the name that cp assigns to the resulting copy of the file.

If the **destination-file** exists *before* you give a cp command, cp overwrites it. Because cp overwrites (and destroys the contents of) an existing **destination-file** without warning you, you must take care not to cause cp to overwrite a file that you need.

The following command line makes a copy of the file named **output**. The copy is named **outputb**.

```
$ cp output outputb
$
```

Sometimes it is useful to incorporate the date in the name of a copy of a file. In the following example, the period is part of the filename—just another character.

```
$ cp memo memo.0130
$
```

Although the date has no significance to the UNIX operating system, it can help you to find a version of a file that you saved on a certain date. It can also help you avoid overwriting existing files by providing a unique filename each day.

Chapter 4 discusses rules for naming files.

USING lp TO PRINT A FILE

So that several people or jobs can use a single printer, the UNIX system provides a means of *queuing* printer output so that only one job gets printed at a time. The lp utility places a file in the printer queue for printing. Earlier versions of the UNIX system used another utility that performed the same function, lpr. Your system may use lpr in place of lp. Either utility will send your files to the printer.

The following command line prints the file named **report**.

```
$ lp report
request id is printer_1-450 (1 file)
$
```

The lp utility displays a line of information that contains a request number each time you ask it to print a file (the lines that begin with the word request in the examples). You can use these request numbers to check on the progress of or cancel a printing job. See cancel and lpstat in Part II.

You can send more than one file to the printer with a single command line. The following command line prints three files.

```
$ lp memo letter text
request id is printer_1-451 (3 files)
$
```

USING grep TO FIND A STRING

The grep utility can search through a file to see if it contains a specified string of characters. This utility does not change the file it searches through but displays each line that contains the string.

Give the following command to see if the file **memo** contains the word disc.

```
$ grep ´disc´ memo
    .
    .
$
```

The grep utility will display each line from the file **memo** that contains the string disc. It will include words like *discover* and *indiscreet* because they contain the string you asked it to search for.

You do not need to enclose the string you are searching for in single quotation marks, but doing so doesn't change the outcome of the search and it does allow you to put SPACEs and special characters in the Search String.

The grep utility can do much more than searching for a simple string. Refer to grep in Part II and "Regular Expressions" in the Appendix for more information.

USING date TO DISPLAY THE TIME AND DATE

The date utility displays the current time and date. An example of date is shown below.

```
$ date
Wed Dec 19 09:23:30 PST 1984
$
```

USING echo TO DISPLAY TEXT ON THE TERMINAL

The echo utility copies anything you put on the command line after **echo** to the terminal. Some examples are shown in Figure 3-5.

```
$ echo Hi
Hi

$ echo This is a sentence.
This is a sentence.

$ echo Good morning.
Good morning.
$
```

Figure 3-5
The echo **Utility**

The echo utility is a good tool for learning about the Shell and other UNIX programs. Chapter 5 uses echo for learning about special characters. Chapter 8 uses it for learning about Shell variables and sending messages from a Shell program to the terminal.

USING man TO DISPLAY THE SYSTEM MANUAL

The man (manual) utility displays pages from the system documentation on the terminal. This documentation is useful if you know what utility you want to use but have forgotten exactly how it works.

To find out more about a utility, give the command **man** followed by the name of the utility. The following command displays information about the who utility. If the information man displays runs off the top of the screen, give the second form of the command. This command uses a pipe (the | symbol—pipes are explained in Chapter 5) and pg to cause the output to pause after each screenful.

```
$ man who
```

or

```
$ man who | pg
```

You can use the command **man man** (or **man man | pg**) to find out more about the man utility.

Using one of the two formats for man shown above, man displays a prompt at the bottom of the screen after each screenful of text and waits for you to request another screenful. When you press the SPACE bar (or RETURN if you are using the second form of the command), man displays a new screenful of information. Pressing DEL once or twice stops man and displays a Shell prompt.

USING sort TO DISPLAY A FILE IN ORDER

The sort utility displays the contents of a file in order by lines. If you have a file named **days** that contains the names of each of the days of the week on a separate line, sort will display the file in alphabetical order as shown in Figure 3-6.

```
$ cat days
Monday
Tuesday
Wednesday
Thursday
Friday
Saturday
Sunday

$ sort days
Friday
Monday
Saturday
Sunday
Thursday
Tuesday
Wednesday
$
```

Figure 3-6
The sort Utility

The sort utility is useful for putting lists in order. Within certain limits, sort can be used to order a list of numbers. Part II describes the features and limitations of sort.

SUMMARY

Below is a list of the utilities that have been introduced up to this point. Because you will be using these utilities frequently, and because they are integral to the following chapters, it is important that you become comfortable using them. The particular editor that you use is not important. If your installation has an editor that you prefer to vi, learn to use that editor.

- cat displays the contents of a file on the terminal.
- cp makes a copy of a file.
- date displays the time, day, and date.
- echo displays a line of text on the terminal.
- lp prints a text file.
- ls displays a list of files.
- mail sends or receives mail.
- mesg permits or denies messages sent by write.
- man displays information on utilities.
- passwd changes your password.
- rm deletes a file.
- sort puts a file in order by lines.
- vi creates or edits a text file.
- who displays a list of who is logged on.
- write sends a message to another user who is logged on.

4

THE FILE
STRUCTURE

This chapter discusses the organization and terminology of the file structure of the UNIX system. It defines plain and directory files and explains the rules for naming them. It shows how to create and delete directories, move through the file structure, and use pathnames to access files in different directories. This chapter also covers file access permissions that allow you to share selected files with other users. The final section describes links, which can make a single file appear in more than one directory.

THE HIERARCHICAL FILE STRUCTURE

A *hierarchical* structure frequently takes the shape of a pyramid. One example of this type of structure is found by tracing a family's lineage: A couple has a child; that child may have several children; and each of those children may have more children. This hierarchical structure, shown in Figure 4-1, is called a family tree.

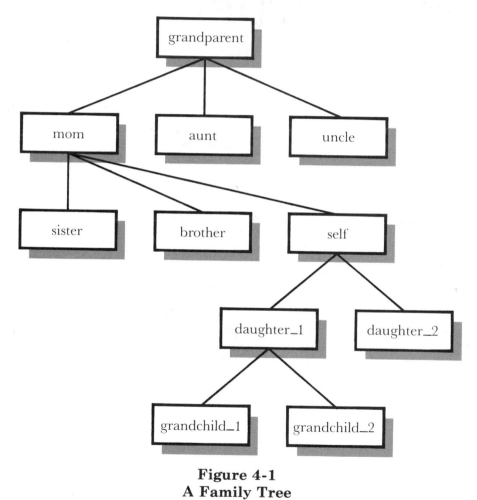

Figure 4-1
A Family Tree

Like the family tree it resembles, the UNIX system file structure is also called a *tree*. It is composed of a set of connected files. This structure allows you to organize files so that you can easily find any particular one. In a standard UNIX system, you start with one directory. From this single directory, you can make as many subdirectories as you like, dividing subdirectories into additional subdirectories. In this manner, you can continue expanding the structure to any level according to your needs.

Using the Hierarchical File Structure

Typically, each subdirectory is dedicated to a single subject. The subject dictates whether a subdirectory should be further subdivided. For instance, Figure 4-2 shows a secretary's subdirectory named **correspondence**. This directory contains three subdirectories: **business, memos**, and **personal**. The **business** directory contains files that store each letter the secretary types. If there are many letters going to one client (as is the case with **milk__co**), a subdirectory can be dedicated to that client.

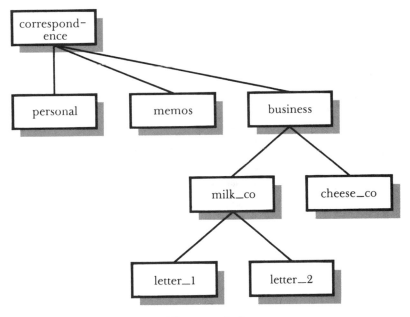

Figure 4-2
The Directory of a Secretary

One of the strengths of the UNIX system file structure is its ability to adapt to different users' needs. You can take advantage of this strength by strategically organizing your files so they are most convenient and useful for you.

DIRECTORY AND PLAIN FILES

The tree representing the file structure is usually pictured upside down, with its *root* at the top. Figure 4-3 shows that the tree "grows" downward from the root, with paths connecting the root and other files. At the end of each path is a plain file or a directory file. *Plain files*, frequently just called *files*, are at the ends of paths that cannot support other paths. *Directory files*, usually referred to as *directories*, are the points that other paths *can* branch off from. (The illustration shows some empty directory files.) When you refer to the tree, *up* is toward the root and *down* is away from the root. Files directly connected by a path are called parents (closer to the root) and children (farther from the root).

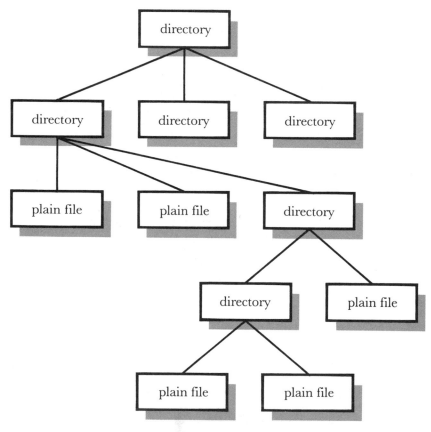

Figure 4-3
Directory and Plain Files

Filenames

Every file has a *filename*. A filename is composed of from 1 to 14 characters. Although you can use almost any character in a filename, you will avoid confusion if you choose characters from the following list.

- uppercase letters [A-Z]
- lowercase letters [a-z]
- numbers [0-9]
- underscore [_]
- period [.]
- comma [,]

The only exception is the root directory, which is always named / and referred to by this single character. No other file can use this name.

Like children of one parent, no two files in the same directory can have the same name. Files in different directories, like children of different parents, can have the same name.

The filenames you choose should mean something. Too often, a directory is filled with important files with names such as **foobar**, **wombat**, and **junk**. A meaningless name won't help you recall what you stored in a file. The following filenames conform to the required syntax *and* convey information about the contents of the file.

- correspondence
- january
- davis
- reports
- 1985
- acct_payable

Although they are not used in examples in this book, you can use uppercase letters within filenames. The UNIX operating system is, however, case-sensitive and considers files named **JANU-ARY**, **January**, and **january** as three distinct files.

Filename Extensions. In the following filenames, filename extensions help describe the contents of the file. A *filename extension* is the part of the filename following an embedded period. Some programs, such as the C programming language compiler, depend on specific filename extensions. In most cases, however, filename extensions are optional.

compute.c	a C programming language source file
compute.o	the object code for the program
compute	the same program as an executable file
memo.0410	a text file

Use extensions freely to make filenames easy to understand. If you like, you can use several periods within the same filename (for example, **notes.4.10.83**).

Invisible Filenames. A filename beginning with a period is called an *invisible filename* because ls does not normally display it. The command **ls −a** displays *all* filenames, even invisible ones. Startup files are usually invisible so that they do not clutter a directory (see page 58). Two special invisible entries, a single and double period (. and ..), appear in every directory. These entries are discussed on page 60.

Absolute Pathnames

As shown in Figure 4-4, every file has a *pathname*. You can build the pathname of a file by tracing a path from the root directory, through all the intermediate directories, to the file. String all the filenames in the path together, separating them with slashes (/) and preceding them with the name of the root directory (/).

This path of filenames is called an *absolute pathname* because it locates a file absolutely, tracing a path from the root directory to the file. The part of a pathname following the final slash is called a *simple filename*, or just a filename.

DIRECTORIES

This section covers creating, deleting, and using directories. It explains the concepts of the *working* and *home directories* and their importance in *relative pathnames*.

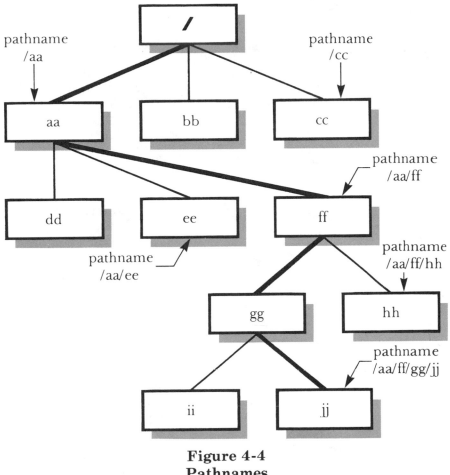

Figure 4-4
Pathnames

The Working Directory

While you are logged on to a UNIX system, you will always be associated with one directory or another. The directory you are associated with, or are working in, is called the *working directory*, or the *current directory*. Sometimes this association is referred to in a physical sense: "you are *in* (or *working in*) the **jenny** directory."

To access any file in the working directory, you do not need a pathname—just a simple filename. To access a file in another directory, however, you *must* use a pathname.

The pwd (print working directory) utility displays the pathname of the working directory (Figure 4-5).

Your Home Directory

When you first log on to a UNIX system, the working directory is your *home* directory. To display the absolute pathname of your home directory, use pwd just after you log on. Figure 4-5 shows Alex logging on and displaying the name of his home directory.

```
login: alex
password:

Welcome to UNIX!

$ pwd
/usr/alex
$
```

Figure 4-5
Logging On

The ls utility displays a list of the files in the working directory. Because your home directory has been the only working directory you have used, ls has always displayed a list of files in your home directory. (All the files you have created up to now are in your home directory.)

Startup Files. An important file that appears in your home directory is a *startup file*. It gives the operating system specific information about you as a user. Frequently, it tells the Shell what kind of terminal you are using and executes the stty utility to establish your line kill and erase keys.

Either you or the system administrator can put a startup file, containing Shell commands, in your home directory. The Shell executes the commands in this file each time you log on. With the Bourne Shell (standard UNIX System V), the filename must be **.profile**. Use **.login** with the C Shell. Because the startup files have invisible filenames, you must use the **ls −a** command if you want to see if either of these files is in your home directory.

For more information on startup files and other files the Shell automatically executes, refer to Chapters 8 and 9.

Creating a Directory

The mkdir (make directory) utility creates a directory file. It does *not* change your association with the working directory. The *argument* (the word following the name of the command) you use with mkdir becomes the pathname of the new directory.

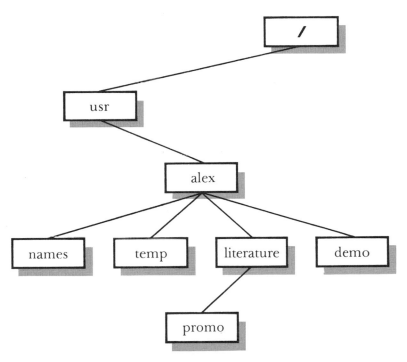

Figure 4-6
The File Structure Used in the Examples

In Figure 4-7, mkdir creates a directory named **literature** as a child of the working directory. When you use mkdir, enter the absolute pathname of *your* home directory in place of **/usr/alex**.

The ls utility verifies the presence of the new directory and shows the files Alex has been working with: **names, temp,** and **practice**.

By itself, ls does not distinguish between a directory file and a plain file. With the **−p** option, ls displays a slash after the name of each directory file. When you call ls with an argument that is the name of a directory, ls lists the contents of the directory. If there are no files in the directory, ls does not list anything.

```
$ mkdir /usr/alex/literature

$ ls
literature
names
practice
temp

$ ls —p
literature/
names
practice
temp

$ ls literature
$
```

Figure 4-7
The mkdir **Utility**

The . and .. Directory Entries. The mkdir utility automatically puts two entries in every directory you create. They are a single and double period, representing the directory itself and the parent directory, respectively. These entries are invisible because their filenames begin with periods.

Because mkdir automatically places these entries in every directory, you can rely on their presence. The . is synonymous with the pathname of the working directory and can be used in its place; .. is synonymous with the pathname of the parent of the working directory.

Figure 4-8 lists the contents of the **/usr** directory from **/usr/alex** by using .. to represent the parent directory.

Changing to Another Working Directory

The cd (change directory) utility makes another directory the working directory—it does *not* change the contents of the working directory. In this context, you can think of the working directory as a place marker. The first **cd** command in Figure 4-9 makes the **/usr/alex/literature** directory the working directory, as verified by pwd.

```
$ pwd
/usr/alex

$ ls ..
alex
barbara
bin
.
.
```

Figure 4-8
Using .. with ls

Without an argument, cd makes your home directory the working directory, as it was when you first logged on. The second cd in Figure 4-9 does not have an argument and makes Alex's home directory the working directory.

```
$ cd /usr/alex/literature
$ pwd
/usr/alex/literature

$ cd
$ pwd
/usr/alex
$
```

Figure 4-9
The pwd Utility

Deleting a Directory

The rmdir (remove directory) utility deletes a directory file. You cannot delete the working directory or a directory that contains any files. If you need to delete a directory with files in it, first delete the files (using rm) and then delete the directory. You do not have to delete the . and .. entries; rmdir removes them automatically. The following command deletes the directory that was created in Figure 4-7.

```
$ rmdir /usr/alex/literature
$
```

Relative Pathnames

A *relative pathname* traces a path from the working directory to a file. The pathname is *relative* to the working directory. Any pathname that does not begin with the root directory (/) is a relative pathname. Like absolute pathnames, relative pathnames can describe a path through many directories.

Alex could have created the **literature** directory (Figure 4-7) more easily using a relative pathname, as shown below.

```
$ pwd
/usr/alex

$ mkdir literature
$
```

The pwd command shows that Alex's home directory (**/usr/alex**) is still the working directory. The mkdir utility will display an error message if the **literature** directory already exists—you cannot have two files with the same name in one directory.

The pathname used in this example is a simple filename. A simple filename is a form of a relative pathname that specifies a file in the working directory.

The following commands show two ways to create the same directory, **promo**, a child of the **literature** directory that was just created. The first assumes that **/usr/alex** is the working directory and uses a relative pathname; the second uses an absolute pathname.

```
$ mkdir literature/promo
$
```

or

```
$ mkdir /usr/alex/literature/promo
$
```

Because the location of the file that you are accessing with a relative pathname is dependent on (relative to) the working directory, always make sure you know which is the working directory before using a relative pathname. When you use an absolute pathname, it does not matter which is the working directory.

Anywhere that a UNIX utility program requires a filename or pathname, you can use an absolute or relative pathname or a simple filename. You can use any of these types of names with cd, ls, vi, mkdir, rm, rmdir, and other UNIX utilities.

Significance of the Working Directory. Typing long pathnames is tedious and increases the chances of making mistakes. You can choose a working directory for any particular task to reduce the need for long pathnames. Your choice of a working directory does not allow you to do anything you could not do otherwise—it just makes some operations easier.

Files that are children of the working directory can be referenced by simple filenames. Grandchildren of the working directory can be referenced by relative pathnames, composed of two filenames separated by a slash. When you manipulate files in a large directory structure, short relative pathnames can save much time and aggravation. If you choose a working directory that contains the files used most for a particular task, you will need to use fewer long, cumbersome pathnames.

Using Pathnames

The following example assumes that **/usr/alex** is the working directory. It uses a relative pathname to copy the file **letter** to the **/usr/alex/literature/promo** directory. The copy of the file has the simple filename **letter.0610**. Use vi to create a file named **letter** if you want to experiment with the following examples.

```
$ cp letter literature/promo/letter.0610
$
```

Assuming that Alex has not changed to another working directory, the following command allows him to edit the copy of the file he just made.

```
$ vi literature/promo/letter.0610
.
.
.
```

If Alex does not want to use a long pathname to specify the file, he can use cd to make the **promo** directory the working directory before calling vi.

```
$ cd literature/promo

$ pwd
/usr/alex/literature/promo

$ vi letter.0610
.
.
.
```

If Alex wants to make the parent of the working directory (**/usr/alex/literature**) the new working directory, he can give the following command, which takes advantage of the .. directory entry.

```
$ cd ..

$ pwd
/usr/alex/literature
$
```

Important Standard Directories and Files

The UNIX system file structure is usually set up according to a convention. Aspects of this convention may vary from installation to installation. Figure 4-10 shows the usual locations of some important directories and files.

/ (root)   The root directory is present in all UNIX system file structures. It is the ancestor of all files in the file system.

/usr   Each user's home directory is typically one of many subdirectories of **/usr**, although many systems use other conventions. Using this scheme, the absolute pathname of Jenny's home directory is **/usr/jenny**.

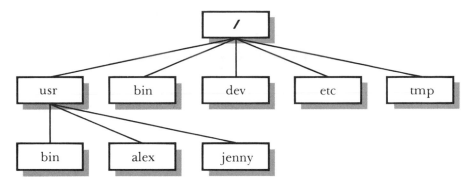

Figure 4-10
The Standard UNIX System File Structure

/bin and /usr/bin   These directories contain the standard UNIX utility programs. By convention, **/bin** contains the most frequently used standard utilities including all those necessary to bring the system up, while **/usr/bin** contains more obscure utilities as well as programs that are specific to an installation.

/dev   All files that represent peripheral devices such as terminals and printers are kept in this directory.

/etc   Administrative and configuration programs and other system files are kept here. The most useful is the **passwd** file, containing a list of all users who have permission to use the system. See Chapter 10 for more information.

/tmp   Many programs use this directory to hold temporary files.

ACCESS PERMISSIONS

There are three types of users that can access a file: the owner of the file (*owner*), a member of a group to which the owner belongs (*group*—see Chapter 10 for more information on groups), and everyone else (*other*). A user can attempt to access a plain file in three ways—by trying to *read* from, *write* to, or *execute* it. Three types of users, each able to access a file in three ways, equals a total of nine possible ways to access a plain file. A list of these ways follows.

The owner of a file can try to:
        read from the file
        write to the file
        execute the file

A member of the owner's group can try to:
        read from the file
        write to the file
        execute the file

Anyone else can try to:
        read from the file
        write to the file
        execute the file

The ls Utility and the −l Option

When you call ls with the −l (long) option and the name of a file, ls displays a line of information about the file.

```
$ ls −l letter.0610
-rw-r--r-- 1 alex    pubs    3355  Dec  2 10:52 letter.0610
```

From left to right, the line contains the following information.

- the type of file (first character)
- the file's access permissions (the next nine characters)
- the number of links to the file (the next section covers links)
- the name of the owner of the file (usually the person who created it)
- the name of the group that has group access to the file
- the size of the file in characters
- the date and time the file was created or last modified
- the name of the file

If the first character is a **d**, the file is a directory; if the character is a −, it is a plain file. The next three characters represent the access permission for the owner of the file: **r** indicates that the owner *has* read permission, − indicates that the owner *does not have* read permission; **w** indicates that the owner *has* write permission, − indicates that the owner *does not have* write permission; **x** indicates execute permission for the owner, and − indicates no execute permission.

In a similar manner, the next three characters represent permissions for the group and the final three characters represent permissions for everyone else. The preceding example shows a plain file that has read and write permissions set for the owner and read permission set for the group and everyone else.

Changing Access Permissions

The owner of a file controls which users have permission to access the file and how they can access it. If you own a file, you can use the chmod utility to change access permissions for that file. Below, chmod adds (+) read and write permission (**rw**) for all (**a**) users.

```
$ chmod a+rw letter.0610
$ ls -l letter.0610
-rw-rw-rw- 1 alex    pubs      3355   Dec   2 10:52 letter.0610
$
```

For more information on changing access permissions, refer to the discussion of chmod in Part II.

The UNIX system access permission scheme lets you give other users access to the files you want to share and keep your private files confidential. You can allow other users to read from *and* write to a file (you may be one of several people working on a joint project); only to read from a file (perhaps a project specification you are proposing); or only to write to a file (similar to an in-basket or mail box, where you don't want someone else to read your mail). Similarly, you can protect entire directories from being scanned.

There is an exception to the access permissions described above: the system administrator or another user who knows the special password can log on as the *Superuser* and have full access to *all* files, regardless of owner or access permissions. Refer to Chapter 10 for more information.

Directory Access Permissions

Access permissions have slightly different meanings when used with directory files. Although a directory file can be accessed by the three types of users and can be read from or written to, it can never be executed. Execute access permission is redefined for a directory: it means you can search through and list the contents of the directory. It has nothing to do with executing a file.

Alex can give the following command to ensure that Jenny, or anyone else, can look through, read files from, and write files to his home directory. The **x** stands for execute access.

```
$ chmod a+rwx /usr/alex
$
```

You can view the access permissions associated with a directory by using both the **−d** (directory) and **−l** options as shown in
the following example. The **d** at the left end of the line indicates
that **/usr/alex** is a directory.

```
$ ls −ld /usr/alex
drwxrwxrwx 3 alex    pubs      112  Dec  2 11:05 /usr/alex
```

LINKS

A *link* is a pointer to a file. Every time you create a file using vi,
cp, or any other means, you are putting a pointer in a directory.
This pointer associates a filename with a place on the disk. When
you specify a filename in a command, you are pointing to the
place on the disk where the information that you want is (or will
be) located.

Creating Additional Links

Creating additional links to a file allows users to share a file.
Sharing files can be useful if two or more people are working on a
project and need to share information. (If you want to share a file
with someone else, it may be necessary for you to use the chmod
utility to change the access permissions of the parent directory of
the file as well as the file itself.) A link can also be useful to a single user with a large directory structure. It is sometimes convenient to create a link so that a file appears in more than one
directory. In some cases, this duplication of names can reduce the
need for long pathnames.

Removing Links

When you first create a file, there is one link to it. You can delete
the file or, using UNIX system terminology, remove the link with
the rm utility. When you remove the last link to a file, you can no
longer access the information stored in the file, and the operating
system releases the space the file occupied on the disk for use by
other files. If there is more than one link to a file, you can remove
a link and still access the file from any remaining link.

Using ln to Create a Link

The ln (link) utility creates an additional link to an existing file. The link appears as another file in the file structure. If the file appears in the same directory as the one the file is linked with, the links must have different filenames. This restriction does not apply if the file is in another directory.

The following command makes the link shown in Figure 4-11. It assumes that **/usr/jenny** is the working directory and creates a link to the file named **draft**. The link appears in the **/usr/alex** directory with the filename **letter**. Practically, it may be necessary for Alex to use chmod, as shown in the previous section, to give Jenny write access permission to the **/usr/alex** directory.

```
$ ln draft /usr/alex/letter
$
```

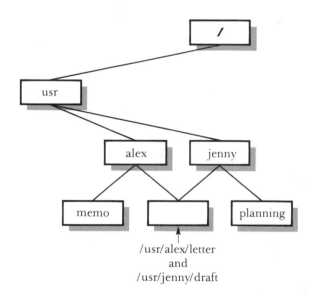

Figure 4-11
Links and the File Structure:
/usr/alex/letter and /usr/jenny/draft
Are Two Links to the Same File

The ln utility creates an additional pointer to an existing file. It does *not* make another copy of the file. Because there is only one file, the file status information (such as access permissions, owner, and the time the file was last modified) is the same for all links. Only the filenames differ. You can verify that ln does not make an additional copy of a file by creating a file, using ln to make an additional link to the file, changing the contents of the file through one link (use vi), and verifying the change through the other link.

```
$ cat file_a
This is file A.

$ ln file_a file_b

$ cat file_b
This is file A.

$ vi file_b
.
.
.

$ cat file_b
This is file B after the change.

$ cat file_a
This is file B after the change.
$
```

If you try the same experiment using cp instead of ln (and making a change to a *copy* of the file), the difference between the two utilities will become clearer. Once you change a *copy* of a file, the two files are different.

```
$ cat file_c
This is file C.

$ cp file_c file_d

$ cat file_d
This is file C.

$ vi file_d
.
.
.

$ cat file_d
This is file D after the change.

$ cat file_c
This is file C.
$
```

You can also use ls with the −l option, followed by the names of the files you want to compare, to see that the status information is the same for two links to a file and different for files that are not linked. In the following example, the 2 in the links field (just to the left of **alex**) shows there are two links to **file_a** and **file_b** (they are linked to each other).

```
$ ls -l file_a file_b file_c file_d
-rw-r--r-- 2 alex    pubs      33  Dec   2 10:52  file_a
-rw-r--r-- 2 alex    pubs      33  Dec   2 10:52  file_b
-rw-r--r-- 1 alex    pubs      16  Dec   2 10:55  file_c
-rw-r--r-- 1 alex    pubs      33  Dec   2 10:57  file_d
```

All links to a file are of equal value—the operating system cannot distinguish the order in which two links were made. If a file has two links, you can remove either one and still access the file through the remaining link. You can even remove the link used to create the file and, as long as there is a remaining link, still access the file through that link. Part II has more information on **ln**.

SUMMARY

The UNIX system has a *hierarchical,* or treelike, file structure that makes it possible to organize files so you can find them quickly and easily. The file structure contains *directory* files and *plain* files. Directories contain other files, including other directories, while plain files generally contain text or programs. The ancestor of all files is the *root* directory, named /.

You can use up to 14 characters to name a file, but it is a good idea to keep the filenames simple and meaningful. *Filename extensions* can help make filenames more meaningful.

An *absolute pathname* starts with the root directory and contains all the filenames that trace a path to a given file. It starts with a slash representing the root directory and contains additional slashes between the other filenames in the path.

When you are logged on, you are always associated with a *working directory.* Your *home directory* is your working directory from the time you first log on until you use **cd** to change directories.

A *relative pathname* is similar to an absolute pathname, but the path it traces starts from the working directory. A *simple filename* is the last element of a pathname and is a form of a relative pathname.

A *link* is a pointer to a file. You can have several links to a single file so that you can share the file with other users or have the file appear in more than one directory. Because there is only one copy of a file with multiple links, changing the file through any one link causes the changes to appear in all the links.

This chapter introduced the following utilities.

- ► pwd displays the pathname of the working directory.
- ► mkdir creates a directory.
- ► cd associates you with another working directory.
- ► rmdir deletes a directory.
- ► ln makes a link to an existing file.

5

THE SHELL

This chapter takes a close look at the Shell and explains how to use some of its features. It discusses command line syntax, how the Shell processes a command line, and how it initiates execution of a program. The chapter shows how to redirect input to and output from a program, construct pipes and filters on the command line, and run a program as a background task. The final section covers filename generation and explains how you can use this feature in your everyday work. Everything in this chapter applies to both the Bourne and C Shells. Refer to Chapters 8 and 9 for information on writing Shell scripts (programs).

THE COMMAND LINE

The Shell executes a program when you give it a command in response to its prompt. The line that contains the command, including any arguments, is called the *command line*.

Command Line Syntax

Command line syntax dictates the spelling, ordering, and separation of the elements on a command line. When you press the RETURN key after entering a command, the Shell scans the command line for proper syntax. The format for a command line is:

> **command [arg1] [arg2] ... [argn]** RETURN

The square brackets enclose optional elements. One or more SPACES or TABS must appear between elements on the command line. The **command** is the command name, **arg1** through **argn** are optional arguments, and RETURN is the keystroke that terminates all command lines.

Command Name. All a useful command line need contain is the name of a command. An example of a minimal command line is an **ls** command without any arguments.

Arguments. An *argument* is a filename, string of text, number, or some other object that a command acts on. For example, the argument to a **vi** command is the name of the file you want to edit.

The following command line shows cp copying the file named **temp** to **tempcopy**.

```
$ cp temp tempcopy
$
```

The cp utility requires two arguments on the command line. The first is the name of an existing file, and the second is the name of the file that it is creating. Here, the arguments are not optional; both arguments must be present for the command to work. If you do not supply the right number or kind of arguments, cp displays an error message.

Options. An option is an argument that modifies the effects of a command. Frequently, you can specify more than one option, modifying the command in several different ways. Options are specific to and interpreted by the program that the command calls.

By convention, options are separate arguments that follow the name of the command. Most UNIX utility programs require you to prefix options with a hyphen. This requirement is, however, specific to the utility and not the Shell.

Figure 5-1 shows that the **−r** (reverse order) option causes the ls utility to display the list of files in reverse alphabetical order. The **−C** (column) option causes ls to display the list of files in columns. It allows you to view a list of many filenames without having the them scroll off the top of the screen before you can read them. (See page 90 if your version of ls does not have this option.)

```
$ ls −r
test
temp
names

$ ls −C
names    temp    test
$
```

Figure 5-1
Using Options

If you need to use several options, you can usually group them into one argument that starts with a single hyphen; do not put SPACES between the options. Specific rules for combining options depend on the utility. Figure 5-2 shows both the **−r** and **−C** options with the ls utility. Together, these options generate a list of filenames in columns, in reverse alphabetical order. The order of the options doesn't matter; **ls −Cr** produces the same results as **ls −rC**. Also, the command **ls −C −r** will generate the same list.

```
$ ls  −rC
test   temp   names
$
```

Figure 5-2
Using Two Options at Once

Processing the Command Line

As you enter a command line, the UNIX operating system examines each character to see if it must take any action (Figure 5-3).
When you enter a # (to erase a character) or a @ (to kill a line),
the operating system immediately adjusts the command line as
required—the Shell never sees the character you erased or line you
killed. If the character does not require immediate action, the
operating system stores the character in a buffer and waits for
additional characters. When you press RETURN, the operating system passes the command line to the Shell for processing.

When the Shell processes a command line, it looks at the line
as a whole and breaks it down into its component parts (Figure 5-
4). Next, the Shell looks for the name of the command. It
assumes that the name of the command is the first thing on the
command line after the prompt (i.e., argument zero), so it takes
the first characters on the command line, up to the first SPACE,
and sees if it can find a program with that name. If the Bourne
Shell can't find the program, it displays the message, xx: not found
where **xx** is the name of the program you called. The C Shell
gives you the message xx: Command not found. If the Bourne Shell
finds the program but cannot execute it (if you do not have execute access to the file that contains the program), you will see the
following message: xx: execute permission denied or, under the C
Shell, xx: Permission denied.

The Shell has no way of knowing whether a particular option
or other argument is valid for a given program. Any error messages about options or arguments come from the program itself.
Many UNIX utility programs ignore bad options.

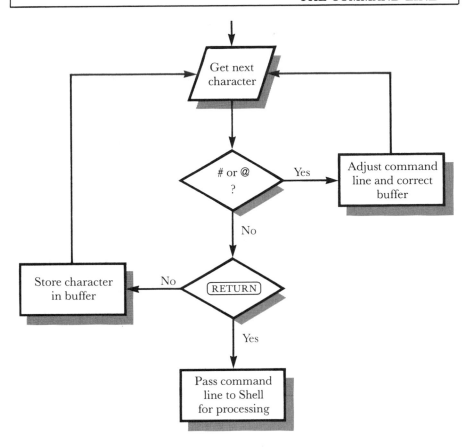

Figure 5-3
Entering a Command Line

Executing the Command Line

If the Shell finds a program with the same name as the command, it starts a new process. A *process* is the UNIX system execution of a program. The Shell makes each command line argument, including options and the name of the program, available to the program. While the program is executing, the Shell waits, inactive, for the process to finish. The Shell is in a state called *sleep*. When the program finishes executing, the Shell returns to an active state (wakes up), issues a prompt, and waits for another command.

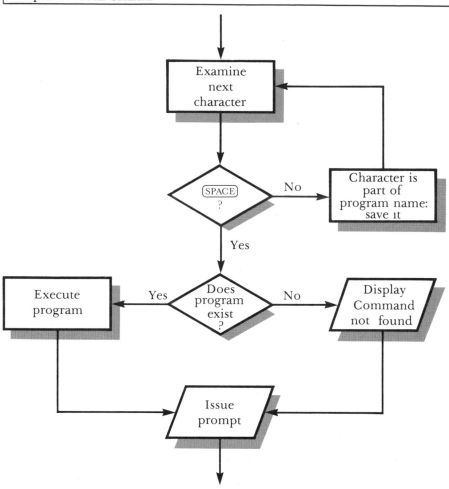

Figure 5-4
Processing the Command Line

STANDARD INPUT AND STANDARD OUTPUT

A program's *standard output* is a place to which it can send information, frequently text. The program never "knows" where the
information it sends to its standard output is going. The information can go to a printer, a plain file, or a terminal. This section
shows that the Shell directs the standard output from a program
to the terminal, and how you can cause the Shell to redirect this
output to another file. It also explains how to redirect the *standard input* to a program so that it comes from a plain file instead
of the terminal.

The Terminal as a File

Chapter 4 introduced plain and directory files. The UNIX system has an additional type of file, a *device file*. A device file resides in the UNIX system file structure, usually in the /**dev** directory, and represents a peripheral device such as a terminal, printer, or disk drive.

The device name that the who utility displays after your login name is the filename of your terminal. If who displays the device name **tty6**, the pathname of your terminal is probably /**dev/tty6**. Although you wouldn't normally have occasion to, you could read from and write to this file as though it were a text file. Writing to it would display what you wrote on the terminal screen, and reading from it would read what you entered on the keyboard.

The Terminal as the Standard Input and Output

When you first log on, the Shell directs your programs' standard output to the device file that represents your terminal (Figure 5-5). Directing output in this manner causes it to appear on your terminal screen.

The Shell also directs the standard input to come from the same file, so that your programs receive anything you type on your terminal keyboard as input.

The cat utility provides a good example of the way the terminal functions as the standard input and output. When you use cat, it copies a file to its standard output. Because the Shell directs the standard output to the terminal, cat displays the file on the terminal.

Up to this point, cat has taken its input from the filename (argument) you specified on the command line. If you do not give cat an argument (i.e., if you give the command **cat** immediately followed by a RETURN), cat takes input from its standard input.

The cat utility can now be defined as a utility that, when called without an argument, copies its standard input file to its standard output file. On most systems, it copies one line at a time.

To see how cat works, type **cat** RETURN in response to the Shell prompt. Nothing happens. Enter a line of text and a RETURN. The same line appears just under the one you entered. The cat utility is working. (Some versions do not display anything until you signal the end of the file by pressing CONTROL-D;

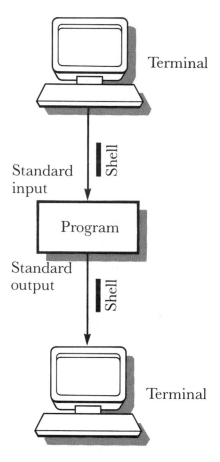

Figure 5-5
Standard Input and Output

see below.) What happened is that you typed a line of text on the terminal, which the Shell associated with cat's standard input, and cat copied your line of text to its standard output file, which the Shell also associated with the terminal. This exchange is shown in Figure 5-6.

The cat utility keeps copying until you enter CONTROL-D on a line by itself. Pressing CONTROL-D sends an *end of file* signal to cat that indicates it has reached the end of the standard input file and that there is no more text for it to copy. When you enter CONTROL-D, cat finishes execution and returns control to the Shell, which gives you a prompt.

```
$ cat
This is a line of text.
This is a line of text.
Cat keeps copying lines of text
Cat keeps copying lines of text
until you press CONTROL-D at the beginning
until you press CONTROL-D at the beginning
of a line.
of a line.
CONTROL-D
$
```

Figure 5-6
cat **Copies Its Standard Input to Its Standard Output**

REDIRECTION

The term *redirection* encompasses the various ways you can cause the Shell to alter where a program gets its standard input from or where it sends its standard output to. As the previous section demonstrated, the Shell, by default, associates a program's standard input and standard output with the terminal. You can cause the Shell to redirect the standard input and/or the standard output of any program by associating the input or output with a program or file other than the device file representing the terminal. This section demonstrates how to redirect output from and input to plain text files and UNIX utility programs.

Redirecting the Standard Output

The *redirect output* symbol (>) instructs the Shell to redirect a program's output to the specified file instead of the terminal (Figure 5-7). The format of a command line that redirects output follows.

program [arguments] > filename

The **program** is any executable program (e.g., an application program or a UNIX utility program), **arguments** are optional arguments, and **filename** is the name of the plain file the Shell redirects the output to.

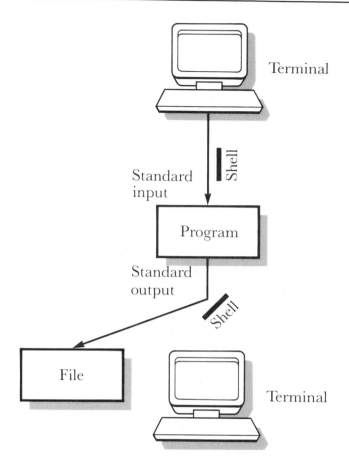

Figure 5-7
Redirecting the Standard Output

**Use caution when you redirect output. If the file
already exists, the Shell overwrites it and destroys its contents.**

In Figure 5-8, cat demonstrates output redirection. This figure
contrasts with Figure 5-6, where both the standard input *and*
standard output were associated with the terminal. In Figure 5-8,
only the input comes from the terminal. The redirect output symbol on the command line causes the Shell to associate **cat**'s standard output with the file specified on the command line,
sample.txt.

Now, **sample.txt** contains the text you entered. You can use
cat with an argument of **sample.txt** to display the file. The next
section shows another way to use cat to display the file.

```
$ cat > sample.txt
This text is being entered at the keyboard.
Cat is copying it to a file.
Press CONTROL-D to indicate the
end of file.
CONTROL-D
$
```

Figure 5-8
cat with Its Output Redirected

Figure 5-8 shows that redirecting the output from cat is a handy way to make files without using an editor. Its drawback is that, once you enter a line and press RETURN, you cannot edit the text. While you are entering a line, the erase and kill keys work to delete text. This procedure is useful for making short, simple files.

Figure 5-9 shows how to use cat and the redirect output symbol to *catenate* (join one after the other) several files into one larger file.

```
$ cat tony
This is a letter to Tony.
$ cat alice
This is a letter to Alice.
$ cat linda
This is a letter to Linda.

$ cat tony alice linda > all

$ cat all
This is a letter to Tony.
This is a letter to Alice.
This is a letter to Linda.
$
```

Figure 5-9
Using cat to Catenate Files

The first three commands display the contents of three files, **tony**, **alice**, and **linda**. The next command shows cat with three filenames as arguments. When you call cat with more than one filename, it copies the files, one at a time, to its standard output. Here, the standard output is redirected to the file **all**. The final **cat** command shows that **all** contains the contents of all three files.

Redirecting the Standard Input

Just as you can redirect cat's standard output, you can redirect its standard input. The *redirect input* symbol (<) instructs the Shell to redirect a program's input from the specified file instead of the terminal (Figure 5-10).

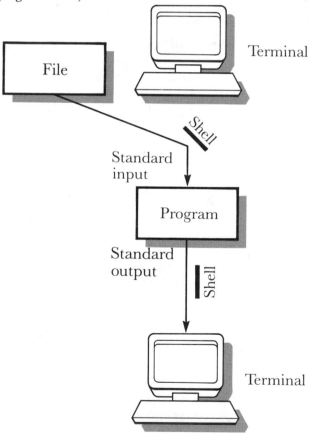

Figure 5-10
Redirecting the Standard Input

The format of a command line that redirects input follows.

program [arguments] < filename

The **program** is any executable program (e.g., an application program or a UNIX utility program), **arguments** are optional arguments, and **filename** is the name of the plain file the Shell redirects the input from.

Figure 5-11 shows cat with its input redirected from the **sample.txt** file that was created in Figure 5-8 and its standard output going to the terminal. This setup causes cat to display the sample file on the terminal.

```
$ cat < sample.txt
This text is being entered at the keyboard.
Cat is copying it to a file.
Press CONTROL-D to indicate the
end of file.
$
```

Figure 5-11
cat **with Its Input Redirected**

The system automatically supplies an end of file signal at the end of a plain file, so no CONTROL-D is necessary.

Using cat with input redirected from a file yields the same result as giving a cat command with the filename as an argument. The cat utility is a member of a class of UNIX utility programs that function in this manner. Other members of this class of utilities are lp, sort, and grep. These utilities first examine the command line you use to call them. If you include a filename on the command line, the utility takes its input from the file you specify. If there is no filename, the utility takes its input from its standard input. It is the program, not the Shell or the operating system, that functions in this manner.

Following is an example of how to use redirected input with mail. Frequently it is convenient to compose your thoughts in a file before you send someone electronic mail. You can use lp to print the file, check that it is correct, and send it at your leisure. The following command sends the contents of the file **memo.alex** to Alex using mail. The redirect input symbol redirects mail's standard input to come from **memo.alex** instead of the terminal.

```
$ mail alex < memo.alex
$
```

Cautions Regarding Redirecting Standard Output

When you give the following command, the Shell displays an error message and overwrites the **orange** file.

```
$ cat orange pear > orange
cat: input orange is output
$
```

If you want to catenate two files into one, use cat to put the two files into a third, temporary file, and then use mv to rename the third file as you desire.

```
$ cat orange pear > temp

$ mv temp orange
$
```

What happens with the typo in the next example can be even worse. The person giving the command meant to redirect the output from the nroff program (Chapter 7 covers the nroff text formatter) to the file **a.out**. Instead, the person entered the filename as **a out**, omitting the period and leaving a SPACE in its place. The Shell obediently removed the contents of **a** and then called nroff. The error message takes a while to appear, giving you a sense that the program is running correctly. Even after you see the error message, you may not know that you destroyed the contents of **a**.

```
$ nroff —mm a b c > a out
cannot open file out
$
```

Appending the Standard Output to a File

The redirect output symbol causes the Shell to overwrite any information in the file you redirect output to. The *append output* symbol (>>) causes the Shell to add the new information to the end of the file, leaving the information that was already there intact.

The example in Figure 5-12 shows how to create a file that contains the date and time (the output from the date utility) followed by a list of who is logged on (the output from who).

```
$ date > whoson

$ cat whoson
Wed Dec 19 09:24:19 PST 1984

$ who >> whoson

$ cat whoson
Wed Dec 19 09:24:19 PST 1984
hls          console       Dec 19 08:47
jenny        tty2          Dec 19 07:21
alex         tty6          Dec 18 11:01
$
```

Figure 5-12
Redirecting and Appending Output

The first line in Figure 5-12 redirects the output from date to the file named **whoson**. Then cat displays the file. Next, the example appends the output from who to the **whoson** file. Finally, cat displays the file containing the output of both utilities.

Pipes

The Shell uses a *pipe* to redirect the standard output of one program directly to the standard input of another program. A pipe has the same effect as redirecting the standard output of one program to a file and then using that file as the standard input to another program. It does away with separate commands and the intermediate file. The symbol for a pipe is a vertical bar (|).

The format of a command line using a pipe follows.

program__a [arguments] | program__b [arguments]

The command line above uses a pipe to generate the same result as the following command lines.

program__a [arguments] > temp
program__b [arguments] < temp
rm temp

The preceding sequence of commands first redirects the standard output from **program__a** to an intermediate file named **temp**. Then it redirects the standard input for **program__b** to come from **temp**. The final command line deletes **temp**.

You can use a pipe with a member of the class of UNIX utility programs that accept input either from a file specified on the command line or from the standard input. The **lp** (line printer) utility is one of these. When you follow **lp** with the name of a file, **lp** places that file in the printer queue. If you do not specify a filename on the command line, **lp** takes input from its standard input. This feature allows you to use a pipe to redirect input to **lp**. The line of information **lp** displays tells you whether it is getting its input from a file or its standard input.

```
$ ls > temp

$ lp temp
request id is printer_1-452 (1 file)

$ rm temp
$

or

$ ls | lp
request id is printer_1-453 (standard input)
$
```

Figure 5-13
A Pipe

The first set of commands in Figure 5-13 shows how you can use ls and lp, with an intermediate file, to send a list of the files in the working directory to the printer. The second set of commands sends the same list to the printer using a pipe.

```
$ who > temp
$ sort temp
barbara      tty3         May 22 12:53
chas         tty6         May 22 10:31
hls          console      May 22 12:48
scott        tty2         May 21 09:07
$
```

Figure 5-14
Simulating a Pipe with who **and** sort

The commands in Figure 5-14 redirect the output from the who utility to **temp** and then display this file in sorted order. The sort utility takes its input from the file specified on the command line or, if you do not specify a file, from its standard input. It sends its output to its standard output. The **sort** command in Figure 5-14 specifies **temp** as the input file. The output that sort sends to the terminal lists the users in sorted (alphabetical) order.

Figure 5-15 achieves the same result with a pipe. Using a pipe, the Shell directs the output from who to the input of sort. The sort utility takes input from its standard input because no filename follows it on the command line.

```
$ who | sort
barbara      tty3         May 22 12:53
chas         tty6         May 22 10:31
hls          console      May 22 12:48
scott        tty2         May 21 09:07
$
```

Figure 5-15
A Pipe

If there are a lot of people using the system and you only want information about one of them, you can redirect the output from who to grep. The grep utility will display the line containing the string you specify—chas in the following example.

```
$ who | grep ´chas´
chas            tty6             May 22 10:31
$
```

Early versions of System V ls did not include the −C option for displaying a list in multiple columns. If you have a lot of files, a single column list can easily run off the top of the screen. The following command uses a pipe to list the filenames in five columns, allowing you to see all the names on the screen at once. See pr in Part II for more information on how pr works.

```
$ ls | pr −5 −t
 .
 .
 .
$
```

Filters

A *filter* is a program that processes an input stream of data to produce an output stream of data. A command line that includes a filter uses a pipe to redirect the filter's input from the standard output of one program. Another pipe redirects the filter's output to the standard input of another program.

Below, sort is a filter, taking its standard input from the standard output of who and using a pipe to redirect its standard output to the standard input of lp. The command line sends the sorted output of who to the printer.

```
$ who | sort | lp
request id is printer_1-454 (standard input)
$
```

This example demonstrates the power of the Shell combined with the versatility of UNIX utility programs. The three utilities, who, sort, and lp, were not specifically designed to work with each other. By using the Shell to redirect input and output, you can piece standard utilities together on the command line to achieve the results you want.

RUNNING A PROGRAM IN THE BACKGROUND

When you run a program in the *background*, you do not have to wait for the program to finish before you start running another program. Running a program in the background can be useful if the program will be running a long time and doesn't need supervision. The terminal will be free so that you can use it for something else.

To run a program in the background, type an ampersand (**&**) just before the RETURN that ends the command line. The Shell will display a PID (Process ID) number that identifies the program running in the background and give you another prompt.

The following example runs an **ls −l** command in the background. A pipe redirects the output from the command to the **lp** utility, which sends it to the printer.

```
$ ls −l | lp &
31725
request id is printer_1-455 (standard input)
$
```

If a background task sends output to the standard output and you do not redirect it, the output appears on your terminal, even if you are running another job. If a background task requests input from the standard input and you have not redirected the standard input, the Shell supplies a null string.

You will probably want to redirect the output of a job you run in the background to keep it from interfering with whatever you are doing at the terminal. Chapter 8 goes into more detail about background tasks in the section on "Command Separation and Grouping."

The DEL key will not work to abort a process you are running in the background; you must use the kill utility for this purpose. When you call kill, you must give it the PID number of the process you want to abort. If you forget the PID number, you can use the ps (process status) utility to display it. The following example runs an nroff job in the background, uses ps to display the PID number of the process, and aborts the job with kill. Refer to Part II for more information on kill and ps; see Chapter 7 for nroff information.

```
$ nroff —mm textfile > textfile.out &
1466

$ ps
   PID   TTY        TIME COMMAND
   1456  tty03      0:05 sh
   1465  tty03      0:00 sh
   1466  tty03      0:39 nroff
   1514  tty03      0:03 ps

$ kill 1466
$
```

FILENAME GENERATION

When you give the Shell abbreviated filenames that contain *special characters* (or *metacharacters*—characters that have a special meaning to the Shell), the Shell can generate filenames that match the names of existing files. When one of these special characters appears in an argument on the command line, the Shell expands that argument into a list of filenames and passes the list to the program that the command line is calling. Filenames that contain these special characters are called *ambiguous file references* because they do not refer to any one specific file.

The special characters are referred to as *wild cards*, because they act like the jokers in a deck of cards. The process of expanding an ambiguous file reference is sometimes called *globbing*. Expanding an ambiguous file reference allows you to quickly reference a group of files with similar names or a file whose name you don't remember in its entirety.

The ? Special Character

The question mark is a special character that causes the Shell to generate filenames. It matches any single character in the name of an existing file. The following command uses this special character in an argument to the lp utility.

```
$ lp memo?
request id is printer_1-456 (4 files)
$
```

The Shell expands the memo? argument and generates a list of the files in the working directory that have names composed of

memo followed by any single character. The Shell passes this list to lp. The lp utility never "knows" that the Shell generated the filenames it was called with. If there is no filename that matches the ambiguous file reference, the Bourne Shell passes the string itself (memo?) to the program. The C Shell can display an error message (No match).

The following example uses ls to display the filenames that memo? does and does not match.

```
$ ls
mem
memo
memo12
memo5
memo9
memoa
memoalex
memos
newmemo5

$ ls memo?
memo5
memo9
memoa
memos
$
```

The memo? ambiguous file reference does not match **mem,** **memo, memo12, memoalex,** or **newmemo5**.

You can also use a question mark in the middle of an ambiguous file reference.

```
$ ls
7may4report
may.report
may14report
may4report
may4report.79
may__report
mayqreport
mayreport

$ ls may?report
may.report
may4report
may__report
mayqreport
$
```

The * Special Character

The asterisk performs a function similar to that of the question mark, except that it matches any number of characters, *including zero characters,* in a filename. An asterisk does not match a leading period (one that indicates an invisible filename). The following examples use the **–a** option with ls to force ls to display invisible filenames.

```
$  ls  –a
.memo.0612
.profile
amemo
mem
memo
memo.0612
memoa
memorandum
memosally
sallymemo
user.memo

$  ls  –a  memo*
memo
memo.0612
memoa
memorandum
memosally
```

The ambiguous file reference memo* does not match **.memo.0612**, **.profile**, **amemo**, **mem**, **sallymemo**, or **user.memo**.

```
$  ls  –a
.aaa
.profile
aaa
memo.0612
memo.sally
report
sally.0612
saturday
thurs

$  ls  –a  *a*
aaa
memo.sally
sally.0612
saturday
```

The command **ls –a *a*** does not display **.aaa**, **.profile**, **memo.0612**, **report**, or **thurs**.

```
$ ls —a
.private
.profile
memo.0612
private
reminder
report

$ ls —a .*
.private
.profile
.
.
.
$
```

In the final example, .* does not match **memo.0612**, **private**, **reminder**, or **report**, but does cause ls to list the contents of the . directory (the working directory) and the .. directory (the parent of the working directory).

If you establish conventions for naming files, you can take advantage of ambiguous file references. For example, if you end all your text file filenames with **.txt**, you can reference that group of files with *.txt. Following this convention, the command below will send all the text files in the working directory to the printer. The ampersand causes lp to run in the background.

```
$ lp *.txt&
4312
request id is printer_1-457 (5 files)
$
```

The [ ] Special Characters

A pair of square brackets causes the Shell to expand selected filenames. Whereas **memo?** matches **memo** followed by any character, **memo[17a]** matches only **memo1**, **memo7**, and **memoa**. The brackets define a *character class* that includes all the characters within the brackets. The Shell expands an argument that includes a character class definition, substituting each member of the character class, *one at a time*, in place of the brackets and their contents. The Shell passes a list of filenames that match existing filenames to the program it is calling.

Each character class definition can only replace a single character within a filename. The brackets and their contents are like a question mark that will only substitute the members of the character class.

The first of the following commands lists the names of all the files in the working directory that begin with a, e, i, o, or u. The second command displays the contents of the files named **page2.txt**, **page4.txt**, **page6.txt**, and **page8.txt**.

```
$ ls [aeiou]*
.
.
.

$ cat page[2468].txt
.
.
.
$
```

A hyphen defines a range of characters within a character class definition. For example, [6−9] represents [6789], and [a−z] represents all lowercase letters.

The following command lines show three ways to print the files named **part0**, **part1**, **part2**, **part3**, and **part5**. Each of the command lines calls lp with five filenames.

```
$ lp part0 part1 part2 part3 part5
request id is printer_1-457 (5 files)

$ lp part[01235]
request id is printer_1-458 (5 files)

$ lp part[0−35]
request id is printer_1-459 (5 files)
$
```

The first command line explicitly specifies the five filenames. The second and third command lines use ambiguous file references, incorporating character class definitions. The Shell expands the argument on the second command line to include all files that have names beginning with part and ending with any of the characters in the character class. The character class is explicitly defined as 0, 1, 2, 3, and 5. The third command line also uses a character class definition, except it defines the character class to be all characters in the range from 0-3 and 5.

The following command line will print 36 files, **part0** through **part35**.

```
$ lp part[0-9] part[12][0-9] part3[0-5]
request id is printer_1-460 (36 files)
$
```

The next two examples list the names of some of the files in the working directory. The first lists the files whose names start with a through m. The second lists files whose names end with x, y, or z.

```
$ ls [a-m]*
.
.
.

$ ls *[x-z]
.
.
.
$
```

Practicing with Filename Generation

The echo utility displays the arguments that the Shell passes to it. Try giving the following command.

```
$ echo *
.
.
.
```

The Shell expands the asterisk into a list of all files in the working directory and passes this list to echo, as though you had entered the list of filenames as arguments to echo. The echo utility responds to this command by displaying the list of files in the working directory.

You can use echo to experiment with ambiguous filenames. Try giving a command such as the following.

```
$ echo *a*
.
.
.
```

The echo utility displays all the filenames in the working directory that contain an a.

SUMMARY

The Shell is the UNIX system command interpreter. It scans the command line for proper syntax, picking out the command name and any arguments. Many programs use options to modify the effects of a command. Most UNIX programs identify options by their leading hyphens.

When you give the Shell a command, it tries to find an executable program with the same name as the command. If it does, it executes the program. If it doesn't, it tells you that it cannot find or execute the program.

When the Shell executes a program, it assigns a file to the program's *standard input* and *standard output*. By default, the Shell causes a program's standard input to come from, and standard output to go to, the terminal. You can instruct the Shell to *redirect* a program's standard output to any reasonable file, device, or program. You can also redirect the standard input.

When a program runs in the *foreground*, the Shell waits for it to finish before it gives you another prompt and allows you to continue. If you put an ampersand (**&**) at the end of a command line, the Shell executes the command in the *background* and gives you another prompt immediately.

The Shell interprets special characters on a command line for *filename generation*. It uses a question mark to represent any single character and an asterisk to represent zero or more characters. A reference to a file that includes one of these characters is called an *ambiguous file reference*.

6

THE vi EDITOR

This chapter shows you how to use the vi editor to change existing text files. It assumes that you have read the part of Chapter 2 that explains how to specify your terminal and get started using vi. This chapter goes into detail about many of the vi commands and explains the use of parameters for customizing vi for your needs. At the end of the chapter is a quick reference summary of vi commands.

INTRODUCTION TO vi

This section contains historical information on vi, some useful facts about how vi operates, and suggestions on what you can do when you encounter exceptional conditions such as system crashes or not being able to exit from vi. It also summarizes some of the information on vi that was presented in Chapter 2.

History of vi

The vi editor was developed at U.C. Berkeley as part of Berkeley UNIX. Although many systems supported vi in the past, it only became an official part of AT&T UNIX with the release of System V.

Before vi was developed, the standard UNIX system editor was ed. The ed editor was line-oriented, making it difficult to see the context for your editing. Then ex came along, and in UNIX Version 6 (several releases before System V), ex was a superset of ed. The most notable advantage that ex had over ed was a display editing facility that allowed you to work with a full screen of text instead of with only a line at a time. While you were using ex, you could use the display editing facility by giving the command **vi** (for visual mode). People used the display editing facility of ex so extensively that the developers of ex made it possible to call it up so that you were using the display editing facility at once, without having to call ex and give the **vi** command. Appropriately, they named the new facility vi.

You can still call the visual mode from ex, and you can go back to ex while you are using vi. Give vi a **Q** command to use ex, or give ex a **vi** command to switch to visual mode.

Modes of Operation

The ex editor has five modes of operation:

- ex Command Mode
- ex Input Mode
- vi Command Mode
- vi Input Mode
- vi Last Line Mode

While you are using vi, you will mostly use vi *Command Mode* and *Input Mode.* On occasion you will use *Last Line Mode.* While in Command Mode, vi accepts keystrokes as commands, responding to each command as you enter it. In Input Mode, vi accepts keystrokes as text, displaying the text as you enter it. All commands that start with a colon put vi in Last Line Mode. The colon moves the cursor to the bottom line of the screen where you enter the rest of the command.

In addition to the position of the cursor, there is another important difference between Last Line Mode and Command Mode. When you give a command in Command Mode, you do not have to terminate the command with RETURN. You must terminate all Last Line Mode commands with a RETURN.

You will not normally use the ex modes. When this chapter refers to *Input* and *Command Modes,* it refers to the vi modes and never to the ex modes.

At the start of an editing session, vi is in Command Mode. There are several commands, such as Insert and Append, that put vi in Input Mode. When you press the ESCAPE key, vi always reverts to Command Mode.

The Change and Replace commands combine Command and Input Modes. The Change command deletes the text you want to change and puts vi in Input Mode so that you can insert new text. The Replace command deletes the character(s) you overwrite and inserts the new one(s) you enter.

Correcting Text as You Insert It

While vi is in Input Mode, you can use the erase and line kill keys to back up over text that you are inserting so you can correct it. You can also use CONTROL-W to back up to the beginning of the word you are entering. Using these techniques, you cannot back up past the beginning of the line you are working on, nor can you back up past the beginning of the text you entered since you most recently put vi into Input Mode.

Command Case

Be certain to observe the case of commands as this chapter describes them. The same letter will serve as two different commands depending on whether you enter it as a uppercase or lowercase character.

If vi seems to be behaving very strangely, check to see if the SHIFT LOCK on the terminal is on.

The Work Buffer

The vi editor does all its work in the *Work Buffer*. At the start of an editing session, vi reads the file you are editing from the disk into the Work Buffer. During the editing session, vi makes all changes to this copy of the file. It does not change the disk file until you write the contents of the Work Buffer back to the disk. When you edit a new file, vi does not create the file until it writes the contents of the Work Buffer to the disk, usually at the end of the editing session. Normally, when you end an editing session, vi automatically writes out the contents of the Work Buffer and makes the changes to the text final.

Storing the text you are editing in the Work Buffer has advantages and disadvantages. If you accidentally end an editing session without writing out the contents of the Work Buffer, all your work is lost. However, if you unintentionally make some major changes (such as deleting the entire contents of the Work Buffer), you can end the editing session without implementing the changes. The vi editor will leave the file as it was when you last wrote it out.

Abnormal Termination of an Editing Session

You can end an editing session in one of two ways—so vi saves or does not save the changes you made during the editing session. Chapter 2 explained that the **ZZ** command saves the contents of the Work Buffer and exits from vi.

You can end an editing session without writing out the contents of the Work Buffer by giving the following command. (The **:** puts vi in Last Line Mode—you must press RETURN to execute the command.)

:q!

When you use this command to end an editing session, vi does not preserve the contents of the Work Buffer—you will lose all the work you did since the last time you wrote the Work Buffer to disk. The next time you edit or use the file, it will appear as it did the last time you wrote the Work Buffer to disk. Use the **:q!** command with caution.

You may run into a situation where you have created or edited a file, and vi will not let you exit. When you give the **ZZ** command, you will see the message No current filename, if you forgot to specify a filename when you first called vi, or Permission denied, when you do not have write permission for the file. If vi will not let you exit normally, you can write the file to the disk manually before you quit (**:q!**) using vi. To write the file manually, give the following command, substituting the name of the file in place of **filename**:

> **:w filename**

If you don't have write permission to the working directory, vi may still not be able to write your file to the disk. Give the command again, using an absolute pathname of a dummy (nonexistent) file in your home directory in place of **filename**. (Alex might give the command **:w /usr/alex/temp**.)

After writing your file, you can quit using vi and not lose any of your work.

Recovering Text After a Crash

You can often recover text that you would otherwise lose if the system crashes while you are editing a file with vi. When the system is brought back up after a crash, give the following command to see if the system saved the contents of your Work Buffer.

> **vi −r filename**

If your work was saved, you will be editing a recent copy of your Work Buffer. Exit from vi with **ZZ** and continue your work.

THE DISPLAY

The vi editor uses the status line and several special symbols to give you information about what is happening during an editing session.

The Status Line

The vi editor displays status information on the bottom line—the twenty-fourth line of most terminals. This information includes error messages, information about the deletion or addition of blocks of text, and file status information. In addition, vi displays Last Line Mode commands on the status line.

The @ Symbol

The vi editor refreshes the screen display as little and as infrequently as possible. This means that users, especially those using a UNIX system over slow telephone lines, do not have to wait through unnecessary pauses when text is deleted from the screen.

In some cases, vi uses an @ symbol at the left of the screen to replace deleted lines. This symbol only appears on the screen and is never written to the Work Buffer or file. If the screen becomes cluttered with these symbols, enter CONTROL-R (some terminals use CONTROL-L) while vi is in Command Mode to redraw the screen.

The ~ Symbol

If the end of the file is displayed on the screen, vi marks lines that would appear past the end of the file with a tilde (~) at the left of the screen. The vi editor marks every line on the screen, except for the first line, with these symbols when you start editing a new file.

COMMAND MODE— MOVING THE CURSOR

While vi is in Command Mode, you can position the cursor over any character on the screen. You can also display a different portion of the Work Buffer on the screen. By manipulating the screen and cursor position, you can place the cursor on any character in the Work Buffer.

You can move the cursor forward or backward through the text. As illustrated in Figure 6-1, *forward* always means toward the bottom of the screen and the end of the file. *Backward* means toward the top of the screen and the beginning of the file. When you use a command that moves the cursor forward past the end (right) of a line, the cursor generally moves to the beginning (left) of the next line. When you move it backward past the beginning of a line, it moves to the end of the previous line.

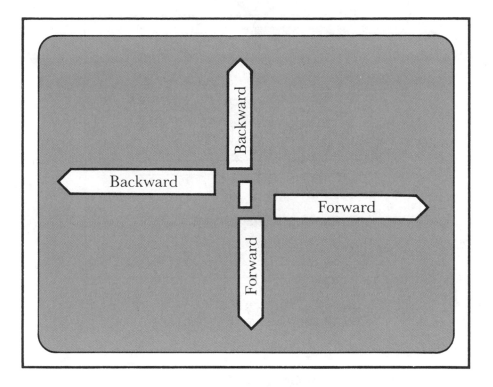

Figure 6-1
Forward and Backward

You can move the cursor through the text by any *Unit of Measure* (i.e., character, word, line, sentence, paragraph, or screen.) If you precede a cursor-movement command with a number, called a *Repeat Factor*, the cursor moves that number of units through the text. Refer to the sections at the end of this chapter on "Units of Measure" and "Repeat Factors" for more precise definitions of these terms.

Moving the Cursor by Characters

The SPACE bar moves the cursor forward, one character at a time, toward the right side of the screen. The l (ell) key and the right arrow key (see Figure 6-2) do the same thing. The command 7SPACE or 7l moves the cursor seven characters to the right. These keys *will not* move the cursor past the end of the current line to the beginning of the next.

The **h** key and the left arrow key are similar to the l key but work in the opposite direction.

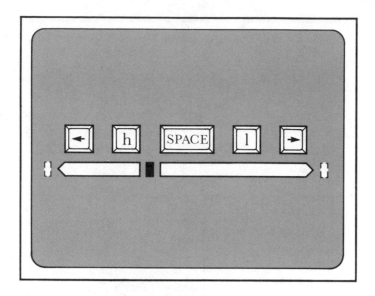

Figure 6-2
Moving the Cursor by Characters

Moving the Cursor by Words

The **w** key moves the cursor forward to the first letter of the next word (Figure 6-3). Groups of punctuation count as words. This command *will* go to the next line if that is where the next word is, unless the line ends with a SPACE. The command **15w** moves the cursor to the first character of the fifteenth subsequent word.

The **W** key is similar to the **w** key, except that it moves the cursor by blank delimited words, including punctuation, as it skips forward over words. (See "Blank Delimited Word," page 131.)

The **b** key moves the cursor backward to the first letter of the previous word. The **B** key moves the cursor backward by blank delimited words.

Moving the Cursor by Lines

The RETURN key moves the cursor to the beginning of the next line (Figure 6-4), while the **j** and down arrow keys move it down one line to the character just below the current character. If there is no character immediately below the current character, the cursor moves to the end of the next line. The cursor will not move past the last line of text.

The **k** and up arrow keys are similar to the **j** key but work in the opposite direction.

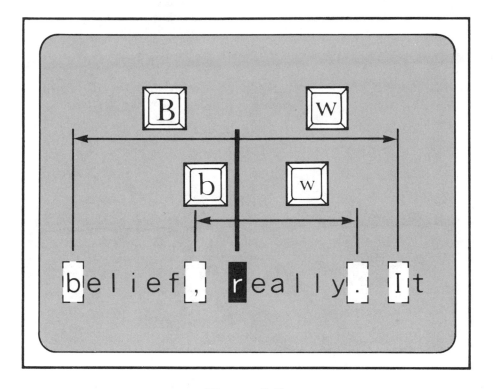

Figure 6-3
Moving the Cursor by Words

Moving the Cursor by Sentences and Paragraphs

The) and } keys move the cursor forward to the beginning of the next sentence or paragraph, respectively (Figure 6-5). The (and { keys move the cursor backward to the beginning of the current sentence or paragraph.

Moving the Cursor Within the Screen

The **H** key positions the cursor at the left end of the top, or Home, line of the screen. The **M** key moves the cursor to the Middle line and **L** moves it to the bottom, or Lower line. See Figure 6-5.

Viewing Different Parts of the Work Buffer

The screen displays a portion of the text that is in the Work Buffer. You can display the text preceding or following the text on the screen by *scrolling* the display. You can also display a portion of the Work Buffer based on a line number.

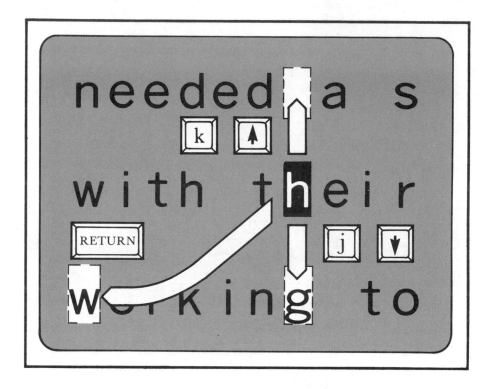

Figure 6-4
Moving the Cursor by Lines

Press CONTROL-D to scroll the screen Down (forward) through the file so that vi displays half a screenful of new text. Use CONTROL-U to scroll the screen Up (backward) the same amount. The CONTROL-F (Forward) or CONTROL-B (Backward) keys display almost a *whole* screenful of new text, leaving a couple of lines from the previous screen for continuity. See Figure 6-6.

When you enter a line number followed by **G** (Goto), vi displays a specific line in the Work Buffer. If you press **G** without a number, vi positions the cursor on the last line in the Work Buffer. Line numbers are implicit; your file does not need to have actual line numbers for you to use this command. Refer to "Line Numbers," page 125, if you want vi to display line numbers.

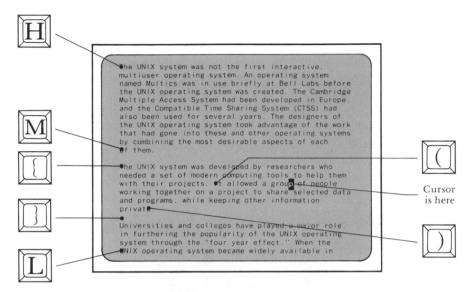

The UNIX system was not the first interactive,
multiuser operating system. An operating system
named Multics was in use briefly at Bell Labs before
the UNIX operating system was created. The Cambridge
Multiple Access System had been developed in Europe,
and the Compatible Time Sharing System (CTSS) had
also been used for several years. The designers of
the UNIX operating system took advantage of the work
that had gone into these and other operating systems
by combining the most desirable aspects of each
of them.

The UNIX system was developed by researchers who
needed a set of modern computing tools to help them
with their projects. It allowed a group of people
working together on a project to share selected data
and programs, while keeping other information
private.

Universities and colleges have played a major role
in furthering the popularity of the UNIX operating
system through the "four year effect." When the
UNIX operating system became widely available in

Cursor
is here

Figure 6-5
Moving the Cursor by Sentences,
Paragraphs, H, M, and L

INPUT MODE

The Insert, Append, Open, Change, and Replace commands put vi
in Input Mode. While vi is in Input Mode, you can put new text
into the Work Buffer. Always press the ESCAPE key to return vi to
Command Mode when you finish entering text. Refer to "Show
Mode" in the "Parameters" section of this chapter if you want vi
to remind you when it is in Input Mode.

The Insert Command

The **i** command puts vi in Input Mode and places the text you
enter *before* the character the cursor is on (the *current character*).
See Figure 6-7. Although the **i** command sometimes overwrites
text on the screen, the overwritten text reappears when you press
ESCAPE and vi returns to Command Mode. Use the **i** command to
insert a few characters or words into existing text or to insert text
in a new file.

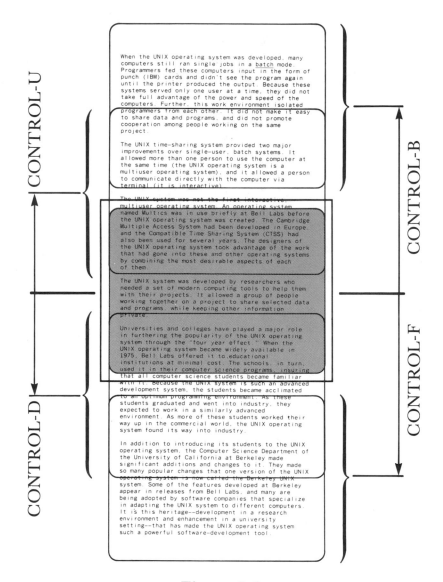

Figure 6-6

Moving the Cursor by CONTROL Characters

The Append Commands

The **a** command is similar to the **i** command, except that it places the text you enter *after* the current character (Figure 6-7). The **A** command places the text *after* the last character on the current line.

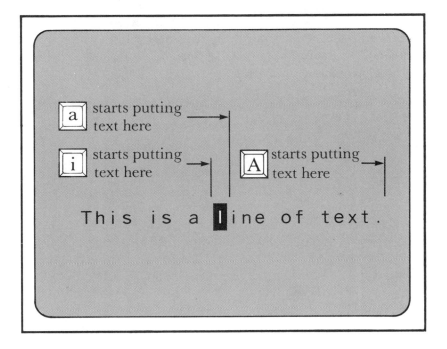

Figure 6-7
The i, a, and A Commands

The Open Commands

The **o** and **O** commands open a blank line within existing text, place the cursor at the beginning of the new (blank) line, and put vi in Input Mode. The **O** command opens a line *above* the current line; **o** opens one below. Use the Open commands when entering several new lines within existing text.

The Replace Commands

The **R** and **r** commands cause the new text you enter to overwrite (replace) existing text. The single character you enter following an **r** command overwrites the current character. After you enter that character, vi automatically returns to Command Mode. You do not need to press the ESCAPE key.

The **R** command causes *all* subsequent characters to overwrite existing text until you press ESCAPE and vi returns to Command Mode.

These commands may appear to behave strangely if you replace TAB characters. TAB characters can appear as several SPACEs—until you try to replace them. They are actually only one character and will be replaced by a single character. Refer to "Invisible Characters," page 126, for information on how to display TABs as visible characters.

COMMAND MODE—DELETING AND CHANGING TEXT

The Undo Command

The Undo command, **u**, undoes what you just did. It restores text that you deleted or changed by mistake. The Undo command only restores the most recently deleted text. If you delete a line and then change a word, Undo restores only the changed word—not the deleted line. The **U** command restores the current line to the way it was before you started changing it, even after several changes.

The Delete Character Command

The **x** command deletes the current character. You can precede the **x** command by a Repeat Factor to delete several characters on the current line, starting with the current character.

The Delete Command

The **d** command removes text from the Work Buffer. The amount of text that **d** removes depends on the Repeat Factor and the Unit of Measure you enter after the **d**. After the text is deleted, vi is in Command Mode.

Caution. The command **d** RETURN deletes two lines—the current line and the following one. Use the **dd** command to delete just the current line, or precede **dd** by a Repeat Factor to delete several lines.

A list of some Delete commands follows. Each of the commands, except the last group, deletes *from* the current character.

Command	Action
d0	delete to beginning of line
dw	delete to end of word
d3w	delete to end of third word
db	delete to beginning of word
dW	delete to end of blank delimited word
dB	delete to beginning of blank delimited word
d7B	delete to beginning of seventh previous blank delimited word
d)	delete to end of sentence
d4)	delete to end of fourth sentence
d(	delete to beginning of sentence
d}	delete to end of paragraph
d{	delete to beginning of paragraph
d7{	delete to beginning of seventh preceding paragraph
dd	delete the current line
5dd	delete 5 lines starting with the current line
dL	delete through last line on screen
dH	delete through first line on screen
dG	delete through end of Work Buffer
d1G	delete through beginning of Work Buffer

The Change Command

The **c** command replaces existing text with new text. The new text does not have to occupy the same space as the existing text. You can change a word to several words, a line to several lines, or a paragraph to a single character.

The Change command deletes the amount of text specified by the Unit of Measure that follows it and puts vi in Input Mode. When you finish entering the new text and press ESCAPE, the old word, line, sentence, or paragraph is changed to the new one.

When you change less than a line of text, vi does not delete the text immediately. Instead, the **c** command places a dollar sign at the end of the text that it will change and leaves vi in Input Mode. You may appear to overwrite text, but vi will restore it, except for the old (changed) text, when you press ESCAPE. When you change a line or more, vi deletes the lines as soon as you give the Change command.

A list of some Change commands follows. Each of the commands, except the last group, changes text *from* the current character.

Command	Action
cw	change to end of word
c3w	change to end of third word
cb	change to beginning of word
cW	change to end of blank delimited word
cB	change to beginning of blank delimited word
c7B	change to beginning of seventh previous blank delimited word
c)	change to end of sentence
c4)	change to end of fourth sentence
c(	change to beginning of sentence
c}	change to end of paragraph
c{	change to beginning of paragraph
c7{	change to beginning of seventh preceding paragraph
cc	change the current line
5cc	change 5 lines starting with the current line

SEARCHING FOR A STRING

The Search Commands

The vi editor will search backward or forward through the Work Buffer to find a specific string of text. To find the next occurrence of a string (forward), press the forward slash (/) key, enter the text you want to find (called the *Search String*), and press RETURN. When you press the slash key, vi displays a slash on the status line. As you enter the string of text, it too is displayed on the status line. When you press RETURN, vi searches for the string. If vi finds the string, it positions the cursor on the first character of the string. If you use a question mark (**?**) in place of the forward slash, vi searches for the previous occurrence of the string.

The **N** and **n** keys repeat the last search without the need for you to enter the Search String again. The **n** key repeats the original search exactly, while the **N** key repeats the search in the opposite direction of the original search.

If you need to include a forward slash in a forward search or a question mark in a backward search, you must quote it by preceding it with a backslash (\).

Normally, if you are searching forward and vi does not find the Search String by the time it gets to the end of the Work Buffer, it will *wrap around* and continue the search at the beginning of the Work Buffer. During a backward search, vi will wrap around from the beginning of the Work Buffer to the end. Also, vi normally performs case-sensitive searches. Refer to "Wrap Scan" (page 127) and "Ignore Case in Searches" (page 126) for information about how to change these search parameters.

Special Characters in Search Strings.   Because the Search String is a regular expression (refer to the Appendix), some characters take on a special meaning within the Search String. The following paragraphs list some of these characters. The first two (^ and $) always have their special meaning, while the rest can have their special meaning turned off. Refer to "Allow Special Characters in Searches," page 126.

The Beginning of Line Indicator (^).   When the first character in a Search String is a caret or circumflex, it matches the beginning of a line. The command /^**the** finds the next line that begins with the string the.

The End of Line Indicator ($).   Similarly, a dollar sign matches the end of a line. The command /!$ finds the next line that ends with an exclamation point.

The Any Character Indicator (.).   A period matches *any* character, anywhere in the Search String. The command /l..e finds line, followed, like, included, all memory, or any other word or character string that contains an l followed by any two characters and an e. To search for an actual period, use a backslash to quote the period (\.).

The End of Word Indicator (\>). This pair of characters matches the end of a word. The command **/s\>** finds the next word that ends with an s.

The Beginning of Word Indicator (\<). This pair of characters matches the beginning of a word. The command **/\<The** finds the next word that begins with The.

The Character Class Definition ([ ]). Square brackets surrounding two or more characters match any *single* character located between the brackets. The command **/dis[ck]** finds the next occurrence of *either* disk or disc.

There are two special characters that you can use within a character class definition. A caret (^) as the first character following the left bracket defines the character class to be *any but the following characters*. A hyphen between two characters indicates a range of characters.

Command	Result
/ and	finds the next occurrence of the string and
	Examples: sand, and, standard, slander, andiron
/\<and\>	finds the next occurrence of the word and
	Example: and
/^The	finds the next line that starts with The
	Examples: The... There...

(continued)

Command	Result
/^[0−9][0−9])	finds the next line that starts with a two-digit number followed by a right parenthesis

Examples:
77)...
01)...
15)...

Command	Result
/\<[adr]	finds the next word that starts with an a, d, or r

Examples: apple, drive, road, argument, right

SUBSTITUTING ONE STRING FOR ANOTHER

A Substitute command is a combination of a Search command and a Change command. It searches for a string just as the / command does, allowing the same special characters that the previous section discussed. When it finds a string, the Substitute command changes it. The format of the Substitute command is shown below. As with all commands that begin with a colon, vi executes a Substitute command from the status line.

   :[address]s/search-string/replace-string[/g]

The next sections discuss the **address**, **s** command, **search-string**, **replace-string**, and **g** flag.

The Substitute Address

If you do not specify an address, Substitute only searches the current line. If you use a single line number as the address, Substitute searches that line. If the address is two line numbers separated by a comma, Substitute searches lines between and including the ones you specify. Refer to "Line Numbers," page 125, if you want vi to display line numbers.

   Within the address, a period represents the current line and a dollar sign represents the last line in the Work Buffer. In many versions of vi, a percent sign represents the entire Work Buffer. You can perform address arithmetic using plus and minus signs. Some examples of addresses are shown below.

Address	Portion of Work Buffer addressed
5	line 5
77,100	lines 77 through 100 inclusive
1,.	the beginning of the Work Buffer through the current line
.,$	the current line through the end of the Work Buffer
1,$	the entire Work Buffer
%	the entire Work Buffer (not all versions)
.,.+10	the current line through the tenth following line

The Search and Replace Strings

An **s**, indicating that a Substitute command follows, comes after the address. A delimiter, marking the beginning of the Search String, follows the **s**. Although the examples in this book use a forward slash, you can use any character that is not a letter or number as a delimiter. You must use the same delimiter at the end of the Search String.

Next comes the Search String. It has the same format as the Search String in the / command and can include the same special characters. (The Search String is a regular expression; refer to the Appendix for more information.) Another delimiter marks the end of the Search String and the beginning of the Replace String. The Replace String is the string that will replace the Search String. The only special characters in the Replace String are the ampersand (**&**), which represents the text that was matched by the Search String, and the backslash, which quotes the character following it. Refer to the following examples and the Appendix.

To replace only the *first occurrence* of the Search String on each line within the specified address, press the RETURN or ESCAPE key after you enter the Replace String. If you want a *global* substitute—that is, if you want to replace *all* occurrences of the Search String on all addressed lines—enter a third delimiter (/) and a **g** before you press RETURN or ESCAPE.

Command	Result
:s / bigger / biggest	replaces the string bigger on the current line with biggest **Example:** bigger → biggest
:1,.s / Ch 1 / Ch 2 / g	replaces every occurrence of the string Ch 1, before or on the current line, with Ch 2 **Examples:** Ch 1 → Ch 2 Ch 12 → Ch 22
:1,$s / ten / 10 / g	replaces every occurrence of the string ten by the string 10 **Examples:** ten → 10, often → of 10 tenant → 10ant
:1,$s / \<ten\> / 10 / g	replaces every occurrence of the word ten by the string 10 **Examples:** ten → 10
:.,+10s / every / each / g	replaces every occurrence of the string every by the string each on the current line through the tenth following line **Examples:** every → each everything → eachthing

MISCELLANEOUS COMMANDS

The Join Command

The Join command, **J**, joins two lines of text. **J** joins the line below the current line to the end of the current line. It inserts a SPACE between what was previously two lines and leaves the cursor on this SPACE. If the current line ends with a period, exclamation point, or question mark, vi inserts two SPACES.

You can always "unjoin" (break) a line into two lines by replacing the SPACE or SPACES where you want to break the line with a RETURN.

The Status Command

The Status command, CONTROL-G, displays the name of the file you are editing, the line number of the current line, the total number of lines in the Work Buffer, and the percent of the Work Buffer preceding the current line.

The . Command

The . (period) command repeats the most recent command that made a change. If, for example, you had just given a **d2w** command (delete the next two words), the . command would delete the next two words. If you had just inserted text, the . command would repeat the insertion of the same text.

This command is useful if you want to change some, but not all, occurrences of a word or phrase in the Work Buffer. Search for the first occurrence of the word (use /), then make the change you want (use **cw**). Following these two commands, you can use **n** to search for the next occurrence of the word and . to make the same change to it. If you do not want to make the change, use **n** again to find the next occurrence.

THE PUT, DELETE, AND YANK COMMANDS

The vi editor has a General Purpose Buffer and 26 Named Buffers that you can use to hold text during an editing session. These buffers are useful if you want to move or copy a portion of text to another location in the Work Buffer. A combination of the Delete and Put commands removes text from one location in the Work Buffer and places it in another. The Yank and Put commands copy text to another location in the Work Buffer without changing the original text.

The General Purpose Buffer

The vi editor stores the text that you most recently changed, deleted, or yanked (see page 121) in the General Purpose Buffer. The Undo command uses the General Purpose Buffer when it restores text.

The Put Commands.   The Put commands, **P** and **p**, copy text from the General Purpose Buffer into the Work Buffer.

If you delete or yank characters or words into the General Purpose Buffer, **P** inserts them before the current *character* and **p** inserts them after. If you delete or yank lines, sentences, or paragraphs, **P** inserts the contents of the General Purpose Buffer before the *line* the cursor is on and **p** inserts it after.

The Put commands do not destroy the contents of the General Purpose Buffer, so it is possible to place the same text at several points within the file by using one Delete or Yank command and several Put commands.

Because vi has only one General Purpose Buffer and vi changes the contents of this buffer each time you give a Change, Delete, or Yank command, **you can use only cursor positioning commands between a Delete or Yank command and the corresponding Put command**. Any other commands change the contents of the General Purpose Buffer and therefore change the results of the Put command.

The Delete Commands.   Any of the Delete commands that were described earlier in this chapter (page 112) automatically place the deleted text in the General Purpose Buffer. Just as you can use the Undo command to put the deleted text back where it came from, you can use a Put command to put the deleted text at another location in the Work Buffer.

For example, if you delete a word from the middle of a sentence using the **dw** command and then move the cursor to a SPACE between two words and give a **p** command, vi will place the word you just deleted at the new location. Or, if you delete a line using the **dd** command and then move the cursor to the line *below* the line where you want the deleted line to appear and give a **P** command, vi will place the line at the new location.

The Yank Commands.   The Yank commands are identical to the Delete commands except that they do not delete text from the Work Buffer. The vi editor places a *copy* of the yanked text in the General Purpose Buffer so that you can use Put to put another copy of it elsewhere in the Work Buffer. Use the Yank command, **y**, just as you use **d**, the Delete command.

Caution. Just as **d** RETURN deletes two lines, **y** RETURN yanks two lines. Use the **yy** command to yank the current line.

For example, if you yank three lines using a **3yy** command and then move the cursor to the line *above* the line where you want a copy of the yanked lines to appear and give a **p** command, vi will copy the lines to the new location.

The Named Buffers

You can use a Named Buffer with any of the Delete, Yank, or Put commands. There are 26 Named Buffers, each named by a letter of the alphabet. Each Named Buffer can store a different block of text so that you can recall each block as needed. Unlike the General Purpose Buffer, vi does not change the contents of a Named Buffer unless you use a command that specifically overwrites that buffer. The vi editor maintains the contents of the Named Buffers throughout an editing session.

The vi editor stores text in a Named Buffer if you precede a Delete or Yank command with a double quotation mark (") and a buffer name (e.g., **"kyy** yanks a copy of the current line into buffer **k**). You can use a Named Buffer in two ways. If you give the name of the buffer as a lowercase letter, vi overwrites the contents of the buffer when it deletes or yanks text into the buffer. If you use an uppercase letter, vi appends the newly deleted or yanked text to the end of the buffer. Using uppercase buffer names, you can collect blocks of text from various sections of a file and then deposit them at one place in the file with a single command.

An example of using a Named Buffer follows. If you have one sentence that you will be using throughout a document, you can yank the sentence into a Named Buffer and put it wherever you need it by using the following procedure. After inserting the first occurrence of the sentence and pressing ESCAPE to return to Command Mode, put the cursor on the first letter of the first word of the sentence. (The sentence must appear on a line or lines by itself for this procedure to work.) Then yank the sentence into buffer **a** by giving a **"ayy** command (or **"a2yy** if the sentence takes up two lines). Now as you are entering text, any time you need the sentence, you can return to Command Mode and give the command **"ap** to put a copy of the sentence below the line the cursor is on.

READING AND WRITING FILES

The vi editor reads a disk file into the Work Buffer when you call vi from the Shell. The **ZZ** command that terminates the editing session writes the contents of the Work Buffer back to the disk file. This section discusses other ways of reading text into the Work Buffer and writing it out.

The Read Command

The Read command reads a file into the Work Buffer. The new file does not overwrite any text in the Work Buffer but is positioned following the current line. The format of the Read command is shown below.

>   **:r [filename]**

As with other commands that begin with a colon, when you enter the colon, it appears on the status line. The **filename** is the pathname of the file that you want to read and must be terminated by RETURN. If you omit the **filename**, vi reads the file you are editing from the disk.

The Write Command

The Write command writes part or all of the Work Buffer to a file. You can use an address to write out part of the Work Buffer and a filename to specify a file to receive the text. If you do not use an address or filename, vi writes the entire contents of the Work Buffer to the file you are editing, updating the file on the disk.

During a long editing session, it is a good idea to use a **:w** command occasionally. Then, if a problem develops, a recent copy of the Work Buffer is safe on the disk. If you use a **:q!** command to exit from vi, the disk file will reflect the version of the Work Buffer at the time you used the Write command.

The format of the Write command is shown below.

>   **:[address]w[!] [filename]**

You can use the following format of the Write command to append text to an existing file.

:[address]w>> filename

The next sections discuss the components of the Write command.

The Address.   If you use an address, it specifies the portion of the Work Buffer that you want vi to write to the disk. The address follows the form of the address that the Substitute command uses. If you do not use an address, vi writes out the entire contents of the Work Buffer.

The w and !.   Because Write can quickly destroy a large amount of work, vi demands that you enter an exclamation point following the **w** as a safeguard against accidentally overwriting a file. The only times you don't need an exclamation point are when you are writing out the entire contents of the Work Buffer to the file being edited (using no address, no filename) and when you are writing part or all of the Work Buffer to a new file. When you are writing part of the file to the file being edited, or overwriting another file, you must use an exclamation point.

The Filename.   The optional filename is the pathname of the file you are writing to. If you do not specify a filename, vi writes to the file you are editing.

SETTING PARAMETERS

You can adapt vi to your needs and habits by setting vi parameters. These parameters can perform many functions, such as causing vi to display line numbers, automatically inserting RETURNs for you, and establishing nonstandard searches.

You can set parameters in two different ways. You can set them while you are using vi, to establish the environment for the current editing session, or you can set the parameters in your **.profile** (Bourne Shell) or **.login** (C Shell) file, so that each time you use vi the environment has been established and you can begin editing immediately.

Setting Parameters from vi

To set a parameter while you are using vi, enter a colon (:), the word **set**, a SPACE, and the parameter (see the "Parameters" section, below). The command appears on the status line as you type it and takes effect when you press RETURN.

Setting Parameters in a Startup File

If you are using the Bourne Shell, put the following lines in the **.profile** file in your home directory.

```
EXINIT='set parm1 parm2 . . .'
export EXINIT
```

Replace **parm1** and **parm2** with parameters selected from the list in the next section. **EXINIT** is a variable that vi reads.

If you are using the C Shell, put the following line in the **.login** file in your home directory.

```
setenv EXINIT 'set parm1 parm2'
```

Again, replace **parm1** and **parm2** with parameters from the following section.

Parameters

This section contains a list of some of the most useful vi parameters. The vi editor displays a complete list of parameters and how they are currently set when you give the command **:set all** followed by a RETURN while using vi.

Line Numbers. The vi editor does not normally display the line number associated with each line. To display line numbers, set the parameter **number**. To cause line numbers not to be displayed, set the parameter **nonumber**.

Line numbers—whether displayed or not—are not part of the file, are not stored with the file, and are not displayed when the file is printed. They only appear on the screen while you are using vi.

Line Wrap Margin. The line wrap margin causes vi to break the text that you are inserting at approximately the specified number of characters from the right margin. The vi editor breaks the text by inserting a NEWLINE character at the closest blank delimited word boundary. Setting the line wrap margin is handy if you want all your text lines to be about the same length. It relieves you of the burden of remembering to press RETURN after each line of input.

Set the parameter **wrapmargin=nn**, where **nn** is the number of characters *from the right side of the screen* where you want vi to break the text. This number is not the column width of the text but the distance from the end of the text to the right edge of the screen. Setting the wrap margin to 0 (zero) turns this feature off.

Show Mode. The vi editor does not normally give you a visual clue to let you know when it is in Input Mode. To display INPUT MODE at the lower right of the screen when vi is in Input Mode, set the parameter **showmode**. Set **noshowmode** to cause vi to not display the message.

Flash. The vi editor normally causes the terminal to beep when you give an invalid command or press ESCAPE when you are in Command Mode. Setting the parameter **flash** causes the terminal to flash instead of beep. Set **noflash** to cause it to beep.

Ignore Case in Searches. The vi editor normally performs case-sensitive searches, differentiating between uppercase and lowercase letters. It performs case-insensitive searches when you set the **ignorecase** parameter. Set **noignorecase** to restore case-sensitive searches.

Allow Special Characters in Searches. The following characters and character pairs normally each have a special meaning when you use them within Search Strings. Refer to "Special Characters in Search Strings," page 115.

> . \< \> [ ]

When you set the **nomagic** parameter, these characters no longer have special meanings. The **magic** parameter gives them back their special meanings.

The ^ and $ characters always have a special meaning within Search Strings, regardless of how you set this parameter.

Invisible Characters. To cause vi to display TABs as ^I and mark the end of each line with a $, set the parameter **list**. To display TABs as white space and not mark ends of lines, set **nolist**.

Wrap Scan. Normally, when a search for the next occurrence of a Search String reaches the end of the Work Buffer, vi continues the search at the beginning of the Work Buffer. The reverse is true of a search for the previous occurrence of a Search String. The **nowrapscan** parameter stops the search at either end of the Work Buffer. Set the **wrapscan** parameter if you want searches to once again wrap around the ends of the Work Buffer.

Automatic Indention. The automatic indention feature works with the **shiftwidth** parameter to provide a regular set of indentions for programs or tabular material. This feature is normally off. You can turn it on by setting **autoindent** (or **ai**) and off by setting **noautoindent** (or **noai**).

When automatic indention is on and vi is in Input Mode, CONTROL-T moves the cursor from the left margin (or an indention) to the next indention position, RETURN moves the cursor to the left side of the next line under the first character of the previous line, and CONTROL-D backs up over indention positions. The CONTROL-T and CONTROL-D characters function in a manner analogous to TAB and BACKTAB keys, but they only function before any text is placed on a line.

Shift Width. The **shiftwidth** parameter controls the functioning of CONTROL-T and CONTROL-D in Input Mode when automatic indention is on. Set the parameter **shiftwidth=nn**, where **nn** is the spacing of the indention positions. Setting the shift width is similar to setting the TAB stops on a typewriter.

ADVANCED EDITING TECHNIQUES

This section presents several commands that you may find useful once you have become comfortable using vi.

Using Markers

While you are using vi, you can set and use up to 26 markers. Set a marker by giving the command **ma**, where **a** is any letter from a-z. Once you have set a marker, you can use it in a manner similar to a line number. The vi editor does not preserve markers when you stop editing a file.

You can move the cursor to a marker by preceding the marker name with a single quotation mark. For example, to set marker **t**, position the cursor on the line you want to mark and give the command **mt**. Unless you reset marker **t**, during this editing session you can return to the line you marked with the command **'t**.

You can delete all text from the current line to marker **r** with the following command.

    d ' r

You can use markers in Substitute commands in place of line numbers. The following command will replace all occurrences of The with THE on all lines from marker **m** to the current line (marker **m** must precede the current line).

    : ' m , . s / T h e / T H E / g

Editing Other Files

The following command causes vi to edit the file you specify with **filename**.

    :e[!] [filename]

If you want to save the contents of the Work Buffer, you must write it out (using **:w**) before you give this command. If you do not want to save the contents of the Work Buffer, vi insists that you use an exclamation point to show that you know that you will lose the work you did since the last time you wrote out the Work Buffer. If you do not supply a **filename**, vi edits the same file you are currently working on.

You can give the command **:e!** to start an editing session over again—this command returns the Work Buffer to the state it was in the last time you wrote it out, or, if you have not written it out, the state it was in when you started editing the file.

Because this command does not destroy the contents of the Named Buffers, you can store text from one file in a Named Buffer, use a **:e** command to edit a second file, and put text from the Named Buffer in the second file. A **:e** command does destroy the contents of the General Purpose Buffer.

Executing Shell Commands from vi

There are several ways you can execute Shell commands while you are using vi. You can create a new, interactive Shell by giving the following command and pressing RETURN.

:sh

After you have done what you want to do in the Shell, you can return to vi by exiting from the Shell (press CONTROL-D or give the command **exit**).

When you create a new Shell in this manner, you must remember that you are still using vi. A common mistake is to start editing the same file from the new Shell, forgetting that vi is already editing the file from a different Shell. Because each invocation of vi uses a different Work Buffer, you will overwrite any work you did from the more recent invocation of vi when you finally get around to exiting from the original invocation of vi.

You can execute a Shell command line from vi by giving the following command, replacing **command** with the command line you want to execute. Terminate the command with a RETURN.

:!command

The vi editor will spawn a new Shell that will execute the **command**. When the command runs to completion, the newly spawned Shell will return control to the editor.

You can execute a command from vi and have vi replace the current line with the output from the command. If you do not want to remove any text, put the cursor on a blank line before giving the command.

!!command

Nothing will happen when you enter the first exclamation point. When you enter the second one, vi will move the cursor to the status line and allow you to enter the command you want to execute. Because this command puts vi in Last Line Mode, you must end the command with a RETURN.

Finally, you can execute a command from vi with the standard input to the command coming from all or part of the file you are editing and the standard output from the command replacing the input in the file you are editing. You can use this type of command to sort a list in place in a file you are working on.

To specify the block of text that is to become the standard input for the command, move the cursor to one end of the block of text. If you want to specify the whole file, move the cursor to the beginning or end of the file. Then enter an exclamation point followed by a command that would normally move the cursor to the other end of the block of text. For example, if the cursor is at the beginning of the file and you want to specify the whole file, give the command **!G**. If you want to specify the part of the file between the cursor and marker **b**, the command would be **!´b**. After you give the cursor movement command, vi will display an exclamation point on the status line and allow you to give a command.

For example, to sort a list of names in a file, move the cursor to the beginning of the list and set marker **q** with an **mq** command. Then move the cursor to the end of the list and give the following command.

```
! ´qsort
```

Press RETURN and wait. After a few moments, you will see the sorted list replace the original list on the screen. If the command didn't do what you expected, you can undo the change with a **u** command.

UNITS OF MEASURE

Many vi commands operate on a block of text—from a character to many paragraphs. You can specify the size of a block of text with a *Unit of Measure*. You can specify multiple Units of Measure by preceding a Unit of Measure with a number, called a *Repeat Factor*. This section defines the various Units of Measure.

Character

A character is one character, visible or not, printable or not, including SPACEs and TABs.

Examples of characters

a	q
A	.
TAB	5
SPACE	R
—	>

Word

A word is an English word or its equivalent. It is a string of one or more characters that is bounded on both sides by any combination of one or more of the following elements: a punctuation mark, SPACE, TAB, numeral, or NEWLINE. In addition, vi considers each group of punctuation marks to be a word.

Text	Word count
pear	(1 word)
pear!	(2 words)
pear!)	(2 words)
pear!) The	(3 words)
pear!) "The	(4 words)
This is a short, concise line (no frills).	(11 words)

Blank Delimited Word

A blank delimited word is the same as a word, except that it includes adjacent punctuation. Blank delimited words are separated from each other by one or more of the following elements: a SPACE, TAB, or NEWLINE.

Text	Blank delimited word count
pear	(1 blank delimited word)
pear!	(1 blank delimited words)
pear!)	(1 blank delimited words)
pear!) The	(2 blank delimited words)
pear!) "The	(2 blank delimited words)
This is a short, concise line (no frills).	(8 blank delimited words)

Line

A line is a string of characters bounded by NEWLINEs. It is not necessarily a single, physical line on the terminal. You can enter a very long single (logical) line that wraps around (continues on the next physical line) several times. It is a good idea to avoid long logical lines by terminating lines with a RETURN before they reach the right side of the terminal screen. Terminating lines in this manner ensures that each physical line contains one logical line and avoids confusion when you edit and format text. Some commands do not *appear* to work properly on physical lines that are longer than the width of the screen. For example, with the cursor on a long logical line that wraps around several physical lines, pressing RETURN once will appear to move the cursor down more than one line.

Sentence

A sentence is an English sentence or the equivalent. A sentence starts at the end of the previous sentence and ends with a period, exclamation point, or question mark, followed by two SPACEs or a NEWLINE.

Text	Sentence count
That's it. This is one sentence.	(one sentence: only one SPACE after the first period—NEWLINE after the second period)
That's it. This is two sentences.	(two sentences: two SPACEs after the first period—NEWLINE after the second period)
What? Three sentences? One line!	(three sentences: two SPACEs after the first two question marks—NEWLINE after the exclamation point)
This sentence takes up a total of three lines.	(one sentence: NEWLINE after the period)

Paragraph

A paragraph is preceded and followed by one or more blank lines. A blank line is composed of two NEWLINE characters in a row.

Text	**Paragraph count**
one paragraph	(one paragraph: blank line before and after text)
This may appear to be more than one paragraph. Just because there are two indentions does not mean it qualifies as two paragraphs.	(one paragraph: blank line before and after text)
Even though in	(three paragraphs: three blocks of text separated by blank lines)
English this is only one sentence,	
vi considers it to be three paragraphs.	

Screen

The terminal screen is a window that opens onto part of the Work Buffer. You can position this window so that it shows different portions of the Work Buffer.

Repeat Factor

A number that precedes a Unit of Measure is a Repeat Factor. Just as the *5* in *5 inches* causes you to consider *5 inches* as a single unit of measure, a Repeat Factor causes vi to group more than one Unit of Measure and consider it as a single Unit of Measure. For example, the command **w** moves the cursor forward one word. The command **5w** moves the cursor forward five words, and **250w** moves it 250 words. If you do not specify a Repeat Factor, vi assumes that you mean one Unit of Measure.

SUMMARY

This summary of vi includes all the commands covered in this chapter, plus some new ones.

Calling vi

Command	Function
vi *filename*	edit *filename* starting at line 1
vi +*n filename*	edit *filename* starting at line *n*
vi + *filename*	edit *filename* starting at the last line
vi +/ *pattern filename*	edit *filename* starting at the first line containing the *pattern*
vi −r *filename*	recover *filename* after a system crash

Moving the Cursor by Units of Measure

You must be in Command Mode to use these commands. They are the Units of Measure that you can use in Change, Delete, and Yank commands. Each of these commands can be preceded with a Repeat Factor.

Command	Moves the cursor
SPACE, l, or →	space to the right
h or ←	space to the left
w	word to the right
W	blank delimited word to the right
b	word to the left
B	blank delimited word to the left
$	end of line
e	end of word to the right
E	end of blank delimited word to the right
0	beginning of line (cannot be used with a Repeat Factor)
RETURN	beginning of next line
j or ↓	down one line
k or ↑	up one line
)	end of sentence
(	beginning of sentence
}	end of paragraph
{	beginning of paragraph

Viewing Different Parts of the Work Buffer

Command	Moves the cursor
CONTROL-D	forward ½ screenful
CONTROL-U	backward ½ screenful
CONTROL-F	forward one screenful
CONTROL-B	backward one screenful
nG	to line n (without n to the last line)
H	to the top of screen
M	to the middle of screen
L	to the bottom of screen

Adding Text

All the following commands (except **r**) leave vi in Input Mode. You must press ESCAPE to return it to Command Mode.

Command	Insert text
i	before cursor
I	before first nonblank character on line
a	after cursor
A	at end of line
o	open a line below the current line
O	open a line above the current line
r	replace current character (no ESCAPE needed)
R	replace characters, starting with current character (overwrite until ESCAPE)

Deleting and Changing Text

In the following list, M is a Unit of Measure that you can precede with a Repeat Factor. The n is a Repeat Factor.

Command	Effect
nx	delete the number of characters specified by n, starting with the current character
nX	delete the number of characters specified by n, starting with the character following the current character
dM	delete text specified by M
$n$dd	delete the number of lines specified by n
D	delete to end of line

The following commands leave vi in Input Mode. You must press ESCAPE to return it to Command Mode.

Command	Effect
ns	substitute the number of characters specified by n
cM	change text specified by M
$n$cc	change the number of lines specified by n
C	change to end of line

Yanking and Putting Text

In the following list, M is a Unit of Measure that you can precede with a Repeat Factor. The n is a Repeat Factor. You can precede any of these commands with the name of a buffer in the form "x, where x is the name of the buffer (a-z).

Command	Effect
yM	yank text specified by M
$n$yy	yank the number of lines specified by n
Y	yank to end of line
P	put text before or above
p	put text after or below

Searching for a String

In the following list, *rexp* is a regular expression that can be a simple string of characters.

Command	Effect
/*rexp* RETURN	search forward for *rexp*
?*rexp* RETURN	search backward for *rexp*
n	repeat original search exactly
N	repeat original search, opposite direction
/RETURN	repeat original search forward
?RETURN	repeat original search backward

String Substitution

The format of a Substitute command is shown below.

:[address]s/search-string/replace-string[/g]

address   is one line number or two line numbers separated by a comma. A . represents the current line, $ represents the last line, and % represents the entire file. You can use a marker in place of a line number.

search-string is a regular expression that can be a simple string of characters.

replace-string is the replacement string.

g   indicates a global replacement (more than one replacement per line).

Advanced Commands

Command	Effect
m*x*	set marker *x*, where *x* is a letter from a-z
`` `` ``	move cursor back to its previous location
´*x*	move cursor to marker *x*, where *x* is a letter from a-z
:w *file*	write contents of Work Buffer to *file* (current file if there is no *file*)
:e! *file*	edit file, discarding changes to current file (use **:w** first if you want to keep the changes)
:sh	fork a Shell
:!*command*	fork a Shell and execute command
!!*command*	fork a Shell, execute command, place output in file replacing the current line

7

THE nroff TEXT FORMATTER

This chapter shows how to use the nroff text formatting program to prepare documents. It discusses the theory of filling and justifying lines, describes the structure of an input file, and shows how to use nroff commands. Most of the commands described in this chapter are part of the **mm** macro package. The summary at the end of the chapter covers plain nroff commands and **mm** commands.

INTRODUCTION TO nroff

Input to nroff is a file of text that you create using an editor such as vi. Output from nroff is paginated, formatted text that you can send to a terminal, printer, or plain file. Commands embedded in the input file determine what the output text looks like.

The nroff formatter has default values for all margins, line lengths, indentions, and spacing of text on a page. If your input file contains text without embedded commands, nroff uses these default values to format the output text. You can use as few or as many commands as the complexity of the formatting job requires.

The nroff formatter can accomplish many formatting tasks. Among its capabilities, nroff can

- fill lines
- right-justify lines
- hyphenate words
- center text
- generate footnotes
- automatically number headings
- number pages
- put the date on each page
- put headers on each page
- put footers on each page
- produce numbered lists

The output from nroff is designed to go to a terminal or line printer. A related formatter, troff, sends its output to a photo-typesetter. Because a phototypesetter has a much higher resolution than a line printer, troff gives you much more control over the way the output looks. The troff formatter has commands that change the size and style of type you use. It can also produce special symbols such as em dashes (—). Where nroff underlines type, troff uses *italic* type. You can use all the commands in this chapter with troff—each command may, however, have slightly different effects with troff than with nroff.

Two preprocessors work with either nroff or troff. The eqn preprocessor assists you in formatting equations, while tbl formats tables.

Instructing nroff to format a file can be tedious and unnecessarily complex. To make the job easier, nroff allows you to define and use *macros*. A macro is a short command that nroff expands into a longer sequence of commands. Even with this facility, you would ordinarily need an in-depth knowledge of nroff to format a document of moderate complexity.

Because so many people's formatting needs are similar, nroff provides several predefined packages of macros. Using one of the existing *macro packages* can make a job easier, so that you can concentrate on the content, rather than the format, of a document. This chapter shows how to use nroff with the **mm** (memorandum) macro package.

USING nroff WITH THE mm PACKAGE

You can distinguish **mm** commands from regular nroff commands because all **mm** commands (and most commands from other macro packages) use uppercase letters while plain nroff commands use only lowercase letters. The regular nroff commands that are described in this chapter and **mm** commands can be mixed in a file that is processed by nroff *and* the **mm** macro package.

The following command line indicates to nroff that you want to use the macro package.

```
$ nroff -mm filename
   .
   .
   .
```

The **−mm** is the option that selects the macro package, and the **filename** is the name of the input file that you want to format. This command line sends the formatted text to the standard output. Unless you redirect it, the text appears on the terminal. You can use the pg utility to view one screenful of text at a time. (Press RETURN to view additional pages after pg displays the first.)

```
$ nroff -mm file | pg
   .
   .
   .
```

You can inspect nroff output before sending it to the printer by redirecting it and using pg.

```
$ nroff —mm file > hold
$ pg hold
.
.
.
$
```

If the output is what you want, you can send it to the printer
using lp.

```
$ lp hold
request id is printer_1-540 (1 file)
$
```

You can also use a pipe to redirect the output directly to the lp
utility without first inspecting it.

```
$ nroff —mm file | lp
request id is printer_1-541 (standard input)
$
```

THEORY OF FILLING AND JUSTIFYING LINES

The ability to *fill* and *justify* lines is the most important feature of
any formatter. It is this process that gives the output text its
finished appearance. A filled line of output text is brought as close
to the right margin as is possible without padding the line with
SPACES; a filled and justified line is padded so that it reaches the
right margin.

Input File:

```
The ability to fill and justify lines is the
most important
feature of any formatter.
```

Filled Output Text:

```
The ability to fill and
justify lines is the
most important feature
of any formatter.
```

Filled and Justified Output Text:

```
The ability to fill and
justify  lines  is  the
most important  feature
of any formatter.
```

Filling a Line

The format of the output text is not dependent upon the length of lines in the input file. To nroff, the input file is a stream of words. To produce a line of output text, nroff takes words from the input stream and keeps adding them to the output line until it gets to a word that brings the line past the right margin. If nroff can hyphenate and include part of this word on the line, it does. Otherwise it saves this word for the next line of output text. At this point, the line is *filled.* It cannot hold the entire next word, or part of the next word if it was hyphenated, without exceeding the right margin. When each of the output lines is filled, the right edge of the output text is ragged. It is said to have a *ragged right* margin.

Justifying Text

All the lines in justified text come exactly to (are flush with) the right margin. The only exception is the last line of a paragraph, which is never justified. Justified text is said to have a *flush right* margin. Unless you instruct nroff with the **mm** macros otherwise (refer to the section of this chapter on "Justification"), it fills but does not justify lines.

Before a line can be justified, it must be filled. To justify text, nroff expands single SPACEs between words in the filled line, one at a time, to double, triple, or more SPACEs as it brings the right end of the line to the right margin. (Some versions also increase the space between letters of words by fractions of SPACEs.)

THE INPUT FILE

You can prepare the input file with an editor such as vi. Each line in the input file contains either an nroff command or text. This section discusses both types of lines.

Command Lines

A line in the input file containing an nroff command begins with a period or a single quotation mark. This chapter does not discuss command lines that begin with a single quotation mark—they are just mentioned here so that you can avoid giving nroff a command by mistake. A line beginning with a SPACE and a line with nothing on it (a *blank line*) also have special meanings to nroff—refer to the section of this chapter on "Breaks."

Because nroff considers a line in the input file that begins with a period, a single quotation mark, or a SPACE to be a command line—regular lines of text cannot begin with any of these characters.

Commands. Commands follow a period at the beginning of a line in the input file. A command is composed of one or two letters or a number and a letter. Plain nroff commands use lowercase letters; **mm** macro package commands use uppercase letters. A list of sample commands follows.

Plain nroff **commands**	**mm macro package** **commands**
.bp	.P
.ce	.AL
.fi	.I
.nf	.DS
.nr	.BI

Command Arguments. Some commands require additional information on the same line with the command. SPACEs separate these pieces of information, or arguments, from the command and from each other. You can quote arguments that include SPACEs by preceding and following them with double quotation marks (")— nroff will interpret everything between the double quotation marks as a single argument.

There are two kinds of arguments—measurements and text. A measurement gives some information to nroff but is not printed. When text appears after a command, nroff places it in the output text in some special manner.

The following command takes a number as an argument. It

centers the next three lines in the output text. The **3** is a measurement that tells nroff how many lines to center.

    .ce 3

The next command takes text as an argument. It underlines the word that follows it on the same line. The **I** stands for *italic* (nroff underlines the text because it can't produce italic type).

    .I important

The next command uses both types of arguments. The Head command places a numbered head in the text. The heading level is specified by the first argument and the body of the head by the second. The second argument contains SPACEs—the double quotation marks cause nroff to consider the heading text as a single argument.

    .H 4 "This is a Level Four Head"

Text Lines

All lines in the input file that are not command lines are text lines. The nroff formatter processes these lines into the output text according to the specifications of the command lines.

THE mm MACROS

Because the **mm** macros are designed to be used by people with varying amounts of experience, most commands have default values. As an example, the command

    .P

by itself indicates the start of a left-block paragraph (all lines flush left).

A *register* is a location in memory that nroff uses to store a number. Most default values can be changed by using a **.nr** (number register) command to change the value of a number register. As an example, the command

```
.nr Pt 1
```

changes the paragraph type register so that all the following **.P** commands generate standard paragraphs (first line indented). The **mm** macros use registers to control various aspects of document format. Just as you can change the paragraph style by changing the value of the **Pt** register, you can change the way headings appear, vertical spacing, footnote style, and more by changing the values of other registers.

In addition, many commands accept parameters to make a one-time exception to a default value. The command

```
.P 1
```

makes only the paragraph following the command a standard paragraph—all subsequent paragraphs go back to the default value—either standard or left block.

The difference between changing a number register and changing a parameter is usually one of extent. In the preceding example, changing the number register changed the effect of all subsequent Paragraph commands while changing the parameter only changed the effect of the current Paragraph command.

PARAGRAPHS

An nroff paragraph is a block of output text that usually has one or more blank lines above and below it. With the **mm** macros, nroff fills, but does not justify, lines of the paragraph unless you instruct it otherwise (refer to the **.SA** command, page 172).

The nroff formatter provides two types of paragraphs, left block and standard (indented). All the lines in a *left-block* paragraph are flush with the left margin. The first line of a *standard* paragraph is indented, while all the following lines are flush with the left margin.

The format of a Paragraph command is shown below. (The square brackets indicate that the argument they surround is optional.)

.P [type]

If you do not specify **type**, the **.P** command initially produces left-block paragraphs. You can change the default type with the **Pt** register (following).

The **type** controls the type of the paragraph immediately following the command only. It temporarily overrides the default paragraph type. When you specify **type** equal to 0, nroff produces a left-block paragraph; a 1 produces a standard paragraph.

Input File:

```
.P
This is a left—block paragraph.
When you give a .P command without
an argument and without changing the
value of the Pt register, this is what
you get.
.P 1
This is a standard paragraph.
The first line is indented; the rest
come out to the left margin.
The 1 following the .P command
overrides the default paragraph type
and forces this to be a standard
paragraph.
```

Output Text:

```
This is a left—block paragraph. When you give a .P command
without an argument and without changing the value of the Pt
register, this is what you get.

     This is a standard paragraph. The first line is
indented; the rest come out to the left margin. The 1
following the .P command overrides the default paragraph
type and forces this to be a standard paragraph.
```

The **Pt** (paragraph type) register controls the default paragraph type for all the Paragraph commands that follow it. Initially, the **Pt** register has a value of 0 (zero), causing **.P** commands to yield left-block paragraphs. Using the following command to change the value of **Pt** to 1 causes **.P** commands to produce standard paragraphs.

```
.nr Pt 1
```

Below, nroff produces standard paragraphs without the use of an argument after each **.P** command.

Input File:

```
.nr Pt 1
.P
This is a standard paragraph.
Setting the Pt register to 1 causes
all subsequent .P commands to produce
standard paragraphs.
Now it is necessary to follow a .P command
with a 0 if you want to print a left—block
paragraph.
.P 0
This is a left—block paragraph.
The 0 following the .P command only affects
this paragraph — the next one is a standard
paragraph by default.
.P
Each .P command from now on (unless you
change the value of the Pt register) produces
standard paragraphs.
```

Output Text:

```
        This is a standard paragraph.  Setting the Pt register
to 1 causes all subsequent .P commands to produce standard
paragraphs.  Now it is necessary to follow a .P command with
a 0 if you want to print a left—block paragraph.

This is a left—block paragraph.  The 0 following the .P
command only affects this paragraph — the next one is a
standard paragraph by default.

        Each .P command from now on (unless you change the
value of the Pt register) produces standard paragraphs.
```

The **Pi** (paragraph indention) register controls the number of SPACEs that precede the first line of indented paragraphs. Initially, **Pi** is set to 5. The following command changes the paragraph indention to 12.

```
.nr Pi 12
```

If you set **Pi** to 0, standard paragraphs appear to be left-block paragraphs because they are not indented.

LISTS

A list is a set of items, such as words, lines, paragraphs, or sections, each one of which is preceded by a design element, such as a number, dash, word, or phrase. The **mm** macros provide automatically numbered or lettered lists, lists where each item is preceded by the same design element (e.g., a dash) and lists where each item is preceded by a different word or phrase. You can nest lists up to six levels deep.

All lists start with a List-initialization command (**.AL**, **.DL**, **.ML**, or **.VL**) that tells nroff what kind of list follows. A **.LI** (list item) command precedes each item within the list, and a **.LE** (list end) command ends the list.

An example of a simple, automatically numbered list follows.

Input File:

```
.AL
.LI
This is the first list item.
.LI
This is the second list item.
Each item must be preceded by
a .LI command.
.LI
This is the last item in the list.
.LE
```

Output Text:

```
    1.    This is the first list item.

    2.    This is the second list item.   Each item must be
          preceded by a .LI command.

    3.    This is the last item in the list.
```

Automatic Lists

The **.AL** (automatic list) command generates lists that are numbered or lettered in a variety of ways (see the preceding and following examples). The format of the command is shown below.

.AL [type] [indention] [separation]

You can select **type** from the following list:

type   **Result**

1	Arabic numbers (default)
A	uppercase letters
a	lowercase letters
I	uppercase Roman numbers
i	lowercase Roman numbers

The **indention** is the number of SPACEs that the text is to be indented. If it is null or missing, nroff uses the value of the **Li** register. The **separation** is 0 (default) for a blank line separating items in the list and 1 for no lines separating items. There is always a blank line before the first item in a list.

The following example shows a three-level list. The **Ls** register controls spacing above and below items based on the level of each item. (If you set **Ls** to 1, nroff only leaves blank lines around level 1 items, setting **Ls** to 2 leaves blank lines around level 1 and level 2 items, and so on.) Initially, **Ls** is set to 6, which means that nroff leaves a blank line above and below each item (levels 1-6). The following example sets **Ls** equal to 2, which causes nroff to leave blank lines around level 1 and 2 list items only.

Input File:

```
.nr Ls 2
.AL I
.LI
This example shows an automatic list that is nested
to three levels.
The first level uses uppercase Roman numerals to
identify list items.
.AL
.LI
Each of the second-level list items is preceded by
an Arabic number.
.LI
As with all automatic lists, each List Item (.LI) command
increments the number (or letter) preceding each list item.
.AL a
.LI
This item is at the third level of this list.
.LI
The third-level items are identified by lowercase letters.
.LI
The Ls register was set to 2 before this list was started
so that third-level items would not be separated from each
other by blank lines.
.LE
.LI
Because the Ls register was set to 2, level 1 and 2 items
are still separated from each other by blank lines.
.LE
.LI
Each .LE (list end) command ends a list level.
As each level ends, the previous (higher level) list takes over.
The next .LE command corresponds to the first .AL command and
ends the entire list.
.LE
```

Output Text:

I. This example shows an automatic list that is nested to three levels. The first level uses uppercase Roman numerals to identify list items.

    1. Each of the second—level list items is preceded by an Arabic number.

    2. As with all automatic lists, each List Item (.LI) command increments the number (or letter) preceding each list item.

       a. This item is at the third level of this list.

       b. The third—level items are identified by lowercase letters.

       c. The Ls register was set to 2 before this list was started so that third—level items would not be separated from each other by blank lines.

    3. Because the Ls register was set to 2, level 1 and 2 items are still separated from each other by blank lines.

II. Each .LE (list end) command ends a list level. As each level ends, the previous (higher level) list takes over. The next .LE command corresponds to the first .AL command and ends the entire list.

The Dash List

A dash and a single SPACE precede each element in a dash list. The format of the List-initialization command for a dash list is shown below.

.DL [indention] [separation]

The **indention** is the number of SPACEs that the text is indented. If it is null or missing, nroff uses the value of the **Pi** register (see page 149) so that the text lines up with the first line of an indented paragraph. The **separation** is 0 (default) for a blank line separating items in the list and 1 for no lines separating items. There is always a blank line before the first item in a list.

Input File:

```
This is regular text.
It is here to show the effect of indenting a list.
.DL 15
.LI
This is the first item.
.LI
This is a dash list.
.LI
Each item is indented 15 SPACEs.
.LI
This is the last item.
.LE
```

Output Text:

```
This is regular text.  It is here to show the effect of
indenting a list.

                — This is the first item.

                — This is a dash list.

                — Each item is indented 15 SPACEs.

                — This is the last item.
```

The Marked List

Each item in a marked list begins with a mark that is specified in the List-initialization command. The mark can be more than one character, but you must quote all SPACEs within the mark by preceding each with a backslash so that nroff does not expand them. The format for a marked list is shown below.

.ML mark [indention] [separation]

The **mark** is the element that is to appear before each item in the list. The **indention** is the number of SPACEs that the text is indented. If it is null or missing, nroff indents the text one SPACE more than the number of characters in the mark. The **separation** is 0 (default) for a blank line separating items in the list and 1 for no lines separating items. There is always a blank line before the first item in a list.

Input File:

```
.ML >
.LI
This is a marked list
.LI
It uses a greater—than symbol as a mark.
.LI
You can use any mark you like.
.LE

.ML READ\ THIS\ —> 15
.LI
A marked list can use a mark composed of many characters.
.LI
If the mark contains SPACEs, each SPACE must be preceded
by a backslash.
.LI
See the next section ("The Variable—Item List") if you
want to have
a different mark appear before each item.
.LE
```

Output Text:

```
> This is a marked list

> It uses a greater—than symbol as a mark.

> You can use any mark you like.

  READ THIS —> A marked list can use a mark composed of many
               characters.

  READ THIS —> If the mark contains SPACEs, each SPACE must
               be preceded by a backslash.

  READ THIS —> See the next section ("The Variable—Item
               List") if you want to have a different mark
               appear before each item.
```

The Variable-Item List

A variable-item list allows you to put a different mark before each item in the list. The text that acts as the mark for a particular item is specified in each List Item command. The format of a variable-item List-initialization command is shown below.

.VL indention [mark-indention] [separation]

The **indention** is the number of SPACEs that the text is indented. The **mark-indention** is the number of SPACEs that each mark is indented. The default value is 0 (the mark is left-justified). The **separation** is 0 (default) for a blank line separating items in the list and 1 for no lines separating items. There is always a blank line before the first item in a list.

Input File:

```
.VL 15
.LI Useful
Variable lists are useful for many purposes.
.LI Glossaries
They are frequently used for glossaries.
.LI Flexible
You can customize variable lists to suit your needs.
.LI Low\ Overhead
They are also easy to use.
Remember to quote SPACEs within marks by preceding
each with a backslash.
.LE
```

Output Text:

Useful	Variable lists are useful for many purposes.
Glossaries	They are frequently used for glossaries.
Flexible	You can customize variable lists to suit your needs.
Low Overhead	They are also easy to use. Remember to quote SPACEs within marks by preceding each with a backslash.

The List Item Command

The format of the List Item command that must precede each item in a list is shown below.

.LI [mark] [prefix]

The **mark** is the mark for a variable-list list. If you use it with another type of list, it will replace the mark for the current item only. If you include a second argument (the **prefix**), it causes the **mark** to precede the current mark and has the effect of emphasizing it. You can use any character as the **prefix**—your choice of characters has no effect on the outcome of the list.

Input File:

```
In order to successfully complete the test,
you must follow all the starred instructions.
Instructions that are not starred may or may
not be helpful to you.
.AL
.LI
Use a pencil.
.LI * x
Draw a square.
.LI note
The square does not have to be precise.
Approximate the shape of a square to the
best of your ability using the tools you
have.
.LI
Try not to use the eraser.
.LI * x
Draw a triangle.
.LE
```

Output Text:

```
In order to successfully complete the test, you must follow
all the starred instructions.  Instructions that are not
starred may or may not be helpful to you.

     1.   Use a pencil.

 *   2.   Draw a square.

note   The square does not have to be precise.  Approximate
       the shape of a square to the best of your ability
       using the tools you have.

     4.   Try not to use the eraser.

 *   5.   Draw a triangle.
```

The List End Command

The List End command must terminate all lists. Its format is shown below.

.LE [separation]

The **separation** is 0 (default) for no blank lines following the list and 1 for a blank line.

UNDERLINED AND BOLD FONTS

The **.I** (italic) command causes nroff to underline text. (If you were using troff, the typesetting version of nroff, the text would be printed in an italic font, hence the name of the command.)

You can use the **.I** command with or without arguments. With a single argument, the **.I** command underlines that argument only. Without an argument, it underlines all subsequent text until a **.R** (Roman) command stops the underlining. The following example demonstrates these uses of the **.I** command.

Input File:

```
This is an example of the use of
the .I command.
It
.I will
underline text.
If you want to underline more than
a single word,
.I
do not give the .I command an argument.
.R
Use the .R
command to return to text
that is not underlined.
```

Output Text:

```
This is an example of the use of the .I command.  It will
underline text.  If you want to underline more than a single
word, do not give the .I command an argument.  Use the .R
command to return to text that is not underlined.
```

With two arguments, the **.I** command underlines the first argument, displaying the second without underlining it and without any intervening SPACEs.

The **.RI** (Roman-italic) command allows you to have text immediately preceding and following an underlined word. This command displays its arguments alternating between Roman and underlined text.

Input File:

```
When you give the .I command two
arguments, it underlines the first,
removes the space between the arguments,
and prints the second in a regular (called
.I Roman )
font.

The .RI command alternates between Roman
and underlined
.RI ( italic )
fonts.
```

Output Text:

```
When you give the .I command two arguments, it underlines
the first, removes the space between the arguments, and
prints the second in a regular (called Roman) font.

The .RI command alternates between Roman and underlined
(italic) fonts.
```

The **.B** (bold) command displays text in a bold font. (Some printers are not capable of producing bold type. On these machines, there is no difference between bold and Roman text.)

In a manner similar to the **.RI** command, the following commands alternate between other fonts.

Command	Font
.IB	underlined-bold
.BI	bold-underlined
.IR	underlined-Roman
.RI	Roman-underlined
.RB	Roman-bold
.BR	bold-Roman

HEADINGS

A *heading* (or *head*) is a title within text. Headings are usually set off from the surrounding text by typeface and position. The **mm** macros provide extensive heading capabilities, including automatic generation of heading numbers for up to seven levels of headings, heading formatting, and automatic generation of a table of contents based on headings. As with paragraphs, you can change many aspects of headings by changing the values of registers.

Numbered Headings

A numbered heading is a heading that is preceded by a number in the form 2.5.7. A **.H** (heading) command indicates that a numbered heading follows. Each time you use a **.H** command, it automatically increments the number corresponding to the heading level you specify (e.g., if the previous heading number was 2.5.7 and you specified a third-level head, the new heading number would be 2.5.8; if you specified a second-level head, it would be 2.6). The format of a Heading command is shown below.

.H level [heading-text]

The **level** is the desired heading level from 1 through 7, and the **heading-text** is the text of the heading. If the **heading-text** includes any SPACEs, you must enclose the text in double quotation marks. See the following example.

By default, nroff prints level 1 and 2 heads in boldface followed by a single blank line. These two levels are distinguished by the section number that precedes them and the way (by convention) you enter them: level 1 in all uppercase letters and level 2 in lowercase letters with initial capital letters. Level 3 through 7 heads are underlined run-in headings followed by two SPACEs. The section numbers that precede each of these five levels distinguish them.

Input File:

```
.H 1 "PARTS"
This example demonstrates how numbered headings work.
It uses a parts list as sample text.
.H 2 "Screws"
By default, level 2 heads are printed in boldface type
and separated from the following text by a single blank line.
.H 3 "Sheet Metal Screws"
Level 3 heads are underlined and run in to the following text.
.H 3 "Wood Screws"
Each subsequent level 3 head increments the third-level heading
number.
.H 4 "Phillips Head"
Level 4 heads are displayed the same way as level 3 heads.
.H 4 "Slotted Head"
This is a level 4 head.
It increments the fourth-level heading number.
.H 3 "Specially Hardened Screws"
This is another third-level head.
.H 2 "Nails"
This level 2 head increments the second-level heading number.
```

Output Text:

---

1. **PARTS**

This example demonstrates how numbered headings work. It uses a parts list as sample text.

1.1 **Screws**

By default, level 2 heads are printed in boldface type and separated from the following text by a single blank line.

1.1.1 <u>Sheet</u> <u>Metal</u> <u>Screws</u> Level 3 heads are underlined and run in to the following text.

1.1.2 <u>Wood</u> <u>Screws</u> Each subsequent level 3 head increments the third—level heading number.

1.1.2.1 <u>Phillips</u> <u>Head</u> Level 4 heads are displayed the same way as level 3 heads.

1.1.2.2 <u>Slotted</u> <u>Head</u> This is a level 4 head. It increments the fourth—level heading number.

1.1.3 <u>Specially</u> <u>Hardened</u> <u>Screws</u> This is another third—level head.

1.2 **Nails**

This level 2 head increments the second—level heading number.

Unnumbered Headings

A **.HU** (heading-unnumbered) command indicates that an unnumbered heading follows. Unnumbered headings are similar to numbered headings except they are not preceded by level numbers. The format of a **.HU** command follows.

.HU heading-text

As with a numbered heading, the **heading-text** is the text of the heading—enclosed in double quotation marks if it contains SPACES.

Input File:

```
.HU "Unnumbered Heading"
By default, unnumbered headings are level 2 heads.
If you change the value of the Hu register, the level of
subsequent unnumbered heads changes to the new value of Hu.
```

Output Text:

Unnumbered Heading

By default, unnumbered headings are level 2 heads. If you
change the value of the Hu register, the level of subsequent
unnumbered heads changes to the new value of Hu.

By default, unnumbered headings are level 2 heads. If you
want unnumbered headings at a different level (for appearance or
for the table of contents described later on), you must change the
value of the **Hu** register before giving a **.HU** command. The following commands produce a third-level unnumbered heading.

```
.nr Hu 3
.HU "This is a Third—level Head"
```

Subsequent **.HU** commands will also produce third-level heads
until you change the value of the **Hu** register.

Changing Heading Format

The following paragraphs explain how to change the format of
both numbered and unnumbered headings of various levels. If you
are satisfied with the heads produced by the **.HU** and **.H** commands, you can skip this section.

Forcing Heads to the Tops of Pages. You can force all first-level heads to start at the top of a page by setting the **Ej** (ejection) register to 1.

```
.nr Ej 1
```

If you set the **Ej** register to a larger number, all headings at that level and lower will begin on a new page (e.g., setting **Ej** to 3 causes level 1, 2, and 3 heads to start new pages).

Breaks After Heads. By default, level 1 and 2 heads appear on lines by themselves while level 3 through 7 heads are run in to the text. The **Hb** (head-break) register controls which heads have breaks following them. The following command causes only level 5, 6, and 7 heads to run in to the text. It causes a break following all heads at level 4 and lower.

```
.nr Hb 4
```

Blank Lines After Heads. By default, level 1 and 2 heads are followed by single blank lines, while level 3 through 7 heads are not. Actually, the format of level 3 through 7 heads is controlled by the **Hb** register (above)—you can't separate run-in heads from the text by a blank line. But if you set the **Hs** (head-space) register to a value less than the **Hb** register, you can produce three kinds of heads: heads followed by a break and a blank line, heads followed by a break and no blank line, and run-in heads. For example, the following commands will cause level 1, 2, and 3 heads to be followed by a blank line, level 4 and 5 heads to be followed by a break but no blank line, and level 6 and 7 heads to run in to the following text.

```
.nr Hb 5
.nr Hs 3
```

Heading Indents. The **Hi** (heading-indent) register controls the indention of the line of text that follows heads that are followed by breaks. If it is set to 0, the line is left-justified; if it is 1, indention is controlled by the **Pt** (paragraph type) register (see page 147); if it is 2, nroff indents the text to line up with the first word of the heading text.

Centered Heads. The **Hc** (head-center) register controls which heads are centered. By default, there are no centered heads (**Hc** is equal to 0). If you set **Hc** to a value greater than 0, nroff will center all heads at that level and lower except that it will never center run-in heads.

Table of Contents

The **mm** macros can cause nroff to create a table of contents automatically at the end of a document (you have to manually move it to the front, where it belongs). The table of contents lists all headings lower than and including the heading level specified by the **Cl** (contents-level) register along with the appropriate page numbers. The default value for **Cl** is 2; that is, nroff includes all first- and second-level heads in the table of contents. If you want a different value of **Cl**, you must change it at the beginning of the text file, before the first header command. As an example, the following command changes the value of the **Cl** register to 3, causing the table of contents to include first-, second-, and third-level heads.

```
.nr Cl 3
```

A .**TC** command at the *end* of the text file causes nroff to print the table of contents. Without this command, nroff will not print a table of contents.

DISPLAYS

A display is a block of text that nroff normally treats as an integral unit—it does not break a display between pages. A display can be a chart, table, or paragraph that must appear intact. You can define a display by placing the appropriate nroff commands before and after the block of text in the input file.

Unless you instruct nroff otherwise, displays are not filled or indented in the output text—nroff preserves the spacing and formatting of the text from the input file.

Headings (.**H** or .**HU** commands) and footnotes (see page 169) must not appear within displays.

Static Displays

When nroff finds a block of text in the input file that you have specified as a static display, it places the text on the current page only if there is room for the entire block. If there is not room, nroff starts a new page and places the block of text there.

A **.DS** (display-static) command precedes the text of a static display and a **.DE** (display-end) command follows it. The format of a static display is shown below.

> **.DS [position] [fill] [right-position]**
> **text**
> **.DE**

You can chose the **position** from the following table—it determines how nroff positions the display. If you don't specify a **position**, nroff positions the display flush with the left margin.

L   (left) positions the display flush against the left margin (default).

I   (indent) indents the display by the value of the **Si** (static-indent) register, which is initially set to 5.

C   (center) centers each line between the left and right margins.

CB   (center block) centers the entire display as a block of text (a single unit), using the longest line for positioning.

The **fill** controls whether or not nroff fills the text in the display (see page 142 for an explanation of filling text). If you omit this argument, or if you specify it as N (nofill), nroff does not fill the text. If it is an F (fill), nroff fills the text.

The **right-position** is the number of characters that you want the right margin indented. This value has no effect when the display is not being filled.

There are two registers that affect the format of static displays. The **Si** (static-indent) register controls the number of spaces that nroff indents an indented static display. The **Ds** register controls spacing before and after the display—if you set it to 0 (zero), no blank line will appear before or after the display.

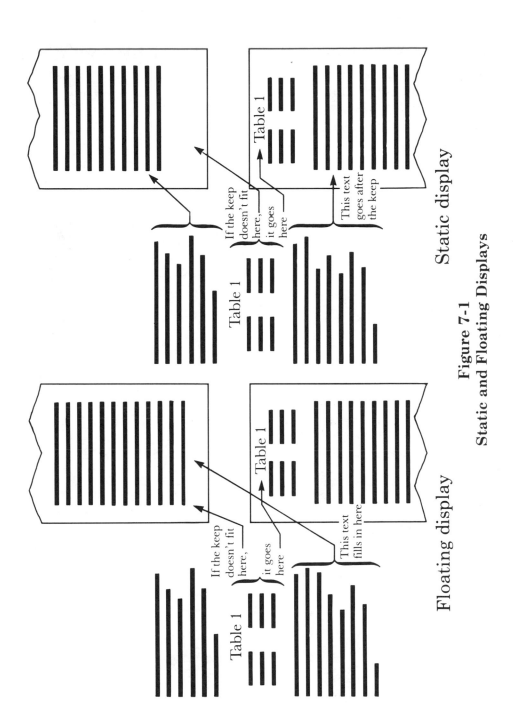

Figure 7-1
Static and Floating Displays

Floating Displays

A floating display is similar to a static display; it is a block of text that nroff keeps on one page. However, if there is no room for a floating display on the current page, nroff sets aside the display and finishes filling the page with the text from the input file that follows the display. When the page is full, nroff places the display at the top of the next page and continues with the text from the previous page.

The placement of a floating display can change the order of the output text. A floating display is useful for displaying a table or chart that is not context-sensitive when you do not want a blank space at the bottom of a page.

The format of a floating display is shown below.

.DF [position] [fill] [right-position]
text
.DE

The **De** and **Df** registers affect the format of floating displays.

When set to 1 (one), the **De** (display-eject) register causes nroff to eject the current page after a floating display so that any following text appears on the next page and only one floating display appears on a page. The initial value of **De** is 0 (zero), which causes nroff not to take any special action after a display.

The **Df** (display-float) register causes nroff to float floating displays in different manners. It can take on any one of the values from the following table.

0   Output floating displays at the end of the document.

1   Output floating displays on the page they occur or at the end of the document if there is not room on the page.

2   Output only one floating display at the top of a new page.

3   Output only one floating display on the page it occurs or at the top of the next page if there is not room on the current page.

4   Output all floating displays starting at the top of a new page. More than one display per page is allowed.

5   Output floating displays on the page they occur or at the top of the next page if there is no room on the current page (default).

FOOTNOTES

You must embed footnotes in the input text immediately after you reference them. The nroff formatter places a footnote at the bottom of the page it occurs on in the output file unless there is not enough room, in which case it moves it (or part of it) to the next page. If you like, nroff can sequentially number footnotes throughout the document.

The nroff formatter processes footnotes in Fill Mode. It does not permit other footnotes, headings, or displays within a footnote.

There are two kinds of footnotes available under the **mm** macros: *automatically numbered* and *labeled* footnotes.

The nroff formatter sequentially numbers automatically numbered footnotes throughout the document. This scheme is useful if you add and delete footnotes frequently because it automatically compensates for these footnotes by renumbering the remaining footnotes.

Labeled footnotes are more conventional. You specify a label for each footnote: an asterisk, a number, or whatever you like.

The format of an automatically numbered footnote follows.

```
text\*F
.FS
footnote
.FE
text
```

You must put the *F in your input file as shown. The **mm** macros will cause nroff to replace the *F with the proper footnote number.

The format of a labeled footnote is shown below.

```
text**
.FS**
footnote
.FE
text
```

The ** is the label. You can replace it with any string of characters you like. You must put the label in two places: at the end of the text, just before the footnote; and immediately following the **.FS** macro that starts the footnote.

If you do not like the default footnote style, you can use the **.FD** command to change the footnote style. It has the following format.

.FD [format] [renumber]

The **format** is a number from 0 through 11 from the following table.

Format	Hyphen	Adjust	Indent	Label
0	no	yes	yes	left
1	yes	yes	yes	left
2	no	no	yes	left
3	yes	no	yes	left
4	no	yes	no	left
5	yes	yes	no	left
6	no	no	no	left
7	yes	no	no	left
8	no	yes	yes	right
9	yes	yes	yes	right
10	no	no	yes	right
11	yes	no	yes	right

The **renumber** can be set to 1 to cause automatically numbered footnotes to start over again with number 1 following each first-level head.

Figure 7-2 on page 176 contains an example of a footnote.

RUNNING TITLES

There are two categories of running titles: *headers* and *footers*. Headers (sometimes called *running heads*) appear at the top of all, all even-numbered, or all odd-numbered pages. You can have three headers in use at one time (page header, even header, and odd header). In the same manner, footers appear at the bottoms of pages.

The **mm** macros provide three-part titles for headers and

footers. For example, a **.PH** (page-header) command takes the following format.

.PH "´left´center´right´"

The **left** is a string that nroff left justifies at the top of each page. In a similar manner, **center** and **right** represent strings that are centered and right-justified.

All headers (except the page header) and footers are initially blank lines. The initial value of the page header is the page number, centered between hyphens.

The following table lists all of the header and footer commands.

Title command	What it stands for	Where nroff puts the title
.PH	page header	top of every page but the first
.EH	even header	top of even-numbered pages
.OH	odd header	top of odd-numbered pages
.PF	page footer	bottom of every page
.EF	even footer	bottom of even-numbered pages
.OF	odd footer	bottom of odd-numbered pages

Page Numbers and the Date

You can cause the page number not to appear at the top of pages by changing the value of the center portion of the page header. An easy way to do this is to set the page header to a null string as shown below.

```
.PH ""
```

You can also cause the page number to appear in a different position on the page by incorporating the **P** (page-number) register in a title. Without going into a lengthy explanation, the page number is generated by placing the following sequence of characters within a title.

```
\\\\nP
```

The first of the following commands removes the page number from the center-top of each page and places the title of the work flush left at the top of all pages. The second and third commands position the page number at the bottom-left of even-numbered pages and the bottom-right of odd-numbered pages.

```
.PH "'The Story of My Life''''"
.EF "'\\\\nP'''"
.OF "'''\\\\nP'"
```

The current date is stored in the **DT** (date) string. The following command causes nroff to display the date, centered at the bottom of every page.

```
.PF "''\\\\*(DT''"
```

TEXT AND PAGE LAYOUT

This section explains how to justify text, skip pages, and skip lines. The next two sections ("Using Plain nroff Commands with mm Macros" and "Setting Parameters from the Command Line") discuss other commands that affect the appearance of the output text.

Justification

By default, text produced by the **mm** macros is not right-justified (see page 143). You can turn on justification by giving the following command.

```
.SA 1
```

You can turn it off again with the same command and an argument of 0.

```
.SA 0
```

Input File:

```
This text demonstrates the default mm
macro style — the text is not
right—justified.
The text is filled but is not, however,
brought out to the right margin.
Look at the difference between this and the
following text.

.SA 1
You can use an .SA 1 command to
cause nroff to justify text.
This command causes nroff to produce an
even right margin (i.e., the text is
right—justified).
Some people like this style.
However, many people think that a ragged
right margin makes text easier to read.

.SA 0
An .SA 0 command causes nroff to revert
to its initial style, ragged right
margins.
```

Output Text:

```
This text demonstrates the default mm macro style — the
text is not right—justified.  The text is filled but is not,
however, brought out to the right margin.  Look at the
difference between this and the following text.

You can use an .SA 1 command to cause nroff to justify text.
This  command  causes  nroff to produce an even right margin
(i.e., the text is right—justified).  Some people like  this
style.   However,  many  people  think  that  a ragged right
margin makes text easier to read.

An .SA 0 command causes nroff to revert to its  initial
style, ragged right margins.
```

Skipping Lines

The **.SP** (space) command leaves the number of blank lines that you give it as an argument. The following example shows how to use **.SP**.

Input File:

```
This example demonstrates the use of
the .SP command.
.SP 3
There are three blank lines above this line.
```

Output Text:

```
This example demonstrates the use of the .SP command.


There are three blank lines above this line.
```

It is frequently simpler to just leave blank lines in the input file rather than give a **.SP** command to create one or two blank lines.

Skipping Pages

When used without an argument, the **.SK** (skip page) command skips to the top of the next page. With an argument, **.SK** leaves the number of blank pages that you give it as an argument. The nroff formatter still displays titles (headers and footers) on the blank pages. The following command leaves two blank pages.

```
.SK 2
```

Skipping to the Top of an Odd-Numbered Page. The .OP (odd-page) command skips to the top of the next odd-numbered page. You can use this command to make sure that a chapter starts on an odd-numbered page.

Input File:

```
.PH ""
.EH "´\\\\nP´´TITLE´"
.OH "´TITLE´´\\\\nP´"
.PF "´´\\\\*(DT´´"
.nr Pt 1
.nr Pi 10
.P
This sample illustrates some of the page layout features of the
mm macros.
It also demonstrates footnotes\*F
.FS
This is an example of an automatically numbered footnote.
.FE
and various paragraph features.
.P
The first command\*F
.FS
The .PH command at the beginning of this example.
.FE
removes the default page header\*F.
.FS
The default page header is the page number enclosed in hyphens.
.FE
by replacing it with a null string.
The even- and odd-page headers do not displace the page
header because
the mm macros display them on the line below the page header.*
.FS *
You can use take advantage of two lines of page headers on
each page.
(As you can see from this footnote, you can mix
labeled and automatically numbered footnotes in an input file.
.FE
.P
Setting the Pt register to 1 causes .P commands to yield
standard (indented) paragraphs.
The Pi register controls the amount of indention.
In this example it´s set to 10 spaces.
```

TITLE   1

          This sample illustrates some of the page layout
features of the mm macros. It also demonstrates footnotes1
and various paragraph features.

          The first command2 removes the default page header3.
by replacing it with a null string. The even- and odd-page
headers do not displace the page header because the mm
macros display them on the line below the page header.*

          Setting the Pt register to 1 causes .P commands to
yield standard (indented) paragraphs. The Pi register
controls the amount of indention. In this example it's set
to 10 spaces.

---

1. This is an example of an automatically numbered
   footnote.

2. The .PH command at the beginning of this example.

3. The default page header is the page number enclosed in
   hyphens.

 * You can use take advantage of two lines of page headers
    on each page. (As you can see from this footnote, you
    can mix labeled and automatically numbered footnotes in
    an input file.

                    February 20, 1985

Figure 7-2
Output Text: A Sample Page

USING PLAIN nroff COMMANDS
WITH mm MACROS

In general, you should not mix plain nroff commands with **mm**
macros because they may change the way the macros work. You
may, however, find the following plain nroff commands useful—
they should not alter the functioning of the **mm** macros.

Breaks

This section covers plain nroff commands that end lines, leave blank lines, and center text. When you command nroff to end a line, it stops filling the line and does not justify it. What happens next depends on which command you use.

The End-line Command.   The simplest End-line command is the **.br** (break) plain nroff command. It does nothing except end (or break) a line. Subsequent text begins on the next line.

Input File:

```
This is an example of the simplest
kind of break, or End—line, command.
nroff can be halfway through filling
a line, but when you give a
.br
Break command, it ends the line it
was filling and continues on the
next line.
```

Output Text:

```
This is an example of the simplest kind of break, or End—
line, command.  nroff can be halfway through filling a line,
but when you give a
Break command, it ends the line it was filling and continues
on the next line.
```

The Implicit End-line Command.   Any line in the input file that begins with a SPACE automatically ends the current line of output text. The new line begins with a SPACE. If you begin a line in the input file with five SPACEs, the new line in the output text will begin with five SPACEs. This feature allows you to indent a paragraph without an explicit command.

The implicit End-line command is of limited use, but it is important to understand how it works so that you do not use it unintentionally.

Input File:

```
This is an example of how a line of
input text, beginning with a SPACE,
 causes the line to end
and a new line to start.
     If you start a line of input text
with five SPACEs, the output line starts
with five SPACEs.
```

Output Text:

```
This is an example of how a line of input text, beginning
with a SPACE,
 causes the line to end and a new line to start.
     If you start a line of input text with five SPACEs, the
output line starts with five SPACEs.
```

Blank Lines. A blank line in the input file causes a break in the output text. After the break, the nroff formatter copies one or more blank lines from the input file to the output text.

The **mm** macros try not to leave blank lines at the top of a page of output text—refer to page 183, "Leaving Blank Lines at the Top of a Page," if you need blank lines at the top of a page.

Centering Lines. The .ce (center) plain nroff command centers one or more following lines of text. Without an argument, this command centers the line that follows it. With an argument, the **.ce** command centers the number of lines its argument specifies.

Input File:

```
This example demonstrates two ways to use the .ce command.
Without an argument, the command
.ce
centers
only the line that follows it.
You can use an argument to specify the number of lines you
want centered.
.ce 3
This line is centered,
as is this line,
and this one.
This line is not centered; it is part
of the text that follows the centered lines.
```

Output Text:

```
This example demonstrates two ways to use the .ce command.
Without an argument, the command
                           centers
only the line that follows it.  You can use an argument to
specify the number of lines you want centered.
                   This line is centered,
                      as is this line,
                       and this one.
This line is not centered; it is part of the text that
follows the centered lines.
```

Filling Lines

The **.nf** (nofill) plain nroff command causes nroff *not* to fill (see page 143) output lines of text. The output lines are exactly the same as the input lines. The initial condition, filling lines of text, can be restored with the **.fi** (fill) plain nroff command.

Double-Spacing

You can double- (or triple-) space output text by using the **.ls** (line-spacing) plain nroff command. The following command specifies double-spaced output text.

```
.ls 2
```

An argument of 3 specifies triple-spacing, while a 1 restores the initial condition of single-spacing.

Tab Settings

Tabs in nroff are similar to tabs on a typewriter: they define horizontal positions for columns of information. Once you set tab positions, they remain in effect until you change them or until the end of the document. If you don't set tabs, nroff uses its default tab positions (every eight characters, starting at the current indent or left margin).

The **.ta** command clears all previous tab positions and sets new tab positions as its arguments specify. Without any arguments, **.ta** clears all tab positions. After you establish the tab positions you want to use, a TAB character (CONTROL-I) causes the following text to appear in the next tab position to the right.

The following example demonstrates what happens when there are no more tab positions on a line. The word *demonstrate* takes up more than one column, forcing the next word (*the*) over to what would be the next column, if there was one. Because there is not another column, the TAB in the input text has no effect and the word following the TAB appears immediately after the preceding word. In the following **.ta** command, **i** stands for inches. You can also use **n** for characters.

Temporary Indentions

The **.ti** (temporary-indent) command causes nroff to indent the next line of output text. An argument to the command specifies

Input File:

```
This example demonstrates the use of tabs.
After setting three tab positions, nroff
produces four aligned columns
of words.
You will generally want to produce tabular
material in Nofill Mode.

.ta 1i 2i 3i
This TAB example TAB demonstrates TAB the
use TAB of TAB tabs. TAB After
setting TAB three TAB tab TAB positions,
nroff TAB produces TAB four TAB aligned
columns TAB of TAB words.
```

Output Text:

```
This example demonstrates the use of tabs.  After setting
three tab positions, nroff produces four aligned columns of
words.  You will generally want to produce tabular material
in Nofill Mode.

This        example     demonstratesthe
use         of          tabs.      After
setting     three       tab        positions,
nroff       produces    four       aligned
columns     of          words.
```

the amount of indention. The line after the indented line comes back to the current margin.

The following command sets a temporary indent of seven characters to the right of the current indent. The + adds the 7 to the current indent; without it, nroff would set the temporary indent absolutely to seven characters from the left margin (page offset). The **n** stands for characters; you can also use **i** for inches.

```
.ti  +7n
```

Input File:

```
This example demonstrates the use of the Temporary
Indent command.

.ti +1i
All the text following the first
line comes back to the left margin
because the .ti command only affects one. line.
```

Output Text:

```
This example demonstrates the use of the Temporary Indent
command.

        All the text following the first line comes back
to the left margin because the .ti command only affects one
line.
```

Comments

A comment in an input file is a note that nroff ignores and does not send to the output text. You can use comments to leave notes in a file for yourself or someone else—items you want to add to the file, references you want to check, or markers so you can easily find where you stopped reading or editing.

A \" precedes a comment, and the end of a line ends a comment. If you want a line that has nothing but a comment on it, place a period before the comment indicator. Refer to the following example.

Input File:

```
This is input text.\"Check to see if this comment appears
.\"in the output text.
This is some more input text.
It follows a comment.
```

Output Text:

```
This is input text.  This is some more input text.  It
follows a comment.
```

Leaving Blank Lines at the Top of a Page

The nroff formatter has a special mechanism to prevent it from leaving blank lines at the top of a page. This mechanism keeps the blank lines that precede headings from appearing at the top of a page—the result is that text always starts at the same position on each page.

Sometime you may want blank lines at the top of a page. Give an **.rs** (restore spacing) command and then skip the number of lines you want with an **.SP** command, or simply leave the blank lines in the input file.

Input File:

```
.rs
.SK 5
This is the first line of text.
```

Output Text:

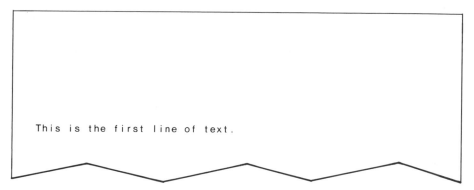

This is the first line of text.

SETTING PARAMETERS FROM THE COMMAND LINE

You can set several important parameters that control the output text from the command line when you call nroff.

Page Length

The **mm** macros store the page length in the **L** (length) register. The default value is 66 lines (11 inches). If you want to change the page length, you must do so from the command line. The −rL84 in the following command line changes the page length to 14 inches (84 lines). The command line formats the **report** file and sends the output to the printer. The **&** causes the entire process to run in the background.

```
$ nroff -mm −rL84 report  |  lp &
1324
request id is printer_1-542 (standard input)
$
```

Page Offset

The **mm** macros store the page offset in the **O** (offset) register. The default value is 9 characters (¾ of an inch) from the left edge of the screen or page. You can change the page offset from the command line. The following command line changes the offset to 18 characters.

```
$ nroff —mm —rO18 report
.
.
.
```

Page Width

The **mm** macros store the initial line length in the **W** (width) register. The default value is 72 characters (6 inches). You can change the line length from the command line. The following command line changes the line length to 60 characters.

```
$ nroff —mm —rW60 report
.
.
.
```

Outputting Selected Pages

You can control which pages of output text nroff outputs with the —o (output) option on the command line. Follow the —o with the numbers of the pages you want to see. Separate page numbers with commas for single pages or with hyphens for ranges of pages. A hyphen before the first page number displays all pages from the beginning of the document through that page. A hyphen following the last page number in the list prints the last pages of the document. The following command prints pages 5, 10, 15 through 20, and 35 through the end of the output text from the file **report**.

```
$ nroff —mm —o5,10,15—20,35— report | lp
request id is printer_1-543 (standard input)
$
```

SUMMARY

This summary describes the commands covered in this chapter and introduces some additional ones. First, the summary describes plain nroff commands. These commands work with or without a macro package. Following the plain commands, the summary reviews **mm** macro package commands.

Plain nroff **Commands**

Each command must start at the beginning of a line in the input file. A command line starts with a SPACE, a single quotation mark, or a period.

Breaks.

Command	Break line and ...
.br	break line, nothing else
.sp n	leave n blank lines
.ce n	center next n lines (one line if n is missing)
.bp	begin new page

Margins.

Command	Effect
.na	do not justify lines
.ad b	justify lines
.nf	do not fill lines
.fi	fill lines
.in[$\pm$]xi	adjust left margin to the right (+) or left (–) x inches (if no $\pm$, set indent absolutely to x inches)
.ti[$\pm$]xi	for the next line only, adjust left margin as above
.po[$\pm$]xi	adjust page offset as above (not with **mm** macros)

Headings.

Command	Effect
.tl ′*left*′*center*′*right*′	produce a three-part heading; replace *left, center,* and *right* with the text of the title to appear at the left, center, and right of the page

Changing Dimensions.

Command	Effect
.ls x	replace x with 1, 2, or 3 to single-, double-, or triple-space text
.ll[±]xi	adjust line length to the right (+) or left (−) x inches (if no ±, set length absolutely to x inches)

Hyphenation.

Command	Effect
.nh	turn off hyphenation
.hy	turn on hyphenation

Number Registers. The **mm** macros take advantage of this plain nroff command to set parameters for macro commands.

Command	Effect
.nr x n	set register x to value n (register names can be one or two characters long)

The mm Macro Commands

As the beginning of this chapter explains, **mm** macro commands use number registers to alter the way commands work. You set a number register as explained in the "Number Registers" section above.

Paragraphs.

Command	Effect
.P [*type*]	set *type* to 0 for a left-block paragraph or 1 for a standard (indented) paragraph
Registers:	
Pt	establishes the default paragraph type: 0 for left-block (initial value) or 1 for standard
Pi	establishes the indention of the first line of standard paragraphs (initially 5 spaces)

Lists.

Command:	.AL [*type*] [*indention*] [*separation*]
Effect:	start automatic list; choose *type* from: 1, A, a, I, or i

Command:	.DL [*indention*] [*separation*]
Effect:	start dash list

Command:	.ML *mark* [*indention*] [*separation*]
Effect:	start marked list; *mark* is the element used to mark list items

Command:	.VL *indention* [*mark-indention*] [*separation*]
Effect:	start variable-item list; set marks for each list item with **.LI**

Command:	.LI [*mark*] [*prefix*]
Effect:	start new list item

Command:	.LE [*separation*]
Effect:	end list

Registers:

Li	text indention if *indention* is not supplied (automatic list)
Pi	text indention if *indention* is not supplied (dash list)
Ls	spacing above and below items based on item level

Fonts.

Command	**Effect**
.R	print the argument in a Roman (regular) font; without an argument, print all subsequent text in a Roman font
.B	as above, bold font
.I	as above, underlined font
.BI	alternate bold and underlined fonts for each argument
.BR	alternate bold and Roman fonts for each argument

Fonts (continued)

Command	Effect
.IB	alternate underlined and bold fonts for each argument
.IR	alternate underlined and Roman fonts for each argument
.RB	alternate Roman and bold fonts for each argument
.RI	alternate Roman and underlined fonts for each argument

Headings.

Command:	.H *level* [*heading-text*]
Effect:	produce a numbered heading; specify a number (1-7) for *level*

Command:	.HU *heading-text*
Effect:	produce an unnumbered heading

Registers:

Hu	level of subsequent unnumbered headings
Ej	level of heads that are forced to the tops of new pages
Hb	level of heads that appear followed by line breaks
Hc	level of centered heads
Hi	indent of text following heads that are followed by line breaks:
	0 left-justified
	1 indention controlled by **Pt** register
	2 line up with first word of head

All running headers and footers (at the tops and bottoms of pages) have the following format.

.PH "'left'center'right' "

Substitute the text you want for any or all of **left**, **center**, and **right**. You can use the following macros in place of **.PH** above.

Command	Effect
.EF	even footer appears at the bottom of even-numbered pages
.EH	even header appears at the top of even-numbered pages
.OF	odd footer appears at the bottom of odd-numbered pages
.OH	odd header appears at the top of odd-numbered pages
.PF	page footer appears at the bottom of every page
.PH	page header appears at the top of every page but the first

Footnotes and Displays.

Command: .FS
Effect: start footnote

Command: .FE
Effect: end footnote

Command: .FD [*format*] [*renumber*]
Effect: set footnote style—see page 170

Command: .DS [*position*] [*fill*] [*right-position*]
Effect: start static display; set *fill* to N (nofill) or
    F (fill) and choose *position* from the following list
      L flush left
      I indent according to **Si** register
      C center each line
      CB center display as a block

Command: .DF [*position*] [*fill*] [*right-position*]
Effect: start floating display (see **.DS** above)

Command: .DE
Effect: end display

Registers:
Si   controls indent when *position* is I
Ds   set to 0 for no space above and below display,
      1 for space
De   set to 1 to eject page after a floating display
Df   set as described on page 168

Miscellaneous Commands.

Command	Effect
.SA x	turn on ($x=1$) or turn off ($x=0$) justification
.SP x	leave x blank lines
.SK x	skip x pages
.OP	skip to the top of an odd-numbered page
.TC	print table of contents (put at end of input file)

Register:

Cl	specify heading levels to be included in table of contents (must appear before first heading in input file)

Command Line Parameters. You must set the registers described in this section as command line options. They are shown the way you must enter them on the command line.

Option	Effect
$-$rLxx	set the page length to xx lines
$-$rOxx	set the page offset to xx characters
$-$rWxx	set the page width to xx characters

8

THE BOURNE SHELL

The Bourne Shell is both a command interpreter and a high-level programming language. As a command interpreter, it processes commands you enter in response to its prompt. When you use the Shell as a programming language, it processes groups of commands stored in files called *Shell scripts*. This chapter shows how to use the Shell interactively, explains how to write and execute Shell scripts, and explores aspects of Shell programming, such as variables, control structures, processes, executable files, and signals. Although this chapter is primarily about the Bourne Shell, much of the theory it explains and the sections on "Executable Files" and "Command Separation and Grouping" also apply to the C Shell. The C Shell is not a part of UNIX System V but is available on many machines—see Chapter 9.

Shell scripts allow you to group command lines together so that a single command can execute them. These files of commands make it possible for any user to initiate a complex series of tasks or to execute a repetitive procedure simply and quickly. You can redirect input and output within a Shell script to combine standard UNIX utility programs to meet your needs.

EXECUTABLE FILES

An executable file is one that you or another user has permission to execute. It typically contains either a compiled program (e.g., vi, who, or an application program) or a Shell script. This section discusses how to use the chmod utility to make a Shell script executable.

Shell Scripts

The **com1** file (below) is an example of a Shell script. It contains a Shell command line. As it stands, you cannot execute the **com1** file by giving its name as a command because you do not have execute access permission to it.

```
$ cat com1
echo 'This is the output of com1.'

$ com1
com1: execute permission denied
$
```

The Shell does not recognize **com1** as an executable file and issues an error message when you try to execute it.

Execute Access

In order to execute a Shell script by giving its name as a command, you must have execute access permission to the file containing the script. Execute access is similar to read or write access—only it tells the Shell that the user, group, or public has permission to execute the file. It also implies that the content of the file is executable.

As shown in Chapter 4, the chmod utility changes the access privileges associated with a file. Below, ls with the —l option displays the access permissions of **com1** before and after chmod gives the owner execute access permission to the file.

```
$ ls —l com1
-rw-r--r-- 1 alex    pubs        36  Aug 22 10:55 com1

$ chmod u+x com1

$ ls —l com1
-rwxr--r-- 1 alex    pubs        36  Aug 22 10:55 com1

$ com1
This is the output of com1.
$
```

The first ls displays a hyphen as the fourth character, indicating that the owner does not have execute access permission to the file. Then chmod uses two arguments to give the owner execute access permission. The u+x causes chmod to add (+) execute access permission (x) for the owner (u). The second argument is the name of the file. The second ls shows an x in the fourth position, indicating that the owner now has execute access permission.

Finally, the Shell executes the file when its name is given as a command. If other users are going to execute the file, you must also change group and/or public access privileges. For more information on access permissions, refer to "Access Permissions" in Chapter 4 and to ls and chmod in Part II.

VARIABLES

Because the Bourne Shell has no true numeric variables, it uses string variables (variables that are able to take on the value of a string of characters) to represent numbers as well as text. There are three types of variables: *user variables*, *Shell variables*, and *read-only Shell variables*. You can declare, initialize, read, and change user variables from the command line or from a Shell script. The Shell declares and initializes Shell variables, but you can read and change them. The Shell declares and initializes read-only Shell variables, which you can read but not change.

User Variables

You can declare any sequence of nonblank characters as the name of a variable. The first line in the example below declares the variable **person** and initializes it with the string alex. When you assign a value to a variable, **you must not precede or follow the equal sign with a** SPACE.

```
$ person=alex

$ echo person
person

$ echo $person
alex
$
```

The second line shows that **person** does not represent alex. The string person is echoed as person. The Shell only substitutes the value of a variable when you precede the name of the variable with a dollar sign. The final command (above) displays the value of the variable **person**.

As the following example shows, you must quote a string containing embedded SPACEs in order to assign it to a variable.

```
$ person='alex and jenny'

$ echo $person
alex and jenny
$
```

You can remove a variable with the Unset command. For example, to remove the **person** variable, you would give the command **unset person**.

Variable Substitution

The echo utility copies its arguments to the standard output. The command **echo $person** displays the value of the variable **person**. It does not display $person because the Shell does not pass $person to echo as an argument. Because of the leading dollar sign, the Shell recognizes that $person is the name of a variable, *substitutes* the value of the variable, and passes that value to echo. The echo utility displays the value of the variable, not its name, never knowing that you called it with a variable. The Shell would have passed echo the same command line, and echo would have displayed the same string, if you had given the command **echo alex and jenny**.

You can prevent the Shell from substituting the value of a variable by quoting the leading dollar sign. Double quotation marks will not prevent the substitution.

```
$ echo $person
alex and jenny

$ echo \$person
$person

$ echo '$person'
$person

$ echo "$person"
alex and jenny
$
```

Read-Only User Variables

The next example declares the variable **person** to be read-only. You must assign a value to a variable *before* you declare it to be read-only; you cannot change its value after the declaration. When you attempt to change the value of a read-only variable, the Shell displays an error message.

```
$ person=jenny

$ echo $person
jenny

$ readonly person

$ person=helen
person: is read only

$ readonly
readonly person
$
```

A Readonly command without an argument displays a list of all read-only variables.

Read-Only Shell Variables

A read-only Shell variable is similar to a read-only user variable, except that the Shell assigns it a value—you can *never* assign a value to a read-only Shell variable.

Name of the Calling Program. The Shell stores the name of the command that you use to call a program in the variable named **$0**. It is variable number zero because it appears before the first argument on the command line.

```
$ cat abc
echo 'The name of the command used'
echo 'to execute this Shell script was' $0

$ abc
The name of the command used
to execute this Shell script was abc
$
```

The Shell script above uses echo to verify the name of the program you are executing. The **abc** file must be executable (use chmod) before this example will work.

Arguments. The Shell stores the first nine command line arguments in the variables **$1**, **$2**, ..., **$9**. These variables appear in this, the "Read-Only Shell Variables" section, because you cannot assign them values using an equal sign. You can, however, use the Set command (page 200) to assign new values to them.

```
$ cat display_args
echo 'The first five command line'
echo 'arguments are' $1 $2 $3 $4 $5

$ display_args jenny alex helen
The first five command line
arguments are jenny alex helen
$
```

The **display_args** script displays the first five command line arguments. The variables representing arguments that were not present on the command line, **$4** and **$5**, have a null value.

The variable **$*** represents all the command line arguments, as the **display_all** program demonstrates.

```
$ cat display_all
echo $*

$ display_all helen jenny alex barbara
helen jenny alex barbara
$
```

The variable **$#** contains the number of arguments on the command line. This string variable represents a decimal number. You can use the expr utility to perform computations involving this number and test to perform logical tests on it. There is more information on expr and test in the "Control Structures" part of this chapter and in Part II.

```
$ cat num_args
echo 'This Shell script was called with'
echo $# 'arguments.'

$ num_args helen alex jenny
This Shell script was called with
3 arguments.
$
```

Shift. The Shift command promotes each of the command line arguments. The second argument (which was represented by **$2**) becomes the first (now represented by **$1**), the third becomes the second, up through the last argument becoming the next to last.

You can access only the first nine command line arguments (as **$1** through **$9**) from a Shell script. The Shift command gives you access to the tenth command line argument by making it the ninth, and it makes the first unavailable. Successive Shift commands make additional arguments available. There is, however, no "Unshift" command to bring back the arguments that are no longer available.

```
$ cat demo_shift
echo 'arg1=' $1 '     arg2=' $2 '     arg3=' $3
shift
echo 'arg1=' $1 '     arg2=' $2 '     arg3=' $3
shift
echo 'arg1=' $1 '     arg2=' $2 '     arg3=' $3
shift
echo 'arg1=' $1 '     arg2=' $2 '     arg3=' $3
shift
```

```
$ demo_shift alice helen jenny
arg1= alice      arg2= helen      arg3= jenny
arg1= helen      arg2= jenny      arg3=
arg1= jenny      arg2=      arg3=
arg1=      arg2=      arg3=
demo_shift: cannot shift
$
```

The example above calls the **demo_shift** program with three arguments. The program displays the arguments and shifts them repeatedly, until there are no more arguments to shift. The Shell displays an error message when the script executes Shift after it has run out of variables.

Set. Without any arguments, Set displays a list of all variables that are set.

```
$ set
HOME=/usr/alex
IFS=

LOGNAME=alex
MAIL=/usr/mail/alex
MAILCHECK=600
PATH=:/bin:/usr/bin
PS1=$
PS2=>
SHELL=/bin/sh
TERM=vt100
TZ=PST8PDT
```

When you call Set with one or more arguments, it sets the values of the command line argument variables (**$1-$n**) to its arguments. The script below uses Set to set the first three command line argument variables. See "Command Substitution," page 213, for another example of the Set command.

```
$ cat s25
set this is it
echo $#: $*

$ s25
3: this is it
$
```

Shell Variables

The Shell declares and initializes variables that determine your home directory, what directories the Shell looks in when you give it a command, how frequently the Shell checks to see if you have received any mail, your prompt, and more. You can assign new values to these variables from the command line or from the **.profile** file in your home directory.

HOME. By default, your home directory is your working directory when you first log on. The system administrator determines your home directory when you establish your account and stores this information in the **/etc/passwd** file. When you log on, the Shell gets the pathname of your home directory and assigns it to the variable **HOME**.

 When you give a **cd** command without an argument, cd makes the directory whose name is stored in **HOME** the working directory. If you change the value of **HOME** to a different directory pathname, cd will make the new directory the working directory.

```
$ echo $HOME
/usr/jenny

$ cd
$ pwd
/usr/jenny

$ HOME=/usr/jenny/literature
$ cd
$ pwd
/usr/jenny/literature
$
```

 The example above shows the value of the **HOME** variable and the effect of the cd utility. After you execute cd without an argument, the pathname of the working directory is the same as the value of **HOME**. After assigning a different pathname to **HOME**, cd makes the working directory correspond to the new pathname.

PATH. When you give the Shell a command, it searches through the file structure for the program you want to execute. The Shell looks in several directories for a file that has the same name as the command and that you have execute access permission for. The

PATH Shell variable controls this search path. The first directory the Shell normally searches is the working directory. If the program is not there, the search continues with the **/bin** and the **/usr/bin** directories. These directories usually contain executable programs. If the Shell does not find the program in any of these directories, it reports that it cannot find (or execute) the program.

If you use a pathname that includes slashes (e.g., not a simple filename) to call a program, the Shell does not use **PATH**. If the executable file does not have the exact pathname that you specify, the Shell reports that it cannot find (or execute) the program.

The **PATH** variable specifies the directories in the order the Shell is to search them. Each must be separated from the next by a colon. The following command causes the search for an executable file to start with the working directory [specified by a null string (nothing) preceding the first colon]. If the Shell fails to find the file in the working directory, it consults the **/usr/jenny/bin**, **/bin**, and **/usr/bin** directories.

```
$ PATH=:/usr/jenny/bin:/bin:/usr/bin
$
```

If each user is given a unique search path, each user can execute a different program by giving the same command. Because the search stops when it is satisfied, you can use the name of a standard UNIX utility program for your own program by including the program in one of the first directories that the Shell searches.

MAIL, MAILPATH, and MAILCHECK. The **MAIL** variable contains the name of the file that the mail (and mailx) utility uses to store your mail. Normally, the absolute pathname of this file is **/usr/mail/name**, where **name** is your login name.

The **MAILPATH** variable contains a list of filenames separated by colons. If this variable is set, the Shell informs you when any of the files is modified (e.g., when mail arrives). You can follow any of the filenames in the list with a percent sign (%) and a message that will replace the you have mail message when you get mail while you are logged on. You will not normally want to set this variable.

The **MAILCHECK** variable specifies how often, in seconds, the Shell checks for new mail. The default is 600 seconds (10 minutes). If you set this variable to zero, the Shell will check each time before it gives you a prompt.

TZ. This variable describes what time zone the computer is in. It is usually set by the system administrator. The format for setting the **TZ** variable is shown below.

TZ = zzzX[ddd]

The **zzz** is the three-letter name of the local time zone, **X** is the number of hours that the local time zone differs from Greenwich Mean Time (GMT), and **ddd** is the three-letter name of the local daylight saving time zone.

The following command sets the **TZ** variable for California.

```
$ TZ=PST8PDT
$
```

PS1. The Shell prompt lets you know that the Shell is waiting for you to give it a command. The Bourne Shell prompt used in the examples throughout this book is a dollar sign followed by a SPACE. Your prompt may differ. The Shell stores the prompt as a string in the **PS1** variable. When you change the value of this variable, the appearance of your prompt changes.

If you are working on more than one machine, it can be helpful to incorporate a machine name in your prompt. The following example shows how to change the prompt to the machine name *bravo* followed by a colon and a SPACE.

```
$ PS1='bravo: '

bravo: echo test
test
bravo:
```

PS2. Prompt string 2 is a secondary prompt that the Shell stores in **PS2**. On the first line of the following example, an unclosed quoted string follows an **echo** command. The Shell assumes that the command is not finished and, on the second line, gives the default secondary prompt (>). This prompt indicates that the Shell is waiting for the user to continue the command line. The Shell waits until it receives the single quotation mark that closes the string and then executes the command.

```
$ echo 'demonstration of prompt string
> 2'
demonstration of prompt string
2

$ PS2='secondary prompt:  '

$ echo 'this demonstrates
secondary prompt: prompt string 2'
this demonstrates
prompt string 2
$
```

The second command above changes the secondary prompt to secondary prompt: followed by a SPACE. A multiline echo command demonstrates the new prompt.

IFS. You can always use a SPACE or TAB to separate fields on the command line. When you assign **IFS** (internal-field separator) the value of another character, you can also use this character to separate fields.

The **num_args** program (page 199) reports the number of arguments it was called with. Below, it demonstrates how setting **IFS** can affect interpretation of a command line.

```
$ num_args a:b:c:d
This Shell script was called with
1 arguments.

$ IFS=:

$ num_args a:b:c:d
This Shell script was called with
4 arguments.
$
```

The first time **num_args** is executed, the Shell interprets the string a:b:c:d as a single argument. After **IFS** is set to : the Shell interprets the same string as four separate arguments.

Reading User Input

The Read command reads one line from the standard input and assigns the line to one or more variables. It enables a Shell script to read user input from its standard input. The following program shows how Read works.

```
$ cat read1
echo 'Go ahead: \c'
read firstline
echo 'You entered:' $firstline

$ read1
Go ahead: This is a line.
You entered: This is a line.
$
```

The first line of the **read1** program uses echo to prompt you to enter a line of text. The \c suppresses the NEWLINE following the string that echo displays. The second line reads the text into the variable **firstline**. The third line verifies the action of the Read command by displaying the value of **firstline**.

The **read2** Shell script shown below prompts for a command line and then reads it into the variable **command**. The Shell script then executes the command line by placing **command** on a line by itself. When the Shell executes the Shell script, it replaces the variable with its value and executes the command line as part of the Shell script.

```
$ cat read2
echo 'Enter a command: \c'
read command
$command
echo 'Thanks'

$ read2
Enter a command: echo Please display this message.
Please display this message.
Thanks

$ read2
Enter a command: who
alex        tty11        Oct 30 07:50
scott       tty7         Oct 20 11:54
Thanks
$
```

First, **read2** reads a command line that calls the echo utility. The Shell executes the command and then displays Thanks. Next, **read2** reads a command line that executes the who utility.

In the following example, the **read3** program reads values into three variables. The Read command assigns one word to each variable.

```
$ cat read3
echo 'Enter something: \c'
read word1 word2 word3
echo 'Word 1 is:' $word1
echo 'Word 2 is:' $word2
echo 'Word 3 is:' $word3

$ read3
Enter something: this is something
Word 1 is: this
Word 2 is: is
Word 3 is: something
```

If you enter more words than Read has variables, Read assigns one word to each variable with all the left-over words going to the last variable. Actually, **read1** and **read2** both assigned the first word and all the left-over words to the one variable they each had to work with.

Below, Read accepts five words into three variables. It assigns the first word to the first variable, the second word to the second variable, and the third through fifth words to the third variable.

```
$ read3
Enter something: this is something else, really.
Word 1 is:    this
Word 2 is:    is
Word 3 is:    something else, really.
```

PROCESSES

A process is the execution of a command by the UNIX system. When you give a command, you initiate a process. The operating system can also initiate processes.

Process Structure

Like the file structure, the process structure is hierarchical. It has parents, children, and even a *root*. A parent process *forks* (or *spawns*—the words are interchangeable) a child process, which in turn can fork other processes. One of the first things the UNIX operating system does to begin execution is to start a single process, PID number 1. This process holds the same position in the process structure as the root directory does in the file structure. It is the ancestor of all processes that each user works with. It forks a getty process for each terminal. Each of these processes becomes a Shell process when a user logs on. Refer to "Overview of the Login Procedure" in Chapter 10 for more information.

Executing a Command

When you give the Shell a command, it usually forks a child process to execute the command. While the child process is executing the command, the parent process *sleeps*. While a process is sleeping, it does not use any computer time; it remains inactive, waiting to wake up. When the child process finishes executing the command, it dies. The parent process (which is running the Shell) wakes up and prompts you for another command.

When you request that the Shell run a process in the background (by ending a command with an **&**), the Shell forks a child process without going to sleep and without waiting for the child process to run to completion. The parent process, executing the Shell, reports the PID number of the child and prompts you for another command. The child process runs in the background, independent of its parent.

Process Identification

The UNIX system assigns a unique process identification (PID) number at the inception of each process. As long as a process is in existence, it keeps the same PID number. During one session, the same process is always executing the login Shell. When you fork a new process—for example, when you use an editor, the new (child) process has a different PID number from its parent process. When you return to the login Shell, it is still being executed by the same process and has the same PID number as when you logged on.

The Shell stores the PID number of the process that is executing it in the **$$** variable. In the following interaction, echo displays the value of this variable and the ps (process status) utility confirms its value. The line of the ps display with sh in the COMMAND column refers to the process running the Shell. The column headed by PID lists the process ID number. Both commands show that the Shell has a PID of 14437.

```
$ echo $$
14437

$ ps
    PID   TTY       TIME COMMAND
  14437   tty14    0:06 sh
  14565   tty14    0:02 ps
```

The PID numbers of the Shell are the same in both cases because they both identify the same process. In the first case, the Shell substitutes its own PID number for **$$**. The Shell makes this substitution *before* it forks a new process to execute echo. Thus, echo displays the PID number of the Shell that called it, not of the process that is executing it. In the second case, the ps utility lists all of your processes, including the one that is executing the Shell.

The next interaction shows that the process running the Shell forked (is the parent of) the process running ps. When you call ps with the −l option, it displays more information. (See Part II, ps, for a complete description of all the columns this option displays.) The column headed PPID lists the PID number of the *parent* of each of the processes. From the PID and PPID columns, you can see that the process running the Shell (PID 14437) is the parent of the process running ps (PID 14566): The parent PID number of ps is the same as the PID number of the Shell.

```
$ ps −l
F S UID    PID  PPID  C PRI  NI  ADDR  SZ WCHAN TTY      TIME COMD
1 S 107 14437     1   0  30  20   59a  10 e2b6 tty14   0:06 sh
1 R 107 14566 14437 97  20  20   5e7  11      tty14   0:02 ps
$
```

When you give another **ps −l** command, you can see that the Shell is still being run by the same process but that it forked another process to run ps.

```
$ ps −l
F S UID    PID  PPID  C PRI  NI  ADDR  SZ WCHAN TTY      TIME COMD
1 S 107 14437     1   0  30  20   4e4  10 e2b6 tty14   0:07 sh
1 R 107 14708 14437 91  20  20   3ae  11      tty14   0:02 ps
$
```

The **$!** variable has the value of the PID number of the last process that you ran in the background. The next example executes ps as a background task and then uses echo to display the value of **$!**.

```
$ ps &
14727
$     PID  TTY      TIME COMMAND
  14437  tty14   0:07 sh
  14727  tty14   0:02 ps

echo $!
14727
$
```

Although the prompt in the preceding example appears to be out of sequence, it is not. The Shell displays a prompt after displaying the PID number of a background process. The output from the background process follows the prompt. The **echo** command is given in response to the prompt, although the command does not appear to immediately follow the prompt. You can press RETURN if you want to see another prompt before issuing a command.

When you execute a program in the background, the Shell displays the PID number of the background process and then gives you a prompt. Above, this PID number is confirmed by **ps** and again by the **echo $!** command.

Exit Status

When a process stops executing for any reason, it returns an *exit status* to its parent process. The exit status is also referred to as a *condition code* or *return code*. The Shell stores the exit status of the last command in the read-only Shell variable **$?**.

By convention, a nonzero exit status represents a false value and means that the command failed. A zero is true and means that the command was successful.

You can specify the exit status that a Shell script is to return by using an Exit command, followed by a number, to terminate the script. The following example shows that the number specifies the exit status.

```
$ cat es
echo 'This program returns an exit'
echo 'status of 7.'
exit 7
```

```
$ es
This program returns an exit
status of 7.

$ echo $?
7

$ echo $?
0
```

The **es** Shell script displays a message and then terminates execution with an Exit command that returns an exit status of 7. Then echo displays the value of the exit status of **es**. The second echo displays the value of the exit status of the first echo. The value is zero because the first echo was successful.

Invocation

There are five ways to execute a program under the UNIX operating system. Each method is slightly different from the others and has its own uses. The beginning of this chapter explored the chmod utility as a method of making a Shell script executable. Using Shell scripts, this section demonstrates the four other methods. Except for sh and ., you can also use these techniques with compiled programs (binary executable files), such as those generated by the C compiler.

sh. You can fork a new Shell and command it to execute a Shell script by using sh. Because sh expects a command file, you do not need to have execute access permission to the file. The example below uses **id2**, a command file that displays the PID number of the process that called it. The **id2** program displays the PID number of the Shell that sh forked. The echo utility displays the PID number of the first Shell. The difference in these PID numbers shows that sh forked a new Shell.

```
$ cat id2
echo 'id2 PID =' $$

$ sh id2
id2 PID = 28953

$ echo $$
28907
$
```

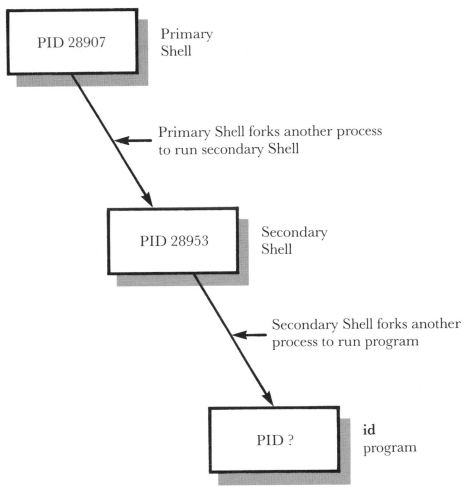

Figure 8-1
sh **Flowchart**

As with any utility, the Shell forks a new process to execute sh (see Figure 8-1). The program that sh executes is another Shell. This second Shell forks yet another process to execute the program you specify. In the preceding example, sh causes the Shell to fork a secondary Shell that forks a process that runs **id2**. While the program is running, the second Shell sleeps. When execution is complete, the forked process dies, waking the second Shell. Then this Shell dies, waking the original Shell, which issues a prompt.

The . and Exec Commands. There are two ways to execute a program without forking a new process. The . command executes a new Shell script as part of the current process. When the new script finishes execution, the current process continues to execute the original script. The Exec command executes the new program in place of (overlays) the current process and never goes back to the original program.

The . command will not execute a compiled program (binary executable file) and does not require that you have execute access permission to the Shell script it executes. Exec will execute a compiled program and does require execute access permission to either a compiled program or Shell script.

The Shell script below displays its PID number and then calls the **id2** Shell script (see the previous example) by using a . command. When **id2** finishes execution, the . command returns control to the calling Shell script, which displays a message.

```
$ cat testpgm4
echo $0 'PID =' $$
. id2
echo 'This line is executed.'

$ testpgm4
testpgm4 PID = 28907
id2 PID = 28907
This line is executed.
$
```

By examining the PID numbers, you can see that the . command did not fork a new process to execute **id2**.

```
$ chmod u+x id2

$ cat testpgm3
echo $0 'PID =' $$
exec id2
echo 'This line is never executed.'

$ testpgm3
testpgm3 PID = 28925
id2 PID = 28925
$
```

After giving the owner execute access permission to **id2**, the Shell script above calls it using an Exec command. The script never executes the line following the call to **id2** because Exec never returns control to **testpgm3**.

The login process takes advantage of the ability of one program to overlay itself with (exec) another. Refer to Chapter 10 for more information.

Command Substitution.   You can execute a command by enclosing it between two grave accent marks [sometimes called *backquotes* (`)]. The Shell replaces the command, including the accent marks, with the output of the command.

The Shell script below assigns the output of the pwd utility to the variable **dir** and displays a message containing this variable.

```
$ cat dir
dir=`pwd`
echo 'You are using the' $dir 'directory.'

$ dir
You are using the /usr/jenny directory.
$
```

The next example contains a variation of the previous one. It incorporates the output of the pwd utility where it is needed in the **echo** command without assigning it to a variable.

```
$ cat dir2
echo 'You are using the' `pwd` 'directory.'

$ dir2
You are using the /usr/jenny directory.
```

The next script shows how to use the date utility and the Set command to provide the date in a useful format. The first command shows the output from date. Then cat displays the **dateset** script. The first command in the script uses grave accent marks to set the command line argument variables to the output of date. Subsequent commands display the values of the first four of these variables. The final command displays the date in a format that you can use in a letter or report.

```
$ date
Mon Nov 26 23:04:09 PST 1984

$ cat dateset
set `date`
echo $*
echo
echo 'Argument 1:' $1
echo 'Argument 2:' $2
echo 'Argument 3:' $3
echo 'Argument 4:' $4
echo
echo $2 $3, $6
```

```
$ dateset
Mon Nov 26 23:04:13 PST 1984

Argument 1: Mon
Argument 2: Nov
Argument 3: 26
Argument 4: 23:04:13

Nov 26, 1984
```

Environment and Exporting Variables

Within a given process, you can declare, initialize, read, and change variables. But a variable is local to a process. When a process forks a child process, the parent does not automatically pass the value of a variable to the child.

The **extest1** Shell script assigns a value of american to the variable named **cheese**. Then it displays the name of the file being executed (**$0**), its PID number (**$$**), and the value of **cheese**. The **extest1** script then calls **display**, which attempts to display the same information. When **display** finishes, it returns control to the parent process executing **extest1**, which again displays the value of **cheese**.

```
$ cat extest1
cheese=american
echo $0 $$ $cheese
display
echo $0 $$ $cheese

$ cat display
echo $0 $$ $cheese

$ extest1
extest1 12247 american
display 12248
extest1 12247 american
$
```

The **display** script never receives the value of **cheese** from **extest1**, while **extest1** never loses the value. When a process attempts to display the value of a variable that has not been declared, as is the case with **display**, it displays nothing—the value of an undeclared variable is that of a null string.

The **extest2** and **change** scripts, following, are similar to **extest1** and **display**. The difference is in **change**, which declares and initializes **cheese** in the child process.

```
$ cat extest2
cheese=american
echo $0 $$ $cheese
change
echo $0 $$ $cheese

$ cat change
echo $0 $$ $cheese
cheese=swiss
echo $0 $$ $cheese

$ extest2
extest2 12252 american
change 12253
change 12253 swiss
extest2 12252 american
```

The **change** script first displays the (null) value of the as-yet undeclared variable **cheese**. Then it declares the variable by assigning swiss to **cheese** and displays this value. This **cheese** variable is local to the child process that is executing **change**. As can be seen above, the parent process preserves the value of its **cheese** variable.

Export.　You can pass the value of a variable to a child process by using the Export command. This command places the value of the variable in the calling environment for the child process. This *call by value* gives the child process a *copy* of the variable for its own use.

Although the child can change the value of the variable, any changes it makes only affect its own copy and not the parent's copy.

```
$ cat extest3
export cheese
cheese=american
echo ·$0 $$ $cheese
change
echo $0 $$ $cheese

$ extest3
extest3 12258 american
change 12259 american
change 12259 swiss
extest3 12258 american
$
```

Above, the child process inherits the value of **cheese** as american and, after displaying this value, changes *its copy* to **swiss**. When control is returned to the parent, the parent's copy of **cheese** still retains its original value, **american**.

If you need several routines to share variables, you can use the method demonstrated below.

```
$ cat extest4
cheese=american
echo $0 $$ $cheese
. change
echo $0 $$ $cheese

$ extest4
extest4 12264 american
extest4 12264 american
extest4 12264 swiss
extest4 12264 swiss
```

Calling **change** using the . command executes it as part of the calling process, not a child process. The PID number remains the same throughout the display. When the value of **cheese** is altered in **change**, it remains changed when control returns to **extest4**.

The value of **$0**, the name the process was called with, does not change when the . command executes another Shell script. The name stays the same because, although a different program is being executed, the same process is executing it.

COMMAND SEPARATION AND GROUPING

When you are giving the Shell commands interactively or writing a Shell script, you must separate commands from one another. This section reviews the ways that were covered in Chapter 5 and introduces a few more.

The NEWLINE Character

The NEWLINE character is a unique command separator because it initiates execution of the command preceding it. You have seen this throughout this book each time you press the RETURN key at the end of a command line.

The | and & Characters

Other command separators are the pipe symbol (|) and the background task symbol (**&**). These command separators *do not* start execution of a command but *do* change some aspect of how the command functions. They alter where the input or output comes from or goes to or determine whether the Shell executes the task in the background or foreground.

If **a**, **b**, and **c** are commands, then the following command line initiates a job that comprises three tasks. The Shell directs the output from task **a** to task **b**, and **b**'s output to **c**. Because the Shell runs the entire job in the foreground, you do not get a prompt back until all three tasks have run to completion.

```
$ a | b | c
```

The next command line executes tasks **a** and **b** in the background and task **c** in the foreground. You get a prompt back as soon as **c** is finished.

```
$ a & b & c
```

The command line below executes all three tasks as background jobs. You get a prompt immediately.

```
$ a & b & c &
```

You can use a pipe to send the output from one subtask to the next and run the whole job as a background task. Again, the prompt comes back immediately.

```
$ a | b | c &
```

The semicolon is a command separator that *does not* initiate execution of a command and *does not* change any aspect of how the command functions. You can execute a series of commands sequentially by entering them on a single command line and separating each from the next by a semicolon. You must terminate the command line with a RETURN to initiate execution of the sequence of commands.

```
$ a ; b ; c
```

The preceding command line yields the same results as the following three command lines.

```
$ a
$ b
$ c
```

Command Grouping

You can use parentheses to group commands. The Shell treats each group of commands as a job, forking child processes as needed to execute tasks.

Assume that **a**, **b**, **c**, and **d** are commands. The first command line below executes commands **a** and **b** sequentially in the background while executing **c** in the foreground. The Shell prompt returns when **c** finishes execution.

```
$ (a ; b) & c
```

The example above differs from a previous example (**a & b & c**) because tasks **a** and **b** are not initiated concurrently but sequentially.

Similarly, the following command line executes **a** and **b** sequentially in the background and, at the same time, executes **c** and **d** sequentially in the background. The prompt returns immediately.

```
$ (a; b)& (c; d)&
```

You can see a demonstration of sequential and concurrent processes run in both the foreground and background. Create a group of executable files named **a**, **b**, **c**, and **d**. Have each file echo its name over and over as file **a** (below) does.

```
$ cat a
echo 'aaaaaaaaaaaaaaaaaaaaaaaaaa\c'
echo 'aaaaaaaaaaaaaaaaaaaaaaaaaa\c'
echo 'aaaaaaaaaaaaaaaaaaaaaaaaaa\c'
echo 'aaaaaaaaaaaaaaaaaaaaaaaaaa\c'
echo 'aaaaaaaaaaaaaaaaaaaaaaaaaa\c'
$
```

Execute the files sequentially and concurrently, using the example command lines from this and the previous section. When you execute two of these Shell scripts sequentially, their output follows one another. When you execute two of them concurrently, their output is interspersed as control is passed back and forth between the tasks. The results will not always be identical because the UNIX system schedules jobs slightly differently each time they run. Two sample runs are shown below.

```
$ a&b&c&
16717
16718
16719
$ aaaaaaaaaaaaaaaaaaaaaaaaaccccccccccccccccccccccccccccccccc
cccccccccccccccccccccccccccccccccccccccccccccccccccccccccccc
cccccccccccccccccccccccccccccaaaaaaaaaaaaaaaaaaaaaaaaaaaaaaa
aaaaaaaaaaaaaaaaaaaaaaaaaaaaaaaaaaaaaaaaaaaaaaaaaaaaaaaaaaaa
aaaaaaaaaaaabbbbbbbbbbbbbbbbbbbbbbbbbbbbbbbbbbbbbbbbbbbbbbbbb
bbbbbbbbbbbbbbbbbbbbbbbbbbbbbbbbbbbbbbbbbbbbbbbbbbbbbbbbbbbbb
bbbbbbbbbbbbbbbbbbbb
```

```
$ a&b&c&
16738
16739
16740
$ cccccccccccccccccccccccccccccccccccccccccccccccccccccccccc
ccccccccccccccccccccccccccccccccccccccccccccccccccccccccccccc
cccccccbbbbbbbbbbbbbbbbbbbbbbbbbbbbbbbbbbbbbbbbbbbbbbbbbbbaaa
aaaaaaaaaaaaaaaaaaaaaaaaaaaaaaaaaaaaaaaaaaaaaaaaaaaaaaaaaaaa
aaaaaaaaaaaaaaaaaaaaaaaaaaaaaaaaaaaaaaaaaaaaaaaaaaaaaaaaaaaa
aabbbbbbbbbbbbbbbbbbbbbbbbbbbbbbbbbbbbbbbbbbbbbbbbbbbbbbbbbbb
bbbbbbbbbbbbbbbbbbbb
```

CONTROL STRUCTURES

A Shell control structure alters the flow of control within a Shell script. The Shell provides simple two-way branch If statements, multiple branch Case statements, as well as For, While, and Until statements.

If Then

The format of the If Then control structure follows. The **bold** words in the format description are the items you supply to cause the structure to have the desired effect. The other words are the keywords the Shell uses to identify the control structure.

if **test-command**
    then **commands**
fi

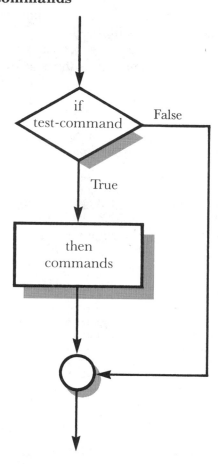

Figure 8-2
If Then Flowchart

As seen in Figure 8-2, the If statement tests the status that the **test-command** returns and transfers control based on this status. When you spell *if* backward, it's *fi;* the Fi statement marks the end of the If structure.

The following program uses an If structure at the beginning of a script to check that the user supplied at least one argument on the command line. The test utility returns a true status if its first and third arguments have the relationship specified by its second argument (i.e., if the number of arguments—represented by **$#**—is equal to 0).

The If statement executes the statements immediately following it if *its* argument returns a true status (its argument is everything enclosed within the parentheses). The effect of this If statement is to display a message and exit from the script if the user did not supply an argument.

If the return status of If's argument is false, the structure transfers control to the statement following the Fi statment.

```
$ cat chkargs
if (test $# = 0)
      then echo 'You must supply at least one argument.'
      exit
fi
echo 'Program running.'

$ chkargs
You must supply at least one argument.

$ chkargs abc
Program running.
```

The next program prompts you and reads in two words. Then it uses an If structure to evaluate the result returned by the **test** utility when it compares the two words. The **test** utility returns a status of true if the two words are the same and false if they are not. Double quotation marks surround $word1 and $word2 so that test will work properly if the user enters a string that contains a SPACE. The double quotation marks (instead of single quotation marks) allow the Shell to substitute values for the variables.

```
$ cat if1
echo 'word 1: \c'
read word1
echo 'word 2: \c'
read word2
if (test "$word1" = "$word2")
      then echo 'Match'
fi
echo 'End of program.'

$ if1
word1: peach
word2: peach
Match
End of program.
$
```

In the example, the parentheses enclose the **test-command** for clarity. If this command returns a true status (=0), the Shell executes the commands between the Then and Fi statements. If the command returns a false status (not =0), the Shell passes control to the statement after Fi without executing the statements between Then and Fi.

If Then Else

The format of the If Then Else control structure is shown below.

```
if test-command
        then commands
        else commands
fi
```

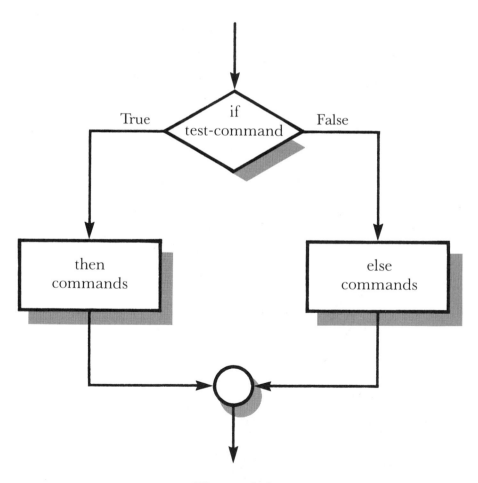

Figure 8-3
If Then Else Flowchart

The introduction of the Else statement turns the If structure into the two-way branch shown in Figure 8-3. If the **test-command** returns a true status, the If structure executes the commands between the Then and Else statements and then diverts control to the statement after Fi. If the **test-command** returns a false status, it executes the commands following the Else statement.

The following script builds on the **chkargs** script. When you call **out** with arguments that are names of files, it displays the files on the terminal. If the first argument is a −v, **out** uses pg to display the files.

After determining that it was called with at least one argument, **out** tests its first argument to see if it is not −v. If the test is true (if the first argument is not −v), the script uses cat to display the files. If the test is false (if the first argument is −v), **out** shifts the arguments to get rid of the −v and displays the files using pg.

```
$ cat out
if (test $# = 0)
     then echo 'You must supply at least one argument.'
     exit
fi
if (test "$1" != "−v")
     then
          cat $*
     else
          shift
          pg $*
fi
```

The expanded word-match program shown below also demonstrates an If Then Else structure. The leading SPACEs on the lines within the If structure make the program easier to read—If does not require them.

```
$ cat if2
echo 'word 1: \c'
read word1
echo 'word 2: \c'
read word2
if (test "$word1" = "$word2")
     then echo 'Match'
     else echo 'No match'
fi
echo 'End of program.'
```

```
$ if2
word 1: peach
word 2: pear
No match
End of program.
$
```

If Then Elif

The format of the If Then Elif control structure is shown below.

> if **test-command**
> > then **commands**
> elif **test-command**
> > then **commands**
> else **command**
> fi

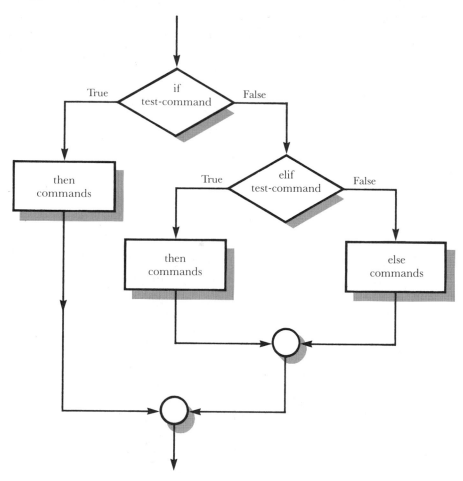

Figure 8-4
If Then Elif Flowchart

The Elif statement combines the Else and If statements and allows you to construct a nested set of If Then Else structures.

The example below shows an If Then Elif Then Else Fi structure. This Shell script compares three words. In the first If statement it uses an AND operator (−a) as an argument to test. The test utility only returns a true status if the first and the second logical comparisons are true (i.e., if **word1** matches **word2** and **word2** matches **word3**). If **test** returns a true status, the program executes the command following the next Then statement and passes control to the statement after Fi, terminating execution of the Shell script.

If the three words are not the same, the structure passes control to the first Elif, which begins a series of tests to see whether any pair of words is the same. As the nesting continues, if any one of the If statements is satisfied, the structure passes control to the next Then statement and subsequently to the statement after Fi. Each time an Elif statement is not satisfied, the structure passes control to the next Elif statement.

```
$ cat if3
echo 'word 1: \c'
read word1
echo 'word 2: \c'
read word2
echo 'word 3: \c'
read word3
if (test "$word1" = "$word2" -a "$word2" = "$word3")
          then echo 'Match: words 1, 2, & 3'
      elif (test "$word1" = "$word2")
          then echo 'Match: words 1 & 2'
      elif (test "$word1" = "$word3")
          then echo 'Match: words 1 & 3'
      elif (test "$word2" = "$word3")
          then echo 'Match: words 2 & 3'
      else echo 'No match'
fi
$
```

For In

The For In structure has the following format.

> for **loop-index** in **argument-list**
>> do
>> **commands**
>> done

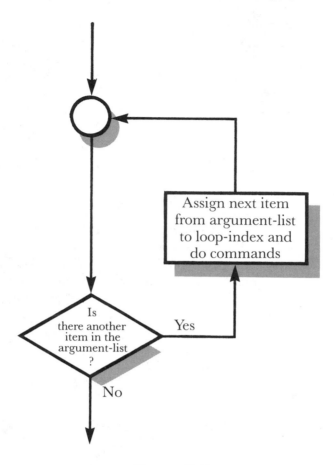

Figure 8-5
For In Flowchart

This structure assigns the value of the first item in the **argument-list** to the **loop-index** and executes the **commands** between the Do and Done statements. The Do and Done statements mark the beginning and end of the For loop.

After the structure passes control to the Done statement, it assigns the value of the second item in the **argument-list** to the **loop-index** and repeats the **commands**. The structure repeats the **commands** between the Do and Done statements—once for each of the items in the **argument-list**. When the structure exhausts the **argument-list**, it passes control to the statement following the Done statement.

The For In structure shown below assigns **apples** to the user variable **fruit** and then displays the value of **fruit**, which is apples. Next, it assigns oranges to **fruit** and repeats the process. When it exhausts the argument list, the structure transfers control to the statement following Done, which displays a message.

```
$ cat fruit
for fruit in apples oranges pears bananas
        do
        echo $fruit
        done
echo 'Task complete.'

$ fruit
apples
oranges
pears
bananas
Task complete.
$
```

For

The For structure has the following format.

> for **loop-index**
>   do
>   **commands**
>   done

The For In structure is often used to loop through the command line parameters (**$1, $2, ...**), performing a series of commands involving each of the parameters in turn. When you omit the keyword In and the **argument-list**, the **loop-index** automatically takes on the value of each of the command line parameters, one at a time.

The Shell script below shows a For structure displaying each of the command line arguments. The first line of the Shell script, for args, implies for args in $*, where the Shell expands $* into a list of command line arguments. The balance of the script mimics the standard For structure.

```
$ cat for_test
for args
        do
        echo $args
        done
```

```
$ for_test candy gum chocolate
candy
gum
chocolate
$
```

While

The While structure (see Figure 8-6) has the following format:

while **test-command**
      do
      commands
      done

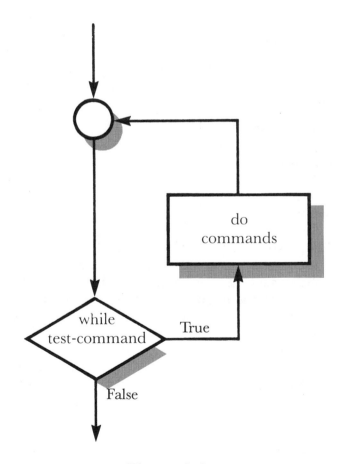

Figure 8-6
While Flowchart

While the **test-command** returns a true exit status, the structure continues to execute the series of **commands** delimited by the Do and Done statements. Before each loop through the **commands**, the structure executes the **test-command**. When the exit status of the **test-command** is false, the structure passes control to the statement following the Done statement.

The Shell script shown below first initializes the variable **number** to the character value of zero—Shell variables can only take on values of character strings. The test utility then determines if the value of the variable **number** is less than 10. The **count** script calls test, using −**lt** to perform a *numerical* test. [You must use −**ne** (not equal), −**eq** (equal), −**gt** (greater than), −**ge** (greater than or equal), −**lt** (less than), or −**le** (less than or equal) for numerical comparisons and = or != for string comparisons.] The test utility has an exit status of true as long as **number** is less than 10. While test returns true, the structure executes the commands between the Do and Done statments.

The first command following Do displays the string represented by **number**. The next command uses the expr utility to increment the value of **number** by one. Here, expr converts its arguments to numbers, adds them, converts the result to characters, and echoes them to the standard output. The grave accent marks cause the command that they enclose to be replaced by the output of the command. This value is then assigned to the variable **number**. The first time through the loop, **number** has a value of zero, so expr converts the strings 0 and 1 to numbers, adds them, and converts the result back to a string (1). The Shell then assigns this value to the **number** variable. The Done statement closes the loop and returns control to the While statement to start the loop over again.

```
$ cat count
number=0
while (test "$number" -lt "10")
     do
     echo "$number\c"
     number=`expr $number + 1`
     done
echo

$ count
0123456789
$
```

Until

The Until structure is shown below.

until **test-command**
> do
> **commands**
> done

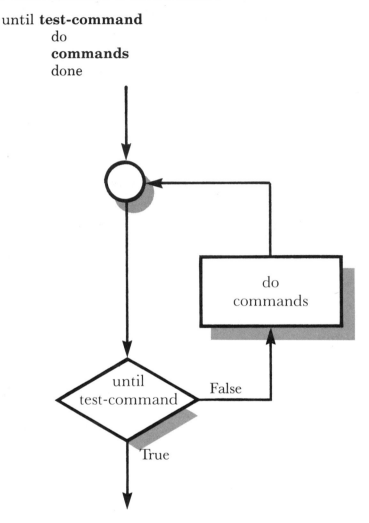

Figure 8-7
Until Flowchart

The Until and While structures are very similar. They only differ in the sense of the test at the top of the loop. Figure 8-7 shows that Until continues to loop *until* the **test-command** returns a true or nonerror condition. While loops *while* the **test-command** continues to return a true or nonerror condition.

The following program demonstrates an Until structure that

includes a Read command. When the user enters the correct name, the **test-command** is satisfied and the structure passes control out of the loop.

```
$ cat until1
secretname='jenny'
name='noname'
echo 'Try to guess the secret name!'
echo
until (test "$name" = "$secretname")
     do
     echo 'Your guess: \c'
     read name
     done
echo 'Very good.'

$ until1
Try to guess the secret name!

Your guess: helen
Your guess: barbara
Your guess: jenny
Very good.
$
```

Break and Continue

You can interrupt a For, While, or Until loop with a Break or Continue statement. Break transfers control to the statement after the Done statement, terminating execution of the loop. Continue transfers control to the Done statement, which continues execution of the loop.

Case

The Case structure is shown below.

```
case test-string in
        pattern-1) commands-1;;
        pattern-2) commands-2;;
        pattern-3) commands-3;;

     .

     .

     .

esac
```

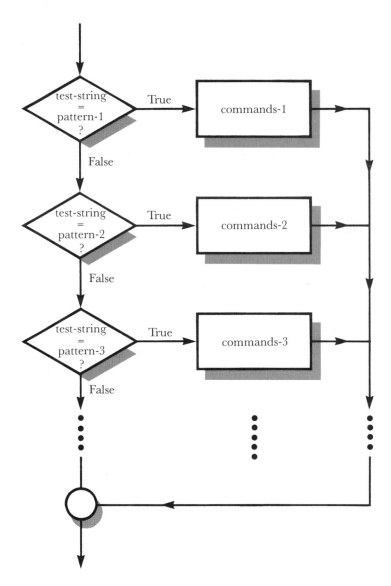

Figure 8-8
Case Flowchart

Figure 8-8 shows that the Case structure provides a multiple branch decision mechanism. The path that the structure choses depends on a match between the **test-string** and one of the **patterns**.

The following Case structure uses the value of the character that the user enters as the test string. This value is represented by **letter**. If the test string has a value of A, the structure executes the command following A). If the test string has a value of B or C, the structure executes the appropriate command. The asterisk indicates *any string of characters* and functions as a catchall, in case there is no match. The second sample execution of **case1** shows the user entering a lowercase b. Because b does not match the uppercase B in the Case statement, the program tells you there is no match.

```
$ cat case1
echo 'Enter A, B, or C: \c'
read letter
case $letter in
     A) echo 'You entered A';;
     B) echo 'You entered B';;
     C) echo 'You entered C';;
     *) echo 'You did not enter A, B, or C';;
esac

$ case1
Enter A, B, or C: B
You entered B

$ case1
Enter A, B, or C: b
You did not enter A, B, or C
$
```

The pattern in the Case structure is analogous to that of an ambiguous file reference. You can use the following special characters and strings.

*   An asterisk matches any string of characters. You can use it for the default case.

?   A question mark matches any single character.

[...] Square brackets define a character class. Any characters enclosed within square brackets are tried, one at a time, in an attempt to match a single character. A hyphen specifies a range of characters.

| A vertical bar separates alternate choices that will satisfy a particular branch of the Case structure.

The next program is a variation of the previous one. This script accepts uppercase and lowercase letters.

```
$ cat case2
echo 'Enter A, B, or C: \c'
read letter
case $letter in
     a|A) echo 'You entered A.';;
     b|B) echo 'You entered B.';;
     c|C) echo 'You entered C.';;
     *) echo 'You did not enter A, B, or C.';;
esac

$ case2
Enter A, B, or C: b
You entered B.
$
```

The Here Document

A Here document allows you to redirect input to a Shell script from within the Shell script itself. It is called a Here document because it is *here*, immediately accessible in the Shell script, instead of *there*, in another file.

The following program, **bd**, contains a Here document. The two less-than symbols on the first line indicate to the Shell that a Here document follows. One or more characters that delimit the Here document follow the less-than symbols—this example uses plus signs. The Shell sends everything between the two delimiters to the process as its standard input. It is as though you had redirected the standard input to grep from a file, except that the file is embedded in the Shell script.

```
$ cat bd
grep $1 <<+
Mary      August 21, 1953
Peter     June 21, 1962
Ann       April 15, 1949
Tom       June 6, 1980
Penny     May 29, 1955
+

$ bd Ann
Ann       April 15, 1949

$ bd June
Peter     June 21, 1962
Tom       June 6, 1980
$
```

When you run **bd**, it lists all the lines in the Here document that contain the argument you call it with. The first time it is run (on the preceding page), it displays Ann's birthday because it is called with an argument of Ann. The second run displays all the birthdays in June.

SIGNALS

A signal is a report to a process about a condition. The UNIX system uses signals to report bad system calls, broken pipes, illegal instructions, and other conditions. This discussion covers the three signals that are useful when you work with Shell scripts. They are the *terminal interrupt* signal (number 2), the *kill* signal (number 9), and the *software termination* signal (number 15).

You can use the Trap command to trap a signal. When a program traps a signal, it takes whatever action you specify. It can close files or finish any other processing as needed, display a message, terminate execution immediately, or ignore the signal.

The format of a Trap command is shown below.

trap ['commands'] signal-numbers

The **signal-numbers** are the numbers of the signals that the Trap command will catch. One or more **signal-numbers** must be present. The **commands** part is optional. If it is not present, the command resets the trap to its initial condition, which is to exit from the program. If the **commands** part is present, the Shell executes the **commands** when it catches one of the signals. After executing the **commands**, the Shell resumes executing the script where it left off.

You can interrupt the program you are running in the foreground by pressing the DEL key. Pressing this key sends signal number 2, a terminal interrupt signal, to the program. The Shell terminates execution of the program if the program does not trap this signal. The following script demonstrates the use of the Trap command to trap signal number 2. It returns an exit status of 1.

```
$ cat inter
trap 'echo PROGRAM INTERRUPTED; exit 1' 2
while (true)
        do
        echo 'Program running.'
        done
```

The first line of **inter** sets up a trap for signal number 2. When the signal is caught, the Shell executes the two commands between the single quotation marks in the Trap command. The echo utility displays the message PROGRAM INTERRUPTED. Then Exit returns control to the Shell, which displays a prompt. If the Exit command were not there, the Shell would return control to the While loop after displaying the message.

You can send a software termination signal to a background process by using kill without a signal number. A Trap command, set up to catch signal number 15, will catch this signal. Refer to the kill utility in Part II for more information.

You can send a kill signal to a process by using kill with signal number 9. The Shell cannot trap a kill signal.

REDIRECTING THE ERROR OUTPUT

Chapter 5 described the concept of standard output and explained how to redirect a program's standard output. In addition to the standard output, programs can send their output to another place: the *error output*. A program can send error messages to its error output to keep them from getting mixed up with the information it sends to its standard output. Just like the standard output, unless you redirect it, the Shell sends a program's error output to the terminal. Unless you redirect one or the other, you will not know the difference between the output a program sends to its standard output and the output it sends to it error output.

The following examples demonstrate how to redirect the standard output and the error output to different files or to the same file. When you call cat with the name of a file that does not exist and the name of a file that does exist, it sends an error message to the error output and copies the file to the standard output. Unless you redirect them, both messages appear on the terminal.

```
$ cat y
This is y.

$ cat x y
cat:   cannot open x
This is y.
$
```

When you redirect the standard output of a command using the greater-than symbol, the error output is not affected—it still appears on the terminal.

```
$ cat x y > hold
cat:   cannot open x

$ cat hold
This is y.
$
```

The following example redirects the standard output and the error output to different files. The notation **2>** tells the Shell where to redirect the error output. The **1>** is the same as **>** and tells the Shell where to redirect the standard output. You can use **>** in place of **1>**.

```
$ cat x y 1> hold1 2> hold2

$ cat hold1
This is y.

$ cat hold2
cat:   cannot open x
$
```

Next, **2>&1** declares file descriptor 2 to be a duplicate of file descriptor 1. The **1>** redirects both the standard output and standard error to the same file.

```
$ cat x y 1> hold 2>&1

$ cat hold
cat:   cannot open x
This is y.
$
```

JOB CONTROL

UNIX System V, Release 2, introduced *job control* to AT&T UNIX (Berkeley UNIX has had job control for quite a while). Job control allows you, from a single terminal, to control up to seven Shells at once. These Shells, called *layers,* can each be running a different program at the same time. The *current* layer is the one that receives the characters you enter on the keyboard. There can be zero or one current layers at any given time. Using the job-control commands, you can make any layer the current layer, create new layers, delete layers, and list layers.

When you give an **shl** (Shell layer) command, the Shell layer manager takes over and issues its prompt, which is >>>. To create a new layer, give the **create** command, optionally followed by the name of the layer you want to create. If you do not name the layer, shl will name it **(1)**. You can refer to it as just **1**. If you create additional unnamed layers, shl will name them **(2)** through **(7)**. When you create a layer, you will see the Shell prompt, which shl sets to the name of the layer. Use the new Shell as you would any Shell—give it commands to edit files, compile programs, send mail, etc. When you want to create a new layer, press CONTROL-Z and you will see the Shell layer manager prompt.

You can give the Shell layer manager another **create** command to create another layer, a **layers** command to display a list of layers, a **resume** command followed by the name of a layer to make that layer the current layer, a **delete** command followed by the name of a layer to remove a layer, or a **quit** command to stop using the Shell layer manager.

In addition, you can give a **block** command to block output from a layer. Blocking output causes a program to stop execution when it it is not the current layer and it tries to send output to the terminal. When you make the blocked layer the current layer, execution resumes and you can view the output. Blocking output prevents programs that are running in layers other than the current layer from flooding the terminal with output while you are working on something else. The **unblock** command reverses the effects of the **block** command.

You can abbreviate all Shell layer manager commands to as few characters as are necessary to ensure that the command is unique (usually one character).

Any time after you have logged on, you can start using the

Shell layer manager. Give the command **shl** in response to the Shell prompt. The Shell layer manager will display its prompt.

Below, Jenny calls the Shell layer manager and gives a Create command (**c**) to create a layer. Because she did not specify a name for the layer, the Shell layer manager gives it the default name for layer 1, **(1)**. Once layer 1 displays its prompt, (1), Jenny calls mail. After starting to enter a message to send to Alex, Jenny presses CONTROL-Z to call the Shell layer manager and creates a new layer so she can check on a directory name she needs to include in her note to Alex.

```
$ shl

>>> c

(1) mail alex
The file you asked me for in the  CONTROL-Z  >>>  c

(2) pwd
/usr/jenny/literature
```

After Jenny creates layer 2, she gives a **pwd** command (above) and an **ls** command (below). Before returning to the note she is still sending Alex, she calls vi to edit a file named **reminder**.

While she is still using vi in layer 2, Jenny presses CONTROL-Z to return to the Shell layer manager. (If you lose track of which layer is running what, you can give an l −l command in response to the Shell layer manager prompt to display a list of active layers and what processes each is running.) After the Shell layer manager displays its prompt, Jenny gives the command **1** to return to layer 1. The Shell layer manager displays resuming 1, and she is back in the middle of using mail. She finishes her message to Alex and enters a period to exit from mail.

```
(2) ls
.
.
(2) vi reminder
.
.
CONTROL-Z  >>>  1
resuming 1
 directory named /usr/jenny/literature.

       Jenny
.
(1)
```

When Jenny gets the prompt for layer 1, she returns to the Shell layer manager, deletes layer 1 (**d 1**), and goes back to layer 2 where she was using vi. She presses CONTROL-L (some terminals use CONTROL-R) to refresh the screen, finishes editing her file, and exits from vi.

Finally, Jenny goes back to the Shell layer manager, deletes layer 2, checks that there are no active layers (**l**), and returns to her regular Shell with a **q** command.

```
( 1 )  CONTROL-Z  >>> d 1
>>>  2
resuming 2
CONTROL-L
.

.
( 2 )  CONTROL-Z  >>> d 2
>>>  l
>>>  q
$
```

For more information, refer to shl in Part II.

FUNCTIONS

UNIX System V, Release 2, introduced *Shell functions*. A Shell function is similar to a Shell script in that it stores a series of commands for execution at a later time. However, because the Shell stores a function in main memory instead of a file, you can access it more quickly than a script. Also, the Shell preprocesses (parses) a function so that it starts up more quickly than a script. Finally, the Shell executes a Shell function in the same Shell that called it—see "Environment and Exporting Variables," page 214, for more information.

You can declare Shell functions in your **.profile** file or enter them directly from the command line. You can remove functions with the Unset command. The Shell will not keep functions once you log off.

The format you use to declare a Shell function is shown below.

> **function-name ()**
> {
>   **commands**
> }

The **function-name** is the name you will use to call the function.

The **commands** is the list of commands the function will execute when you call it. These **commands** can include anything you can include in a Shell script.

The next example shows how to create a simple function that displays the date and lists the people who are using the system. The name of the function is **dw**.

```
$ dw ()
{
date
who
}

$ dw
Thu Dec 13 09:51:09 PST 1984
hls        console Dec  8 08:59
alex       tty20   Dec 13 09:33
jenny      tty24   Dec 13 09:23
```

If you want to have the **dw** function always available without having to enter it each time you log on, put its definition in your **.profile** file. Below is a **.profile** file that defines the **dw** function, declares a terminal type, and sets the line kill character.

```
$ cat .profile
TERM=vt100
export TERM
stty kill '^u'
dw ()
{
date
who
}
$
```

Make sure that a function does not call itself. If you want to give a function the same name as a utility it calls, call the utility with its absolute pathname. For example, a function named **ls** that substitutes **ls −C** for **ls** should contain the line **/bin/ls −C $*** (assuming **ls** is in the **/bin** directory).

SUMMARY

The Shell is both a *command interpreter* and a *programming language*. As a command interpreter, the Shell executes commands that you enter in response to its prompt. When you use it as a programming language, the Shell executes commands from files called *Shell scripts*.

You can declare Shell scripts to be functions so that they are immediately available and the Shell can execute them more quickly.

When you are using the Shell interactively, you can call the Shell layer manager (shl) to work with more than one Shell at a time.

The Shell executes commands by means of processes. Each process has a unique process ID (PID) number. When you give the Shell a command, it generally *forks* a new process that executes the command. The Shell has some commands that are built in. It does not fork a new process to execute these commands.

Built-in
command Function

:	null command
.	execute a program as part of the current process
`pgm`	execute *pgm* in line
break	exit from For, While, or Until loop
cd	change working directories
continue	start with next iteration of For, While, or Until loop
echo	display arguments
exec	execute a program in place of the current process
exit	exit from current Shell (same as CONTROL-D)
export	place the value of a variable in the calling environment
pwd	print the name of the working directory
read	read a line from the standard input
readonly	declare a variable to be read-only
return	exit from a function
set	set Shell flags or command line argument variables; without an argument, display a list of all variables
shift	promote each command line argument
test	compare arguments
times	display times for the current Shell and its children
trap	trap a signal
type	display how each argument would be interpreted as a command
umask	file-creation mask
unset	remove a variable or function

You can execute a Shell script (or a compiled program) by giving yourself execute access permission to the file (using chmod) and using the name of the file as a command. If you precede the filename of a Shell script with an **sh** command, you do not need execute access permission to the file.

The Shell allows you to define *variables*. When you give the Shell a command, it examines the command line for words that begin with unquoted dollar signs. It assumes that these words are variables and substitutes a value for each of them. You can declare and initialize a variable by assigning a value to it. You can remove a variable declaration by using the Unset command.

The Shell also defines some variables. These variables are listed below. Read-only variables are preceded by a dollar sign because you can only reference them in this manner—you cannot assign a value to them.

Variable	Contents
$0	name of the calling program
$n	value of the nth command line argument (can be changed by Set)
$*	all of the command line arguments (can be changed by Set)
$#	count of the command line arguments
$$	PID number of the current process
$!	PID number of the most recent background task
$?	exit status of the last task that was executed
HOME	pathname of your home directory
IFS	internal-field separator
PATH	search path for commands
PS1	prompt string 1
PS2	prompt string 2
CDPATH	list of directories for the Shell to check when you give a **cd** command
MAIL	file where mail stores your mail
MAILCHECK	specifies how often the Shell checks your mail box
MAILPATH	list of other potential mail boxes

The Shell provides the *control structures* listed below so that you can alter the flow of control within a Shell script.

if then
if then else
if then elif
for in
for
while
until
case

Some of the special characters that the Shell recognizes are listed below.

Special character	Function
RETURN	initiates execution of a command
;	separates commands
( )	groups commands for execution
&	executes a command in the background
|	pipe
>	redirect standard output
>>	append standard output
<	redirect standard input
<<	Here document
*	any string of characters in an ambiguous file reference
?	any single character in an ambiguous file reference
\	quote special characters
'	quote a string
`	execute a program in line
"	quote a string
[ ]	character class in an ambiguous file reference
$	reference a variable
.	execute a command (only at the beginning of a line)
#	comment follows

9

THE C SHELL

The C Shell performs the same function as the Bourne Shell: It provides an interface between you and the UNIX operating system. It is an interactive command interpreter as well as a high-level programming language. At any one time you will be using the Bourne Shell or the C Shell, not both, although it is possible to switch back and forth between the two. This chapter contrasts the C Shell with the Bourne Shell, paying particular attention to those facets of the C Shell that are absent from the Bourne Shell. Although Chapter 8 is not specifically about the C Shell, it discusses many important concepts that are common to both shells and provides a good background for this chapter.

This book discusses the C Shell because, although it is not a part of standard UNIX System V, it is available on many machines running System V.

C Shell variables are much more versatile than those of the Bourne Shell. The C Shell processes arrays of numbers and strings and evaluates logical and numerical expressions. You can customize the C Shell to make it more tolerant of mistakes and easier to use. By setting the proper Shell variables, you can make the C Shell warn you when you appear to be accidentally logging off or overwriting a file. The Alias mechanism makes it easy to change the names of existing commands and create new ones. The History mechanism allows you to edit and rerun previous command lines.

ENTERING AND LEAVING THE C SHELL

If your version of UNIX has the C Shell, and you are not already using it, you can execute the C Shell by giving the command **csh**. If you are not sure which Shell you are using, use the **ps** utility to find out. It will show that you are running **csh** (the C Shell) or **sh** (the Bourne Shell).

If you want to use the C Shell as a matter of course, the system administrator can set up the **/etc/passwd** file so that you are using the C Shell immediately when you log on. On some systems, you can give a **chsh csh** (change shell to C Shell) command to effect the same change. Use **chsh sh** if you want to go back to using the Bourne Shell.

So that you can run both Bourne and C Shell scripts under the C Shell, the first character in a C Shell script must be a sharp sign (#). If the first character of a Shell script is anything other than a sharp sign, the C Shell will run the script under the Bourne Shell. Refer to page 267, "C Shell Scripts."

There are several ways to leave a C Shell. The way that you use is dependent on two factors: whether the Shell variable **ignoreeof** is set and whether you are using the Shell that you logged on to or another Shell that you created after you logged on. If you are not sure how to exit from a C Shell, press CONTROL-D. You will either exit or receive instructions on how to exit.

If you have not set **ignoreeof**, and it has not been set for you in your **.cshrc** startup file (see page 268), you can exit from any Shell using CONTROL-D (the same procedure you use to exit from the Bourne Shell).

If **ignoreeof** is set, CONTROL-D will not work. It causes the Shell to display a message telling you how to exit. You can exit from a C Shell (other than the login Shell) by giving an **exit** command. A **logout** command allows you to exit from the login Shell. There is more information on **ignoreeof** on page 265.

HISTORY

Many of the examples in this chapter show numbered prompts. The History mechanism maintains a list of recently used command lines, also called *events*. The **history** variable (page 264) determines the number of events preserved in this list. Typically, you will want to preserve 10 to 15 events. If you attempt to preserve too many events, you may run out of memory.

The C Shell assigns a sequential *event number* to each of your command lines. If you wish, the C Shell can display this number as part of its prompt (see page 264). Many of the examples in this chapter show numbered prompts. The History mechanism preserves events whether or not you use a numbered prompt.

Give the following command manually, or place it in your **.cshrc** startup file, to establish a History list of the ten most recent events.

```
% set history = 10
%
```

Give the command **history** to display the events in the History list. When you first set the **history** variable, the History list will just record the events back to the command line you used to set it.

```
32 % history
    23 ls -l
    24 cat temp
    25 rm temp
    26 vi memo
    27 lpr memo
    28 vi memo
    29 lpr memo
    30 mail jenny < memo
    31 rm memo
    32 history
33 %
```

Reexecuting Events

You can reexecute any event in the History list. Even if there is no History list, you can always reexecute the previous event. There are three ways to reference an event: by its absolute event number, by its number relative to the current event, or by the text it contains.

All references to events begin with an exclamation point. One or more characters follow the exclamation point to specify an event.

Reexecuting the Previous Event. You can always reexecute the previous event by giving the command !!. In the following example, event 4 reexecutes event 3.

```
3 % ls −l text
-rw-rw-r-- 1 alex   pubs       5  Feb 27  12:51  text

4 % !!
ls −l text
-rw-rw-r-- 1 alex   pubs       5  Feb 27  12:51  text
5 %
```

Using Event Numbers. A number following an exclamation point refers to an event. If that event is in the History list, the C Shell executes it. A negative number following an exclamation point references an event relative to the current event (e.g., !−3 refers to the third preceding event). Both of the following commands reexecute event 3.

```
7 % !3
ls −l text
-rw-rw-r-- 1 alex   pubs       5  Feb 27  12:51  text

8 % !−5
ls −l text
-rw-rw-r-- 1 alex   pubs       5  Feb 27  12:51  text
9 %
```

Using Event Text. When a string of text follows an exclamation point, the C Shell searches for and executes the most recent event that *began* with that string. If you enclose the string between question marks, the C Shell executes the most recent event *containing* that string. The final question mark is optional if a RETURN would immediately follow it.

```
53 % history
      48 cat letter
      49 cat memo
      50 lpr memo
      51 mail jenny < memo
      52 ls -l
      53 history

54 % !l
ls -l
 .
 .
 .

55 % !lp
lpr memo

56 % !?letter?
cat letter
 .
 .
 .

57 %
```

Words Within Events

You can select any word or series of words from an event. The words are numbered starting with 0, representing the first command on the line, and continuing with 1, representing the first word following the command, through n, representing the last word on the line.

To specify a particular word from a previous event, follow the event specification (such as !14) with a colon and the number of the word in the previous event. (Use !14:3 to specify the third word from event 14.) You can specify a range of words by separating two word numbers with a hyphen. The first word following the command (word number one) can be specified by a caret (^), and the last word by a dollar sign.

```
72 % echo apple grape orange pear
apple grape orange pear

73 % echo !72:2
echo grape
grape

74 % echo !72:^
echo apple
apple
```

```
75 %  !72:0  !72:$
echo pear
pear

76 %  echo !72:2-4
echo grape orange pear
grape orange pear

77 %  !72:0-$
echo apple grape orange pear
apple grape orange pear
78 %
```

As the next example shows, !$ refers to the last word of the
previous event. You can use this shorthand to edit, for example, a
file you just displayed with cat.

```
%  cat  report.718
 .
 .
 .

%  vi  !$
vi  report.718
 .
 .
 .
```

If an event contains a single command, the word numbers
correspond to the argument numbers. If an event contains more
than one command, this correspondence is not true for commands
after the first. Event 78, below, contains two commands,
separated by a semicolon so that the Shell executes them sequentially. The semicolon is the fifth word.

```
78 %  !72 ; echo helen jenny barbara
echo apple grape orange pear ; echo helen jenny barbara
apple grape orange pear
helen jenny barbara

79 %  echo !78:7
echo helen
helen

80 %  echo !78:4-7
echo pear ; echo helen
pear
helen
81 %
```

Modifying Previous Events

On occasion, you may want to reexecute an event, changing some aspect of it. Perhaps you entered a complex command line with a typo or incorrect pathname. Or you may want to reexecute a command, specifying a different argument. You can modify an event, or a word of an event, by following the event or word specifier with a colon and a modifier. The following example shows the substitute modifier correcting a typo in the previous event.

```
145 % ct /usr/jenny/memo.0506 /usr/alex/letter.0506
ct: Command not found.

146 % !!:s/ct/cat
cat /usr/jenny/memo.0506 /usr/alex/letter.0506
.
.
.
147 %
```

As a special case, you can use an abbreviated form of the substitute modifier, shown below, to change the most recent event.

```
%  ^old^new
```

produces the same results as

```
%  !!:s/old/new
```

Thus, event 146 could have been entered as

```
146 %  ^ct^cat
cat /usr/jenny/memo.0506 /usr/alex/letter.0506
.
.
.
147 %
```

Following is a list of modifiers.

Modifier	Mnemonic	Effect
h	head	remove the last element of a pathname
r	root	remove the filename extension
t	tail	remove all elements of a pathname except the last
&	repeat	repeat the previous substitution
p	print	do not execute the modified event
q	quote	quote the modifications so that no further modifications take place
[g]s/old/new/	substitute	substitute **new** for **old**

The **s** modifier substitutes the first occurrence of the old string with the new one. Placing a **g** before the **s** (**gs/old/new/**) causes a global substitution, replacing all occurrences of the old string. The **/** is the delimiter in these examples, but you can use any character. The final delimiter is optional if a RETURN would immediately follow it. Like the vi Substitute command, the History mechanism replaces an ampersand (**&**) in the new string with the old string. The Shell replaces a null old string (**s//new/**) with the previous old string or string within a command that you searched for with ?string?.

The following examples demonstrate the use of History modifiers.

```
66 % echo /usr/jenny/letter.0406 /usr/jenny/memo.prv
/usr/jenny/letter.0406 /usr/jenny/memo.prv

67 % !!:h
echo /usr/jenny /usr/jenny/memo.prv
/usr/jenny /usr/jenny/memo.prv

68 % echo !66:2:h
echo /usr/jenny
/usr/jenny

69 % echo !66:2:t
echo memo.prv
memo.prv

70 % echo !66:1:r
echo /usr/jenny/letter
/usr/jenny/letter

71 % echo !66:1:p
echo /usr/jenny/letter.0406
72 %
```

Event 66 displays two filenames. Event 67 recalls the previous event, modified by **h**. Because the command did not specify a word from the event, it modified word 1 and recalled the entire previous event. Events 68 through 70 recall and modify specific words from event 66. In these cases, only the specified words are recalled. Event 71 uses the **p** modifier to display, but not execute, the resulting command.

ALIAS

The C Shell Alias mechanism makes standard commands perform nonstandard functions and allows you to define new commands. Alias performs a string substitution on the command line according to your specifications. Because an Alias is local to the Shell you declare it in, Alias does not function within a Shell script unless you give an Alias command in the script. The format of an Alias command is shown below.

alias [entered-command [executed-command]]

The **entered-command** is the command that you enter in response to the C Shell prompt. The **executed-command** is the string that Alias substitutes for the **entered-command**.

The following example shows how to use an Alias. The Alias command in event 6 causes the C Shell to substitute ls —l every time you give an **ls** command. Events 7 and 8 demonstrate this substitution. Event 9 shows that you can avoid Alias' substitution by placing a backslash before a command that has an Alias.

```
5 % ls
one
three
two

6 % alias ls ls —l

7 % ls
total 3
-rwxrw-r--  1 jenny pubs      17  Mar  5 11:36 one
-rw-rw-r--   1 jenny pubs      42  Mar  5 11:14 three
-rwxrw-r--  1 jenny pubs      11  Mar  5 11:35 two

8 % ls three
-rw-rw-r--   1 jenny   pubs  42 Mar  5 11:14 three
```

```
9 %  \ls three
three

10 %  alias w who

11 %  alias
ls        (ls −l)
w'        who

12 %  alias ls
(ls −l)

13 %  unalias ls

14 %  alias
w         who
15 %
```

When you give an Alias command without any arguments
(event 11), the C Shell displays a list of all the Aliases. When
given with one argument (event 12), the Alias for that argument is
displayed. An Unalias command (event 13) removes an Alias from
the list of Aliases.

Implementation of Alias

When you enter a command line, the C Shell breaks it into commands. Next, the C Shell substitutes an Alias for each command
that has an Alias. After it makes these substitutions, the C Shell
substitutes Aliases over and over again until there are no Aliases
left. Alias flags a self-referencing Alias to prevent an infinite loop.

```
82 %  alias a b

83 %  alias b c

84 %  alias c echo finished

85 %  alias
a         b
b         c
c         (echo finished)

86 %  a
finished
87 %
```

Events 82, 83, and 84 define a series of Aliases that reference
each other; event 85 uses Alias without any arguments to display
all of the Aliases. The C Shell executes event 86 as follows:

1. a is replaced by its Alias b

2. b is replaced by its Alias c

3. c is replaced by its Alias echo finished

4. there are no further Aliases, so the Shell
   executes the echo command

Argument Substitution

Alias substitutes command line arguments using the same scheme
as History, with a single exclamation point representing the
current event. Modifiers are the same as those used by History
(page 252). The exclamation points are quoted in the following
example so that the Shell does not interpret them but passes them
on to Alias.

```
21 % alias last echo \!:$
22 % last this is just a test
test
23 % alias fn2 echo \!:2:t
24 % fn2 /usr/jenny/test /usr/alex/temp /usr/barbara/new
temp
25 %
```

Event 21 defines an Alias for **last** that echoes the last argument. Event 23 defines an Alias for **fn2** that echoes the simple
filename, or tail, of the second argument on the command line.

VARIABLES

The C Shell, like the Bourne Shell, only uses string variables. The
C Shell can, however, work with these variables as numbers. You
must use expr to perform arithmetic operations on numbers in the
Bourne Shell. The arithmetic functions of expr, and more, are
built into the C Shell.

This section uses the term *numeric variable* to describe a
string variable that contains a number that the C Shell uses in
arithmetic or logical-arithmetic computations. However, no true
numeric variables exist.

A C Shell variable name consists of 1 to 20 characters, chosen
from the same set of characters as a filename.

Variable Substitution

Three commands declare and manipulate variables: Set, @, and Setenv. Set assumes that a variable is a nonnumeric string variable. The @ command only works with numeric variables. Both Set and @ declare local variables. Setenv declares a variable *and* places it in the calling environment of all child processes. Using Setenv is similar to using Export in the Bourne Shell (see page 214 for a discussion of local and global variables).

Once the value—or merely the existence—of a variable has been established, the C Shell substitutes the value of that variable when it sees the variable on a command line or in a Shell script. The C Shell, like the Bourne Shell, recognizes a word that begins with a dollar sign as a variable. If you quote the dollar sign by preceding it with a backslash (\$), the Shell will not perform the substitution. When a variable is within double quotation marks, the substitution occurs even if you quote the dollar sign. If the variable is within single quotation marks, the substitution will not occur, regardless of whether or not you quote the dollar sign.

String Variables

The C Shell treats string variables similarly to the way the Bourne Shell does. The major difference is in their declaration and assignment. The C Shell uses an explicit command, Set (or Setenv), to declare and/or assign a value to a string variable.

```
1 % set name = fred

2 % echo $name
fred

3 % set
argv     ()
home     /usr/jenny
name     fred
Shell    /bin/csh
status   0

4 % set name

5 % echo $name

6 % unset name
```

```
7 % set
argv    ()
home    /usr/jenny
Shell   /bin/csh
status  0
8 %
```

Event 1 declares the variable **name** and assigns the string fred to it. Unlike the Bourne Shell, **the C Shell requires** SPACEs **around the equal sign.** Event 2 displays this value. When you give a Set command without any arguments, it displays a list of all the declared variables and their values. When you give a Set command with only the name of a variable and no value, it sets the variable to a null string. Refer to events 4 and 5, above. Events 6 and 7 show that the Unset command removes a variable from the list of declared variables.

Arrays of String Variables

Before you can access individual elements of an array, you must declare the entire array. To declare an array, you need to assign a value to each element of the array.

```
8 % set colors = (red green blue orange yellow)

9 % echo $colors
red green blue orange yellow

10 % echo $colors[3]
blue

11 % echo $colors[2-4]
green blue orange

12 % set shapes = ( ' ' ' ' ' ' ' ' ' ' )

13 % echo $shapes

14 % set shapes[4] = square

15 % echo $shapes[4]
square
16 %
```

Event 8 declares the array of string variables named **colors** to have five elements and assigns values to each of these elements. If you do not know the values of the elements at the time you declare an array, you can declare an array containing the necessary number of null elements. See event 12.

You can reference an entire array by preceding its name with a dollar sign (event 9). A number in square brackets following a reference to the array refers to an element of the array (events 10, 14, and 15). Two numbers in square brackets, separated by a hyphen, refer to two or more adjacent elements of the array (event 11). See "Special Forms of User Variables," page 262, for more information on arrays.

Numeric Variables

The **@** command assigns a value to a numeric variable. You can declare single numeric variables with the **@** command, just as the Set command declares nonnumeric variables. If you give **@** a nonnumeric argument, it displays an Expression syntax. error message.

Many of the expressions that the **@** command can evaluate and the operators it recognizes are derived from the C programming language. The format of a declaration or assignment using the **@** command is shown below.

@ variable-name operator expression

The **variable-name** is the name of the variable that you are declaring or assigning a value to. The **operator** is one of the C assignment operators: =, +=, -=, *=, /=, or %=. (See page 336 for an explanation of these operators.) The **expression** is an arithmetic expression that can include most C operators; refer to "Expressions," following. You can use parentheses within the expression for clarity or to change the order of evaluation. Parentheses must surround parts of the expression that contain any of the following characters: <, >, **&**, or | .

Expressions. An expression can be composed of constants, variables, and the following operators (listed in order of decreasing precedence).

Parentheses
()   change the order of evaluation

Unary operators
~   one's complement
!   logical negation

Arithmetic operators
%   remainder
/   divide
*   multiply
–   subtract
+   add

Shift operators
>>   right shift
<<   left shift

Relational operators
>   greater than
<   less than
>=   greater than or equal to
<=   less than or equal to
!=   not equal to (compare strings)
==   equal to (compare strings)

Bitwise operators
&   AND
^   exclusive OR
| inclusive OR

Logical operators
&&   AND
| | OR

Expressions follow these rules:

1. The Shell considers a number that begins with a 0 (zero) to be an octal number.
2. The Shell evaluates a missing or null argument as 0.
3. All results are decimal numbers.
4. Except for != and ==, the operators act on numeric arguments.
5. You must separate each element of an expression from adjacent elements by a SPACE, unless the adjacent element is an **&**, | , <, >, (, or).

Expressions can also return a value based on the status of a file. The format of this type of expression is shown below.

−n filename

where **n** is from the following list.

n Meaning

d The file is a directory file.
e The file exists.
f The file is a plain file.
o The user owns the file.
r The user has read access to the file.
w The user has write access to the file.
x The user has execute access to the file.
z The file is 0 bytes long.

If the specified file does not exist or is not accessible, the C Shell evaluates the expression as 0. Otherwise, if the result of the test is true, the expression has a value of 1; if it is false, the expression has a value of 0.

```
16 % @ count = 0

17 % echo $count
0

18 % @ count = ( 5 + 2 )

19 % echo $count
7

20 % @ result = ( $count < 5 )

21 % echo $result
0

22 % @ count += 5

23 % echo $count
12

24 % @ count++

25 % echo $count
13
26 %
```

Event 16 declares the variable **count** and assigns a value of 0 to it. Event 18 shows the result of an arithmetic operation being assigned to a variable. Event 20 uses **@** to assign the result of a logical operation involving a constant and a variable to **result**. The value of the operation is false (=0) because the variable **count** is not less than 5. Event 22 is a compressed form of the following assignment statement.

```
% @ count = ( $count + 5 )
%
```

Event 24 uses a postfix operator to increment **count**.

Arrays of Numeric Variables. You must use the Set command to declare an array of numeric variables before you can use the **@** command to assign values to the elements of the array. The Set command can assign any values to the elements of a numeric array, including zeros, other numbers, and null strings.

Assigning a value to an element of a numeric array is similar to assigning a value to a simple numeric variable. The only difference is that you must specify the element, or index, of the array. The format is shown below.

@ variable-name[index] operator expression

The **index** specifies the element of the array that is being addressed. The first element has an index of 1. The **index** must be either a numeric constant or a variable. It cannot be an expression. In the preceding format, the square brackets around **index** are part of the format and do not indicate **index** is optional.

```
26 % set ages = (0 0 0 0 0)

27 % @ ages[2] = (15)

28 % @ ages[3] = ($ages[2] + 4)

29 % echo $ages[3]
19

30 % echo $ages
0  15  19  0  0
31 %
```

Elements of a numeric array behave as though they were simple numeric variables. The difference is that you must use Set to declare a numeric array. Event 26 declares an array with five elements, each having a value of 0. Events 27 and 28 assign values to elements of the array, and event 29 displays the value of one of the elements. Event 30 displays all the elements of the array.

Braces

You can use braces to distinguish a variable from surrounding text without the use of a separator (e.g., a SPACE).

```
100 % set prefix = Alex

101 % echo $prefix is short for $prefix{ander}.
Alex is short for Alexander.
102 %
```

Without braces in the above example, **prefix** would have to be separated from ander with a SPACE so that the Shell would recognize **prefix** as a variable. This change would cause Alexander to become Alex ander.

Special Forms of User Variables

A special variable in the following format stores the number of elements in an array.

$#variable-name

You can determine whether a variable has been declared or not by testing a variable of the next format.

$?variable-name

This variable has a value of 1 if **variable-name** has been declared. Otherwise it has a value of 0.

```
205 % set days = (mon tues wed thurs fri)

206 % echo $#days
5

207 % echo $?days
1

208 % unset days

209 % echo $?days
0
210 %
```

Event 206 displays the number of elements in the **days** array that was set in event 205. Event 207 shows that **days** has been declared because **$?days** echoes as 1 (=true). Events 208 and 209 show what happens when **days** is unset.

Shell Variables

This section lists the Shell variables that are either set by the Shell or set by the user and used by the Shell. The section is divided into two parts. The first contains variables that take on significant values (e.g., the PID number of a background process). The second part lists variables that act as switches—*on* if they are declared, *off* if they are not).

Shell Variables That Take On Values

$argv   This Shell variable contains the command line arguments from the command that invoked the Shell. For example, **argv[0]** contains the name of the calling program and **argv[1]** contains the first command line argument. You can change any element of this array except **argv[0]**. Use **argv[*]** to reference all the arguments together. You can abbreviate references to **argv** as **$*** (short for **$argv[*]**) and **$n** (short for **$argv[n]**).

$#argv   The Shell sets this variable to the number of elements in **argv**.

$cdpath   This variable affects the operation of the cd utility. It takes on the value of a list of absolute pathnames (similar to the **path** variable) and is usually set in the **.login** file with a command line such as the following.

```
set cdpath = (/usr/jenny/reports /usr/jenny/letters)
```

When you specify a simple filename as an argument to a **cd** command, cd always searches the working directory for a sub-directory with the same name as the argument. If the subdirectory does not exist and **cdpath** is not set, cd issues an error message. If **cdpath** is set, cd continues its search and tries to find an appropriately named directory in the **cdpath** list. If it does, that directory becomes the working directory.

$child   The Shell sets this variable in the environment of the parent process when you execute a detached, or background, process. The variable **child** takes the value of the PID of the child process. The Shell unsets this variable when the child process terminates.

$history   This variable controls the size of your History list. As a rule of thumb, its value should be kept under 15. If you assign too large a value, the Shell can run out of memory. Refer to "History," page 247.

$home   This variable is similar to the **HOME** variable in the Bourne Shell. It has the value of the pathname of the home directory of the user. The cd command refers to this variable, as does the filename expansion of ~ (see "Filename Generation," page 267).

$path   This variable is similar to the **PATH** variable in the Bourne Shell. Unless it is set, you can execute a file only if it is in the working directory or if you specify its full pathname.

$prompt   This variable is similar to the **PS1** variable in the Bourne Shell. If it is not set, the prompt will be % [# for the system administrator (Superuser)]. The Shell expands an exclamation point in the prompt string to the current event number. Following is a typical command line from a **.cshrc** file that sets the value of **prompt**.

```
set prompt = ´! % ´
```

You must quote the exclamation point so the Shell does not expand it before assigning it to the variable **prompt**.

$shell   This variable contains the pathname of the Shell.

$status   This variable contains the exit status returned by the last command.

$$ As in the Bourne Shell, this variable contains the PID number of the current Shell.

Shell Variables That Act as Switches

The following Shell variables act as switches; their values are not significant. If the variable has been declared, the Shell takes the specified action. If not, the action is not taken or is negated. You can set these variables in your **.cshrc** file, in a Shell script, or from the command line.

$echo   When you call the C Shell with the **−x** option, it sets the **echo** variable. You can also set **echo** using a Set command. In either case, when you declare **echo**, the C Shell displays each command before it executes the command.

$ignoreeof   When you set the **ignoreeof** variable, you cannot exit from the Shell using CONTROL-D, so you cannot accidentally log off. When this variable is declared, you must use **exit** or **logout** to leave a Shell.

$noclobber   The **noclobber** variable prevents you from accidentally overwriting a file when you redirect output. It also prevents you from creating a file when you attempt to append output to a nonexistent file. To override **noclobber**, add an exclamation point to the symbol you use for redirecting or appending output (i.e., **>!** and **>>!**).

When you do *not* declare **noclobber**, these command lines have the following effects.

Command line	Effect
x > fileout	Redirects the standard output from process **x** to **fileout**. Overwrites **fileout** if it exists.
x >> fileout	Redirects the standard output from process **x** to **fileout**. Appends new output to the end of **fileout** if it exists. Creates **fileout** if it does not exist.

When you declare **noclobber**, the command lines have different effects.

Command line	Effect
x > fileout	Redirects the standard output from process **x** to **fileout**. The C Shell displays an error message if **fileout** exists.
x >> fileout	Redirects the standard output from process **x** to **fileout**. Appends new output to the end of **fileout** if it exists. The C Shell displays an error message if **fileout** does not exist.

$noglob   When you declare **$noglob**, the C shell will not expand ambiguous filenames. You can use *****, **?**, **~**, and **[ ]** on the command line or in a Shell script without quoting them.

$nonomatch   When you declare **nonomatch**, the C Shell passes an ambiguous file reference that does not match a filename to the program that is being called. The Shell does not expand the file reference. When you do not declare **nonomatch**, the C Shell generates a no match error message and does not execute the command.

$verbose   The C Shell declares the **verbose** variable when you call it with the **−v** option. You can also declare it using the Set command. In either case, **verbose** causes the C Shell to display the words of each command after a History substitution. (Refer to "History," page 247.)

FILENAME GENERATION

The C Shell generates filenames the same way the Bourne Shell does, with an added feature. Refer to Chapter 5 for more information on filename generation.

The C Shell uses the tilde (~) as a special character for filename generation. By itself, ~ expands into the pathname of your home directory. When you follow the tilde with the login name of a user, the C Shell expands it into the pathname of the home directory of that user. The following example shows how to copy the file named **idea.txt** into Helen's home directory (Helen's login name is hls).

```
152 % cp idea.txt ~hls
153 %
```

You can turn off the filename-expansion feature of the C Shell by setting the **noglob** variable. When **noglob** is set, the Shell treats *, ?, [ ], and ~ as regular characters.

C SHELL SCRIPTS

Just as the Bourne Shell can execute a file of Bourne Shell commands, the C Shell can execute a file of C Shell commands. The concepts of writing and executing programs in the two shells are similar. However, the methods of declaring and assigning values to variables and the syntax of control structures are different.

Executing a C Shell Script

The first nonblank character in a C Shell script must be a sharp sign (#). If a Shell script starts with any other character, it will be executed by the Bourne Shell. This syntax allows Shell scripts written for both shells to be executed from a C Shell command line. It means that when you switch from the Bourne Shell to the C Shell, all your Bourne Shell scripts will still execute properly and you can write new C Shell scripts as needed. Both shells treat Shell script lines that begin with sharp signs as comments.

Automatically Executed Shell Scripts

While the Bourne Shell automatically executes one file (the **.profile** file in your home directory) when you log on, the C Shell executes three files at different times during a session.

.login When you log on and start a session, the C Shell executes the contents of the **.login** file that is located in your home directory. This file should contain commands that you want to execute once, at the beginning of each session. The environment is established from this Shell script: You can use Setenv to declare global variables here. You can also declare the type of terminal that you are using in your **.login** file. A sample **.login** file follows.

```
setenv TERM vt100
stty erase '^X' kill '^U' -lcase -tabs
echo "This is who's on the machine:"
who
```

This file establishes the type of terminal that you are using by setting the **TERM** variable. In this case, the Terminfo name for the terminal is vt100. The sample **.login** file then executes the stty utility, displays a message, and executes the who utility so that you know who else is using the machine. There is more information about the Setenv command in "Variables," starting on page 255.

.cshrc The C Shell executes the **.cshrc** file that is located in your home directory each time you invoke a new C Shell, as when you log on or execute a C Shell script. You can use this file to establish variables and parameters that are local to a specific Shell. Each time you create a new Shell, the C Shell reinitializes these variables for the new Shell. A sample **.cshrc** file follows.

```
set noclobber
set ignoreeof
set history = 10
set prompt = '! % '
set path = ( . /usr/jenny/bin /bin /usr/bin)
alias h history
alias ls ls -l
```

This sample **.cshrc** file sets several Shell variables and establishes two Aliases.

.logout   The C Shell executes the **.logout** file in your home directory when you log off the system, normally when you finish your session.

Below is a sample **.logout** file that displays a reminder. The **sleep** command ensures that echo has time to display the message before the system logs you out (for dial-up lines).

```
echo 'Remember to turn on call'
echo 'forwarding before you go home.'
sleep 10
```

CONTROL STRUCTURES

The C Shell uses many of the same control structures as the Bourne Shell. In each case the syntax is different, but the effects are the same. This chapter summarizes the differences between the control structures in the two shells. There is a more complete discussion of control structures in Chapter 8.

If

The format of the If control structure follows.

> if (**expression**) **simple-command**

The If control structure only works with simple commands, not pipes or lists of commands. You can use the If Then control structure (page 271) to execute more complex commands.

```
# routine to show the use of a simple If
# control structure
#
if ($#argv == 0) echo 'There are no arguments.'
```

The program above checks to see if it was called without any arguments. If the expression (enclosed in parentheses) evaluates to true—that is, if there were zero arguments on the command line—the If structure displays a message to that effect.

Goto

The format of a Goto statement follows.

goto **label**

A Goto statement transfers control to the statement beginning with label:. The following example demonstrates the use of Goto.

```
#
# test for 2 arguments
#
if ($#argv == 2) goto goodargs
echo 'Please use two arguments.'
exit
goodargs:
.
.
.
```

Interrupt Handling

The Onintr statement transfers control when you interrupt a Shell script. The format of an Onintr statement is shown below.

onintr **label**

When you press the DEL key during execution of a Shell script, the Shell transfers control to the statement beginning with label:.

This statement gives you a way to terminate a script gracefully when it is interrupted. You can use it to ensure that when it is interrupted, a Shell script updates and closes its files before returning control to the Shell.

The following program demonstrates Onintr. It loops continuously until you press the DEL key, at which time it displays a message and returns control to the Shell.

```
# demonstration of onintr
onintr close
while (1 == 1)
    echo 'Program is running.'
    sleep 2
end
close:
echo 'End of program.'
```

If Then Else

The three forms of the If Then Else control structure are shown below.

Form 1:

```
if (expression) then
    commands
endif
```

Form 2:

```
if (expression) then
    commands
else
    commands
endif
```

Form 3:

```
if (expression) then
    commands
else if (expression) then
    commands

    .
    .
    .

else
    commands
endif
```

The first form is an extension of the simple If structure; it executes more complex **commands** or a series of **commands** if the **expression** is true. This form is still a one-way branch.

The second form is a two-way branch. If the **expression** is true, the structure executes the first set of **commands**. If it is false, the set of **commands** following Else is executed.

The third form is similar to the If Then Elif structure of the Bourne Shell. It performs tests until it finds an **expression** that is true and then executes the corresponding **commands**.

```
# routine to categorize the first
# command line argument
#
set class
set number = $argv[1]
#
if ($number < 0) then
     @ class = 0
else if (0 <= $number && $number < 100) then
     @ class = 1
else if (100 <= $number && $number < 200) then
     @ class = 2
else
     @ class = 3
endif
#
echo 'The number' $number 'is in class' ${class}'.'
```

The example program above assigns a value of 0-3 to the variable **class**, based on the value of the first command line argument. The variable **class** is declared at the beginning of the program for clarity; you do not need to declare it before its first use. Again, for clarity, the script assigns the value of the first command line argument to **number**. The first If statement tests to see whether **number** is less than 0. If it is, the script assigns 0 to **class**. If it is not, the second If tests to see whether the number is between 0 and 100. The && is a logical AND, yielding a value of true if the expression on each side is true. If the number is between 0 and 100, 1 is assigned to **class**. A similar test determines whether the number is between 100 and 200. If it is not, the final Else assigns 3 to **class**. Endif closes the If control structure.

The final statement uses braces to isolate the variable **class** from the following period. Again, the braces isolate the period for clarity; the Shell does not consider a punctuation mark as part of a variable name. The braces would be required if you wanted other characters to follow immediately after the variable.

Foreach

The Foreach structure parallels the For In structure of the Bourne Shell. Its format follows.

> foreach **loop-index (argument-list)**
> > **commands**
> end

This structure loops through the **commands**. The first time through the loop, the structure assigns the value of the first argument in the **argument-list** to the **loop-index**. When control reaches the End statement, the Shell assigns the value of the next argument from the **argument-list** to the **loop-index** and executes the commands again. The Shell repeats this procedure until it exhausts the **argument-list**.

```
# routine to zero-fill argv to 20 arguments
#
set buffer = (0 0 0 0 0 0 0 0 0 0 0 0 0 0 0 0 0 0 0 0)
set count = 1
#
if ($#argv > 20) goto toomany
#
        foreach argument ($argv[*])
        set buffer[$count] = $argument
        @ count++
        end
#
# REPLACE argtest ON THE NEXT LINE WITH
# THE PROGRAM YOU WANT TO CALL.
exec argtest $buffer[*]
exit
#
toomany:
echo 'There are more than 20 arguments.'
```

The program above calls another program named **argtest** with a command line guaranteed to contain twenty arguments. If this program is called with fewer than twenty arguments, it fills the command line with 0s to complete the twenty arguments for **argtest**. More than twenty arguments cause it to display an error message.

The Foreach structure loops through the commands one time for each of the command line arguments. Each time through the loop, it assigns the value of the next argument from the command line to the variable **argument**. Then it assigns each of these values to an element of the array **buffer**. The variable **count** maintains the index for the **buffer** array. A postfix operator increments **count** using the **@** command (**@ count++**). An Exec command (refer to Chapter 8) calls **argtest** so that a new process is not initiated. (Once **argtest** is called, the process running this routine will no longer be needed, so there is no need for a new process.)

Break and Continue

You can interrupt a Foreach loop with a Break or Continue statement. These statements execute the remaining commands on the line before they transfer control. Break transfers control to the statement after the End statement, terminating execution of the loop. Continue transfers control to the End statement, which continues execution of the loop.

While

The format of the While structure is shown below.

> while (**expression**)
>   **commands**
> end

This structure continues to loop through the **commands** *while* the **expression** is true. If the **expression** is false the first time it is evaluated, the structure never executes the **commands**. You can use Break and Continue statements in a While structure; refer to the previous discussion.

```
# Demonstration of a While control structure.
# This routine sums the numbers between 1 and
# n, n being the first argument on the command
# line.
#
set limit = $argv[1]
set index = 1
set sum = 0
#
        while ($index <= $limit)
        @ sum += $index
        @ index++
        end
#
echo 'The sum is' $sum
```

This program computes the sum of all the integers up to and including n, where n is the first argument on the command line. The += operator assigns the value of **sum + index** to **sum**.

Switch

This structure is analogous to the Case structure of the Bourne Shell.

switch (**test-string**)

    case **pattern**:
        commands
    breaksw

    case **pattern**:
        commands
    breaksw

    .
    .

    default:
        commands
    breaksw

endsw

Refer to the discussion of the Case statement in Chapter 8 for a discussion of special characters you can use within the patterns.

```
# Demonstration of a Switch control structure.
# This routine tests the first command line argument
# for yes or no, any combination of upper and lower-
# case characters.
#
# test that argv[1] exists
if ($#argv == 0) then
        echo 'Argument one does not exist.'
else
# argv[1] exists, set up switch based on its value
        switch ($argv[1])
        #
        # case of YES
                case [yY][eE][sS]:
                echo 'Argument one is yes.'
                breaksw
        #
        # case of NO
                case [nN][oO]:
                echo 'Argument one is no.'
                breaksw
        #
        # default case
                default:
                echo 'Argument one is neither yes nor no.'
                breaksw
        endsw
endif
```

Reading User Input

Some implementations of the C Shell use a Set command to read a line from the terminal and assign it to a variable.

The following portion of a Shell script prompts the user and reads a line of input into the variable **input_line**.

```
echo 'Input the next condition: '
set input_line = $<
```

If your version does not have this feature, you can use the head utility to read user input.

```
echo 'Input the next condition: '
set input_line = `head -1`
```

Above, **head −1** displays the first line it receives from its standard input—in this case, the terminal. The grave accent marks cause the Shell to execute the command in place, replacing the command they enclose with the output from the command. See Chapter 8 for more information on grave accent marks.

Redirecting Error Output

Under the C Shell, you can combine and redirect the standard output and the error output (see page 236) using a greater-than symbol followed by an ampersand.

```
% cat x
x: No such file or directory

% cat y
This is y.

% cat x y >& hold

% cat hold
x: No such file or directory
This is y.
```

BUILT-IN COMMANDS

Built-in commands are part of (built into) the C Shell.

When you give a command, the Shell searches the directory structure for the program you want, using the **path** variable as a guide. When it finds the program, the Shell forks a new process to execute it.

The Shell executes a built-in command as part of the calling process. It does not fork a new process to execute the command. It does not need to search the directory structure for the command program because the program is immediately available to the Shell. The following list describes the built-in commands.

@. This command is similar to the Set command, but it can evaluate expressions. See "Variables," page 255.

Alias. This command creates and displays Aliases. See "Alias," page 253.

Cd (or Chdir). This command changes working directories. Refer to the cd utility in Part II for more information.

Echo. This command is similar to the echo command that is built into the Bourne Shell. Refer to echo in Part II for more information.

Exec. This command is similar to the Exec command of the Bourne Shell. Exec overlays the program that is currently being executed with another program in the same Shell. The original program is lost. Refer to the Exec command in Chapter 8 for more information; also refer to "Source," later in this section.

Exit. You can use this command to exit from a C Shell. When you follow it with an argument that is a number, the number is the exit status that the Shell returns to its parent process. Refer to the **status** variable, page 265.

Foreach. This is the first keyword in a Foreach control structure. See page 272.

Goto. This command transfers control to a labeled line. See page 270.

History. This command displays the History list of commands. See "History," page 247.

If. This is the first keyword in an If control structure. See pages 269 and 271.

Login. This command, which you can follow with a user name, logs in a user.

Logout. This command ends a session if you are using your original (login) Shell.

Onintr. This command controls the behavior of a Shell script when you interrupt it. See "Interrupt Handling," page 270.

Repeat. This command takes two arguments, a count and simple command (no pipes or lists of commands). It repeats the command the number of times specified by the count.

Set. This command declares, initializes, and displays the value of local variables. See "Variables," page 255.

Setenv. This command declares and initializes the value of global variables. See "Variables," page 255. Many systems include a Printenv command that displays the values of global variables.

Shift. This command is analogous to the Bourne Shell Shift command (page 199). Without an argument, Shift promotes the indexes of the **argv[*]** array. You can use it with an argument to perform the same operation on another array.

Source.   Source causes the current C Shell to execute a Shell script given as its argument. It is similar to the . command in the Bourne Shell, except that you do not require execute access permission to the script. Source expects a C Shell script, so no leading sharp sign is required. The current Shell executes Source so that the script can contain commands, such as Set, that affect the current Shell. You can use Source to execute **.cshrc** or **.login** files from within a Shell.

Switch.   This is the first keyword in a Switch control structure. See page 274.

Time.   Time executes the command that you give it as an argument. It displays the elapsed time, the system time, and the execution time for the command. Without an argument, Time displays the times for the current Shell and its children.

Unalias.   This command removes an Alias. See "Alias," page 253.

Unset.   This command removes a variable declaration. See "Variables," page 255.

Wait.   This command causes the Shell to wait for all child processes. When you give a **wait** command in response to a C Shell prompt, the C Shell will not display a prompt and will not accept a command until all background processes have finished execution. If you interrupt it with DEL, Wait displays a list of outstanding processes before returning control to the Shell.

While.   This is the first keyword of the While control structure. See page 274.

SUMMARY

The C Shell, like the Bourne Shell, is both a command interpreter and a programming language. It was developed at the University of California at Berkeley and has most of the facilities of the Bourne Shell, plus some others.

Among its most important features, the C Shell:

- Evaluates logical and numerical expressions.
- Processes arrays of variables representing numbers and strings.
- Protects against overwriting files and accidentally logging off.
- Maintains a history of recent commands.
- Provides an Alias mechanism for altering commands.
- Executes specific files when you log on, log off, and fork a new Shell.
- Uses control structures to control execution within a Shell script.

Although the C Shell is not part of standard UNIX System V, many of its features are available on many machines.

10

SYSTEM ADMINISTRATION

The system administrator is responsible for setting up
new users, installing and removing terminals, making
sure there's enough space on the disk, backing up files,
bringing up and shutting down the system, helping users
when they have problems, and taking care of other computer
housekeeping tasks.

Because UNIX System V is so flexible, and because it
runs on so many different machines, this chapter cannot discuss every system configuration or every action you will have
to take as a system administrator. This chapter comple-
ments the administration section of the manual that came
with your computer.

This chapter assumes you are familiar with the following terms. Refer to the Glossary for definitions.

- block
- daemon
- device filename
- device
- environment
- fork
- kernel
- login Shell
- mount (a device)
- process
- restricted Shell
- root file system
- run level
- signal
- spawn
- system console

THE SYSTEM ADMINISTRATOR AND THE SUPERUSER

There is usually one person who is designated as the system administrator. On large systems this can be a full-time job. On smaller systems, the administrator of the system is also frequently a user of the system.

When you are logged on as the system administrator, you have certain system-wide powers that are beyond those of ordinary system users.

- Some commands, such as commands that halt the system, can only be executed by the system administrator.

- Read and write file access permissions do not affect the system administrator. The system administrator can create a file in or remove a file from any directory. The system administrator can also read from or write to any file.

- Some restrictions and safeguards that are built into some commands do not apply to the system administrator. For example, the system administrator can change any user's password without knowing the old password.

Because the system administrator has powers that can affect the security of any user's files as well as the security of the entire system, there is a special login name and password for the user who can log on the system to perform these functions. The login name is generally *root.* Although you can set up a UNIX system with any name in place of root, it is not advisable to do so. Many programs depend on this name being root. There is also a special term for the user who has logged on as root; this user is called the *Superuser.*

Because of the extensive powers of destruction you have when you are the Superuser, it is a good idea only to become the Superuser as needed. If you're just doing your ordinary day-to-day work, log on as yourself. That way you won't erase someone else's files or bring down the machine by mistake.

There are three ways to become the Superuser.

1. When you bring up the system, if it comes up in single-user mode (see page 286), you are automatically logged on as the Superuser.

2. Once the system is up and running in multiuser mode (page 288), you can log on as *root,* and if you supply the proper password, you will be the Superuser.

3. You can give an **su** (substitute user) command while you are logged on as yourself, and, with the proper password, you will have the privileges of the Superuser.

When you give an **su** command to become the Superuser, you return to your normal status when you log off (by pressing CONTROL-D or giving an **exit** command). To remind you of your special powers, the Shell normally displays a different prompt (usually #) while you are logged on as the Superuser.

The /etc Directory

Many of the commands you will use as the Superuser are typically kept in the /etc directory. They are kept there to lessen the chance that a user other than the Superuser will try to use one by mistake. You can execute these commands by giving their full pathnames on the command line (e.g., **/etc/mkfs**) *or* by including the /etc directory in your **PATH** when you are logged on as the

Superuser. If you are using the Bourne Shell, the following line in the /.**profile** file will put /**etc** in your **PATH** whenever you log on as root.

```
PATH=$PATH:/etc
```

OVERVIEW OF THE LOGIN PROCEDURE

Logging in may seem like a trivial task, but the UNIX system must do much preparation before you can even see login: on the terminal. Once you respond with your login name and password, the UNIX system must verify that you are a legitimate user and then set up an environment for you to work in.

This section gives a brief overview of the steps the operating system goes through before you are logged on. Following the overview is a detailed explanation of the same process and a description of many important system files.

The init, getty, and login Utilities

The execution of three programs leads to the Shell displaying a prompt on the terminal. Each of these programs reads a file. The table below lists these programs, the files each consults, and the information that each file contains.

Program	File read by program	Contents of file
init	/etc/inittab	what processes to start (mostly getty processes for users to log on)
getty	/etc/gettydefs	login prompt, terminal characteristics including speed (baud rate)
login	/etc/passwd	list of legitimate users and passwords
sh	/etc/profile $HOME/.profile	user environment (all users) user environment (specific user)

The init process is process number 1. Based on the **/etc/inittab** file, init forks a getty process for each line that someone can use to log on. When one of these processes dies (when a user logs off), init again takes action based on the **/etc/inittab** file.

The getty utility consults the **/etc/gettydefs** file to set up login prompts and terminal speeds. After getty establishes the terminal speed and the user has entered a login name, getty overlays itself with login. The getty program passes login the login name the user entered.

After checking the **/etc/passwd** file for a valid password, login overlays itself with a Shell. The Shell establishes an environment for the user to work in by executing the commands in the **/etc/profile** file and the **.profile** file in the user's home directory.

When the user logs off, the process running the Shell dies, and the operating system sends init a signal telling it that one of its children died. The init program starts the cycle over again, as specified by **/etc/inittab**.

DETAILED DESCRIPTION OF SYSTEM OPERATION

This section covers the topics listed below.

- booting the system
- single-user mode and maintenance
- the transition from single-user to multiuser mode
- multiuser mode
- logging on
- bringing the system down
- rebooting the system
- crashes

It covers these topics so that you understand the basics of how the system functions and can make intelligent decisions as a system administrator. It does not cover every aspect of system administration to the depth necessary to set up or modify all system functions. It provides a guide to bringing a system up and keeping it running on a day-to-day basis. Refer to your system manual for procedures specific to your machine.

Subsequent sections of this chapter and Part II of this book describe many of the system administration files and utilities in detail.

Bringing Up (Booting) the System

Booting a system is the process of reading the UNIX system kernel (the heart of the UNIX system, usually stored in **/unix**) into the system memory and starting it running.

Some systems come up automatically, while others require you to enter information at the system console before they get started.

As the last step of the boot procedure, the UNIX operating system runs init as process number 1. The init process looks for an **initdefault** entry in the **inittab** file. This entry specifies the initial run level (single-user or multiuser). Based on this specification, the system comes up in single-user or multiuser mode.

Usually, the system comes up in single-user mode with only the system console operational and only the root file system mounted (accessible). Subsequently, you can call init to change the run level so the system is in multiuser mode.

The **/etc/rc** Shell script handles tasks that need to be taken care of when you first bring the system up and subsequently, when the system goes from single-user to multiuser mode and vice versa. Different manufacturers put different commands in the **/etc/rc** script, so it can have different effects. A typical script will, on booting up the system, ask you to enter the date and time. When you go from single-user to multiuser mode, it will mount the necessary file systems.

The **/etc/rc** script is generally executed by init, which passes **/etc/rc** information on what run level the system was at and what run level it is changing to, so the Shell script can take appropriate actions. After running the script, init typically forks a Shell, which issues a prompt (usually #). You are then running a Shell, in single-user mode, as the Superuser.

Single-User Mode. The **initdefault** entry in the **/etc/inittab** file controls whether the machine is in single- or multiuser mode immediately after you boot it. Even if the system is in single-user mode and only the system console is enabled, you can still run programs from this terminal as you would from any terminal in multiuser mode. The only difference is that all file systems may not be mounted. You will not have access to files on file systems that are not mounted.

The Virtual System Console. Traditionally, a system console is the terminal that you use to bring the system up and shut it down. It is the terminal that the system sends all system error messages to, and it is frequently a hard-copy terminal so there is a record of all errors and maintenance.

System V implements a virtual system console as **/dev/syscon**, automatically linking this device to the terminal you are working from when you perform system maintenance. When you run init to bring a multiuser system down to single-user mode, the terminal that you give the commands from automatically becomes the system console. With this setup, you do not need to perform single-user functions from a specific terminal (*the* system console) but instead can work from any terminal, including one attached to a dial-up line.

Maintenance. With the system in single-user mode, you can perform maintenance that requires file systems unmounted or just a quiet system (no one except you using it, so that no user programs interfere with disk maintenance and backup programs).

Backing Up Files. Although you can back up files while other people are using the system, it is better if you back them up while users aren't using the files; the files won't be changing, and you will be assured of accurate copies of all the files.

Checking File System Integrity. The fsck (file system check) utility verifies the integrity of a file system and, if possible, repairs any problems it finds. A file system (except the root) must not be mounted while fsck is checking it.

The **/etc/checklist** file contains a list of device pathnames that fsck checks if you don't specify a device.

Because many file system repairs destroy data, fsck asks you before making each repair. There are two options that cause fsck to run without asking you questions. The **−y** option assumes a *yes* response to all questions, and a **−n** assumes *no*. Some versions of fsck have adopted the Berkeley **−p** option to cause fsck to ask you questions only if a repair will destroy data.

Always run fsck on a file system before it is mounted. The fsck utility should be run on *all* file systems before the UNIX system is brought up in multiuser mode after it has been down for any reason. Many **/etc/rc** scripts run fsck on all file systems that will be mounted (frequently with the **−y** option and using **checklist** to specify the files to be checked). Refer to fsck in Part II for more information.

Going Multiuser. After you have determined that all is well with the root and all file systems that will be mounted, you can bring the operating system up to multiuser mode. An entry in the **inittab** file determines which run-level number represents the multiuser state. On most systems, giving the command

```
# init 2
```

in response to the Superuser prompt (when the system is in single-user mode) brings the system up to multiuser mode. When the system is in multiuser mode, you will see a login: prompt.

Once again, the **inittab** file controls exactly which terminals and dial-in lines become active. The init process selects all lines in the **inittab** file that specify run level 2. The **/etc/rc** file is also called again. The **rc** script normally mounts the appropriate file systems at this point.

Multiuser Mode

Multiuser mode is the normal state for a UNIX system. All appropriate file systems are mounted and users can log on from all connected terminals and dial-in lines.

Logging On. When you bring a system up in multiuser mode, init, based on the **/etc/inittab** file, forks a series of getty processes—each associated with a line users can log in on. Each getty process displays a login: prompt on a terminal and waits for someone to try to log on.

The **/etc/gettydefs** file contains instructions for getty. Traditionally, getty accepts BREAK characters as an indication that it should try a different baud rate. It consults the **/etc/gettydefs** file for a list of baud rates to try. However, you can program **/etc/gettydefs** to change any communication option when it receives a BREAK.

When you enter your login name, getty tries to determine if your terminal is capable of sending lowercase characters and whether the line is terminated with a NEWLINE or RETURN character. (See the **nl** and **lcase** descriptions under "Treatment of Characters" in the stty utility in Part II). It uses this information as well as the information in **/etc/gettydefs** to set the terminal characteristics.

Then getty overlays itself with a login process and passes it whatever you entered in response to the login: prompt. The login program consults the **/etc/passwd** file to see if there is a password associated with the login name you entered. If there is, login prompts you for a password; if not, it continues without requiring a password. If your login name requires a password, login verifies the password you enter by checking the **/etc/passwd** file. If either your login name or password were not correct, login displays Login incorrect. and prompts you to log in again.

If the login name and password are correct, login consults the **/etc/passwd** file to initialize your user and group IDs, establish your home directory, and determine what Shell you will be working with. After consulting the **passwd** file, login assigns values to the **HOME** and **MAIL** Shell variables. Finally, when login has finished its work, it overlays itself with a Shell.

The Shell assigns values to the **IFS**, **MAILCHECK**, **PATH**, **PS1**, and **PS2** Shell variables (Chapter 8 covers these variables) and then executes the commands in the **/etc/profile** Shell script. Exactly what this script does is system dependent. It usually displays the contents of the **/etc/motd** (message of the day) file on the terminal, lets you know if you have any mail, runs the news utility, and sets the file creation mask (umask—see Part II) as well as the time zone (**TZ**) variable.

After executing the commands in **/etc/profile**, the Shell reads and executes the commands from the **.profile** Shell script in your home directory. Because the Shell executes a user's **.profile** script *after* the **/etc/profile** script, a sophisticated user can override any variables or conventions that were established by the system, while a new user can remain uninvolved in these complications.

(If you are running the C Shell—available on many machines but not a part of standard System V—you will need to use **.login** and **.cshrc** in place of **.profile**. The C Shell does not read **/etc/profile**.)

Running a Program and Logging Off. When you see a Shell prompt, you can execute a program or log off the system. This situation is the one most of this book deals with.

When you log off, the process running the Shell dies and the operating system signals init that one of its children has died. When init receives one of these signals, it takes action based on the contents of the **/etc/inittab** file—in the case of a process controlling a line for a terminal, it forks a new getty process that waits for someone to log on.

Bringing the System Down

System V provides a Shell script named **/etc/shutdown** that performs all the tasks involved in bringing the system down. Use this script to bring the system down—refer to your system manual for more information. The next section describes the steps you can use to perform the key steps of shutdown manually.

Going to Single-User Mode. Because going from multiuser to single-user mode can affect other users, you must be the Superuser to make this change. Make sure you give other users enough warning before going to single-user mode, otherwise they may lose whatever they were working on.

You can perform the following procedure from any terminal. When you bring the system down to single-user mode, UNIX System V links **/dev/syscon** (the virtual system console) to whatever terminal you are using. In single-user mode, the Shell only communicates with the terminal linked to **syscon**. The result is that you can perform system maintenance from any terminal.

Although it is not recommended, you can use the following procedure in place of shutdown.

1. Log in as root or use su to become the Superuser.

2. After using wall (write all) to warn everyone who is using the system, run killall to terminate all user processes except yours.

3. Use umount to unmount all mounted devices. (You can use mount without an argument to see what devices are mounted.)

4. Give the command **sync** three times in a row. The **sync** utility

forces the system to write out the contents of all disk buffers, thereby ensuring that the data on the disk is up to date.

5. Give the command **init s** to bring the system down to single-user mode.

Turning the Power Off.   Once the system is in single-user mode, shutting it down is quite straightforward. If you have run any programs since you brought it down to single-user mode, you must run sync several times again before turning the power off or resetting the system. Consult your system manual for details on your system.

The only time you will not use sync before turning the power off or resetting the system is after using fsck to repair the root file system. Refer to fsck in Part II for details.

Rebooting the System.   Follow these steps if the system is running and you need to reboot it.

▶ Bring the system down to single-user mode (page 290).

▶ Reset the machine by pressing the reset button (on some systems you may have to turn the power off—refer to your system manual).

▶ Boot the system (page 286).

▶ Bring the system up to multiuser mode (page 288).

The Role of init.   The init utility is both a process spawner (when you bring the system up) and a utility to control the state of the system (**init s** brings the system from multiuser mode to single-user mode).

When init starts running, it checks its PID number. If it is process number 1, init functions as a process spawner. If it is not process number 1, init sends the original init signals to change the state of the machine.

You may see init referred to as telinit. They are both links to the same program—one, init, is located in **/etc/init,** and the other, telinit, is in **/bin/telinit**.

Crashes

A *crash* is the system stopping when you don't intend it to. After a crash, the operating system must be brought up carefully to minimize possible damage to the file systems. Frequently, there will be no damage or minimal damage to the file systems.

After a crash, boot the system so that it is in single-user mode. **DO NOT** mount any devices other than the root (which the UNIX system mounts automatically). Run fsck on the root immediately, repairing the root as suggested by fsck. If you repair the root file system, reboot the system immediately *without* running sync. Then run fsck on all the other file systems *before* mounting them. Repair them as needed. Make note of any plain files or directories that you repair (and can identify) and inform their owners that they may not be complete or correct. Look in the **/lost+found** directory for missing files. Refer to fsck in Part II for more information.

If files are not correct or are missing altogether, you may have to recreate them from a backup copy of the file system. Refer to "Backing Up Files," page 311, for more information.

IMPORTANT FILES AND DIRECTORIES

Many directories and files are important to the administration of the system. This section details the most common of these. Refer also to page 64, "Important Standard Directories and Files."

/etc/checklist This file contains a list of device filenames that fsck checks by default. This list should be the same as the list of devices that **/etc/rc** mounts when you bring the system up to multiuser mode. A sample file is shown below.

```
# cat /etc/checklist
/dev/dsk/0s0
/dev/dsk/0s1
```

/etc/gettydefs The getty process refers to this file for terminal baud rates and the appearance of the login: prompt. Only a few of the many terminal characteristics that you can specify from this file are covered here.

The format of a **gettydefs** entry is shown below. A #

separates each of the fields from the others, and blank lines separate each of the entries. If an entry is too long to fit on one line, allow it to wrap around to the next line. Do not end a partial line with a RETURN.

label # initial-flags # final-flags # prompt # next-label

By convention, the **label** is usually the baud rate the entry specifies. The **initial-flags** specify the baud rate that is used until getty executes login. The **final-flags** determine how the terminal will act once you are logged in. They can specify other information in addition to the baud rate: SANE sets most of the necessary flags, TAB3 ensures that the operating system sends SPACEs to the terminal in place of TABs, and HUPCL hangs up when a user logs off a dial-up line. The **prompt** is the login: prompt that getty displays—you can change it to anything you like. The **next-label** specifies the next entry in the file that getty is to try if the user presses the BREAK key while attempting to log on.

Initially, getty tries to log in a terminal at the baud rate whose label matches the second argument that getty is called with. If getty is called without a second argument, it uses the baud rate specified by the first entry in the **gettydefs** file. If, while you are trying to get a login: prompt, you press the BREAK key, getty scans the **gettydefs** file for an entry whose **label** corresponds to the **next-label** of the entry it just tried. Then getty tries the baud rate specified by *that* entry. Using this procedure, getty can attempt to connect a terminal at a series of different baud rates.

Assuming that getty is called without a second argument, the sample **gettydefs** file below first tries to connect a terminal at 9600 baud. If the person trying to log on presses the BREAK key, getty will try 1200 baud. Pressing the BREAK key again switches to 300 baud. One more BREAK brings getty back to 9600 baud.

```
9600# B9600 HUPCL # B9600 SANE TAB3 #login: #1200

1200# B1200 HUPCL # B1200 SANE TAB3 #login: #300

300# B300 HUPCL # B300 SANE TAB3 #login: #9600
```

If the **gettydefs** file is missing and you haven't specified a baud rate in any other way, getty will attempt to log the terminal in at 300 baud.

/etc/group Groups allow a group of system users to share files or programs without allowing all system users access to them. This scheme is useful if several users are working with files that are not public information.

Each line in the **/etc/group** file names a group and can optionally include a list of users who can use the newgrp utility to temporarily change their group IDs to that of the named group.

An entry in the **/etc/group** file has the four fields shown below. If an entry is too long to fit on one line, end the line with a backslash (\), which will quote the following RETURN, and continue the entry on the next line.

group-name:password:group-ID:login-name-list

The **group-name** is from one to six characters, the first being alphabetic and none being uppercase. The **password** is an optional encrypted password. Because there is no good way to enter a password into the **group** file, group passwords are not very useful and should be avoided. The **group-ID** is a number between 0 and 65,535 with 0-99 being reserved. The **login-name-list** is a list of users who can use newgrp to temporarily change their group ID numbers. A comma separates each of the names in the **login-name-list**.

The **/etc/group** file does not define groups. Groups come into existence when a user is assigned a group ID number in the **/etc/passwd** file. When you first log on, your group ID number is the group ID number from the fourth field of your line in the **/etc/passwd** file. Everyone who has the same group ID number in the **/etc/passwd** file belongs to the same group when they first log on. The **/etc/group** file associates a name with a group. You will see this name in the group column when you give an **ls −l** command to list a file you created. If your group is not listed in the **/etc/group** file, **ls −l** will just list your group ID number in place of your group name.

In addition to naming groups, the **/etc/group** file can define a list of users who can, after they log in, use newgrp to change their group ID numbers to that of the named group. (You can always use newgrp without an argument to change your group ID back to what it was when you first logged on.)

A sample entry in a **group** file is shown below. The group is named **pubs**, has no password, and has a group ID of 141.

    pubs::141:alex,jenny,scott,hls,barbara

/etc/inittab Each time you call the init utility, it consults this file. The **/etc/inittab** file indicates what processes init is to start or stop for each run level. Mostly, **/etc/inittab** works with getty processes, which activate terminal lines. The **/etc/inittab** file also initiates various system daemons.

Each entry in **/etc/inittab** has the following format:

id:run-level:action:process

The **id** consists of from one to four characters and is a unique identifier for the entry. The **run-level** is a number from 1-6 (or a combination of numbers in this range *or* a range of numbers such as 1-3) specifying the run level the entry applies to. The **action** is the action that init is to take, and the **process** is the process init is to take the **action** on.

When you call init and specify a run level, it scans /etc/inittab for entries with matching **run-levels**. If you do not specify a run level, init assumes run levels 1-6. For each entry that matches the run level, init takes the **action** on the **process** specified in that entry.

The most common actions and their effects are listed below. (In some **inittab** files, the actions are abbreviated to a single character.)

respawn   Fork the process if it does not exist. Fork another process when the previous one dies. Ignore the entry if the process exists.

wait   Fork the process and wait for it to die.

off   Send the process a warning signal (SIGTERM), wait 20 seconds, and kill the process (SIGKILL). Ignore the entry if the process does not exist.

initdefault   Use the run level of this entry as the initial run level for the system when it is booted.

The following typical entries in the **inittab** file will bring the system up in single-user mode (in this case, run level 6) and turn on tty05 in multiuser mode (run level 2). The line with **id** number

05 ensures that tty05 is turned off in the transition from multiuser to single-user mode. The console will be turned on in all states (1-6). You can use sharp signs (#) in an **inittab** file to mark the start of a comment. The end of the line marks the end of a comment.

```
is:6:initdefault:
co:1-6:respawn:/etc/getty console # console always on
05:6:off:/etc/getty tty05           # 5 off for single-user
105:2:respawn:/etc/getty tty05      # 5 on for multiuser
```

/etc/mnttab   The **/etc/mnttab** (mount table) file contains a list of all currently mounted devices. When you call **mount** without any arguments, it consults this table and displays a list of mounted devices. This file is not an ASCII text file—you cannot edit it with a text editor.

The operating system maintains its own internal mount table, which may, on occasion, differ from this file. The surest way to bring the **mnttab** file in line with the operating system's mount table is to bring the system down and reboot it. When you reboot the system, **/etc/rc** runs the **setmnt** utility, which initializes **mnttab** to contain only the root file system mounted on /. Each time you (or the **rc** script) calls **mount** or **umount**, these programs make the necessary changes to **mnttab**.

/etc/motd   The **/etc/motd** file contains the *message of the day*. The **/etc/profile** script usually uses **cat** to display this file each time someone logs on. The file should not be too long because users tend to see the message many times. Being subjected to a long message of the day can also be tedious for users who communicate with the system over slower dial-up lines.

/etc/passwd   Each entry in the **passwd** file occupies a line, has seven fields, and describes one user to the system. A colon separates each field from the adjacent fields.

login-name:password:user-ID:group-ID:info:directory:program

The **login-name** is the user's login name—the name the user enters in response to the **login:** prompt. The **password** is an encrypted password that is put in this file by the **passwd** utility.

If unauthorized access is not a problem, the password field can initially be null (::). When the user logs in, he or she can run passwd to select a password. Otherwise, you can run passwd while you are the Superuser to assign a password to the user. Another option is to put a comma and a period in the password field (:,.:). When the user logs on, login runs passwd instead of the Shell, forcing the user to select a password.

The **user-ID** is a user ID number from 0-65,535, with 0 indicating the Superuser and 0-99 reserved. The **group-ID** identifies the user as a member of a group. It is a number between 0 and 65,535, with 0-99 being reserved and 1 being the default. The **info** is information that various programs, such as accounting programs, use to further identify the user.

The **directory** is the absolute pathname of the user's home directory. The **program** is the program that the user will be running after logging on. If **program** is not present, **/bin/sh** is assumed. If your system supports the C Shell, you can put **/bin/csh** here to log on to the C Shell. The restricted Shell, a limited version of the Bourne Shell that prevents full access to the system, is identified as **/bin/rsh**.

A brief sample **passwd** file is shown below. The **guest** login has no password and runs the restricted Shell. The **info** field stores telephone extension numbers.

```
# cat /etc/passwd
root:Urv8ynuD2ti2U:0:1:::/:/bin/sh
bill:GE9tC647kffOl:102:100:x347:/usr/bill:/bin/sh
roy:QpMR2EXP.zANA:104:100:x519:/usr/roy:/bin/sh
alex:.NhVeHghQ045s:106:100:x159:/usr/alex:/bin/sh
jenny:gKnL.E8DLFamM:107:100:x205:/usr/jenny:/bin/sh
guest::110:110::/tmp/guest:/bin/rsh
```

The program specified in the right-hand field of each line in the **passwd** file is usually a Shell, but as shown below, it can be any program. The following line in the **passwd** file will create a "user" whose only purpose is to execute the who utility.

```
who::1000:1000:execute who:/usr:/bin/who
```

Using **who** as a login name will cause the system to log you in, execute the who utility, and log you out. This entry in the **passwd** file does not provide a Shell—there is no way for you to stay logged in after who is finished executing.

/etc/profile A *login Shell* is the first Shell you work with when you log on to a system. The first thing a login Shell does is to execute the commands in this file in the same environment as the Shell. (For more information on executing a Shell script in this manner, refer to the discussion of the . command on page 212.) This file allows the system administrator to establish system-wide environment parameters that can be overridden by individual users. Using this file, you can set Shell variables, execute utilities, and take care of other housekeeping tasks.

Because of the way that the Shell executes **/etc/profile**, the Shell variable **$0** indicates which Shell the **/etc/profile** file was executed from: **−sh** (regular Shell), **−rsh** (restricted Shell), and **−su** (substitute user command).

An example of an **/etc/profile** file that sets the time zone and the file creation mask and displays all the recent news items is shown below.

```
# cat /etc/profile
TZ=PST8PDT
export TZ
umask 022
news
#
```

.profile The Bourne Shell executes the commands in this file in the same environment as the Shell each time a user logs on. This file *must* be located in a user's home directory. (Each user has a different **.profile** file.) It usually specifies a terminal type (for vi and other programs), runs stty to establish terminal characteristics desired by the user, and performs other housekeeping functions when a user logs on.

A typical **.profile** file specifying a vt100 terminal and CONTROL-H as the erase key is shown below.

```
TERM=vt100
export TERM
stty erase '^h'
```

If you log in from more than one type of terminal, you may want to construct a more elaborate routine, such as the following one, that asks you for the terminal type each time you log on.

```
echo 'Terminal type: \c'
read TERM
export TERM
stty erase '^h'
```

.login   This file performs the same function as the **.profile** file in the user's home directory, but it is used by the C Shell.

/etc/rc   The init program executes this file as a Shell script when it is first executed and each time it changes the run level. The **/etc/rc** script performs tasks such as removing temporary files (when the system is booted), mounting file systems (when the system goes multiuser), and unmounting file systems (when the system is returned to single-user mode).

So that **rc** can know what to do, init calls it with three arguments: the new run level, the number of times this run level has been entered, and the previous run level. When the system is booted, these arguments have the values of **1 0 0** (assuming the system is brought up in run level 1. When the system is brought up to multiuser (run level 2), they have the values of **2 0 1**.

When run level 2 is entered *from* run level 2 or when you give an **init q** command to reread the **inittab** file, the system does not execute **/etc/rc**. Because the system does not execute **/etc/rc**, you can change the **/etc/inittab** file to add, delete, or change the characteristics of terminals (and their corresponding getty processes) while the system is up and running multiuser. When you run init, the system will implement your changes to **inittab** but will not attempt to mount already mounted file systems or remove temporary files that might be in use. Refer to "Adding and Removing Users" on page 313 for more information.

/etc/shutdown   Use this Shell script to bring the system down properly—refer to your system manual for more information. If you do not have this file, refer to the section of this chapter on "Bringing the System Down."

/dev/null   Any output you redirect to this file will disappear. You can send error messages from Shell scripts here when you do not want the user to see them.

If you redirect input from this file, it will appear as a null file. You can create a null file named **nothing** by giving the following command. You can also use this technique to truncate an existing file to zero length without changing its permissions.

```
$ cat /dev/null > nothing
```

/unix This file contains the UNIX system kernel that is loaded when you boot the system.

/usr/news The **/usr/news** directory contains files that contain items of interest to system users. Either the **/etc/profile** or **.profile** script usually calls news each time a user logs on. The news utility displays all the items in the **/usr/news** directory that the user hasn't seen yet.

/lost+found This directory is where fsck puts files that become lost within the directory structure. After running fsck and repairing unallocated inodes, look here for missing files.

Because there is no way to determine the filename of a lost file, fsck uses an ASCII representation of the inode number of the file as its name when it attaches a file to the **/lost+found** directory. Because the user ID of the owner of a file is stored in the inode, you can use **ls −l** to determine the owner of a file in **/lost+found**. It is up to the owner to determine what the name of the file was.

Because restructuring a corrupted file system is a delicate operation, fsck attempts to alter as little of the file system as possible. It would not be a good idea, for example, for fsck to create a new entry in a directory while it was repairing a file system. Creating an entry involves getting a block from the free list (page 303), and the free list might be the part of the file structure that is corrupt. The **/lost+found** directory provides a place fsck can put unattached files while altering the file system as little as possible.

Before running fsck, you must expand the **/lost+found** directory so that fsck has places it can put files without creating new entries in the directory. You can create places for fsck to put files by creating files and then removing them as shown in the following example. On most systems you will want to create more places for unattached files—just create and delete more files. Some systems have a script named **mklost+found** that expands the **/lost+found** directory.

The reason the following procedure works is the same reason

that you may have to compress a directory if it gets too big (see page 319): UNIX files cannot shrink, they can only expand or go away altogether. When you create a file and then remove it, the UNIX system leaves an empty slot where the file was. The UNIX system cannot remove the slot because that would mean making the directory (which is a file) smaller, and it cannot make a file smaller.

```
# cat /dev/null > /lost+found/temp1
# cat /dev/null > /lost+found/temp2
# cat /dev/null > /lost+found/temp3
# cat /dev/null > /lost+found/temp4
# cat /dev/null > /lost+found/temp5
# rm /lost+found/temp?
```

THE FILE STRUCTURE

A UNIX system file structure consists of one or more mounted file systems that typically reside on disk(s). Each file system holds one or more files. The root file system, which is always mounted, is the base that you can mount other file systems on.

This section describes the structure of a file system, the different kinds of files that a file system contains, how to format a new file system, and how to mount and unmount a file system.

The Structure of a File System

A file system is a data structure that resides on (usually part of) a disk. The portion of the disk that a file structure occupies is called a *disk slice* or *partition*. Under UNIX System V, a disk slice is divided into 1024-byte blocks. The number of blocks depends on the size of the disk slice.

A file system contains several kinds of blocks in addition to data blocks. These blocks keep track of what files are where on the disk, who owns each, where there is room to put new files, and more. An overview of a file system follows.

Inodes.   An *inode* is a data structure that defines a single file's existence. You can identify an inode by its *inode number* (or *i-number*). An *inode* contains information on the file's

- length
- creation, access, and modification times
- owner and group IDs
- access privileges
- number of links
- pointers to the *data blocks* and *indirect blocks* that contain the file itself

Inodes do not contain filenames—this information is stored in directories, which are files that associate filenames with inodes. When more than one filename is associated with a single inode, you have multiple links to the file.

The Superblock. The *superblock* contains housekeeping information, such as the number of inodes in the file system and free list information—it is an index into the rest of the file system.

The mount utility reads the superblock information into main memory when you mount a file system. As the disk is written to, the system keeps the copy of the superblock in memory up to date, occasionally writing an updated copy back to the disk. When you use umount to unmount a file system, the operating system writes an up-to-date copy of the superblock back to the disk.

If the system crashes or a file system is physically removed before it is unmounted, the superblock on the disk may be out of sync with the file system it represents. If the superblock is corrupted and you are able to access the file system at all, errors will be propagated through the file system at a great rate. You can always verify the integrity of a file system with the fsck utility.

Data Blocks. An inode points to 10 regular data blocks, each containing 1024 bytes of data from a file. (UNIX System V can also support old-style blocks of 512 bytes.) If a file is too large to be described by these blocks (larger than 10,240 bytes), the inode uses an eleventh, twelfth, and possibly a thirteenth pointer to point to *indirect* blocks.

Indirect Blocks. The eleventh pointer in the inode points to a first-level indirect block. This indirect block contains an additional set of 256 pointers, each locating a regular data block.

If the file is too large to be described by the inode and first-level indirect block (larger than 272,384 bytes), the twelfth pointer in the inode points to a second-level indirect block. The second-level indirect block points to 256 first-level indirect blocks, each of which points to 256 data blocks.

If needed, the system can use a third-level indirect block. This scheme of indirect blocks allows a file to grow to a maximum size of

$$1024 \times (10 + 256 + 256**2 + 256**3) = 17{,}247{,}250{,}432$$

bytes or the maximum space available on the disk, whichever is smaller. As of the writing of this book, the size of the disk has always been the limiting factor.

The Free List

The *free list* is a list of pointers that describe disk blocks that are available to store data. As the operating system writes a file to the disk, it removes pointers from this list and writes data to the blocks that the pointers describe. As it removes data from the disk, it restores the pointers to the free list.

The *first free-list block* is the block that contains the list of pointers that the operating system is currently working with. This block is stored in memory; the rest of the list is stored on disk. When this block is filled up (as files are removed from the disk and the free list grows), it is written to the disk and a new block is started. When it is empty, a new block of pointers is read from the disk. When no pointers remain, the file system is full.

Plain Versus Directory Files

A *plain* file stores user data, such as textual information and programs.

A *directory* is a disk file with a standard format that stores a list of names of plain files and other directories. It relates each of these filenames to an inode number.

When you move (mv) a file, you change the filename portion of the directory entry that is associated with the inode that describes the file. You do not change the inode.

When you make an additional link (ln) to a file, you create another reference (an additional filename) to the inode that describes the file. You do not change the inode.

When you remove (rm) a file, you remove the entry in the

directory that describes the file. When you remove the last link to a file (the inode keeps track of the number of links), the operating system puts all the blocks the inode pointed to back in the free list.

Every directory always has at least two entries (. and ..). The . entry is a link to the directory itself. The .. entry is a link to the parent directory. In the case of the root directory where there is no parent, the .. entry is a link to the root directory itself.

Special Files

The UNIX system supports five types of files: plain, directory, block special, character special, and fifo special. Plain files hold user data; directories hold directory information (see the preceding section).

Special files represent routines in the kernel that provide access to some feature of the operating system. Block and character special files represent device drivers that let you communicate with peripheral devices such as terminals, printers, and disk drives. Fifo special files, also called *named pipes*, allow unrelated programs to exchange information.

By convention, special files appear in the **/dev** directory. Each special file represents a device: You read from and write to the file to read from and write to the device it represents. (Fifo special files represent pipes: You read from and write to the file to read from and write to the pipe.) Although you will not normally read directly from and write directly to device files, the kernel and many UNIX system utilities do.

System V, Release 2, added several subdirectories to the **/dev** directory. The **/dev/dsk** and **/dev/rdsk** subdirectories contain entries that represent hard-disk drives. The **/dev/mt** and **/dev/rmt** subdirectories contain entries that represent magnetic tape drives. Prior to Release 2, all the device files in these directories were located directly in **/dev**

The following example shows part of the display an **ls -l** command produces for the **/dev** directory.

The first character of each line is a **b**, **c**, **d**, or **p** for block, character, directory, or pipe (see below). The next nine characters

```
# ls -l /dev
total 4
crw--w--w-  2 root    system  8,   1 May  4 18:36 console
drwxrwxr x  1 root    root       762 May  4 15:05 dsk
crw--w--w-  1 daemon  system  9,   0 May  4 11:16 lp
drwxrwxr x  1 root    root       672 May  4 15:07 mt
crw-rw-rw-  1 bin     system  6,   2 May  2 16:40 null
drwxrwxr x  1 root    root       762 May  4 15:05 rdsk
drwxrwxr x  1 root    root       672 May  4 15:07 rmt
brw-rw-rw-  1 root    system  0,   1 Sep 22 12:31 swap
crw--w--w-  2 root    system  8,   1 May  4 18:36 syscon
crw-rw-rw-  1 root    system  8,   0 Apr 24 11:19 tty00
crw-rw-rw-  1 root    system  8,   2 Nov 21 21:10 tty02
crw-rw-rw-  1 alex    system  8,   3 May  5 11:32 tty03
crw-rw-rw-  1 root    system  8,   4 May  4 18:04 tty04
```

represent the permissions for the file, followed by the number of links and the names of the owner and group. Where the number of bytes in a file would appear for a plain or directory file, a device file shows its *major* and *minor device numbers* separated by a comma (see below). The rest of the line is the same as any other **ls −l** listing.

Fifo Special Files.   Unless you are writing sophisticated programs, you will not be working with fifo special files (named pipes).

The term *fifo* stands for *first in first out*—the way any pipe works. The first information that you put in one end is the first information that comes out the other end. When you use a pipe on a command line to send the output of a program to the printer, the printer prints the information in the same order that the program produced it.

The UNIX system has had pipes for many generations. System V is the first version to use named pipes. Without named pipes, only processes that were children of the same ancestor could exchange information using pipes. Using named pipes, *any* two processes can exchange information. One program writes to a fifo special file. Another program reads from the same file. The programs do not have to run at the same time, nor do they have to be aware of each other's activity. The operating system handles all buffering and information storage.

Major and Minor Device Numbers. A *major device number* represents a class of hardware devices: a terminal, printer, tape drive, disk drive, etc. In the preceding list of the /**dev** directory, all the terminals have a major device number of 8 and the printer (**lp**) is 9.

A *minor device number* represents a particular piece of hardware within a class. Although all the terminals are grouped together by their major device number (8), each has a different minor device number (tty00 is 0, tty02 is 2, etc.). This setup allows one piece of software (the device driver) to service all similar hardware while being able to distinguish between different physical units.

Block and Character Devices. This section makes distinctions based on typical device drivers. Because the distinctions are based on device drivers, and because device drivers can be changed to suit a particular purpose, the distinctions in this section will not pertain to every system.

A *block device* is an I/O (input/output) device that is characterized by

➡ the ability to perform random access reads.
➡ a specific block size.
➡ only handling single blocks of data at a time.
➡ only accepting transactions that involve whole blocks of data.
➡ being able to have a file system mounted on it.
➡ having the kernel buffer its input and output.
➡ appearing to the operating system as a series of blocks numbered from 0 through n-1, where n is the number of blocks on the device.

The standard block devices on a UNIX system are disk and tape drives.

A *character device* is any device that is not a block device. Some examples of character devices are printers, terminals, and modems.

The device driver for a character device determines how a program reads from and writes to the device. For example, the device driver for a terminal allows a program to read the information you type on the terminal in two ways. A program can read single characters from a terminal in *raw* mode (this mode has nothing to do with the *raw device* described in the following section), or it can read a line at a time. When a program reads a line at a time, it does not read a fixed amount of information. It reads everything from the beginning of a line to the RETURN that ends a line—the number of characters in a line can vary.

Raw Block Devices. Device driver programs for block devices usually have two entry points so that they can be used in two ways: as block devices *or* as character devices. The character device form of a block device is called a *raw* device. Raw tape devices are usually located in **/dev/rmt** and raw disk devices in **/dev/rdsk**. A raw device is characterized by

- direct I/O (no buffering through the kernel).
- a one-to-one correspondence between system calls and hardware requests.
- device-dependent restrictions on I/O.

An example of the use of a raw device is writing a tape with tar. If you use tar and specify a block tape device (e.g., **/dev/mt/1m**), tar will write only one block (usually 1024 bytes) to the tape at a time. Even if you specify a blocking factor (using the **−b** option), tar will only write one block at a time. Following each write, the device driver leaves an inter-record gap on the tape. The inter-record gap can be as long as the record. Thus half the tape can be filled with gaps.

Using the raw tape device (e.g., **/dev/rmt/1m**), tar will write as many blocks as you specify each time it writes to the tape. If you specify a blocking factor of 20, you will be able to fit almost twice as much information on the tape as when using the block device.

Making a New Device File

The mknod (make node) utility adds a device file to the file system. The format of a mknod command line is shown below.

mknod /dev/name type major-number minor-number

The **name** is the name of the new file (in the **/dev** directory). The **type** is either **b** for a block device or **c** for a character device. The **major-number** and **minor-number** are the major and minor device numbers of the new device.

For example, the following command will make a new terminal

device file. It will create a character device file with the name /dev/tty05 and major and minor device numbers of 8 and 5.

```
# mknod /dev/tty05 c 8 5
#
```

Making and Mounting File Systems

Although the UNIX system can access information on a tape or disk that does not contain a file system, you cannot mount such a device as part of an existing file system.

Many systems have a program that you must use to format (initialize) hard or floppy disks before you can make a file system on them. Refer to your system manual for more information.

Making a File System. The /etc/mkfs program creates a file system on a device, destroying any information that was previously on the device. The format of an **mkfs** command is shown below.

/etc/mkfs device blocks[:inodes]

The **device** is the pathname of the device file that you want to create the file system on. The **blocks** is the number of blocks you want the file system to contain. The optional **:inodes** specifies the number of inodes you want in the file system. If you do not specify **inodes**, mkfs creates a file system with the number of inodes equal to one-fourth of **blocks**. This default allows an average of 4 Kbytes (4 blocks) per file (inode).

For example, the following command creates a file system on **/dev/dsk/1s1** that contains 20,000 blocks and, by default, 5000 inodes.

```
# /etc/mkfs /dev/dsk/1s1 20000
```

If you have a lot of little files, you can add an inode specification to an **mkfs** command by following the number of blocks with a colon and a number of inodes. The following example specifies 10,000 inodes and cuts the average file size to 2 Kbytes.

```
# /etc/mkfs /dev/dsk/1s1 20000:10000
```

The specifics of how mkfs works are dependent on the type of device you are making the file system on and the way your system is set up. Refer to your system manual for more information.

Labeling a File System. The labelit utility can write a label on an unmounted file system or display an existing label. The format of a **labelit** command is shown below.

/etc/labelit device [file-system-name volume-name]

The **device** is the name of the device with the file system you want to write a label to or read a label from. The label is composed of two six-character fields: the **file-system-name** and the **volume-name**. If you do not specify a label, labelit displays information about the file system, including its label. When you specify a label, it writes the label to the file system.

The following command writes a label on the unmounted disk on **/dev/dsk/1s1**.

```
# /etc/labelit /dev/dsk/1s1 acct05 vol273
```

Several utilities, including fsck and mount, use the labels produced by labelit.

Mounting a File System. When you call the mount utility with appropriate arguments, it informs the operating system that a file system is present on a device. It also tells the system where you want to be able to access the new file system within the existing file structure. When you call mount without any arguments, it lists the names of all mounted file systems as contained in **/etc/mnttab**.

After mounting a file system, you **must not** physically remove it until you have unmounted it using umount. If you do, you will probably damage the structure of the file system and lose data. Use fsck to verify the integrity of a file system that you think may be damaged.

The UNIX system automatically mounts the root file system when you boot up. You can never unmount (or mount) the root file system.

A **mount** command takes the following format.

/etc/mount [device directory [−r]]

The **device** is the device (usually in the **/dev** directory) that the file system you want to mount resides on. The **directory** is where mount is to put the root of the newly mounted file system. Use mkdir to create directories for mounting file systems as needed.

You can use the −**r** (read only) option to indicate that the operating system is not to write to the newly mounted file system. You must mount all physically write-protected file systems with this flag, even if you do not intend to write to them explicitly. When the operating system reads a file, it updates the access time associated with that file and will display an error message if the file system is write protected and you have not used the −**r** option.

The following example mounts the file system on **/dev/dsk/1s1** as **/usr**.

```
# /etc/mount /dev/dsk/1s1 /usr
```

Unmounting a File System.   The umount (unmount) utility reverses the effects of mount. It flushes all the buffers pertaining to the file system you specify and then makes the file system inaccessible. You can only unmount a file system that is not being used by a process. You cannot unmount a file system that has an open file, has a file being executed, or contains a process' working directory. Only after using umount can you physically remove a file system such as a disk pack or floppy disk. If you remove a file system that has not been unmounted, you will probably damage its integrity and lose data. When you use fsck to verify the integrity of the file system before you mount it next time, you will find out about any problems as fsck repairs them.

The following command unmounts the file system on **/dev/dsk/1s1**.

```
# /etc/umount /dev/dsk/1s1
```

Swap Area

The *swap area*, or *swap disk* as it is sometimes called, is a disk slice (partition) that the UNIX system uses exclusively for storing active programs while they are not actually being executed. The

UNIX system will *swap out* active programs when another program needs the space in memory the active program occupies. The swap area is not a file system, does not contain a superblock, and cannot be mounted.

As the system administrator, you will not usually be concerned with the swap area. Refer to your system manual if you need to change the amount of swap space (because you get an Out of swap space. message or because you have changed the amount of memory in the system). On some systems, the device that represents the swap area does not appear in the file structure. If it does, it is usually named **/dev/swap**.

DAY-TO-DAY SYSTEM ADMINISTRATOR FUNCTIONS

In addition to bringing up and shutting down the system, you have other responsibilities as the system administrator. This section covers the most important of these responsibilities.

Backing Up Files

One of the most neglected tasks of the system administrator is making backup copies of files on a regular basis. The backup copies are vital in two instances: when the system malfunctions and files are lost, and when a user (or the system administrator) deletes a file by accident.

You must back up the file systems on a regular basis. Backup files are usually kept on floppy disks or magnetic tape as determined by your system. Exactly how often you should back up which files is dependent on your system and needs. The criterion is, "If the system crashes, how much work are you willing to lose?" Ideally, you would back up all the files on the system every few minutes so that you would never lose more than a few minutes of work.

The trade-off is, "How often are you willing to back up the files?" The backup procedure typically slows the machine down for other users, takes a certain amount of your time, and requires that you have and store the media (tape or disk) that you keep the backup on.

The more people using the machine, the more often you should back up the file systems. A common schedule might have you perform a partial backup one or two times a day and a full backup one or two times a week.

A *partial* backup makes copies of the files that have been created or accessed since the last backup. A *full* backup makes copies of all files, regardless of when they were created or accessed.

There are several utilities designed to make backup copies of files; this book discusses the cpio (copy archives in and out) utility that you can use in conjunction with find. The find utility locates files based on criteria you specify—in this case, the last time the file was accessed. The cpio utility makes a copy of plain files that you or find specifies. You can also use the tar utility discussed in Part II to back up files.

Specifics on cpio and find are in Part II of this book. Following are some examples of their use to back up and restore a file system.

Creating a Backup File. The following sample command recursively backs up all subdirectories and plain files within the **/usr** directory. The backup device is **/dev/rmt/1m**; the device you should use is dependent on your system configuration. The example shows the Superuser prompt because the person executing the command must be able to look through all the directories in **/usr** and be able to read the necessary files.

```
# find /usr -cpio /dev/rmt/1m
```

The next command is a variation of the preceding one. It uses find's **-print** option to generate a list of the files it is backing up and sends this list to the printer using lp (the request id... message is from lp). The entire process is executed in the background.

```
# find /usr -cpio /dev/rmt/1m -print | lp &
3456
request id is printer_1-527 (standard input)
```

The next example demonstrates a partial backup. It finds and copies to tape all files on the entire file system (/) that have been accessed within the last two days (**-atime -2**). Again, a list of files is sent to the printer.

```
# find / —atime —2 —cpio /dev/rmt/1m —print  |  lp &
3469
request id is printer_1-528 (standard input)
```

Restoring from a Backup File. The cpio utility can restore a single file, a list of files, or an entire file system. The following commands restore the **/usr** directory from **/dev/rmt/1m**, assuming that only **/usr** was written to **/dev/rmt/1m**.

```
# cd /usr
# cpio —id < dev/rmt/1m
```

If several directories had been saved on the tape on **rmt/1m**, the following commands would extract only **/usr**.

```
# cd /usr
# cpio —id /usr < dev/rmt/1m
```

When you restore files, cpio will not overwrite a newer version of a file with an older version.

Adding and Removing Users

More than a login name is required for a user to be able to log in and use the system. A user must have the necessary files, directories, permissions, and optionally, a password in order to log on. Minimally, a user must have an entry in the **/etc/passwd** file and a home directory.

Adding a New User. Some manufacturers have Shell scripts (such as **/etc/adduser**) for adding new users. If your system has one of these scripts, use it. Otherwise, the following description explains how to add a new user to the system.

The first item a new user requires is an entry in the **/etc/passwd** file. While you are logged on as the Superuser, use vi or another editor to add an entry. Below is a sample entry in the **/etc/passwd** file; refer to page 296 for more information. Do *not* use a group or user ID less than 100.

```
alex::106:100:x159:/usr/alex:/bin/sh
```

If you want to give the user a password, use the passwd utility with the user's login name as an argument. Because you are logged in as the Superuser, passwd does not ask you for the old password, even if there is one. Because of this special treatment, you can give users a new password when they forget their old one.

```
# passwd alex
Changing password for alex.
New password:
Type new password again:
#
```

Now use mkdir to create the user's home directory you specified in the **passwd** file and chown to make the user the owner of the new directory. Use chgrp to associate the new directory with the owner's group. Finally, use chmod to establish the desired access privileges. The following example sets up the directory so that anyone besides the owner can scan through and read files in the home directory, but they cannot change files or write to the directory.

```
# mkdir /usr/alex
# chown alex /usr/alex
# chgrp pubs /usr/alex
# chmod 755 /usr/alex
#
```

To test the new setup, log on as the new user and create an appropriate **.profile** file in the new user's home directory. (You may have to manually assign a value to and export the **TERM** Shell variable if you want to use vi to create this file—see page 27.)

Removing a User. Remove a user by removing the user's entry in the **passwd** file and removing all the files and directories you set up for the user. If appropriate, make a backup copy of all the files belonging to the user before deleting them.

If you just want to prevent a user from logging on temporarily, you can put an **x** in the user's password field in the **passwd** file. You will need to give the user a new password when you want to allow the user to log on again.

Stopping and Starting Terminal Processes

This section explains how to stop and start terminal processes while the system is up and running in multiuser mode.

Refer to your system manual for information about how to physically connect a terminal to your system and how to determine what device file the terminal is associated with.

The **/etc/inittab** file controls which terminals are active, or on-line. Before taking a terminal off-line, make sure no one is using it. Then change the line in **inittab** that controls the getty process for that terminal so that it specifies *off* in place of *respawn* (see page 295). Execute init with an argument of **q**. This argument causes init to reexamine **inittab** and fork any new processes you have added (or changed to *respawn*) and kill any process you have removed (or specified as *off*). After about 20 seconds, the UNIX system will kill the process controlling the terminal and the terminal will become inoperative.

To bring a terminal on-line, change the entry for the terminal in **inittab** from *off* to *respawn* and execute init as above.

The following example shows how to bring the terminal associated with the device file **/dev/tty05** off-line and then how to activate it again. First, use vi or another editor to edit the **/etc/inittab** file. Find the line with a run level of **2** and a process involving **tty05**. It will look something like this:

```
105:2:respawn:/etc/getty tty05
```

Change the word *respawn* to *off*, write the file out, and exit from the editor. Then give the following command to signal init to take the terminal off-line.

```
# init q
```

To bring the terminal back on-line, follow the same procedure, changing the word *off* to *respawn* and executing init.

Checking Your Mail

Remember to log on as **root** periodically to see if there is any mail for the system administrator. (You will not know if you have mail if you always use the **su** command to perform system administration tasks.) Users frequently use mail to communicate with the system administrator.

PROBLEMS

It is your responsibility as the system administrator to keep the system secure and running smoothly. If a user is having a problem, it usually falls to the administrator to help the user get back on the right track. This section presents some suggestions on ways to keep users happy and the system functioning at its peak.

When a User Can't Log On

If a user can't log on the system, follow these steps to determine where the problem is.

Determine if just that one user has a problem, just that one user's terminal has a problem, or if the problem is more widespread.

If just that user has a problem, the user's terminal will respond when you press **RETURN** and you will be able to log on as yourself. Make sure the user has a valid login name and password; then show the user how to log on.

If just that one user's terminal has a problem, other users will be using the system but that user's terminal will not respond when you press **RETURN**. Try pressing the **BREAK** and **RETURN** keys alternately to reestablish the proper baud rate. Make sure the terminal is set for a legal baud rate. Try pressing the following keys:

CONTROL-Q   This key "unsticks" the terminal if someone pressed **CONTROL-S**.

DEL   This key stops a runaway process that has hung up the terminal.

ESCAPE   This key can help if the user is in Input Mode in vi.

CONTROL-L   This key redraws the screen if the user was using vi.

CONTROL-R   This key is an alternate for **CONTROL-L**.

Check the terminal cable from where it plugs into the terminal to where it plugs into the computer. Check the **/etc/inittab** entry for that line. Finally, try turning the terminal off and then turning it back on again.

If the problem appears to be widespread, check to see if you can log on from the system console. If you can, make sure the system is in multiuser mode. If you can't, the system may have crashed—reboot it.

Keeping a Machine Log

A machine log that includes the following information may be helpful in finding and fixing problems with the system. Note the time and date for each entry in the log.

hardware modifications	Keep track of *all* modifications to the hardware—even those installed by factory representatives.
system software modifications	Keep track of any modification that anyone makes to the operating system software, whether it's a patch or a new version of a program.
hardware malfunctions	Keep as accurate a list as possible of any problems with the system. Make note of any error messages or numbers that the system displays on the system console and what users were doing when the problem occurred.
user complaints	Make a list of all reasonable complaints by knowledgeable users (e.g., machine is abnormally slow).

Keeping the System Secure

No system with dial-in lines or public access to terminals is absolutely secure. You can make your system as secure as possible by changing the Superuser password frequently and choosing a Superuser password that is hard to guess. Do not tell anyone who does not *absolutely* need to know the Superuser password what it is. You can also encourage system users to choose difficult passwords and to change them periodically.

A password that is hard to guess is a word that someone else would not be likely to think that you would have chosen. Do not use names of relatives, pets, or friends. Choose nonsense words and include uppercase and lowercase letters as well as numbers.

Make sure that no one (except the Superuser) can write to files containing programs that are owned by root and run in the set user ID mode (e.g., **mail** and **su**). Also make sure that users do not transfer programs that run in the set user ID mode and are owned by root onto the system by means of mounting tapes or disks. These programs can be used to disable system security.

Disk Usage

Disk space is usually a precious commodity. Sooner or later, you will probably start to run out of it. Do not fill up a disk—the UNIX operating system runs best with at least 5 to 30 percent of the disk space in each file system free. The minimum amount of free space you should maintain on each file system is machine dependent. Using more than the maximum optimal disk space in a file system degrades system performance. If there is no space on a file system, you can't write to it at all.

There are several programs that you can use to determine who is using how much disk space on what file systems. Refer to the du and df utilities and the **–size** option of the find utility in Part II.

The *only* ways to increase the amount of free space on a file system are to delete files and condense directories. This section contains some ideas on ways to maintain a file system so that it does not get overloaded.

Growing Files. Some files, such as log files and temporary files, grow automatically over time. Core dump files take up space and are rarely needed. As the system administrator, you must review these files periodically so that they do not get out of hand.

The first thing to do when you start to run out of disk space is to locate unneeded files and delete them. You can archive them using cpio or tar before you delete them.

You can safely remove any files named **core** that haven't been accessed for several days. The following command performs this function.

```
# find / —name core —atime +3 —exec rm {} \;
```

Look through the **/tmp** and **/usr/tmp** directories for old temporary files and remove them. The **/usr/lib/spell/spellhist** file keeps track of all the misspelled words that spell finds—make sure it doesn't get too big. Keep track of disk usage in **/usr/mail**, **/usr/spool**, **/usr/adm**, and **/usr/news**.

Removing Unused Space from a Directory. Directories should not contain more than 320 entries—file system indirection makes large directories inefficient. The following command will list the names of directories larger than 5K bytes (320 entries).

```
# find / —type d —size +5 —print
```

If you find a directory that is too large, you can usually break it into several smaller directories by moving its contents into new directories. Make sure you remove the original directory once you have moved its contents.

Because UNIX files can only grow or be removed altogether, removing a file from a directory will not shrink the directory, even though it will make more space on the disk. To remove unused space and make a directory smaller, you must copy all the files into a new directory and remove the original directory.

The following procedure will remove unused directory space. First, remove all unneeded files from the large directory. Then, following the sample below, make a smaller copy of the directory. The sample procedure removes unused space from a directory named **/usr/alex/large**. The directory **/usr/alex/hold** holds the directory while it is being processed. Make sure that, after creating the new directory, you set its access privileges to that of the original directory. After you complete the procedure, you can use the new directory just as you did the old.

```
# mv /usr/alex/large /usr/alex/hold
# mkdir /usr/alex/large
# cd /usr/alex/hold
# find . —print | cpio —plmd /usr/alex/large
# cd /usr/alex
# rm —rf /usr/alex/hold
```

GETTING INFORMATION TO USERS

As the system administrator, one of your primary responsibilities is communicating with the system users. You need to tell them when the system will be down for maintenance, about a class on a new piece of software that you just installed, and how to use the new system printer. You can even start to fill the role of a small local newspaper, letting users know about new employees, births, the company picnic, etc.

Different items you want to communicate will have different priorities. Information about the company picnic in two months is not as time-sensitive as the fact that you are bringing the system down in five minutes.

The UNIX operating system provides different ways of communicating for different purposes. The most common methods are described and contrasted below.

wall. The wall (write all) utility is most effective for communicating immediately to everyone who is logged on. It works in the same way as write, but it sends a message to everyone who is logged on. Use it if you are about to bring the system down or in other crisis situations. Users who are not logged on never get the message.

Use wall while you are the Superuser *only* in crisis situations—it will interrupt anything anyone is doing.

write. Use the write utility to communicate with any individual user who is logged on. You might use it to ask a user to stop running a program that is bogging down the system. Users can also use write to ask you, for example, to mount a tape or restore a file.

mail. The mail utility is useful for communicating less urgent information to one or more system users. When you send mail, you have to be willing to wait for each user to read the mail. The mail utility is useful for reminding users that they are forgetting to log off, bills are past due, or they are using too much disk space.

As opposed to write, users can make permanent records of mail they receive so that they keep track of important details. It would be appropriate to use mail to inform users about a new, complex procedure—each user could keep a copy of the information for reference.

Message of the Day. All users see this message each time they log on. You can edit the **/etc/motd** file to change the message. The message of the day can alert users to upcoming periodic maintenance, new system features, or a change in procedures.

news. The news utility displays news: class announcements, new hardware or software on the system, new employees, parties, etc.

SUMMARY

The system administrator is responsible for backing up files, adding and removing users, helping users who have problems logging on, and keeping track of disk usage and system security.

This chapter explains many of the files and programs you will have to work with to maintain a UNIX system. Much of the work you will do as the system administrator will require you to log on as the Superuser. The login name for the Superuser is root. When you are logged in as the Superuser, you have extensive system-wide powers that you do not normally have. You can read from and write to any file and execute programs that ordinary users are not permitted to execute.

A series of programs and files control how the system appears at any given time. Many of the files you will work with as the system administrator are located in the **/etc** directory. Among the most important are **inittab**, which is read by init; **gettydefs**, which is read by getty; **passwd**, which is read by login; and **profile**, which is read by the Shell.

When you bring up the system, it is frequently in single-user mode. In this mode, only the system console is functional and not all the file systems are mounted. When the system is in single-user mode, you can back up files and use fsck to check the integrity of file systems before you mount them. The init utility will bring the system to its normal multiuser state.

With the system running in multiuser mode, you can still perform many administration tasks, such as adding users and terminals.

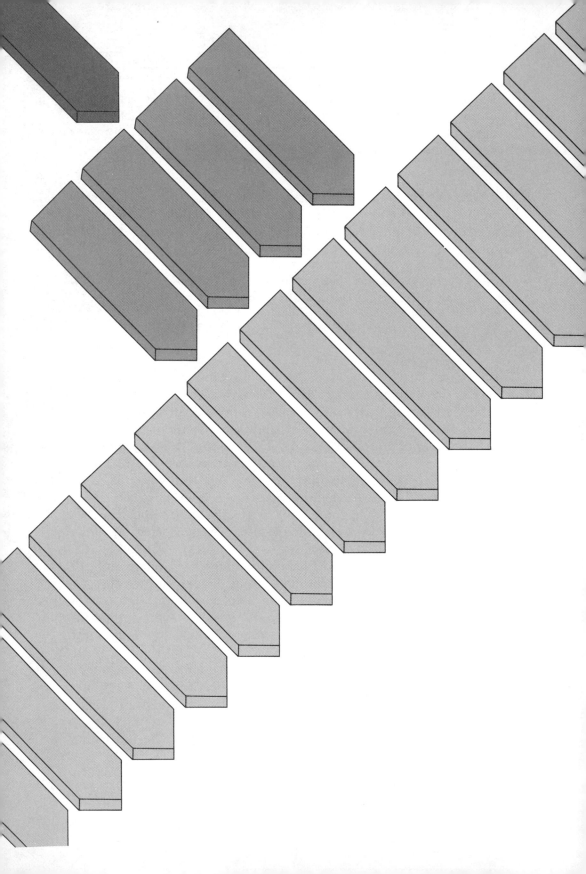

Part II
THE UNIX
UTILITY
PROGRAMS

Following is a list of the utilities grouped by function.

Utilities That Display and Manipulate Files

awk	search for and process a pattern in a file (page 331)
cancel	cancel a printing job (page 362)
cat	display a text file (page 363)
comm	compare files (page 377)
cp	copy files (page 379)
cpio	store and retrieve files in an archive format (page 381)
diff	display the differences between two files (page 387)
find	find files (page 404)
grep	search for a pattern in a file (page 414)
ln	make a link to a file (page 420)
lp	print a file (page 422)
lpr	print a file—alternative to lp (page 424)
lpstat	display the statuses of printing jobs (page 425)
ls	display information about a file (page 426)
mkdir	make a directory (page 453)
more	display a file a screenful at a time (page 454)
mv	rename a file (page 456)
od	dump a file (page 463)
pg	display a file a screenful at a time (page 465)
pr	paginate a file (page 469)
rm	delete a file (page 476)
rmdir	delete a directory (page 478)
sed	editor (noninteractive) (page 479)
sort	sort and/or merge files (page 495)
spell	check a file for spelling errors (page 508)
tail	display the last part of a file (page 516)
tar	create or retrieve files from an archive file (page 518)
uniq	display lines of a file that are unique (page 532)
wc	display a line, word, and character count (page 535)

Communication Utilities

mail	send or receive electronic mail (page 434)
mailx	send or receive electronic mail (page 437)
mesg	enable/disable reception of messages (page 452)
news	display news (page 460)
write	send a message to another user (page 539)

Utilities That Display and Alter Status

cd	change to another working directory (page 369)
chgrp	change the group that is associated with a file (page 371)
chmod	change the access mode of a file (page 372)
chown	change the owner of a file (page 376)
date	display the date (page 385)
df	display the amount of available disk space (page 386)
du	display information on disk usage (page 394)
file	display file classification (page 403)
fsck	check and repair a file system (page 410)
kill	terminate a process (page 418)
newgrp	temporarily change the group identification of a user (page 458)
nice	change the priority of a command (page 461)
nohup	run a command that will keep running after you log off (page 462)
ps	display process status (page 472)
sleep	put process to sleep (page 493)
stty	display or establish terminal parameters (page 510)
umask	establish file-creation permissions mask (page 530)
who	display names of users (page 537)

Utilities That Are Programming Tools

cc	C compiler (page 366)
make	keep a set of programs current (page 445)
touch	update a file's modification time (page 528)

Miscellaneous Utilities

at	execute a Shell script at a specified time (page 328)
cal	display a calendar (page 359)
calendar	reminder calendar (page 361)
echo	display a message (page 396)
expr	evaluate an expression (page 398)
shl	call the Shell layer manager (page 491)
tee	copy the standard input to the standard output and one or more files (page 522)
test	evaluate an expression (page 523)
tty	display the terminal pathname (page 529)

The following sections are a sample of the format that is used throughout Part II. Each section explains what you can expect to find under each heading within each utility.

sample utility

This section gives the name of the utility followed by a very brief description.

Format

This section shows you how to call the utility, including options and arguments. Arguments enclosed in square brackets—[ ]—are optional.

Hyphenated words identify single arguments (e.g., **source-file**) or groups of similar arguments (e.g., **directory-list**). As an example, **file-list** means a list of one or more files.

Summary

Unless stated otherwise, the output from a utility goes to its standard output. The "Standard Input and Standard Output" section on page 78 explains how to redirect output so that it goes to a file other than the terminal.

The statement that a utility "takes its input from files you specify on the command line or from its standard input" indicates that the utility is a member of the class of UNIX utility programs that takes input from files specified on the command line or, if you do not specify a filename, from its standard input. It also means that the utility can receive redirected input. See page 84.

Options

The options section lists the common options that you can use with the utility. Unless specified otherwise, you must precede all options with a hyphen. Most utilities accept a single hyphen before multiple options. See page 75.

Arguments

This section describes the arguments that you use when you call the utility. The argument itself, as shown in the preceding "Format" section, is printed in **bold type**.

Notes

You will find miscellaneous notes, some important and others merely interesting, in this section.

Examples

This section contains examples of how to use the utility. It is tutorial and is more casual than the preceding sections of the utility description.

at

Execute a Shell script at a time you specify.

Format

at time [date] [+ increment]

at [options] job-list

Summary

The at utility causes the operating system to execute commands it receives from its standard input. It executes them as a Shell script in the working directory at the time you specify.

When the operating system executes commands using **at**, it uses mail to send you the standard output and error output of the resulting process. You can redirect the output to avoid getting mail.

Options

These options are not for use when you initiate a job with **at**. You can only use them to determine the status of a job or to a cancel job.

-r   This option cancels jobs that you previously submitted with at. The **job-list** is a list of one or more job numbers of the jobs you want to cancel. If you don't remember the job number, use the **−l** option (below) to list your jobs and their numbers.

-l   This option displays a list of all jobs that you have submitted with **at**. The **job-list** is a list of one or more job numbers of the jobs you want at to list. If you do not include a **job-list**, at lists all your jobs.

Arguments

The **time** is the time of day you want at to execute the job. You can specify the **time** as a one-, two-, or four-digit number. One-

and two-digit numbers specify an hour, while four-digit numbers specify an hour and minute. The at utility assumes a 24-hour clock unless you place **am**, **pm**, **midnight**, or **noon** immediately after the number, in which case, at uses a 12-hour clock. You can also specify the time as **now** or **next** as appropriate.

The **date** is the day of the week or date of the month that you want at to execute the job on. If you do not specify a day, at executes the job today if the hour you specify in **time** is greater than the current hour. If the hour is less than the current hour, at executes the job tomorrow.

To specify a day of the week, you can spell it out or abbreviate it to three letters. You can also use the days **today** and **tomorrow**.

Use the name of a month followed by the number of the day in the month to specify a date. You can follow the month and day number with a year.

The **increment** is a number followed by one of the following (plural or singular is allowed): minutes, hours, days, weeks, months, or years. The at utility adds the **increment** to the **time** (and **date**) you specify.

Notes

The Shell saves environment variables and the working directory so that they are available when it executes commands that you submit using at.

The system administrator must put your login name in the **/usr/lib/cron/at.allow** file for you to be able to use at.

Examples

You can use either of the following techniques to paginate and print **long__file** at two o'clock the next morning. The first example executes the command directly from the command line, while the second uses a file containing the necessary command (**file3**) and executes it using at. If you execute the command directly from the command line, you must signal the end of the list of commands by pressing CONTROL-D at the beginning of a line.

The line that begins with job contains the job number and the time at will execute the job. The request id... is a message from the lp utility.

```
$ at 2am
pr long_file | lp
CONTROL-D
job 474285600.a at Fri Jan 11 02:00:00  1985

$ cat file3
pr long_file | lp

$ at 2am < file3
job 474285601.a at Fri Jan 11 02:00:00  1985
$
```

If you give an **at** −**l** command following the two preceding commands, at will display a list of jobs in its queue.

```
$ at −l
474285600.a    at Fri Jan 11 02:00:00  1985
474285601.a    at Fri Jan 11 02:00:00  1985
$
```

The next example executes **cmdfile** at 3:30 P.M. (1530 hours) a week from next Thursday.

```
$ at 1530 thu +1 week < cmdfile
job 474852600.a at Thu Jan 17 15:30:00 1985
$
```

The final example executes an nroff job at 7 P.M. on Friday. It creates an intermediate file and redirects the error output.

```
$ at 7 pm Friday
nroff −mm report > report.out 2> report.err
lp report.out
CONTROL-D

$
```

awk

Search for and process a pattern in a file.

Format

awk −f program-file [file-list]

awk program [file-list]

Summary

The awk utility is a pattern scanning and processing language. It searches one or more files to see if they contain lines that match specified patterns and performs actions, such as writing the line to its standard output or incrementing a counter, each time it finds a match.

You can use awk to generate reports or filter text. It works equally well with numbers and text—when you can mix the two, awk will almost always come up with the right answer.

The authors of awk (Alfred V. Aho, Peter J. Weinberger, and Brian W. Kernighan) designed it to be easy to use and sacrificed execution speed toward this end.

The awk utility takes many of its constructs from the C programming language. It includes the following features:

- flexible format
- conditional execution
- looping statements
- numeric variables
- string variables
- regular expressions
- C's printf

The awk utility takes its input from files you specify on the command line or from its standard input.

Options

If you do not use the **−f** option, awk uses the first command line argument as its program.

−f (file) This option causes awk to read its program from the **program-file** given as the first command line argument.

Arguments

The first format uses a **program-file**, which is the pathname of a file containing an awk program. See "Description," below.

The second format uses a **program**, which is an awk program included on the command line. This format allows you to write simple, short awk programs without the need for creating a separate **program-file**.

The **file-list** contains pathnames of the plain files that awk processes. These are the input files.

Notes

See page 357 for examples of awk error messages.

Description

An awk program consists of one or more program lines containing a **pattern** and/or **action** in the following format.

pattern { action }

The **pattern** selects lines from the input file. The awk utility takes the **action** on all lines that the **pattern** selects. You must enclose the **action** within braces so that awk can differentiate it from the **pattern**. If a program line does not contain a **pattern**, awk selects all lines in the input file. If a program line does not contain an **action**, awk copies the selected lines to its standard output.

To start, awk compares the first line in the input file (from the file-list) with each **pattern** in the program-file or program. If a **pattern** selects the line (if there is a match), awk takes the **action** associated with the **pattern**. If the line is not selected, awk takes no action. When awk has completed its comparisons for the first line of the input file, it repeats the process for the next line of input. It continues this process, comparing subsequent lines in the input file, until it has read the entire file-list.

If several **patterns** select the same line, awk takes the **actions** associated with each of the **patterns**. It is therefore possible for awk to send a single line from the input file to its standard output more than once.

Patterns

You can use a regular expression (refer to the Appendix), enclosed within slashes, as a pattern. The ~ operator tests to see if a field or variable matches a regular expression. The !~ operator tests for no match.

You can process arithmetic and character relational expressions with the following relational operators.

Operator	Meaning
<	less than
<=	less than or equal to
==	equal to
!=	not equal to
>=	greater than or equal to
>	greater than

You can combine any of the patterns described above using the Boolean operators **||** (OR) or **&&** (AND).

The comma is the range operator. If you separate two patterns with a comma on a single awk program line, awk selects a range of lines beginning with the first line that contains the first pattern. The last line awk selects is the next subsequent line that contains the second pattern. After awk finds the second pattern, it starts the process over by looking for the first pattern again.

Two unique patterns allow you to execute commands before awk starts its processing and after it finishes. The awk utility executes the actions associated with the **BEGIN** pattern before, and with the **END** pattern after, it processes all the files in the file-list.

Actions

The action portion of an awk command causes awk to take action when it matches a pattern. If you do not specify an action, awk assumes {print}. This action copies the record (normally a line— see "Variables" below) from the input file to awk's standard output.

You can follow a Print command with arguments, causing awk to print just the arguments you specify. The arguments can be variables or string constants. Using awk, you can send the output from a Print command to a file (>), append it to a file (>>), or pipe it to the input of another program (|).

Unless you separate items in a Print command with commas, awk catenates them. Commas cause awk to separate the items with the output field separator (normally a SPACE—see "Variables" below).

You can include several actions on one line within a set of braces by separating them with semicolons.

Comments

The awk utility disregards anything on a program line following a sharp sign (#). You can document an awk program by preceding comments with this symbol.

Variables

You declare and initialize user variables when you use them. In addition, awk maintains program variables for your use. You can use both user and program variables in the pattern *and* in the action portion of an awk program. Following is a list of program variables.

Variable	Represents
NR	record number of current record
$0	the current record (as a single variable)
NF	number of fields in the current record
$1-$n	fields in the current record
FS	input field separator (SPACE or TAB)
OFS	output field separator (SPACE)
RS	input record separator (NEWLINE)
ORS	output record separator (NEWLINE)
FILENAME	name of the current input file

The input and output record separators are, by default, NEW-LINE characters. Thus, awk takes each line in the input file to be a separate record and appends a NEWLINE to the end of each record that it sends to its standard output. The input field separators are, by default, SPACEs and TABs. The output field separator is a SPACE. You can change the value of any of the separators at any time by assigning a new value to its associated variable.

Functions

The functions that awk provides for manipulating numbers and strings follow.

Name	Function
length(str)	returns the number of characters in **str**; if you do not supply an argument, it returns the number of characters in the current input record
int(num)	returns the integer portion of **num**
index(str1,str2)	returns the index of **str2** in **str1** or 0 if **str2** is not present
split(str,arr,del)	places elements of **str**, delimited by **del**, in array **arr[1]...arr[n]**; returns the number of elements in the array
sprintf(fmt,args)	formats **args** according to **fmt** and returns the formatted string; mimics the C programming language function of the same name
substr(str,pos,len)	returns a substring of **str** that begins at **pos** and is **len** characters long

Operators

The following awk arithmetic operators are from the C programming language.

*   multiplies the expression preceding the operator by the expression following it

/   divides the expression preceding the operator by the expression following it

%   takes the remainder after dividing the expression preceding the operator by the expression following it

+   adds the expression preceding the operator and the expression following it

=   assigns the value of the expression following the operator to the variable preceding it

++   increments the variable preceding the operator

--   decrements the variable preceding the operator

+=   adds the expression following the operator to the variable preceding it

-=   subtracts the expression following the operator from the variable preceding it

*=   multiplies the variable preceding the operator by the expression following it and assigns the result to the variable preceding the operator

/=   divides the variable preceding the operator by the expression following it and assigns the result to the variable preceding the operator

%=   takes the remainder, after dividing the variable preceding the operator by the expression following it, and assigns the result to the variable preceding the operator

Associative Arrays

An associative array is one of awk's most powerful features. An associative array uses strings as its indexes. Using an associative array, you can mimic a traditional array by using numeric strings as indexes.

You assign a value to an element of an associative array just as you would assign a value to any other awk variable. The format is shown below.

array[string] = value

The **array** is the name of the array, **string** is the index of the element of the array you are assigning a value to, and **value** is the value you are assigning to the element of the array.

There is a special For structure you can use with an awk array. The format is:

for (elem in array) action

The **elem** is a variable that takes on the values of each of the elements in the array as the For structure loops through them, **array** is the name of the array, and **action** is the action that awk takes for each element in the array. You can use the **elem** variable in this **action**.

The "Examples" section contains programs that use associative arrays.

Printf

You can use the Printf command in place of Print to control the format of the output that awk generates. The awk version of Printf is similar to that of the C language. A Printf command takes the following format.

printf "control-string" arg1, arg2, ..., argn

The **control-string** determines how Printf will format **arg1-n** The **arg1-n** can be variables or other expressions. Within the **control-string** you can use \n to indicate a NEWLINE and \t to indicate a TAB.

The **control-string** contains conversion specifications, one for each argument (**arg1-n**). A conversion specification has the following format.

%[–][x[.y]]conv

The – causes Printf to left justify the argument. The **x** is the minimum field width, and the **.y** is the number of places to the right of a decimal point in a number. The **conv** is a letter from the following list.

conv	Conversion
d	decimal
e	exponential notation
f	floating point number
g	use **f** or **e**, whichever is shorter
o	unsigned octal
s	string of characters
x	unsigned hexadecimal

Refer to the following "Examples" section for examples of how to use Printf.

Examples

A simple awk program is shown below.

```
{ print }
```

This program consists of one program line that is an action. It uses no pattern. Because the pattern is missing, awk selects all lines in the input file. Without any arguments, the Print command prints each selected line in its entirety. This program copies the input file to its standard output.

The following program has a pattern part without an explicit action.

```
/jenny/
```

In this case, awk selects all lines from the input file that contain the string jenny. When you do not specify an action, awk assumes Print. This program copies all the lines in the input file that contain jenny to its standard output.

The following examples work with the **cars** data file. From left to right, the columns in the file contain each car's make, model, year of manufacture, mileage, and price. All white space in this file is composed of single TABs (there are no SPACEs in the file).

```
$ cat cars
plym      fury       77      73      2500
chevy     nova       79      60      3000
ford      mustang    65      45      10000
volvo     gl         78      102     9850
ford      ltd        83      15      10500
chevy     nova       80      50      3500
fiat      600        65      115     450
honda     accord     81      30      6000
ford      thundbd    84      10      17000
toyota    tercel     82      180     750
chevy     impala     65      85      1550
ford      bronco     83      25      9500
```

The first example below selects all lines that contain the string chevy. The slashes indicate that chevy is a regular expression. This example has no action part.

Although neither awk nor Shell syntax require single quotation marks on the command line, they prevent many unnecessary problems when you are using awk. If the awk program you create on the command line includes SPACEs or any special characters that the Shell will interpret, you must quote them. Always enclosing the program in single quotation marks is the easiest way of making sure you have quoted any characters that need to be quoted.

```
$ awk '/chevy/' cars
chevy     nova       79      60      3000
chevy     nova       80      50      3500
chevy     impala     65      85      1550
```

The next example selects all lines from the file (it has no pattern part). The braces enclose the action part—you must always use braces to delimit the action part so awk can distinguish the pattern part from the action part. This example prints the third field ($3), a SPACE (indicated by the comma), and the first field ($1) of each selected line.

```
$ awk '{print $3, $1}' cars
77 plym
79 chevy
65 ford
78 volvo
83 ford
80 chevy
65 fiat
81 honda
84 ford
82 toyota
65 chevy
83 ford
```

The next example includes both a pattern and an action part. It selects all lines that contain the string chevy and prints the third and first fields from the lines it selects.

```
$ awk ´/chevy/ {print $3, $1}´ cars
79 chevy
80 chevy
65 chevy
```

The next example selects lines that contain a match for the regular expression h. Because there is no explicit action, it prints all the lines it selects.

```
$ awk ´/h/´ cars
chevy    nova     79      60      3000
chevy    nova     80      50      3500
honda    accord   81      30      6000
ford     thundbd  84      10      17000
chevy    impala   65      85      1550
```

The next pattern uses the matches operator (~) to select all lines that contain the letter h in the first field.

```
$ awk ´$1 ~ /h/´ cars
chevy    nova     79      60      3000
chevy    nova     80      50      3500
honda    accord   81      30      6000
chevy    impala   65      85      1550
```

The caret (^) in a regular expression forces a match at the beginning of the line, or in this case, the beginning of the first field.

```
$ awk ´$1 ~ /^h/´ cars
honda    accord   81      30      6000
```

A pair of brackets surrounds a character class definition (refer to the Appendix, "Regular Expressions"). Below, awk selects all lines that have a second field that begins with t or m. Then it prints the third and second fields, a dollar sign, and the fifth field.

```
$ awk ´$2 ~ /^[tm]/ {print $3, $2, "$" $5}´ cars
65 mustang $10000
84 thundbd $17000
82 tercel $750
```

The next example shows three roles that a dollar sign can play in an awk program. A dollar sign followed by a number forms the name of a field. Within a regular expression, a dollar sign forces a match at the end of a line or field (5$). And, within a string, you can use a dollar sign as itself.

```
$ awk '$3 ~ /5$/ {print $3, $1, "$" $5}' cars
65 ford $10000
65 fiat $450
65 chevy $1550
```

Below, the equals relational operator (==) causes awk to perform a numeric comparison between the third field in each line and the number 65.

```
$ awk '$3 == 65' cars
ford      mustang  65      45      10000
fiat      600      65      115     450
chevy     impala   65      85      1550
```

The next example finds all cars priced at or under $3000.

```
$ awk '$5 <= 3000' cars
plym      fury     77      73      2500
chevy     nova     79      60      3000
fiat      600      65      115     450
toyota    tercel   82      180     750
chevy     impala   65      85      1550
```

When you use double quotation marks, awk performs textual comparisons, using the ASCII collating sequence as the basis of the comparison. Below, awk shows that the *strings* 450 and 750 fall in the range that lies between the *strings* 2000 and 9000.

```
$ awk '$5 >= "2000" && $5 < "9000"' cars
plym      fury     77      73      2500
chevy     nova     79      60      3000
chevy     nova     80      50      3500
fiat      600      65      115     450
honda     accord   81      30      6000
toyota    tercel   82      180     750
```

When you need a numeric comparison, don't use quotation marks. The next example gives the correct results. It is the same as the previous example but omits the double quotation marks.

```
$ awk '$5 >= 2000 && $5 < 9000' cars
plym      fury     77      73      2500
chevy     nova     79      60      3000
chevy     nova     80      50      3500
honda     accord   81      30      6000
```

Next, the range operator (,) selects a group of lines. The first line it selects is the one specified by the pattern before the comma.

The last line is the one selected by the pattern after the comma. The example selects all lines starting with the line that contains volvo and concluding with the line that contains fiat.

```
$ awk '/volvo/ , /fiat/' cars
volvo   gl      78      102     9850
ford    ltd     83      15      10500
chevy   nova    80      50      3500
fiat    600     65      115     450
```

After the range operator finds its first group of lines, it starts the process over, looking for a line that matches the pattern before the comma. In the following example, awk finds three groups of lines that fall between ford and chevy. Although the fifth line in the file contains ford, awk never selects it because, when it is processing the fifth line, it is searching for chevy.

```
$ awk '/chevy/ , /ford/' cars
chevy   nova     79      60      3000
ford    mustang  65      45      10000
chevy   nova     80      50      3500
fiat    600      65      115     450
honda   accord   81      30      6000
ford    thundbd  84      10      17000
chevy   impala   65      85      1550
ford    bronco   83      25      9500
```

When you are writing a longer awk program, it is convenient to put the program in a file and reference the file on the command line. Use the **−f** option followed by the name of the file containing the awk program.

Following is an awk program that has two actions and uses the **BEGIN** pattern. The awk utility performs the action associated with **BEGIN** before it processes any of the lines of the data file. The **a1** awk program uses **BEGIN** to print a header.

The second action, {print}, has no pattern part and prints all the lines in the file.

```
$ cat a1
BEGIN    {print "Make     Model    Year     Miles    Price"}
         {print}
```

```
$ awk -f a1 cars
Make       Model    Year     Miles    Price
plym       fury     77       73       2500
chevy      nova     79       60       3000
ford       mustang  65       45       10000
volvo      gl       78       102      9850
ford       ltd      83       15       10500
chevy      nova     80       50       3500
fiat       600      65       115      450
honda      accord   81       30       6000
ford       thundbd  84       10       17000
toyota     tercel   82       180      750
chevy      impala   65       85       1550
ford       bronco   83       25       9500
```

In the previous and following examples, the white space in the headers is composed of single TABS so that the heads line up with the columns of data.

```
$ cat a2

BEGIN      {
print "Make        Model     Year      Miles      Price"
print "----------------------------------------------"
}
           {print}
```

```
$ awk -f a2 cars
Make       Model    Year     Miles    Price
-----------------------------------------
plym       fury     77       73       2500
chevy      nova     79       60       3000
ford       mustang  65       45       10000
volvo      gl       78       102      9850
ford       ltd      83       15       10500
chevy      nova     80       50       3500
fiat       600      65       115      450
honda      accord   81       30       6000
ford       thundbd  84       10       17000
toyota     tercel   82       180      750
chevy      impala   65       85       1550
ford       bronco   83       25       9500
```

When you call the **length** function without an argument, it returns the number of characters in the current line, including field separators. The **$0** variable always has the value of the current line. In the next example, a pipe sends the output from awk to sort so that the lines of the **cars** file appear in order of length. Because the formatting of the report depends on TABS, including three extra characters at the beginning of each line

throws off the format of some lines. A remedy for this situation
will be covered shortly.

```
$ awk  '{print length, $0}'  cars | sort
19 fiat  600      65        115     450
20 ford  ltd      83         15     10500
20 plym  fury     77         73     2500
20 volvo          gl         78     102       9850
21 chevy          nova       79     60        3000
21 chevy          nova       80     50        3500
22 ford  bronco   83         25     9500
23 chevy          impala     65     85        1550
23 honda          accord     81     30        6000
24 ford  mustang  65         45     10000
24 ford  thundbd  84         10     17000
24 toyota         tercel     82     180       750
```

The **NR** variable contains the record (line) number of the
current line. The following pattern selects all lines that contain
more that 23 characters. The action prints the line number of all
the selected lines.

```
$ awk  'length > 23 {print NR}'  cars
3
9
10
```

You can combine the range operator (,) and the **NR** variable
to display a group of lines of a file based on their line numbers.
The next example displays lines 2 through 4.

```
$ awk  'NR == 2 , NR == 4'  cars
chevy    nova    79      60      3000
ford     mustang 65      45      10000
volvo    gl      78      102     9850
```

The **END** pattern works in a manner similar to the **BEGIN**
pattern, except awk takes the actions associated with it after it
has processed the last of its input lines. The following report only
displays information after it has processed the entire data file.
The **NR** variable retains its value after awk has finished processing the data file so an action associated with an **END** pattern can
use it.

```
$ awk  'END {print NR, "cars for sale."}'  cars
12 cars for sale.
```

The next example uses If commands to change the values of some of the first fields. As long as awk doesn't make any changes to a record, it leaves the entire record, including separators, intact. Once it makes a change to a record, it changes all separators in that record to the default. The default output field separator is a SPACE.

```
$ cat a3
    {
    if ($1 ~ /ply/)  $1 = "plymouth"
    if ($1 ~ /chev/) $1 = "chevrolet"
    print
    }
```

```
$ awk -f a3 cars
plymouth fury 77 73 2500
chevrolet nova 79 60 3000
ford      mustang 65      45      10000
volvo     gl      78      102     9850
ford      ltd     83      15      10500
chevrolet nova 80 50 3500
fiat      600     65      115     450
honda     accord  81      30      6000
ford      thundbd 84      10      17000
toyota    tercel  82      180     750
chevrolet impala 65 85 1550
ford      bronco  83      25      9500
```

You can change the default value of the output field separator by assigning a value to the **OFS** variable. There is one TAB character between the quotation marks in the following example.

This fix improves the appearance of the report but does not properly line up the columns.

```
$ cat a4
BEGIN   {OFS = "          "}
        {
        if ($1 ~ /ply/)  $1 = "plymouth"
        if ($1 ~ /chev/) $1 = "chevrolet"
        print
        }
```

```
$ awk −f a4 cars
plymouth            fury       77       73       2500
chevrolet           nova       79       60       3000
ford        mustang 65         45       10000
volvo       gl      78         102      9850
ford        ltd     83         15       10500
chevrolet           nova       80       50       3500
fiat        600     65         115      450
honda       accord  81         30       6000
ford        thundbd 84         10       17000
toyota      tercel  82         180      750
chevrolet           impala     65       85       1550
ford        bronco  83         25       9500
```

You can use Printf to refine the output format (refer to page 337). (The following example uses a backslash at the end of a program line to mask the following NEWLINE from awk. You can use this technique to continue a long line over one or more lines without affecting the outcome of the program.)

```
$ cat a5
BEGIN {
        print "                                      Miles"
        print "Make        Model        Year      (000)              Price"
        print "-----------------------------------------------------------"
        }
        {
        if ($1 ~ /ply/)  $1 = "plymouth"
        if ($1 ~ /chev/) $1 = "chevrolet"
        printf ."%−10s %−8s      19%2d      %5d      $ %8.2f\n",\
                $1, $2, $3, $4, $5
        }
```

```
$ awk −f a5 cars
                                   Miles
Make        Model        Year     (000)            Price
- - - - - - - - - - - - - - - - - - - - - - - - - - - - - -
plymouth    fury         1977        73      $    2500.00
chevrolet   nova         1979        60      $    3000.00
ford        mustang      1965        45      $   10000.00
volvo       gl           1978       102      $    9850.00
ford        ltd          1983        15      $   10500.00
chevrolet   nova         1980        50      $    3500.00
fiat        600          1965       115      $     450.00
honda       accord       1981        30      $    6000.00
ford        thundbd      1984        10      $   17000.00
toyota      tercel       1982       180      $     750.00
chevrolet   impala       1965        85      $    1550.00
ford        bronco       1983        25      $    9500.00
```

The next example creates two new files, one with all the lines that contain chevy and the other with lines containing ford.

```
$ cat a18
/chevy/          {print > "chevfile"}
/ford/           {print > "fordfile"}
END              {print "done."}


$ awk -f a18 cars
done.


$ cat chevfile
chevy   nova    79      60      3000
chevy   nova    80      50      3500
chevy   impala  65      85      1550
```

The **a6** program produces a summary report on all cars and newer cars. The first two lines of declarations are not required; awk automatically declares and initializes variables as you use them. After awk reads all the input data, it computes and displays averages.

```
$ cat a6
BEGIN   {
        yearsum = 0 ; costsum = 0
        newcostsum = 0 ; newcount = 0
        }
        {
        yearsum += $3
        costsum += $5
        }
$3 > 80 {newcostsum += $5 ; newcount ++}
END     {
        printf "Average age of cars is %3.1f years\n",\
                84 - (yearsum/NR)
        printf "Average cost of cars is $%7.2f\n",\
                costsum/NR
        printf "Average cost of newer cars is $%7.2f\n",\
                newcostsum/newcount
        }

$ awk -f a6 cars
Average age of cars is 7.2 years
Average cost of cars is $6216.67
Average cost of newer cars is $8750.00
```

Following, grep shows the format of a line from the **passwd** file that the next example uses.

```
$ grep ´sobell´ /etc/passwd
mark:gKnL.E8DLFamM:107:101:mark sobell:/z/mark:/bin/csh
```

The next example demonstrates a technique for finding the largest number in a field. Because it needs to work with the **passwd** file, which delimits fields with colons (:), it changes the input field separator (**FS**) before reading any data. This example reads the **passwd** file and determines the next available user ID number (field 3). The numbers do not have to be in order in the **passwd** file for this program to work.

The pattern causes awk to select records that contain a user ID number greater than any previous user ID number that it has processed. Each time it selects a record, it assigns the value of the new user ID number to the **saveit** variable. Then awk uses the new value of **saveit** to test the user ID of all subsequent records.

Finally, awk adds 1 to the value of **saveit** and displays the result.

```
$ cat a7
BEGIN               {FS = ":"
                     saveit = 0}
$3 > saveit          {saveit = $3}
END                  {print "Next UID is " saveit + 1}

$ awk −f a7 /etc/passwd
Next UID is 192
```

The next example shows another report based on the **cars** file. This report uses nested If Else statements to substitute values based on the contents of the price field. The program has no pattern part—it processes every record.

```
$ cat a8
{
if ($5 <= 5000) $5 = "inexpensive"
else if ($5 > 5000 && $5 < 10000) $5 = "please ask"
else if ($5 >= 10000) $5 = "expensive"
printf "%−10s %−8s     19%2d     %5d     %−12s\n",\
        $1, $2, $3, $4, $5
}
```

```
$ awk -f a8 cars
plym        fury        1977         73      inexpensive
chevy       nova        1979         60      inexpensive
ford        mustang     1965         45      expensive
volvo       gl          1978        102      please ask
ford        ltd         1983         15      expensive
chevy       nova        1980         50      inexpensive
fiat        600         1965        115      inexpensive
honda       accord      1981         30      please ask
ford        thundbd     1984         10      expensive
toyota      tercel      1982        180      inexpensive
chevy       impala      1965         85      inexpensive
ford        bronco      1983         25      please ask
```

Below, the **manuf** associative array uses the contents of the first field of each record in the **cars** file as an index. The array is composed of the elements **manuf[plym]**, **manuf[chevy]**, **manuf[ford]**, and so on. The ++ C language operator increments the variable that it follows. The action following the **END** pattern is the special For structure that loops through the elements of an associative array.

This example is a Shell script (see Chapter 8) that calls **awk** and includes the **awk** program and the name of the file that **awk** will process. A pipe sends the output through **sort** to produce an alphabetical list of cars and the quantities in stock.

```
$ cat a10
awk '            {manuf[$1]++}
END       {for (name in manuf) print name, manuf[name]}
' cars |
sort

$ a10
chevy 3
fiat 1
ford 4
honda 1
plym 1
toyota 1
volvo 1
```

The **a11** program is a more complete Shell script that includes error checking. This script lists and counts the contents of a column in a file, with both the column number and the name of the file specified on the command line.

The first **awk** action (the one that starts with {count) uses the Shell variable **$1** in the middle of the **awk** program to specify an array index. The single quotation marks cause the Shell to substitute the value of the first command line argument in place of **$1**.

The leading dollar sign (the one before the first single quotation mark) causes awk to interpret what the Shell substitutes as a field number. Refer to Chapter 8 for more information on Shell scripts.

```
$ cat a11
if (test "$1" = "") then
        echo "You must supply an argument."
        exit
fi
awk < $2 '
        {count[$'$1']++}
END     {for (item in count) printf "%-20s%-20s\n",\
                item, count[item]}' |
sort


$ a11
You must supply an argument.


$ a11 1 cars
chevy           3
fiat            1
ford            4
honda           1
plym            1
toyota          1
volvo           1


$ a11 3 cars
65              3
77              1
78              1
79              1
80              1
81              1
82              1
83              2
84              1
```

The **a12** program displays a word usage list for a file you specify on the command line. The deroff utility removes nroff and troff commands from a file and, with the **−w** option, lists the words one to a line. The sort utility orders the file with the most frequently used words at the top of the list. It sorts groups of words that are used the same number of times in alphabetical order. Refer to sort in Part II for more information.

```
$ cat a12
deroff -w $* |
awk         '
            {count[$1]++}
END         {for (item in count) printf "%-15s%3s\n",\
                         item, count[item]}' |
sort +1nr +0f -1
```

```
$ a12 textfile
the             42
file            29
fsck            27
system          22
you             22
to              21
it              17
SIZE            14
and             13
MODE            13
 .
 .
 .
```

Below is a similar program in a different format. The format mimics that of a C program and may be easier to read and work with for more complex awk programs.

```
$ cat a13
deroff -w $* |
awk ' {
    count[$1]++
}
END {
    for (item in count)
        {
        if (count[item] > 4)
            {
            printf "%-15s%3s\n", item, count[item]
            }
        }
} ' |
sort +1nr +0f -1
```

The tail utility displays the last ten lines of output.

```
$ a13 textfile | tail
directories     5
if              5
information     5
INODE           5
more            5
no              5
on              5
response        5
this            5
will            5
```

The next example shows one way to put a date on a report. The first line of input to the awk program comes from date. The awk program reads this line as record number 1 (NR == 1) and processes it accordingly. It processes all subsequent records with the action associated with the next pattern (NR > 1). The script then sorts the output numerically.

```
$ cat a15
if (test $# = 0) then
    echo "You must supply a filename."
    exit
fi
(date; cat $*) |
awk '
NR == 1      {print "Report for", $1, $2, $3 ", " $6}
NR > 1       {print $5 "     " $1}
' | sort −n
```

```
$ a15 cars
Report for Mon Dec 3, 1984
450        fiat
750        toyota
1550       chevy
2500       plym
3000       chevy
3500       chevy
6000       honda
9500       ford
9850       volvo
10000      ford
10500      ford
17000      ford
```

The next example uses the **numbers** file and sums each of the columns in a file you specify on the command line. It performs error checking, discarding fields that contain nonnumeric entries. It also displays a grand total for the file.

```
$ cat numbers
10          20          30.3        40.5
20          30          45.7        66.1
30          xyz         50          70
40          75          107.2       55.6
50          20          30.3        40.5
60          30          45.O        66.1
70          1134.7      50          70
80          75          107.2       55.6
90          176         30.3        40.5
100         1027.45     45.7        66.1
110         123         50          57a.5
120         75          107.2       55.6
```

```
$ cat a19
awk '       BEGIN {
                ORS = ""
                }
NR == 1     {
        nfields = NF
        }
        {
        if ($0 ~ /[^0-9. \t]/)
                {
                print "\nRecord " NR " skipped:\n\t"
                print $0 "\n"
                next
                }
        else
                {
                for (count = 1; count <= nfields; count++)
                        {
                        printf "%10.2f", $count > "b10.out"
                        sum[count] += $count
                        gtotal += $count
                        }
                print "\n" > "b10.out"
                }
        }
END     {
        for (count = 1; count <= nfields; count++)
                {
                print "   -------" > "b10.out"
                }
        print "\n" > "b10.out"
        for (count = 1; count <= nfields; count++)
                {
                printf "%10.2f", sum[count] > "b10.out"
                }
        print "\n\n          Grand Total " gtotal "\n" > "b10.out"
} ' < numbers
```

```
$ a19
Record 3 skipped:
          30          xyz         50          70

Record 6 skipped:
          60          30          45.O        66.1

Record 11 skipped:
          110         123         50          57a.5
$ cat b10.out
          10.00       20.00       30.30       40.50
          20.00       30.00       45.70       66.10
          40.00       75.00      107.20       55.60
          50.00       20.00       30.30       40.50
          70.00     1134.70       50.00       70.00
          80.00       75.00      107.20       55.60
          90.00      176.00       30.30       40.50
         100.00     1027.45       45.70       66.10
         120.00       75.00      107.20       55.60
         -------     -------     -------     -------
         580.00     2633.15      553.90      490.50

         Grand Total 4257.55
```

The next awk example reads the **passwd** file. It lists users who do not have passwords and users who have duplicate user ID numbers.

```
$ cat passwd
bill::102:100:ext 123:/usr/bill:/bin/sh
roy:QpMB2EaP.zANA:104:100:ext 475:/usr/roy:/bin/sh
tom:QBaUycsXmi9mk:105:100:ext 476:/usr/tom:/bin/sh
lynn:.BhVeaghQ045s:166:100:ext 500:/usr/lynn:/bin/sh
mark:gKBLaE8DLFamM:107:100:ext 112:/usr/mark:/bin/sh
sales:zBKaNBGoJ.29o:108:100:ext 102:/m/market:/bin/sh
anne:7lBNXqWaSWgOk:109:100:ext 355:/usr/anne:/bin/sh
toni::164:100:ext 357:/usr/toni:/bin/sh
ginny:tBitPlajFWa.l:115:100:ext 109:/usr/ginny:/bin/sh
chuck:JBwaFE/5XJYrE:116:100:ext 146:/usr/chuck:/bin/sh
neil:7TBaVtLZarhS6:164:100:ext 159:/usr/neil:/bin/sh
rmi:T3aBxazCvnqz2:118:100:ext 178:/usr/rmi:/bin/sh
vern:aBlncbxAa9eDs:119:100:ext 201:/usr/vern:/bin/sh
bob:nsjBgab1dvsmQ:120:100:ext 227:/usr/bob:/bin/sh
janet:TBQ65yZYaOqjl:122:100:ext 229:/usr/janet:/bin/sh
maggie:BWabz/pGLkb6g:124:100:ext 244:/usr/maggie:/bin/sh
dan::126:100::/usr/dan:/bin/sh
dave:5JBELKmauB4/s:108:100:ext 427:/usr/dave:/bin/sh
mary:rlBYnLS/LD9B6:129:100:ext 303:/usr/mary:/bin/sh
```

```
$ cat a20
awk < passwd ´   BEGIN {
        uid[void] = ""          # tell awk that uid is an array
        }
        {                       # no pattern indicates process all records
        dup = 0                         # initialize duplicate flag
        split($0, field, ":") # split into fields delimited by ":"
        if (field[2] == "") # check for null password field
                {
                if (field[5] == "") # check for null info field
                        {
                        print field[1] " has no password."
                        }
                else
                        {
                        print field[1] " ("field[5]") has no password."
                        }
                }
        for (name in uid)       # loop through uid array
                {
                if (uid[name] == field[3]) # check for 2nd use of UID
                        {
                        print field[1] " has the same UID as "\
                                name " : UID = " uid[name]
                        dup = 1         # set duplicate flag
                        }
                }
        if (!dup)       # same as: if (dup == 0)
                        # assign UID and login name to uid array
                {
                uid[field[1]] = field[3]
                }
```

```
$ a20
bill (ext 123) has no password.
toni (ext 357) has no password.
neil has the same UID as toni : UID = 164
dan has no password.
dave has the same UID as sales : UID = 108
```

The final example shows a complete interactive Shell script
that uses awk to generate a report.

```
$ cat list_cars

trap 'rm —f $$.tem > /dev/null ; echo $0 aborted. ; exit 1' 1 2 15
echo "Price range (e.g., 5000 7500): \c"
read lowrange hirange


echo '
                                Miles
Make          Model      Year  (000)        Price
------------------------------------------------' > $$.tem
awk < cars '
$5 >= '$lowrange' && $5 <= '$hirange' {
        if ($1 ~ /ply/)  $1 = "plymouth"
        if ($1 ~ /chev/) $1 = "chevrolet"
        printf "%—10s %-8s    19%2d    %5d    $ %8.2f\n",\
            $1, $2, $3, $4, $5
        }' | sort —n +5 >> $$.tem
cat $$.tem
rm $$.tem


$ list_cars
Price range (e.g., 5000 7500): 3000 8000

                                Miles
Make          Model      Year  (000)        Price
----------------------------------------------------
chevrolet     nova       1979     60     $   3000.00
chevrolet     nova       1980     50     $   3500.00
honda         accord     1981     30     $   6000.00


$ list_cars
Price range (e.g., 5000 7500): 0 2000

                                Miles
Make          Model      Year  (000)        Price
----------------------------------------------------
fiat          600        1965    115     $    450.00
toyota        tercel     1982    180     $    750.00
chevrolet     impala     1965     85     $   1550.00


$ list_cars
Price range (e.g., 5000 7500): 15000 100000

                                Miles
Make          Model      Year  (000)        Price
----------------------------------------------------
ford          thundbd    1984     10     $  17000.00
```

Error Messages

The following examples show some of the more common causes of awk's infamous error messages (and nonmessages).

The first example leaves the single quotation marks off the command line, so the Shell interprets $3 and $1 as Shell variables. Another problem is that, because there are no single quotation marks, the Shell passes awk four arguments instead of two.

```
$ awk {print $3, $1} cars
awk: syntax error near line 1
awk: illegal statement near line 1
$
```

The next command line includes a typo that awk does not catch (prinnt). Instead of issuing an error message, awk just doesn't do anything.

```
$ awk '$3 >= 83 {prinnt $1}' cars
$
```

No braces around the action:

```
$ awk '/chevy/ print $3, $1' cars
awk: syntax error near line 1
awk: bailing out near line 1
$
```

There is no problem with the next example, awk did just what you asked it to. (None of the lines in the file contained a z).

```
$ awk '/z/' cars
$
```

The following program contains an improper action (the Print command is probably missing).

```
$ awk '{$3}' cars
awk: illegal statement 56250
 record number 1
$
```

Another improper action, but this time awk didn't issue an error message.

```
$ awk ´{$3 " made by " $1}´ cars
$
```

Following is a format that awk didn't particularly care for. Sometimes just changing the positions of the braces can fix a problem such as this one.

```
$ cat a9
BEGIN              {print
"Make    Model    Year    Miles    Price"}
                   {print}

$ awk —f a9 cars
awk: illegal statement 57422
$
```

You must use double quotation marks, not single quotation marks, to delimit strings.

```
$ awk ´$3 ~ /5$/ {print $3, $1, ´$´ $5}´ cars
awk: trying to access field 10000
  record number 3
$
```

cal

Display a calendar.

Format

cal [month] year

Summary

The cal utility displays a calendar for a month or year.

Options

There are no options.

Arguments

The arguments specify the month and year cal displays a calendar for. The **month** is a decimal integer from 1 to 12, and the **year** is a decimal integer.

Notes

Do not abbreviate the year. The year 85 does not represent the same year as 1985.

Examples

The following command displays a calendar for November 1982.

```
$ cal 11 1982
      November 1982
 S   M Tu  W Th   F   S
     1   2   3   4   5   6
 7   8   9  10  11  12  13
14  15  16  17  18  19  20
21  22  23  24  25  26  27
28  29  30
```

The next command displays a calendar for all of 1949.

```
$ cal 1949
                         1949

           Jan                      Feb                      Mar
   S   M Tu  W Th   F   S    S   M Tu  W Th   F   S    S   M Tu  W Th   F   S
                        1        1   2   3   4   5            1   2   3   4   5
   2   3   4   5   6   7   8    6   7   8   9  10  11  12    6   7   8   9  10  11  12
   9  10  11  12  13  14  15   13  14  15  16  17  18  19   13  14  15  16  17  18  19
  16  17  18  19  20  21  22   20  21  22  23  24  25  26   20  21  22  23  24  25  26
  23  24  25  26  27  28  29   27  28                       27  28  29  30  31
  30  31
           Apr                      May                      Jun
   S   M Tu  W Th   F   S    S   M Tu  W Th   F   S    S   M Tu  W Th   F   S
                    1   2    1   2   3   4   5   6   7                1   2   3   4
   3   4   5   6   7   8   9    8   9  10  11  12  13  14    5   6   7   8   9  10  11
   .
   .
   .
$
```

calendar

Reminder calendar

Format
(Not normally called by the user.)

Summary
The UNIX system provides calendar as a service. Once a day, this utility reviews the file named **calendar** in each user's home directory and sends any line containing that or the next day's date to that user using the mail utility.

Options and Arguments
There are no options or arguments.

Notes
During the weekend, the *next day* goes through Monday.

The **calendar** file *must* be in your home directory and must have read access permission for everyone. The dates can appear anywhere on the line in the file, in various formats, but must show the month preceding the day of the month.

When you execute calendar, or have your **.profile** or .login file execute it, calendar displays any lines in the **calendar** file that contain that or the next day's date.

The calendar utility ignores a year as part of the date.

Example
The following example of a **calendar** file shows some of the ways you can express the date. If you place this file in your home directory, each of the three lines will be sent to you by mail on the date you specify and one day previous to it.

```
$ cat calendar
This line will be displayed on 11/20
Nov 28: remember to call Frank
On November 30 five years ago...
$
```

cancel

Cancel a printing job.

Format

cancel job-identification

Summary

The cancel utility aborts a printing job that you started with lp.

Options

There are no options.

Arguments

The **job-identification** is the unique identification number that lp displayed when you started the job. You can use lpstat to determine the identification number of a printing job that you started with lp.

Notes

The cancel utility will not abort a printing job that you started with lpr.

Example

The following command cancels printing job number 579 on printer__1.

```
$ cancel printer_1-579
$
```

cat

Join or display files.

Format

> cat [options] [file-list]

Summary

The cat utility joins plain text files end to end. It takes its input from files you specify on the command line or from its standard input.

You can use cat to display the contents of one or more files on the terminal.

Options

-e   This option marks the ends of lines with dollar signs. In order for this option to work, you must use it with the **-v** option.

-s   This option causes cat not to display a message when it cannot find a file.

-t   This option marks TABs with ^Is. In order for this option to work, you must use it with the **-v** option.

-u   This option causes cat not to buffer output.

-v   This option causes cat to display nonprinting characters other than TABs, NEWLINEs, and FORM-FEEDs. It also allows the **-t** and **-e** options to function.

Arguments

The **file-list** is composed of pathnames of one or more plain text files that cat displays. You can use a hyphen in place of a filename to cause cat to read its standard input [e.g., **cat a − b** gets its input from file **a**, its standard input (terminated by a CONTROL-D if you enter it at the keyboard), and then file **b**].

Notes

Use the od utility (also covered in Part II) to display the contents of a file that does not contain text (e.g., an executable program file).

The name cat is derived from one of the functions of this utility, *catenate*, which means to join together sequentially, or end to end.

Caution.   Despite cat's warning message, a command line such as the following destroys the input file (**letter**) before reading it.

```
$ cat memo letter > letter
cat: input letter is output
$
```

Examples

The following command line displays the contents of the text file named **memo** on the terminal.

```
$ cat memo
   .
   .
   .
$
```

The next example catenates three files and redirects the output to a file named **all**.

```
$ cat page1 letter memo > all
$
```

You can use cat to create short text files without using an editor. Enter the command line shown below, type the text that you want in the file, and then press CONTROL-D on a line by itself. The cat utility takes its input from its standard input (the terminal), and the Shell redirects its standard output (a copy of the input) to the file you specify. The CONTROL-D signals the end of file and causes cat to return control to the Shell. (Also see page 79.)

```
$ cat > new_file
.
.
.
(text)
.
.
.
CONTROL-D
$
```

Below, a pipe redirects the output from who to the standard input of cat. The cat utility creates the **output** file that contains the contents of the **header** file, the output of who, and finally, **footer**. The hyphen on the command line causes cat to read its standard input after reading **header** and before reading **footer**.

```
$ who | cat header — footer > output
$
```

C compiler

Format

cc [options] file-list

Summary

Based on the command line options, cc compiles, assembles, and loads C language source programs. It can also assemble and load assembly language source programs or merely load object programs.

The cc utility uses the following filenaming conventions.

➡ A filename extension of **.c** indicates a C language source program.

➡ A filename extension of **.s** indicates an assembly language source program.

➡ A filename extension of **.o** indicates an object program.

The cc utility takes its input from files you specify on the command line. Unless you use the **−o** option, cc stores the executable program it produces in **a.out**.

Options

Without any options, cc accepts C language source programs, assembly language source programs, and object programs that follow the filenaming conventions outlined above. It compiles, assembles, and loads these programs as appropriate, producing an executable file named **a.out**. The cc utility puts the object programs in files with the same base filename as their source, but with a filename extension of **.o**. If you compile, assemble, and load a single C program with one command, cc deletes the object program.

-c   (compile) Do not load object files. This option causes cc to compile and/or assemble source programs and leave the corresponding object programs in files with filename extensions of **.o**.

-o**file**   (output) Place executable program in **file** instead of **a.out**. You can use any filename in place of **file**.

-O   (optimize) Optimize C source program compilation.

-S   (compile only) Only compile C source programs. This option causes cc to compile C programs and leave the corresponding assembly language source programs in files with filename extensions of **.s**.

-l**arg**   (search library) Search both the /lib/lib**arg**.a and the /usr/lib/lib**arg**.a libraries and load any required functions. You must replace **arg** with the name of the library you want to search. For example, the **−lm** option normally loads the standard math library.

      The position of this option is significant; it generally needs to go at the end of the command line. The loader only uses the library to resolve undefined symbols from modules that *precede* the library option on the command line.

Arguments

The **file-list** contains the pathnames of the programs that cc is to compile, assemble, and/or load.

Examples

The first example compiles, assembles, and loads a single C program, **compute.c**. The executable output is put in **a.out**. The cc utility deletes the object file.

```
$ cc compute.c
$
```

The next example compiles the same program using the C optimizer (**−O** option). It assembles and then loads the optimized code. The **−o** option causes cc to put the executable output in **compute**.

```
$ cc −O compute.c −o compute
$
```

Next, a C program, an assembly language program, and an object program are compiled, assembled, and loaded. The executable output goes to **progo**.

```
$ cc procom.c profast.s proout.o −o progo
$
```

Finally, cc searches the standard math library stored in **/lib/libm.a** when it is loading the **himath** program. It places the executable output in **a.out**.

```
$ cc himath.c −lm
$
```

cd

Change to another working directory.

Format

cd [directory]

Summary

When you call cd and specify a directory, that directory becomes the working directory. If you do not specify a directory on the command line, cd makes your home directory the working directory.

Options

There are no options.

Argument

The **directory** is the pathname of the directory that you want to become the working directory.

Notes

The cd program is not really a utility but a built-in command in both the C and Bourne Shells. Refer to the discussion of the **HOME** Bourne Shell variable in Chapter 8 and the **home** C Shell variable in Chapter 9. Chapter 4 contains a discussion of cd.

Examples

The following command makes your home directory become the working directory.

```
$ cd
$
```

The next command makes the **/usr/alex/literature** directory the working directory. The pwd utility verifies the change.

```
$ cd /usr/alex/literature
$ pwd
/usr/alex/literature
$
```

Next, cd makes a subdirectory of the working directory the new working directory.

```
$ cd memos
$
```

Finally, cd uses the .. reference to the parent of the working directory to make the parent the new working directory.

```
$ cd ..
```

chgrp

Change the group that is associated with a file.

Format

chgrp group file-list

Summary

The chgrp utility changes the group that is associated with the file.

Options

There are no options.

Arguments

The **group** is the name or numeric group ID of the new group. The **file-list** is a list of pathnames of the files whose group association you want to change.

Notes

Only the owner of a file, or the Superuser, can change the group association of a file.

Example

The following command changes the group that the **manuals** file is associated with. The new group is **pubs**.

```
$ chgrp pubs manuals
$
```

Change the access mode of a file.

Format

chmod who[operation][permission] file-list

chmod mode file-list

Summary

The chmod utility changes the ways in which a file can be accessed by the owner of the file, the group to which the owner belongs, and/or all other users. Only the owner of a file or the Superuser can change the access mode, or permissions, of a file.

You can specify the new access mode absolutely or symbolically.

Options

There are no options.

Arguments

Arguments give chmod information about which files are to have their modes changed in what way.

Symbolic. The chmod utility changes the access permission for the class of user specified by **who**. The class of user is designated by one or more of the following letters.

u   (user) owner of the file
g   (group) group to which the owner belongs
o   (other) all other users
a   (all) can be used in place of **u**, **g**, and **o** above

The **operation** to be performed is defined by the following list.

+ add permission for the specified user
− remove permission for the specified user
= set permission for the specified user—reset all other permissions for that user

The access **permission** is defined by the following list.

r read permission
w write permission
x execute permission
s set user ID or set group ID (depending on the **who** argument) to that of the owner of the file while the file is being executed
t set the sticky bit—see page 561 (use with **u** only)

Absolute. In place of the symbolic method of changing the access permissions for a file, you can use an octal number to represent the mode. Construct the number by ORing the appropriate values from the following table. (To OR two octal numbers from the following table, you can just add them. Refer to the second following table for examples.)

Number	Meaning
4000	set user ID when the program is executed
2000	set group ID when the program is executed
1000	sticky bit
0400	owner can read the file
0200	owner can write to the file
0100	owner can execute the file
0040	group can read the file
0020	group can write to the file
0010	group can execute the file
0004	others can read the file
0002	others can write to the file
0001	others can execute the file

The following table lists some typical modes.

Mode	Meaning
0777	owner, group, and public can read, write, and execute file
0744	owner can read, write, and execute; group and public can read file
0644	owner can read and write; group and public can read file
0711	owner can read, write, and execute; group and public can execute file

Notes

You can use the ls utility (with the —l option) to display file access privileges (page 428).

Chapter 4 contains a discussion of file access privileges.

When you are using symbolic arguments, the only time you can omit the **permission** from the command line is when the **operation** is =. This omission takes away all permissions.

Examples

The following examples show how to use the chmod utility to change permissions on a file named **temp**. The initial access mode of **temp** is shown by ls.

```
$ ls —l temp
-rw-rw-r-- 1 alex   pubs        57  Dec   5 16:47 temp
$
```

The command line below removes all access permissions for the group and all other users so that only the owner has access to the file. When you do not follow an equal sign with a permission, chmod removes all permissions for the specified user class. The ls utility verifies the change.

```
$ chmod go= temp

$ ls —l temp
-rw------- 1 alex   pubs        57  Dec   5 16:47 temp
$
```

The next command changes the access modes for all users

(user, group, and all others) to read and write. Now anyone can read from or write to the file. Again, ls verifies the change.

```
$ chmod a=rw temp

$ ls -l temp
-rw-rw-rw- 1 alex    pubs        57 Dec  5 16:47 temp
$
```

Using an absolute argument, the **a=rw** becomes **666**. The next command performs the same function as the previous **chmod** command.

```
$ chmod 666 temp
$
```

The following command removes the write access privilege for all other users. This change means that members of the owner's group can still read from and write to the file, but other users can only read from the file.

```
$ chmod o-w temp

$ ls -l temp
-rw-rw-r-- 1 alex    pubs        57 Dec  5 16:47 temp
$
```

The same command using an absolute argument is shown below.

```
$ chmod 664 temp
$
```

The final command adds execute access privilege for all other users. If **temp** is a Shell script or other executable file, all other users can now execute it.

```
$ chmod o+x temp

$ ls -l temp
-rw-rw-r-x 1 alex    pubs        57 Dec  5 16:47 temp
$
```

Again, the absolute form of the same command:

```
$ chmod 665 temp
$
```

chown

Change the owner of a file.

Format

chown owner file-list

Summary

The chown utility changes the owner of a file.

Options

There are no options.

Arguments

The **owner** is the name or numeric user ID of the new owner. The **file-list** is a list of pathnames of the files whose ownership you want to change.

Notes

Only the owner of a file, or the Superuser, can change the ownership of a file.

Example

The following command changes the owner of the **chapter1** file in the **manuals** directory. The new owner is **jenny**.

```
$ chown jenny manuals/chapter1
```

Compare files.

Format

comm [options] file1 file2

Summary

The comm utility displays a line-by-line comparison of two sorted files. (If the files have not been sorted, comm will not work properly.) The display is in three columns. The first column lists all lines found only in **file1**, the second column lists lines found only in **file2**, and the third lists those common to both files.

Input comes from the files you specify on the command line. (Refer to "Arguments" below for an exception.)

Options

You can use the options **−1**, **−2**, and **−3** individually or in combination.

−1   comm does not display column 1 (does not display lines it finds only in **file1**).

−2   comm does not display column 2 (does not display lines it finds only in **file2**).

−3   comm does not display column 3 (does not display lines it finds in both files).

Arguments

The **file1** and **file2** are pathnames of the files that comm compares. You can use a hyphen in place of **file1** or **file2** to cause comm to use its standard input.

Examples

The following examples use two files, **c** and **d**, that are in the working directory. The contents of these files are shown below. As with all input to comm, the files are in sorted order. Refer to the sort utility for information on sorting files.

File c	**File d**
bbbbb	aaaaa
ccccc	ddddd
ddddd	eeeee
eeeee	ggggg
fffff	hhhhh

The first command (below) calls comm without any options so it displays three columns. The first column lists those lines found only in file **c**, the second column lists those found in **d**, and the third lists the lines found in both **c** and **d**.

```
$ comm c d
        aaaaa
bbbbb
ccccc
                        ddddd
                        eeeee
fffff
        ggggg
        hhhhh
$
```

The next example shows the use of options to prevent comm from displaying columns 1 and 2. The result is column 3, a list of the lines common to files **c** and **d**.

```
$ comm −12 c d
ddddd
eeeee
$
```

cp

Copy one or more files.

Format

cp source-file destination-file

cp source-file-list destination-directory

Summary

The cp utility copies one or more plain files, including text and executable program files. It has two modes of operation. The first copies one file to another, while the second copies one or more files to a directory.

Options

There are no options.

Arguments

The **source-file** is the pathname of the plain file that cp is going to copy. The **destination-file** is the pathname that cp will assign to the resulting copy of the file.

The **source-file-list** is one or more pathnames of plain files that cp is going to copy. The **destination-directory** is the pathname of the directory that cp places the resulting copied files in. When you specify a **destination-directory**, cp gives each of the copied files the same simple filename as its **source-file**. If, for example, you copy the text file **/usr/jenny/memo.416** to the **/usr/jenny/archives** directory, the copy will also have the simple filename **memo.416**, but the new pathname that cp gives it will be **/usr/jenny/archives/memo.416**.

Notes

If the **destination-file** exists before you execute cp, cp overwrites the file, destroying the contents but leaving the access privileges and owner associated with the file as they were. If it does not exist, the access privileges for, and the owner of, the **destination-file** are the same as those of the **source-file**.

Examples

The first command makes a copy of the file **letter** in the working directory. The name of the copy is **letter.sav**.

```
$ cp letter letter.sav
$
```

The next command copies all the files with filenames ending in **.c** into the **archives** file, a subdirectory of the working directory. The copied files each maintain their simple filenames but have new absolute pathnames.

```
$ cp *.c archives
$
```

The next example copies **memo** from the **/usr/jenny** directory to the working directory.

```
$ cp /usr/jenny/memo .
$
```

The final command copies two files named **memo** and **letter** into another directory. The copies have the same simple filenames as the source files (**memo** and **letter**) but have different absolute pathnames. The absolute pathnames of the copied files are **/usr/jenny/memo** and **/usr/jenny/letter**.

```
$ cp memo letter /usr/jenny
$
```

cpio

Store and retrieve files in an archive format.

Format

cpio −o[options]
cpio −i[options] [patterns]
cpio −p[options] directory

Summary

The cpio utility has three functions. It copies one or more files into a single archive file, retrieves specified files from an archive file it previously created, and copies directories. If you specify a tape or other removable media file, you can use cpio to create backup copies of files, to transport files to other, compatible systems, and to create archives.

Options

The cpio utility has three major options and several other options that you can use with the major options. You can only use one major option at a time.

Major Options.

−o   (out) This option causes cpio to read its standard input to obtain a list of pathnames of plain files. It combines these files, together with header information, into a single archive file that it copies to its standard output.

−i   (in) This option causes cpio to read its standard input, which cpio must have previously produced with a −o option. It selectively extracts files from its input based on the patterns you give as arguments.
    Files that you stored using relative pathnames will appear in the working directory or a subdirectory. Files stored with absolute pathnames will appear as specified by their absolute pathnames.

381

-p   (pass) This option causes cpio to read its standard input to obtain a list of pathnames of plain files. It copies these files to the directory you give as an argument. This option is useful for copying directories.

Other Options.

-a   (access time) cpio resets the access times of input files after copying them.

-B   (block) This option blocks data written to a raw magnetic tape device at 5120 bytes/record (do not use with the **-p** option).

-d   (directory) cpio creates directories when needed as it is copying files (do not use with the **-o** option).

-c   (compatible) This option causes cpio to write header information in ASCII so that other (compatible) machines can read the file.

-r   (rename) This option allows you to rename files as cpio copies them. Before it copies each file, cpio prompts you with the name of the file—you respond with the new name. If you just press RETURN, cpio will not copy the file.

-t   (table of contents) This option displays a list of files without copying them. When you use this option with the **-v** option, cpio displays a more extensive list.

-u   (unconditional) This option copies older files over newer ones with the same name—without this option, cpio will not overwrite these newer files.

-v   (verbose) This option displays a list of files that cpio is copying.

-l   (link) When possible, this option links files instead of copying them (only for use with the **-p** option).

-m (modification time) This option keeps the original modification time of plain files (not directories).

-f This option copies all files not specified by the patterns (**−i**
option only).

Arguments

The **patterns** specify the files you want to retrieve with the **−i**
option. The patterns take the same form as ambiguous file references for the Shell, with **?**, *****, and **[ ]** matching the slash that
separates files in a pathname.

If you do not specify a pattern, cpio copies all the files.

The **directory** specifies the directory that is to receive the
files that the **−p** option copies.

Examples

The following example copies all the files in the working directory
to the tape on **/dev/rmt/0m**. It does not copy the contents of
subdirectories because ls does not supply the pathnames of files in
subdirectories. When it finishes, cpio displays the number of
blocks it copied.

```
$ ls | cpio −o > /dev/rmt/0m
7 blocks
$
```

The next example copies all the files in the working directory
and all subdirectories. The **−depth** argument causes find to copy
all entries in a directory before copying the directory itself. The
−B option blocks the tape at 5120 bytes/record.

```
$ find . −depth −print | cpio −oB > /dev/rmt/0m
30 blocks
$
```

The following example demonstrates the find **−cpio** option—it
performs the same function as the preceding command line.

```
$ find . −cpio /dev/rmt/0m
$
```

Next, cpio copies all of Alex's home directory and all subdirectories to the floppy disk on device **/dev/ifdsk00** (do not use the **−B** option on any media other than tape).

```
$ find /usr/alex −depth −print | cpio −o > /dev/ifdsk00
293 blocks
$
```

The next command reads back the files that the previous command wrote to the disk. Because cpio will not overwrite newer files with older ones, the following command will not overwrite any files that have been updated since the previous **cpio** command. You can use the **−u** option to overwrite newer files.

```
$ cpio −i < /dev/ifdsk00
$
```

date

Display or set the time and date.

Format

date [newdate]

Summary

The date utility displays the time and date. The Superuser can use it to change the time and date.

Options

There are no options.

Arguments

When the Superuser specifies a **newdate**, the system changes the system clock to reflect the new date. The **newdate** argument has the following format:

nnddhhmm[yy]

The **nn** is the number of the month (01-12), **dd** is the day of the month (01-31), **hh** is the hour based on a 24-hour clock (00-24), **mm** is the minutes (00-60), and **yy** is optional and specifies the last two digits of the year. If you do not specify a year, date assumes the year has not changed.

Example

The following example shows how to set the date for 3:35 P.M. on January 5.

```
# date 01051535
Sat Jan  5 15:35 PST 1985
#
```

Display the amount of available disk space.

Format

df [options] [file-system-list]

Summary

The df (disk free) utility reports how much free space is left on any mounted device or directory. It displays free disk space in terms of blocks (there are usually 1024 bytes per block).

Options

-t   (total) This option causes df to display the number of blocks that are in use as well as the number of free blocks.

-f   (free list) This option displays the number of blocks in the free list only. Without this option, df displays the number of blocks in the free list *and* the number of free inodes. Refer to Chapter 10 for a discussion of inodes and the free list.

Arguments

When you call df without an argument, it reports on the free space on each of the currently mounted devices.

The **file-system-list** is an optional list of one or more path-names that specify the file systems you want a report on. The df utility permits you to refer to a mounted file system by its device pathname *or* by the pathname of the directory it is mounted on.

Example

Below df displays information about the two mounted file systems.

```
$ df
/usr    (/dev/dsk/c1d0s2):   7138 blocks   3077 inodes
/       (/dev/dsk/c1d0s0):   2742 blocks    818 inodes
```

diff

Display the differences between two files.

Format

diff [options] file1 file2

Summary

The diff utility displays the differences between two files on a line-by-line basis. It displays the differences as instructions that you can use to edit one of the files to make it the same as the other.

Input comes from the files you specify on the command line. (Refer to "Arguments" for an exception.)

Options

Without any options, diff produces a series of lines containing Add (**a**), Delete (**d**), and Change (**c**) instructions. Each of these lines is followed by the lines from the file that you need to add, delete, or change. A less-than symbol (<) precedes lines from **file1**. A greater-than symbol (>) precedes lines from **file2**. The diff output is in the format shown below. A pair of line numbers separated by a comma represents a range of lines—diff uses a single line number to represent a single line.

Instruction	Meaning (to change file1 to file2)
line1 a line2,line3 > lines from file2	append lines from **file2** after line1 in **file1**
line1,line2 d line3 < lines from file1	delete line1 through line2 from **file1**
line1,line2 c line3,line4 < lines from file1 ——— > lines from file2	change line1 through line2 in **file1** to lines from **file2**

The diff utility assumes that you are going to convert **file1** to **file2**. The line numbers to the left of each of the **a**, **c**, or **d** instructions always pertain to **file1**; numbers to the right of the instructions apply to **file2**. To convert **file1** to **file2**, ignore the line numbers to the right of the instructions. (To convert **file2** to **file1**, use a **d** in place of each **a**, an **a** in place of each **d**, and use the line numbers to the right of the instructions.)

–e   This option creates a script for the ed editor that will edit **file1** to make it the same as **file2**. You must add **w** (write) and **q** (quit) instructions to the end of the script if you are going to redirect it as input to ed.

Arguments

The **file1** and **file2** are pathnames of the files that diff works on. You can use a hyphen in place of **file1** or **file2** to cause diff to use its standard input.

Examples

The first example shows how diff displays the differences between two short, similar files.

```
$ cat m
aaaaa
bbbbb
ccccc

$ cat n
aaaaa
ccccc

$ diff m n
2d1
< bbbbb
$
```

The difference between files **m** and **n** is that the second line from file **m** (bbbbb) is missing from file **n**. The first line that diff displays (2d1) indicates that you need to delete the second line from file 1 (**m**) to make it the same as file 2 (**n**). Unless you are editing file 2 to make it the same as file 1, ignore the numbers following the letters on the instruction lines. The next line diff displays starts with a less-than symbol (<), indicating that this line of text is from file 1. In this example you do not need this information—all you need to know is the line number so you can delete the line.

The next example uses the same **m** file and a new file, **p**, to demonstrate diff issuing an **a** (append) instruction.

```
$ cat p
aaaaa
bbbbb
rrrrr
ccccc

$ diff m p
2a3
> rrrrr
$
```

In the preceding example, diff issued the instruction 2a3 to indicate that you must append a line to file **m**, after line 2, to make it the same as file **p**. The second line that diff displayed indicates that the line is from file **p** (the line begins with >, indicating file 2). In this example you need the information on this line—the appended line must contain the text rrrrr.

The next example uses **m** again, this time with file **r**, to show how diff indicates a line that needs to be changed.

```
$ cat r
aaaaa
qqqqq
ccccc

$ diff m r
2c2
< bbbbb
———
> qqqqq
$
```

The difference between the two files is in line 2: file **m** contains bbbbb, while file **r** contains qqqqq. Above, diff displays 2c2 to indicate that you need to change line 2. After indicating that a change is needed, diff shows that you must change line 2 in file **m** (bbbbb) to line 2 in file **r** (qqqqq) to make the files the same. The three hyphens indicate the end of the text in file **m** that needs to be changed and the start of the text in file **r** that is to replace it.

Next, a *group* of lines in file **m** needs to be changed to make it the same as file **t**.

```
$ cat t
aaaaa
lllll
hhhhh
nnnnn

$ diff m t
2,3c2,4
< bbbbb
< ccccc
___
> lllll
> hhhhh
> nnnnn
$
```

Above, diff indicates that you need to change lines 2 through 3 (2,3) in file **m** from bbbbb and ccccc to lllll, hhhhh, and nnnnn.

The next set of examples demonstrates how to use diff to keep track of versions of a file that is repeatedly updated, without maintaining a library of each version in its entirety. With the —e option, diff creates a script for the ed editor that can recreate the second file from the first. If you keep a copy of the original file and the ed script that diff creates each time you update the file, you can recreate any version of the file. Because these scripts are usually shorter than the files they are relating, the scripts can help conserve disk space.

In these examples, **menu1** is the original file. When it needs to be updated, it is copied to **menu2** and the changes are made to the copy of the file. The resulting files are shown below.

```
$ cat menu1
BREAKFAST
        scrambled eggs
        toast
        orange juice

LUNCH
        hamburger on roll
        small salad
        milk shake

DINNER
        sirloin steak
        peas
        potato
        vanilla ice cream
```

```
$ cat menu2
BREAKFAST
        poached eggs
        toast
        orange juice

LUNCH
        hamburger on roll
        French fries
        milk shake

DINNER
        chef's salad
        fruit
        cheese
$
```

Below, diff with the −e option produces an ed script that details the changes between the two versions of the file. The first command line redirects the output from diff to **2changes**; cat displays the resulting file. The ed Change Mode is invoked by the **c** command. In this mode, the lines that you specify in the command are replaced by the text that you enter following the command. A period instructs ed to terminate the Change Mode and return to the Command Mode.

```
$ diff −e menu1 menu2 > 2changes

$ cat 2changes
12,15c
        chef's salad
        fruit
        cheese
.
8c
        French fries
.
2c
        poached eggs
.
$
```

The only commands missing from the ed script that diff creates are Write (**w**) and Quit (**q**). In the following example, cat appends these to **2changes**. (You can also use an editor to add the commands to the file.)

```
$ cat >> 2changes
w
q
CONTROL-D
$
```

The next example repeats the process when the file is updated for the second time. The file is copied (to **menu3**), the changes are made to the copy, and the original (**menu2** in this case) and the edited copy are processed by diff. The cat utility displays the ed script after the necessary commands have been added to it.

```
$ cat menu3
BREAKFAST
        poached eggs
        toast
        grapefruit juice

LUNCH
        tuna sandwich
        French fries

DINNER
        pot luck

$ diff —e menu2 menu3 > 3changes

$ cat >> 3changes
w
q
CONTROL-D

$ cat 3changes
12,14c
        pot luck
.
9d
7c
        tuna sandwich
.
4c
        grapefruit juice
.
w
q
$
```

The **menu2** and **menu3** files are no longer needed; diff can recreate them from **menu1**, **2changes**, and **3changes**. The process of recreating a file follows. First, copy the original file to a file that will become the updated file. (If you make changes to the original file, you may not be able to go back and recreate one of the intermediate files.)

```
$ cp menu1 recreate
$
```

Next, use ed to edit the copy of the original file (**recreate**) with input from **2changes**. The ed editor displays the number of characters it reads and writes. After it has been edited with **2changes**, the file is the same as the original **menu2**.

```
$ ed recreate < 2changes
214
189

$ cat recreate
BREAKFAST
        poached eggs
        toast
        orange juice

LUNCH
        hamburger on roll
        French fries
        milk shake

DINNER
        chef's salad
        fruit
        cheese
$
```

If you just want **menu2**, you can stop at this point. By editing the recreated **menu2** (now **recreate**) with input from **3changes**, the example below recreates **menu3**.

```
$ ed recreate < 3changes
189
139

$ cat recreate
BREAKFAST
        poached eggs
        toast
        grapefruit juice

LUNCH
        tuna sandwich
        French fries

DINNER
        pot luck
$
```

du

Display information on disk usage.

Format

du [options] [file-list]

Summary

The du (disk usage) utility reports how much space a directory, along with all its subdirectories and files, uses. It displays the number of blocks (usually 1024 bytes each) all the files in the directory occupy.

Options

Without any options, du only displays information for each plain file or directory you specify.

-a   (all) This option displays information for each file within each of the directories you specify.

-r   (report) This option causes du to report on directories it cannot open and files it cannot read. Without this option, du does not report this information.

-s   (summary) This option displays summary information for each of the filenames you specify.

Arguments

Without an argument, du only displays information about the working directory.

The **file-list** specifies the directories you want information about. If you use the **-a** option, you can also include the names of plain files as arguments.

Notes

The number du displays is different from the number ls with the
−l option displays. While ls displays the space occupied by the
directory file itself (not all the files the directory file represents),
du displays the space occupied *collectively* by all the files in the
directory.

Examples

Below, du displays size information about directories in the working directory.

```
$ du
127    ./brown
  5    ./memo
  .
  .
  .
```

Next, du displays the total size, in blocks, of all the files in the
working directory.

```
$ du −s
574  .
$
```

The last example displays the total size of all the files in **/usr**.

```
$ du −s /usr
11472 /usr
$
```

echo

Display a message.

Format

echo message

Summary

The echo utility copies its arguments, followed by a NEWLINE, to its standard output.

Options

There are no options.

Arguments

The **message** is one or more arguments. These arguments can include quoted strings, ambiguous file references, and Shell variables. A SPACE separates each argument from the others. The Shell recognizes unquoted special characters in the arguments (e.g., the Shell expands an asterisk into a list of filenames in the working directory).

You can terminate the **message** with a \c to prevent echo from displaying the NEWLINE that normally ends a **message**. To prevent the Shell from interpreting the backslash as a special character, you must quote it. The "Examples" section shows the three ways you can quote the \c.

Notes

You can use echo to send messages to the terminal from a Shell script. For other uses of echo, refer to the discussion of echo at the end of Chapter 5.

Under System V, Release 2, echo is built into the Shell.

Examples

The following examples demonstrate the use of the echo utility. The second through fourth examples show three ways to quote a \c and prevent echo from appending a NEWLINE to the end of the message.

```
$ echo 'Today is Friday.'
Today is Friday.

$ echo 'There is no newline after this.\c'
There is no newline after this.$

$ echo "There is no newline after this.\c"
There is no newline after this.$

$ echo There is no newline after this.\\c
There is no newline after this.$

$ echo 'This is a
> multiline
> echo command.'
This is a
multiline
echo command.
$
```

expr

Evaluate an expression.

Format

expr expression

Summary

The expr utility evaluates an expression and displays the result. It evaluates character strings that represent either numeric or non-numeric values. Operators separate the strings to form expressions.

Options

There are no options.

Arguments

The **expression** is composed of other expressions and strings with operators in between. Each string and operator is a distinct argument that you must separate from other arguments with a SPACE. The following list of expr operators is in order of decreasing precedence. You can change the order of evaluation by using parentheses.

:   comparison operator

This operator compares two strings, starting with the first character in each string and ending with the last character in the second string. If there is a match, it displays the number of characters in the second string. If there is no match, it displays a zero.

*   multiplication operator
/   division operator
%   remainder operator

These operators only work on strings that contain the numerals 0 through 9 and optionally a leading minus sign. They convert the strings to integer numbers, perform the specified arithmetic operation on numbers, and convert the result back to a string before displaying it.

+   addition operator
−   subtraction operator

These operators function in the same manner as those described above.

<   less than
<= less than or equal to
=   equal to
!= not equal to
>= greater than or equal to
>   greater than

These relational operators work on both numeric and non-numeric arguments. If one or both of the arguments is non-numeric, the comparison is non-numeric, using the machine collating sequence (usually ASCII). If both arguments are numeric, the comparison is numeric. The expr utility displays a 1 (one) if the comparison is true and a 0 (zero) if it is false.

&   AND operator

The AND operator evaluates both of its arguments. If neither is 0 or a null string, it displays the value of the first argument. Otherwise, it displays a 0. You must quote this operator.

| OR operator

This operator evaluates the first argument. If it is neither 0 nor a null string, it displays the value of the first argument. Otherwise, it displays the value of the second argument. You must quote this operator.

Notes

The expr utility returns an exit status of 0 (zero) if the expression is neither a null string nor the number 0, 1 if the expression is null or 0, and 2 if the expression is invalid.

     The expr utility is useful in Bourne Shell scripts. Because the C Shell has the equivalent of expr built into it, C Shell scripts do not normally use expr.

Although expr and this discussion distinguish between numeric and non-numeric arguments, all arguments to expr are actually non-numeric (character strings). When applicable, expr attempts to convert an argument to a number (e.g., when using the + operator). If a string contains characters other than 0 through 9 with an optional leading minus sign, expr cannot convert it. Specifically, if a string contains a plus sign or a decimal point, expr considers it to be non-numeric.

Examples

The following examples show command lines that call expr to evaluate constants. You can also use expr to evaluate variables in a Shell script. In the fourth example, expr displays an error message because of the illegal decimal point in 5.3.

```
$ expr 17 + 40
57

$ expr 10 − 24
−14

$ expr −17 + 20
3

$ expr 5.3 \' 4
expr: non−numeric argument
$
```

The multiplication (*), division (/), and remainder (%) operators provide additional arithmetic power, as the examples below show. You must quote the multiplication operator (precede it with a backslash) so that the Shell does not treat it as a special character (an ambiguous file reference).

```
$ expr 5 \' 4
20

$ expr 21 / 7
3

$ expr 23 % 7
2
$
```

The next two examples show how you can use parentheses to change the order of evaluation. You must quote each parenthesis and surround the backslash/parenthesis combination with SPACES.

```
$ expr 2 \* 3 + 4
10

$ expr 2 \* \( 3 + 4 \)
14
$
```

You can use relational operators to determine the relationship between numeric or non-numeric arguments. The command below uses expr to compare two strings to see if they are equal. The expr utility displays a 0 when the relationship is false and a 1 when it is true.

```
$ expr fred = mark
0

$ expr mark = mark
1
$
```

Relational operators, which you must also quote, can establish order between numeric or non-numeric arguments. Again, if a relationship is true, expr displays a 1.

```
$ expr fred \> mark
0

$ expr fred \< mark
1

$ expr 5 \< 7
1
$
```

The next command compares **5** with **m**. When one of the arguments expr is comparing with a relational operator is non-numeric, expr considers the other to be non-numeric. In this case, because **m** is non-numeric, expr treats **5** as a non-numeric argument. The comparison is between the ASCII (on most machines) values of **m** and **5**. The ASCII value of **m** is 109 and **5** is 53 so that expr evaluates the relationship as true.

```
$ expr 5 \< m
1
$
```

The next example shows the matching operator determining that the four characters in the second string match the first four characters in the first string. The expr utility displays a 4.

```
$ expr abcdefghijkl : abcd
4
$
```

The **&** operator displays a 0 if one or both of its arguments are 0 or a null string. Otherwise, it displays the first argument.

```
$ expr ´ ´ \& book
0

$ expr magazine \& book
magazine

$ expr 5 \& 0
0

$ expr 5 \& 6
5
$
```

The I operator displays the first argument if it is not 0 or a null string. Otherwise, it displays the second argument.

```
$ expr ´ ´ \| book
book

$ expr magazine \| book
magazine

$ expr 5 \| 0
5

$ expr 0 \| 5
5

$ expr 5 \| 6
5
$
```

file

Display file classification.

Format

file file-list

Summary

The file utility classifies files according to their contents.

Options

There are no options.

Arguments

The **file-list** contains the pathnames of one or more files that file classifies. You can specify any kind of file, including plain, directory, and special files, in the **file-list**.

Notes

The file utility works by examining the first part of a file, looking for keywords and special numbers (referred to as *magic numbers*) the linker uses. It also examines the access permissions associated with the file. The results of file are not always correct.

Examples

Some examples of file identification follow.

```
$ file memo proc new
memo:             English text
proc:             commands text
new:              empty
$
```

A few of the classifications that file displays are listed below.

```
English text
ascii text
c program text
cannot stat
commands text
data
directory
empty
executable
```

find

Find files.

Format

find directory-list expression

Summary

The find utility selects files that are located in specified directories and are described by an expression. It does not generate any output without an explicit instruction to do so.

Options

There are no options.

Arguments

The **directory-list** contains the pathnames of one or more directories that find is to search. When find searches a directory, it searches all subdirectories, to all levels.

The **expression** contains one or more criteria, as described in "Criteria," below. The find utility tests each of the files in each of the directories in the **directory-list** to see if it meets the criteria described by the **expression**.

A SPACE separating two criteria is a logical AND operator: the file must meet *both* criteria to be selected. A **−o** separating the criteria is a logical OR operator: the file must meet one or the other (or both) of the criteria to be selected.

You can negate any criterion by preceding it with an exclamation point. The find utility evaluates criteria from left to right unless you group them using parentheses.

Within the **expression** you must quote special characters so that the Shell does not interpret them but passes them to the find utility. Special characters that you may frequently use with find are parentheses, square brackets, question marks, and asterisks.

Each element within the **expression** is a separate argument. You must separate arguments from each other with SPACEs. There must be a SPACE on both sides of each parenthesis, exclamation point, criterion, or other element. When you use a backslash to quote a special character, the SPACES go on each side of the pair of characters (e.g., " \[").

Criteria

Following is a list of criteria that you can use within the **expression**. As used in this list, **±n** is a decimal integer that can be expressed as **+n** (meaning more than **n**), **−n** (meaning less than **n**), or **n** (meaning exactly **n**).

−name **filename**	The file being evaluated meets this criterion if **filename** matches its name. You can use ambiguous file references but must quote them.
−type **filetype**	The file being evaluated meets this criterion if **filetype** specifies its file type. You can select a file type from the following list.

File type	Description
b	block special file
c	character special file
p	fifo (named pipe)
d	directory file
f	plain file

−links **±n**	The file being evaluated meets this criterion if it has the number of links specified by **±n**.
−user **name**	The file being evaluated meets this criterion if it belongs to the user with the login name, **name**. You can use a numeric user ID in place of **name**.
−group **name**	The file being evaluated meets this criterion if it belongs to the group with the group name, **name**. You can use a numeric group ID in place of **name**.

–size ±**n**[**c**]   The file being evaluated meets this criterion if it is the size specified by ±**n**, measured in blocks. Follow **n** with the letter **c** to measure files in characters.

–atime ±**n**   The file being evaluated meets this criterion if it was last accessed the number of days ago specified by ±**n**. When you use this option, find changes the access times of directories it searches.

–mtime ±**n**   The file being evaluated meets this criterion if it was last modified the number of days ago specified by ±**n**.

–newer **filename**   The file being evaluated meets this criterion if it was modified more recently than **filename**.

–cpio **device**   The file being evaluated always meets this action criterion (refer to "Discussion" following). When evaluation of the **expression** reaches this criterion, find writes the file being evaluated to the **device** in cpio format (assumes **–oB** options). Refer to cpio in Part II for more information.

–depth   The file being evaluated always meets this action criterion. It causes find to take action on entries in a directory before it acts on the directory itself. Use this option before the **–cpio** option.

–print   The file being evaluated always meets this action criterion. When evaluation of the **expression** reaches this criterion, find displays the pathname of the file it is evaluating. If this is the only criterion in the **expression**, find displays the names of all the files in the **directory-list**. If this criterion appears with other criteria, find displays the name only if the preceding criteria are met. Refer to "Discussion" and "Notes," following.

-exec **command**\; The file being evaluated meets this action criterion if the **command** returns a zero (true value) as an exit status. You must terminate the **command** with a quoted semicolon. A pair of braces ({ }) within the **command** represents the filename of the file being evaluated.

You can use the **−exec** action criterion at the end of a group of other criteria to execute the **command** if the preceding criteria are met. Refer to the following "Discussion."

-ok **command**\; This action criterion is the same as **−exec**, except that it displays each of the **command**s to be executed, enclosed in angle brackets. The find utility only executes the **command** if it receives a **y** from its standard input.

Discussion

Assume that **x** and **y** are criteria. The following command line never tests to see if the file meets criterion **y** if it does not meet criterion **x**. Because the criteria are separated by a SPACE (the logical AND operator), once find determines that criterion **x** is not met, the file cannot meet the criteria, so find does not continue testing. Assume the file is in the **dir** directory. You can read the expression as "(test to see) if the file meets criterion **x** *and* (SPACE means *and*) criterion **y**."

find dir x y

The next command line *always* tests the file against criterion **y** if criterion **x** is not met. The file can still meet the criteria, so find continues the evaluation. It is read as "(test to see) if criterion **x** *or* criterion **y** is met." If the file meets criterion **x**, find does not evaluate criterion **y**, as there is no need.

find dir x −o y

Certain "criteria" do not select files but cause find to take action. The action is triggered when find evaluates one of these *action criteria*. Therefore, the position of an action criterion on the command line, and not the result of its evaluation, determines whether find takes the action.

The **−print** action criterion causes find to display the pathname of the file it is testing. The following command line displays the names of all files in the **dir** directory (and all subdirectories) that meet criterion **x**.

find dir x −print

The following command line displays the names of *all* the files in the **dir** directory (whether they meet criterion **x** or not).

find dir −print x

Notes

You must explicitly instruct find to display filenames if you want it to do so. Unless you include the **−print** criterion or its equivalent on the command line, find does its work silently. Refer to the first example below.

You can use the **−a** operator between criteria for clarity. This operator is a logical AND operator, just as the SPACE is.

Examples

The following command line finds all the files in the working directory, and all subdirectories, that have filenames that begin with a. The command uses a period to designate the working directory and quotes the ambiguous file reference. The command does not instruct find to do anything with these files—not even display their names. This is not a useful example, but it demonstrates a common problem when using find.

```
$ find . −name ´a*´
$
```

The next command line finds *and displays the filenames of* all the files in the working directory, and all subdirectories, that have filenames that begin with a.

```
$ find . —name 'a*' —print
.
.
.
$
```

The command line below finds, displays the filenames of, and deletes all the files in the working directory, and all subdirectories, that belong to Alex or Jenny.

The parentheses, and the semicolon following **—exec**, are quoted so that the Shell does not treat them as special characters. SPACEs separate the quoted parentheses from other elements on the command line. You can read this find command as, "find, in the working directory and all subdirectories (.), all files that belong to Alex (**—user alex**) *or* (**—o**) belong to Jenny (**—user jenny**) [if a file meets these criteria, continue with] *and* (SPACE) print (**—print**) the name of the file *and* (SPACE) delete the file (**—exec rm** { }).''

```
$ find . \( —user alex —o —user jenny \) —print —exec rm {} \;
.
.
.
$
```

The next command finds all files in two user directories that are larger than 10,000 bytes (**—size +10000c**) and have only been accessed more than five days ago—that is, have not been accessed within the past five days (**—atime +5**). This **find** command then asks whether you want to delete the file (**—ok rm** { }). You must respond to each of these queries with a **y** (for yes) or **n** (for no). The Delete command does not work if you do not have execute and write access permission to the directory.

```
$ find /usr/alex /usr/barbara —size +10000c —atime +5 —ok rm {} \;
< rm ... /usr/alex/notes >?    y
< rm ... /usr/alex/letter >?   n
.
.
.
$
```

fsck

Check and repair a file system.

Format

/etc/fsck [options] [file-systems-list]

Summary

The fsck utility verifies the integrity of a file system and reports on any problems it finds. For each problem it finds, fsck asks you if you want it to attempt to fix the problem or ignore it. If you repair the problem, you may loose some data.

Options

Without any options, fsck checks the file systems in the **file-systems-list**. If the file system is consistent, you will see a report such as the following:

```
/dev/dsk/c1d0s0
File system: root Volume: 10.a

**  Phase 1 — Check Blocks and Sizes
**  Phase 2 — Check Pathnames
**  Phase 3 — Check Connectivity
**  Phase 4 — Check Reference Count
**  Phase 5 — Check Free List
**  Phase 6 — Salvage Free List
xxx files yyy blocks zz free
```

If fsck finds problems with the file system, it reports on each of them, giving you the choice of having it repair the problem or ignore it.

-y   (yes) fsck assumes a *yes* response to all questions and makes any necessary repairs to the file system. If the file system is corrupt, you can lose files by automatically responding *yes* to all of fsck's questions.

-n   (no) fsck assumes a *no* response to all questions and only reports on problems, not allowing you to make repairs.

410

-s   This option causes fsck to reconstruct a new free list and rewrite the superblock unconditionally. The file system should not be mounted during this type of check. The root file system, which cannot be unmounted, must be quiescent. The best way to ensure quiescence is to bring the system down to single-user mode.

-S   This option is the same as **−s** except that it will not reconstruct the free list if there are any problems with the file system.

-q   (quiet) This option checks and repairs the file system without as much reporting. If necessary, it will automatically fix counts in the superblock and salvage the free list.

-D   (directory) This option checks for bad blocks in directories.

-f   (fast) This option only runs Phases 1, 5, and if necessary, 6 of fsck.

Arguments

The **file-systems-list** is an optional list of file systems you want fsck to check. If you do not specify a list, it checks the file systems listed in the **/etc/checklist** file.

Except for the root, you should always check the raw device representing the file system. This device is usually the one whose simple filename begins with **r**.

Notes

Refer to "The File Structure" in Chapter 10 for more information on the structure of a file system.

If you are repairing a file system, you must run fsck on the unmounted file system. If you are repairing the root, run fsck while the system is in single-user mode and no other user processes are running. After repairing the root, you must bring the system down immediately, without running sync, and reboot it.

Although it is technically feasible to repair files that are damaged and that fsck says you should remove, it is usually not practical. The best insurance against significant loss of data is frequent backups. Refer to Chapter 10 for more information on backing up the system.

If you do not have write permission to the file system fsck is checking, fsck will report problems but not give you an opportunity to fix them.

Messages

This section explains fsck's standard messages. It does not explain every message that fsck produces. In general, fsck suggests the most logical way of dealing with a problem in the file structure. Unless you have information that suggests another response, respond to its prompts with *yes*. Use the system backup tapes or disks to restore any data that is lost as a result of this process.

Phase 1 – Check Blocks and Sizes. Phase 1 checks inode information.

Phase 1B – Rescan for More Dups. When fsck finds a duplicate block in Phase 1, it repeats its search.

Phase 2 – Check Pathnames. In Phase 2, fsck checks for directories that pointed to bad inodes it found in Phase 1.

Phase 3 – Check Connectivity. Phase 3 looks for unreferenced directories and a nonexistent or full **lost+found** directory.

Phase 4 – Check Reference Counts. Phase 4 checks for unreferenced files, a nonexistent or full **lost+found** directory, bad link counts, bad blocks, duplicate blocks, and incorrect inode counts.

Phase 5 – Check Free List. Phase 5 checks the free block list for bad blocks, bad counts, duplicate blocks, and unused blocks.

Phase 6 – Salvage Free List.   If Phase 5 found problems, Phase 6 fixes them.

Cleanup.   Once fsck has repaired the file system, it informs you about the status of the file system and tells you what you must do.

xxx files yyy blocks zz free.   This message lets you know how many files (xxx) are using how many blocks (yyy), and how many blocks are free (zz) for your use.

*****Boot UNIX (No Sync!)*****.   The fsck utility displays this message when it has modified a mounted file system (including the root). When you see it, you must reboot the system immediately, without using sync. Follow the procedure discussed at the bottom of page 290, omitting step 4.

*****File System Was Modified*****.   The fsck utility displays this message if it has repaired the file system.

Search for a pattern in a file.

Format

grep [options] pattern [file-list]

Summary

The grep utility searches one or more files, line by line, for a **pattern**. The **pattern** can be a simple string or another form of a regular expression. The grep utility takes various actions, specified by options, each time it finds a line that contains a match for the **pattern**.

The grep utility takes its input from files you specify on the command line or from its standard input.

Options

If you do not specify any options, grep sends lines that contain a match for **pattern** to its standard output. If you specify more than one file on the command line, grep precedes each line that it displays with the name of the file that it came from and a colon.

-c   (count) grep only indicates the number of lines in each file that contain a match.

-e   (expression) This option allows you to use a **pattern** beginning with a hyphen. If you do not use this option and specify a **pattern** that begins with a hyphen, grep assumes that the hyphen introduces an option and the search will not work. (This option is not available on all systems.)

-h   (no header) This option causes grep not to list filenames. Use this option when you specify more than one file and want only a list of lines without filenames. This option is useful when you use grep within a pipe. (This option is not available on all systems.)

-i   (ignore case) This option causes lowercase letters in the pattern to match uppercase letters in the file and vice versa. Use this option when searching for a word that may be at the beginning of a sentence (that is, may or may not start with an uppercase letter).

-l   (list) The grep utility displays the name of each file that contains one or more matches. It displays each filename only once, even if the file contains more than one match.

-n   (number) The grep utility precedes each line by its line number in the file. The file does not need to contain line numbers—this number represents the number of lines in the file up to and including the displayed line.

-s   (status) The grep utility returns an exit status without any output (see "Notes" below).

-v   (reverse sense of test) This option causes lines *not* containing a match to satisfy the search. When you use this option by itself, grep displays all lines that do not contain a match for the **pattern**.

Arguments

The **pattern** is a regular expression as defined in the Appendix. You must quote regular expressions that contain special characters, SPACEs, or TABs. An easy way to quote these characters is to enclose the entire expression within single quotation marks.

The **file-list** contains pathnames of plain text files that grep searches.

Notes

The grep utility returns an exit status of 0 if it finds a match, 1 if it does not find a match, and 2 if the file is not accessible or there is a syntax error.

There are two utilities that perform functions similar to that of grep. The egrep utility can be faster than grep but may also use more space. The fgrep utility is fast and compact, but it can process only simple strings, not regular expressions.

Examples

The following examples assume that the working directory contains three files: **testa**, **testb**, and **testc**. The contents of each file are shown below.

File testa	File testb	File testc
aaabb	aaaaa	AAAAA
bbbcc	bbbbb	BBBBB
ff—ff	ccccc	CCCCC
cccdd	ddddd	DDDDD
dddaa		

The grep utility can search for a pattern that is a simple string of characters. The following command line searches **testa** for, and displays each line containing, the string **bb**.

```
$ grep bb testa
aaabb
bbbcc
$
```

The **−v** option reverses the sense of the test. The example below displays all the lines *without* **bb**.

```
$ grep −v bb testa
ff—ff
cccdd
dddaa
$
```

The **−n** flag displays the line number of each displayed line.

```
$ grep −n bb testa
1:aaabb
2:bbbcc
$
```

The grep utility can search through more than one file. Below, grep searches through each file in the working directory. (The ambiguous file reference ***** matches all filenames.) The name of the file containing the string precedes each line of output.

```
$ grep bb *
testa:aaabb
testa:bbbcc
testb:bbbbb
$
```

The search that grep performs is case-sensitive. Because the previous examples specified lowercase **bb**, grep did not find the uppercase string, BBBBB, in **testc**. The −i option causes both uppercase *and* lowercase letters to match either case of letter in the pattern.

```
$ grep −i bb *
testa:aaabb
testa:bbbcc
testb:bbbbb
testc:BBBBB

$ grep −i BB *
testa:aaabb
testa:bbbcc
testb:bbbbb
testc:BBBBB
$
```

The −c option displays the name of each file, followed by the number of lines in the file that contain a match.

```
$ grep −c bb *
testa:2
testb:1
testc:0
$
```

The following command line displays lines from the file **text2** that contain a string of characters starting with st, followed by zero or more characters (.* represents zero or more characters in a regular expression—see the Appendix), and ending in ing.

```
$ grep 'st.*ing' text2
.
.
.
$
```

The final command line calls the vi editor with a list of files in the working directory that contain the string Sampson. The grave accent marks (see page 213) cause the Shell to execute the **grep** command in place and supply vi with a list of filenames that you want to edit. (The single quotation marks are not necessary in this example, but they are required if the string you are searching for contains special characters or SPACEs.)

```
$ vi `grep −l 'Sampson' *`
.
.
.
```

kill

Terminate a process.

Format

kill [option] PID-list

Summary

The kill utility terminates one or more processes by sending them software termination signals (signal number 15). An option allows you to send a different signal. The process must belong to the user executing kill, except that the Superuser can terminate any process. The kill utility displays a message when it terminates a process.

Options

You can specify a signal number (0-15), preceded by a hyphen, as an option before the **PID-list** to cause kill to send the signal you specify to the process.

Arguments

The **PID-list** contains process identification (PID) numbers of processes kill is to terminate.

Notes

The Shell displays the PID number of a background process when you initiate it. You can also use the ps utility to determine PID numbers.

If the software termination signal does not terminate the process, try using a kill signal (signal number 9). A process can choose to ignore any signal except signal number 9.

If you terminate process number 0 with signal 9, all processes that the current login process initiated are terminated and the operating system logs you off.

Examples

The first example shows a command line executing the file **compute** as a background process and the kill utility terminating it.

```
$ compute &
17542

$ kill 17542
$
```

The next example shows the ps utility determining the PID number of the background process running a program named **xprog** and the kill utility terminating **xprog** with a signal number 9.

```
$ ps
   PID   TTY      TIME COMMAND
 22921  tty11    0:10 sh
 23714  tty11    0:00 xprog
 23715  tty11    0:03 ps

$ kill -9 23714
23714 Killed
$
```

Give the following command to terminate all your jobs and log yourself off.

```
$ kill -9 0

login:
```

ln

Make a link to a file.

Format

ln existing-file new-link

ln existing-file-list directory

Summary

The ln utility makes a link to a plain file and has two modes of operation. The first mode makes a link between an existing file and a new filename. The second makes a link between an existing file and a new filename in a directory you specify.

Options

There are no options.

Arguments

The **existing-file** is the pathname of the plain file you want to make a link to. The **new-link** is the pathname of the new link.

Using the second format, the **existing-file-list** contains the pathnames of the plain files you want to make links to. The ln utility establishes the new links so that they appear in the **directory**. The simple filenames of the entries in the **directory** are the same as the simple filenames of the files in the **existing-file-list**.

Notes

A link is an entry in a directory that points to a file. The operating system makes the first link to a file when you create the file using an editor, a program, or redirected output. You can make additional links using ln and remove links with rm. The ls utility, with the −l option, shows you how many links a file has. Refer to the end of Chapter 4 for a discussion of links.

The ln utility displays an error message if you attempt to make a link across physical devices. Use cp to generate another copy of a file if you want it to appear on another physical device.

If you attempt to make a link to a directory, ln displays an error message.

Examples

The first command makes a link between the **memo2** file in the **/usr/alex/literature** directory and the working directory. The file appears as **memo2** (the simple filename of the existing file) in the working directory.

```
$ ln /usr/alex/literature/memo2 .
$
```

The next command makes a link to the same file. This time, the file appears as **new_memo** in the working directory.

```
$ ln /usr/alex/literature/memo2 new_memo
$
```

The final command makes a link so that the file appears in another user's directory. You must have write access permission to the other user's directory for this command to work. If you own the file, you can use chmod to give the other user write access permission to the file.

```
$ ln /usr/alex/literature/memo2 /usr/jenny/new_memo
$
```

Print a file.

Format

lp [options] [file-list]

Summary

The lp utility places one or more files in the line printer queue. It provides orderly access to the printer for several users or processes. You can use cancel to remove files from the printer queue and lpstat to check the status of files in the printer queue.

The lp utility takes its input from files you specify on the command line or from its standard input. The lp utility sends a unique identification number to its standard output and the specified files to the printer. You can use the identification number with cancel and lpstat.

Options

Check with the system administrator about installation-dependent options.

−c   (copy file) The lp utility copies a file before placing it in the printer queue so that it cannot be changed. If you do not use this option, any changes you make to the file before it is its turn to be printed will be reflected in the printed copy.

−m   (mail) The lp utility uses the mail utility to report when the file has finished printing.

−n**x**   (number of copies) This option causes lp to print **x** copies. Replace **x** with a number.

−w   (write) The lp utility uses the write utility to report when the file has finished printing. If you are not logged on, lp uses mail.

Arguments

The **file-list** is a list of one or more pathnames of plain text files that lp prints.

Notes

If your system does not provide lp, it probably has lpr. If it has both utilities, use lp. Do not use both utilities at the same time.

Examples

The following command line prints the file named **memo2**. The message following the command is from lp. It tells you the job number (printer__1-496) in case you want to use cancel to cancel the job.

```
$ lp memo2
request id is printer_1-496 (1 file)
$
```

Below, a pipe sends the output of the ls utility to the printer.

```
$ ls | lp
request id is printer_1-497 (standard input)
$
```

Next, nroff (with the **mm** macro package) formats **report7** and sends it to the printer using a pipe and lp. The job runs in the background.

```
$ nroff —mm report | lp &
12345

request id is printer_1-498 (standard input)
$
```

The final examples use two different methods to paginate and send the **memo** file to the printer. Refer to the pr utility for more information.

```
$ cat memo | pr | lp
request id is printer_1-499 (standard input)
$

$ pr memo | lp
request id is printer_1-500 (standard input)
$
```

Print a file.

Format

lpr [options] [file-list]

Summary

The lpr utility places one or more files in the line printer queue. It performs the same function as lp and is included here because some systems do not support lp.

The lpr utility takes its input from files you specify on the command line or from its standard input. The output from lpr is placed in the printer queue.

Options

Check with the system administrator about installation-dependent options.

-c   (copy file) The lpr utility copies a file before placing it in the printer queue so that it cannot be changed. If you do not use this option, any changes you make to the file before it is its turn to be printed will be reflected in the printed copy.

-m   (mail report) The lpr utility uses the mail utility to report when the file has finished printing.

-r   (remove file) The lpr utility deletes the file after it has placed it in the printer queue.

Arguments

The **file-list** is a list of one or more pathnames of plain text files that lpr prints.

Examples

Refer to lp for examples. The lpr utility uses the same command line syntax as lp.

lpstat

Display the statuses of printing jobs

Format

lpstat [options] [job-identification]

Summary

The lpstat utility displays the status of the printing jobs as specified by the options and job identification numbers. Without any options or arguments, lpstat displays the status of all printing jobs you started with lp.

Options

–u **user**   This option displays the status of all printing jobs that **user** started with lp. Replace **user** with the login name of a user.

Arguments

The **job-identification** numbers are the numbers that lp returns when you use it to print a file. If you specify a **job-identification** number, lp will only display information about that printing job.

Notes

The lpstat utility will only display status information about jobs that you started with lp. It does not report on jobs that you started with lpr.

Example

The example below shows that job printer__1-500 is waiting to be printed. It was submitted by Alex at 11:59 A.M. on January 13.

```
$ lpstat
printer_1-500        alex          5721   Jan 13 11:59
```

Display information about one or more files.

Format

ls [options] [file-list]

Summary

The ls utility displays information about one or more files. It lists the information alphabetically by filename unless you use an option to change the order.

Options

The options determine the type of information ls displays, how it displays it, and the order it displays the information in.

When you do not use an option, ls displays a short listing, containing only the names of files.

-a   (all entries) Without a **file-list** (no arguments on the command line), this option displays information about all the files in the working directory, including invisible files (those with filenames that begin with a period). When you do not use this option, ls does not list information about invisible files.

      In a similar manner, when you use this option with a **file-list** that includes an appropriate ambiguous file reference, ls displays information about invisible files. (The * ambiguous file reference does not match a leading period in a filename—see page 94.)

-C   (columns) This option lists files in vertically sorted columns.

-d   (directory) This option displays the names of directories without displaying their contents. When you give this option without an argument, ls displays information about the working directory. This option displays plain files normally.

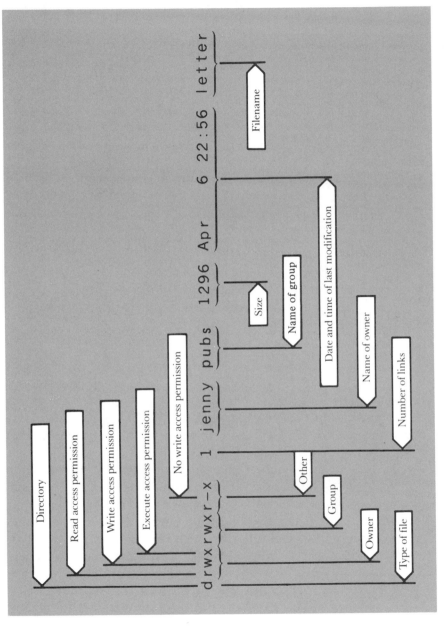

Figure II-1

ls-l

-F   This option displays a slash after each directory and an asterisk after each executable file.

-g   This option generates the same display as the **-l** option except it does not include the owner column.

-i   This option displays the inode number of each file.

-l   (long) This option displays seven columns of information about each file. These columns, shown in Figure II-1, are described below.

    The first column, which contains 11 characters, is divided as follows.

        The first character describes the type of file:

–	indicates a plain file
b	indicates a block device file
c	indicates a character device file
d	indicates a directory file
p	indicates a fifo (named pipe)

    Refer to Chapter 4 for more information on types of files.

    The next nine characters represent all the access permissions associated with the file. These nine characters are divided into three sets of three characters each.

    The first three characters represent the owner's access permissions. If the owner has read access permission to the file, an **r** appears in the first character position. If the owner is not permitted to read the file, a hyphen appears in this position. The next two positions represent the owner's write and execute access permissions. A **w** appears in the second position if the owner is permitted to write to the file, and an **x** appears in the third position if the owner is permitted to execute the file. An **s** in the third position indicates that the file has set user ID permission. An **S** indicates set user ID without execute permission. A hyphen indicates the owner does not have the access permission associated with the character position.

In a similar manner, the second and third sets of three characters represent the access permissions of the user's group and other users. An **s** in the third position of the second set of characters indicates that the file has set group ID permission, and an **S** indicates set group ID without execute permission.

The last bit is **t** if the sticky bit is set and **T** if it is set without execute permission.

Refer to the chmod utility for information on changing access permissions.

The second column indicates the number of links to the file. Refer to Chapter 4 for more information on links.

The third and fourth columns display the name of the owner of the file and the name of the group the file belongs to.

The fifth column indicates the size of the file in bytes or, if information about a device file is being displayed, the major and minor device numbers. In the case of a directory, this number is the size of the actual directory file, not the size of the files that are entries within the directory. (Use du to display the size of all the files in a directory.)

The last two columns display the date and time the file was last modified.

–o   This option generates the same display as the –l option except it does not include the group column.

–p   (indicate directories) This option puts a slash after the names of directories.

–r   (reverse) This option displays the list of filenames in reverse alphabetical order or, when you use it with the –t or –u options, in reverse time order (least recently modified or accessed first).

–s   (size) This option displays the size of each file in (usually 1024-byte) blocks. The size precedes the filename.

        With the –l option, this option displays the size in column 1 and shifts each of the other items over one column to the right.

-q This option displays nonprinting characters in a filename as question marks.

-R This option recursively lists subdirectories.

-t (time modified) This option displays the list of filenames in order by the time of last modification. It displays the files that were modified most recently first.

-u (time accessed) When you use this option with the **-t** option, it sorts by the last time each file was accessed. When you use it with **-l**, it displays access times.

-x This option lists files in horizontally sorted columns.

Arguments

When you do not use an argument, ls displays the names of all the files in the working directory.

The **file-list** contains one or more pathnames of files that ls displays information about. You can use the pathname of any plain, directory, or device file. These pathnames can include ambiguous file references.

When you give an ambiguous file reference that refers to the working directory, ls displays the names of all the files in any directories specified by the ambiguous file reference, in addition to files in the working directory.

When you specify a directory file, ls displays the contents of the directory. The ls utility displays the name of the directory only when it is needed to avoid ambiguity (that is, when ls is displaying the contents of more than one directory, it displays the names of the directories to indicate which files you can find in which directory). If you specify a plain file, ls displays information about just that file.

Notes

Refer to page 92 for examples of using ls with ambiguous file references.

Examples

All the following examples assume that the user does not change from the current working directory.

The first command line shows the ls utility with only the **–C** option and no arguments. You see an alphabetical list of the names of the files in the working directory.

```
$ ls –C
bin           calendar      letters
c             execute       shell
$
```

The **–p** option shows you which files are directories. The **–C** option puts the list in columns.

```
$ ls –pC
bin/          calendar      letters/
c/            execute       shell/
$
```

Next, the **–l** (long) option displays a long list. The files are still in alphabetical order.

```
$ ls –l
total 8
drwxrwxr-x   2 jenny pubs     80 Nov 20 09:17 bin
drwxrwxr-x   2 jenny pubs    144 Sep 26 11:59 c
-rw-rw-r--   1 jenny pubs    104 Nov 28 11:44 calendar
-rwxrw-r--   1 jenny pubs     85 Nov  6 08:27 execute
drwxrwxr-x   2 jenny pubs     32 Apr  6 22:56 letters
drwxrwxr-x  16 jenny pubs   1296 Dec  6 17:33 shell
$
```

The **–a** (all) option lists invisible files when you do not use an argument. Again **–C** puts the list in columns.

```
$ ls –aC
.             .profile      c             execute       shell
..            bin           calendar      letters
$
```

Combining the **–a** and **–l** options displays a long listing of all the files, including invisible files, in the working directory. This list is still in alphabetical order.

```
$ ls -al
total 12
drwxrwxr-x   6 jenny  pubs      480 Dec   6 17:42 .
drwxrwx---  26 root   system    816 Dec   6 14:45 ..
-rw-rw-r--   1 jenny  pubs      161 Dec   6 17:15 .profile
drwxrwxr-x   2 jenny  pubs       80 Nov  20 09:17 bin
drwxrwxr-x   2 jenny  pubs      144 Sep  26 11:59 c
-rw-rw-r--   1 jenny  pubs      104 Nov  28 11:44 calendar
-rwxrw-r--   1 jenny  pubs       85 Nov   6 08:27 execute
drwxrwxr-x   2 jenny  pubs       32 Apr   6 22:56 letters
drwxrwxr-x  16 jenny  pubs     1296 Dec   6 17:33 shell
$
```

If you add the **−r** (reverse order) option to the command line, ls produces a list in reverse alphabetical order.

```
$ ls -ral
total 12
drwxrwxr-x  16 jenny  pubs     1296 Dec   6 17:33 shell
drwxrwxr-x   2 jenny  pubs       32 Apr   6 22:56 letters
-rwxrw-r--   1 jenny  pubs       85 Nov   6 08:27 execute
-rw-rw-r--   1 jenny  pubs      104 Nov  28 11:44 calendar
drwxrwxr-x   2 jenny  pubs      144 Sep  26 11:59 c
drwxrwxr-x   2 jenny  pubs       80 Nov  20 09:17 bin
-rw-rw-r--   1 jenny  pubs      161 Dec   6 17:15 .profile
drwxrwx---  26 root   system    816 Dec   6 14:45 ..
drwxrwxr-x   6 jenny  pubs      480 Dec   6 17:42 .
$
```

Use the **−t** and **−l** options to list files so that the most recently modified file appears at the top of the list.

```
$ ls -tl
total 8
drwxrwxr-x  16 jenny  pubs     1296 Dec   6 17:33 shell
-rw-rw-r--   1 jenny  pubs      104 Nov  28 11:44 calendar
drwxrwxr-x   2 jenny  pubs       80 Nov  20 09:17 bin
-rwxrw-r--   1 jenny  pubs       85 Nov   6 08:27 execute
drwxrwxr-x   2 jenny  pubs      144 Sep  26 11:59 c
drwxrwxr-x   2 jenny  pubs       32 Apr   6 22:56 letters
$
```

Together the **−r** and **−t** options cause ls to list files with the file you modified least recently at the top of the list.

```
$ ls -trl
total 8
drwxrwxr-x   2 jenny pubs     32 Apr  6 22:56 letters
drwxrwxr-x   2 jenny pubs    144 Sep 26 11:59 c
-rwxrw-r--   1 jenny pubs     85 Nov  6 08:27 execute
drwxrwxr-x   2 jenny pubs     80 Nov 20 09:17 bin
-rw-rw-r--   1 jenny pubs    104 Nov 28 11:44 calendar
drwxrwxr-x  16 jenny pubs   1296 Dec  6 17:33 shell
$
```

The next example shows ls with a directory filename as an argument. The ls utility lists the contents of the directory in alphabetical order.

```
$ ls bin
c
e
lsdir
$
```

The −1 option gives a long listing of the contents of the directory.

```
$ ls -l bin
total 3
-rwxrw-r-x 1 jenny pubs     48 Oct  6 21:38 c
-rwxrw-r-- 1 jenny pubs    156 Oct  6 21:40 e
-rwxrw-r-- 1 jenny pubs    136 Nov  7 16:48 lsdir
$
```

To display information about the directory file itself, use the −d (directory) option. This option causes ls to list information only about the directory.

```
$ ls -dl bin
drwxrwxr-x 2 jenny pubs     80 Nov 20 09:17 bin
$
```

mail

Send or receive electronic mail.

Format

mail user-list

mail [options]

Summary

The mail utility sends and receives electronic mail between users. When you log on, the UNIX system tells you if mail is waiting for you.

Use the first format shown above to send mail to other users. When sending mail, mail accepts text from its standard input. You can redirect the input from a file or enter it at the terminal. You must terminate mail you send from the terminal with a line with just a period on it. (Some systems require a CONTROL-D on a line by itself.)

Use the second format to display mail that you have received. When displaying mail, mail prompts you with a question mark following each piece of mail. The following are valid responses to this prompt.

*   An asterisk causes mail to display a summary of valid responses. (Some systems use a question mark.)

!command This response causes mail to exit to the Shell, execute **command**, and return to mail when the **command** has finished executing. Replace **command** with the Shell command line you want to execute.

CONTROL-D This response causes mail to stop and leave unexamined mail in the mail box so that you can look at it the next time you run mail.

d   (delete) A **d** causes mail to delete the piece of mail it just displayed, and to display the next one.

m[**person**]   (mail) This response causes mail to remail the piece of mail to **person**. If you do not specify a **person**, the mail is sent back to you again. Replace **person** with the login name or names of the people you want to send the mail to.

RETURN   Press the RETURN key to display the next piece of mail.

p   (previous) A **p** causes mail to redisplay the previous piece of mail.

q   (quit) A **q** has the same effect as CONTROL-D. It causes mail to stop and leave unexamined mail in the mail box so that you can look at it the next time you run mail.

s[**file**]   (save) This response causes mail to save the piece of mail in the file named **file** or **mbox** if you do not specify a filename. Replace **file** with the name of the file you want to save your mail in.

w[**file**]   (write) This response causes mail to save the piece of mail, without a header, in the file named **file** or **mbox** if you do not specify a filename. Replace **file** with the name of the file you want to save your mail in.

x   (exit) This response causes mail to exit and not change the status of your mail.

Options

The following options affect mail that you have received and are displaying. They are not for use when you are sending mail.

-p   (display mail, no questions) This option causes mail to display mail without prompting you after each piece of mail.

-q   (quit on interrupt) Without this option, DEL stops mail from displaying the current piece of mail and allows it to proceed with the next. When you use this option, DEL stops execution of mail and returns you to the Shell without changing the status of your mail.

−r (reverse order) Without this option, mail displays mail in a last-piece-of-mail-received, first-piece-displayed order. This option causes mail to display mail in chronological order.

Arguments

The **user-list** contains the login names of the users you want to send mail to.

Notes

If mail doesn't recognize the name of the person you are sending mail to, or if you interrupt mail with DEL while you are sending mail, mail puts your letter in a file named **dead.letter** in your home directory.
   Also see mailx in Part II.

Examples

Chapter 3 contains a tutorial session on using mail.
   The first example below shows how to send a message to several users. In this case, mail sends the message to users with the login names of hls, alex, and jenny.

```
$ mail hls alex jenny
(message)
.
$
```

You can also use an editor (such as vi) to compose a message in a file and then send it by redirecting the input to mail. The command line below sends the file **today** to barbara.

```
$ mail barbara < today
$
```

mailx

Send or receive electronic mail.

Format

mailx user-list

mailx [options]

Summary

The mailx utility sends and receives electronic mail. It performs the same basic functions as mail but has many more features. (The mailx utility actually uses mail to receive and deliver its messages.)

When you use mailx to send someone a message, mailx puts the message in that user's mail box, which is usually a file named **/usr/mail/login-name**, where **login-name** is the login name of the user you are sending the message to. When you use mailx to read messages that other people have sent you, mailx normally reads from your mail box and then stores the messages in a file named **mbox** in your home directory after you read them.

The way mailx appears and functions depends to a large extent on mailx *environment variables*. When you call mailx, it establishes an environment that is based on two files: the **/usr/lib/mailx/mailx.rc** file and a **.mailrc** file in your home directory. The system administrator sets up the first file. You can change any aspects of your mailx environment that the administrator has set up by setting variables in your **.mailrc** file. Or, if you are satisfied with the administrator's choices, you do not need to have a **.mailrc** file at all.

Options

-f **filename**   This option causes mailx to read messages from **filename** instead of your system mail box. If you do not specify a filename, mailx reads the **mbox** file in your home directory.

-H   This option displays a list of message headers without giving you the opportunity to read the messages.

–s **header**   When you are sending messages, this option sets
the subject header to **header**.

Arguments

Without any arguments, mailx displays any messages that are
waiting for you. With one or more arguments, mailx sends messages. The **user-list** is a list of the users you are sending messages to.

Sending Messages

You send a message by giving the command **mailx** followed by the
login names of the people you want to send messages to. Depending on how its environment variables are set, mailx may prompt
you for a subject. If it does, enter a line of information in
response to the prompt. This line will appear as the header when
the recipients read the message. After entering the subject, mailx
is in the Input Mode and you can enter the text of your message.
The mailx utility does not prompt you for the text.

   You can give mailx commands while it is in the Input Mode.
All Input Mode commands start with a tilde (˜). They are called
tilde escapes because they temporarily allow you to escape from
the Input Mode so you can give a command. The tilde that introduces a tilde escape must appear as the first character on a line.

   The following list describes some of the more important tilde
escapes.

˜! **command**   Allows you to give a Shell command while you are
composing a message. Replace **command** with a
Shell command line.

˜?   Displays a list of all tilde escapes.

˜b **name-list**   Sends blind carbon copies (bcc) to the users in
the **name-list**. The people who receive blind car-
bon copies are not listed on the copy of the message that goes to the addressee; the people who
receive regular carbon copies (cc) are—see **c**, following.

~c name-list   Sends carbon copies (cc) to the users in the **name-list**.

~h   Causes mailx to prompt you for the subject, to, cc, and bcc fields. Each prompt includes the field as it exists—you can use the erase and line kill keys to back up and edit the fields.

~m msg-list   Reads the messages specified by the **msg-list** into the message you are composing, placing a TAB at the beginning of each line. (Refer to "Reading Messages," following, for a description of **msg-list**.) You can only use **~m** when you are sending a message while reading your messages (see the **m** and **r** commands, also in "Reading Messages").

~p   Displays the entire message you are currently composing.

~q   Quits, saving the message you are composing in the file **dead.letter**.

~r filename   Reads **filename** into the message you are composing.

~s subject   Sets the subject field for the message you are composing to **subject**.

~t name-list   Adds the users in the **name-list** to the list of people who will receive the message.

~v   Calls the vi editor so that you can edit the message you are composing. Using this tilde escape is the only way you can make a change to a message you are composing (except for changes you can make with the erase and line kill keys).

~x   Exits without saving the message you are composing.

Reading Messages

When you have mail you want to read, call mailx without any arguments. The mailx utility will display a list of headers of messages waiting for you. Each line of the display will have the following format.

[>] from-name date lines/characters [subject]

The > indicates that the message is the current message. The **from-name** is the name of the person who sent you the message. The **date** and **lines/characters** are the date the message was sent and its length. The **subject** is the optional subject field for the message.

After the list of headers, mailx displays its prompt, usually a question mark. The mailx utility is in Command Mode, waiting for you to give it a command. The easiest way to read your messages is to press RETURN. After each message, mailx will prompt you. Keep pressing RETURN to read each message in turn.

In addition to pressing RETURN, you can give mailx commands to manipulate and respond to your messages. In the following summary of commands, **msg-list** is a message number, a range of message numbers (use a hyphen to indicate a range: a-b), or the login name of a user. If you do not specify a **msg-list** where one is called for, mailx responds as though you had specified the current message. The *current message* is the message that is preceded by a > in the header list.

Most of the following commands can appear in your **.mailrc** file.

!command　　　　　Allows you to give a Shell command while you are reading messages. Replace **command** with a Shell command line.

?　　　　　　　　　Displays a list of all mailx commands.

alias **a-name name-list** Declares that **a-name** (alias name) represents all the login names in the **name-list**. When you want to send a message to everyone in the **name-list**, all you need to do is send a message to **a-name**. The mailx utility automatically

expands **a-name** into the **name-list**.
This command usually appears in a
.mailrc file.

d **msg-list**   Deletes the messages in the **msg-list**
from your mail box.

x   Exits from mailx without changing your
mail box. If you deleted any messages
during this session with mailx, they are
not removed from your mail box.

h   Displays a list of headers. Refer to the **z**
command if you want to scroll the list of
headers.

m **name**   Sends a message to **name**. Using this
command is similar to calling mailx with
name from the command line.

p **msg-list**   Displays the messages in the **msg-list**.

pr **msg-list**   Preserves messages in the **msg-list** in
your mail box. Use this command after
you have read a message but do not want
to remove it from your mail box. Refer
to the **q** command.

q   Exits from mailx, saving messages that
you read in your **mbox** file and leaving
messages that you have not read in your
mail box. You can use the **pr** command
to force mailx to leave a message in your
mail box even though you have read it.

r **message**   Replies to a message. This command
copies the subject line of the **message**
and addresses a reply message to the person who sent you the **message**. Everyone who got a copy of the original **message** also gets a copy of the new message. The **r** command puts mailx in

	Input Mode so you can compose a message.
s **msg-list filename**	Saves a message in a file. Without any arguments, this command saves the current message in your **mbox** file. If you specify a **msg-list**, it saves the messages you specify in your **mbox** file. If you specify a **filename**, it saves your messages in that file. When you use the **q** command after saving a message, mailx will not save the message in your mail box or **mbox** file.
set	See the introduction to the following section on "The mailx Environment Variables" for a description of this command. It is almost always used in a **.mailrc** file.
to **msg-list**	Displays the top few lines of the specified messages.
u **msg-list**	Undeletes (restores) the specified messages. You can only restore a deleted message if you have not exited from mailx since you deleted the message.
v **msg-list**	Edits the specified messages with vi.
z±	Scrolls the list of headers (see the **h** command) forward (+) or backward (−).

The mailx **Environment Variables**

You can set the mailx environment variables in the **.mailrc** file in your home directory using the mailx Set command. The Set command has the following format.

set name[=value]

The **name** is the name of the mailx environment variable that you are setting, and the **value** is the optional value you are assigning to the variable. The **value** can be either a string or a number. If you use Set without a value, mailx assigns the variable a null value (the value of some mailx environment variables is not relevant, it is only important that they are set).

Following is a list of some of the more important mailx environment variables.

askcc   Set this variable if you want mailx to prompt you for names of people to receive carbon copies of messages you send. By default, mailx sets the **noaskcc** variable.

asksub   Set this variable if you want mailx to prompt you for a subject. By default, mailx sets this variable.

ignore   Set this variable if you want mailx to ignore interrupts while you are composing and sending messages. Setting **ignore** can make your job easier if you are working over a noisy telephone line. By default, mailx sets the **noignore** variable.

record=**filename**   When you set this variable, mailx puts a copy of all your outgoing messages in the file you specify with **filename**.

Examples

The following example shows Alex reading his messages with mailx. After calling mailx and seeing that he has two messages, he gives the command **2** followed by a RETURN to display the second message. After displaying the message, mailx displays a prompt and Alex deletes the message with a **d** command.

```
$ mailx
mailx version 2.14 08/01/84 Type ? for help
"/usr/mail/alex": 2 messages 2 new
> N   jenny    Thurs Jan 10 15:01 16/363 our meeting
  N   hls      Thurs Jan 10 20:01 10/241 your trip
? 2
(text of message 2)
  .

  .
? d
```

After reading his second message, Alex tries to read his first message by pressing RETURN. The mailx utility tells him he is at the end of his mail box (At EOF), so he gives the command **1** followed by a RETURN to view his first piece of mail. After reading it, he decides he did not really want to delete his second message and that he wants to read both messages again later, so he exits from mailx with an **x** command, leaving both messages in his mail box.

```
? RETURN
At EOF
? 1
(text of message 1)
  .

  .
? x
$
```

make

Keep a set of programs current.

Format

make [options] [target-files]

Summary

The make utility keeps a set of executable programs current, based on differences in the modification times of the programs and the source programs that each is dependent on.

In its simplest use, make looks at *dependency lines* in a file named **makefile** in the working directory. The dependency lines indicate relationships between files, specifying a *target file* that is dependent on one or more *prerequisite* files. If you have modified any of the prerequisite files more recently than their target file, make updates the target file based on *construction commands* that follow the dependency line. The make utility stops if it encounters an error.

Options

If you do not use the **−f** option, make takes its input from **makefile** or **Makefile** in the working directory.

−f **file** (input file) Uses **file** as input in place of **makefile**. You can use any filename in place of **file**.

−n (no execution) Causes make to display the commands it would execute to bring the **target-files** up to date, but not actually execute the commands.

−t (touch) Updates modification times of target files, but does not execute any other commands. Refer to the touch utility.

Arguments

The **target-files** refer to targets on dependency lines in **makefile**. If you do not specify a **target-file**, make updates the target on the first dependency line in **makefile**.

Discussion

A simple **makefile** has the following format.

> target: prerequisite-list
> TAB   construction-commands

The dependency line is composed of the **target** and the **prerequisite-list,** separated by a colon. The **construction-commands** line must start with a TAB and must follow the dependency line.

The **target** is the name of the file that is dependent on the files in the **prerequisite-list**. The **construction-commands** are regular commands to the Shell that construct (usually compile and/or load) the target file. The make utility executes the **construction-commands** when the modification time of one or more of the files in the **prerequisite-list** is more recent than that of the target file.

In the following example, **payroll** is the target file. It is dependent on its prerequisites, **sales.c** and **salary.c**. An appropriate **cc** command constructs the **target**. (Refer to the cc utility.)

```
payroll: sales.c salary.c
        cc sales.c salary.c —o payroll
```

Each of the prerequisites on one dependency line can be targets on other dependency lines. The nesting of these dependency specifications can continue, creating a complex hierarchy that specifies dependencies for a large system of programs.

Following, **form** is dependent on two object files, while the object files are each dependent on their respective source files and a header file (**form.h**). In turn, the header file is dependent on two other header files. The last line illustrates the fact that you can put *any* Shell command on a construction line. Here, cat creates the header file.

```
form: size.o length.o
        cc size.o length.o —o form

size.o: size.c form.h
        cc —c size.c

length.o: length.c form.h
        cc —c length.c

form.h: num.h table.h
        cat num.h table.h > form.h
```

Implied Dependencies. The make utility can rely on implied dependencies and construction commands to make your job of writing a **makefile** easier. If you do not include a dependency line for a file, make assumes that object program files are dependent on compiler and assembler source code files. Thus, if a prerequisite for a target file is **xxx.o**, and **xxx.o** is not a target with its own prerequisite, make looks for the one of the following files in the working directory.

Filename	Type of file
xxx.c	C source code
xxx.r	RATFOR source code
xxx.f	FORTRAN source code
xxx.y	YACC source code
xxx.l	Lex source code
xxx.s	assembler source code

If you do not include a construction command for one of the types of files listed above, make provides a default construction command line that calls the proper compiler or the assembler to create the object file.

Macros. The make utility has a macro facility that enables you to create and use macros within the **makefile**. The format of a macro definition is shown below.

ID = list

After this macro definition, **$(ID)** represents **list** in the **makefile**. Replace **ID** with an identifying name and **list** with a list of filenames. An example of the use of a macro appears on page 450.

By default, make invokes the C compiler without any options (except the −c option when it is appropriate to compile but not to load a file). You can use a macro definition, as shown below, to cause make to call the C compiler with any specified flags.

CFLAGS = flags

Replace **flags** with the flags you want to use. See page 450 for an example.

Comments

Because make ignores lines that begin with sharp signs (#), you can use sharp signs to set off comment lines.

Notes

You can use the −t option to touch all relevant files so that make considers everything to be up-to-date. This option is useful if you modify source files in a way that will not affect compilation (e.g., adding comments). If, on the other hand, you want to compile every program in the set that make maintains, you can use the touch utility to update the modification times of all the source files so that make considers that nothing is up-to-date. The make utility will then recompile the entire set of programs.

Examples

The first example shows a **makefile** that keeps a file named **compute** up-to-date. The first three lines (each beginning with a sharp sign) are comment lines. The first dependency line shows that **compute** is dependent on two object files: **compute.o** and **calc.o**. The corresponding construction line gives the command make needs to produce **compute**. The next dependency line shows that **compute.o** is not only dependent on its C source file but also on a header file, **compute.h**. The construction line for **compute.o** uses the C compiler optimizer (−O option). The final dependency and construction lines are not required. In their absence, make would infer that **calc.o** was dependent on **calc.c** and produce the command line needed for the compilation.

```
$ cat makefile
#
# makefile number one
#

compute: compute.o calc.o
        cc compute.o calc.o -o compute

compute.o: compute.c compute.h
        cc -c -O compute.c

# The next two lines are not required.
# Make assumes that calc.o is dependent on
# calc.c and that the C compiler is used to
# construct calc.o.
#
calc.o: calc.c
        cc -c calc.c
$
```

Following are some sample executions of make, based on the previous **makefile**. You can simulate this example by creating a directory with the files listed below and using the −n option with make. When you use −n, make does not examine the contents of the program files but only looks at the names and modification times. Because the contents are not examined, you can use null files. Because the **makefile** tells make what to do, it must contain the proper information as shown above.

```
$ ls -C
calc.c    compute.c    compute.h    makefile

$ make -n
            cc -c -O compute.c
            cc -c calc.c
            cc compute.o calc.o -o compute
$
```

If you run make again without making any changes to the prerequisite files, make indicates that the program is up-to-date by not executing any commands. The following example uses touch to change the modification time of two of the prerequisite files. This simulation shows what would happen if you were to make a change to the file. The make utility only executes the commands necessary to make the out-of-date files up-to-date and construct the target. In the first case, **compute.c** did not need to be compiled. In the second case, **compute.h** was modified. The make utility recompiled **compute.c** because it is dependent on **compute.h**. In both cases make recreated the executable file.

```
$ make
'compute' is up to date.

$ touch calc.c

$ make
cc -c calc.c
cc compute.o calc.o -o compute

$ touch compute.h

$ make
cc -c -O compute.c
cc compute.o calc.o -o compute
$
```

The following **makefile** demonstrates some additional features and uses of make. It uses macros, implied dependencies, and constructions.

```
#
# makefile number two
#

CFLAGS  = -O
FILES = in.c out.c ratio.c process.c tally.c
OBJECTS = in.o out.o ratio.o process.o tally.o
HEADERS = names.h companies.h conventions.h

report: $(OBJECTS)
        cc $(OBJECTS) -o report

ratio.o: $(HEADERS)

process.o: $(HEADERS)

tally.o: $(HEADERS)

print:
        pr $(FILES) $(HEADERS) | lp

printf:
        pr $(FILES) | lp

printh:
        pr $(HEADERS) | lp
```

Following the comment lines, the **makefile** uses **CFLAGS** to make sure that make always selects the C optimizer (**-O** option) when it invokes the C compiler because of an implied construction. (Whenever you put a construction line in a **makefile**, the construction line overrides **CFLAGS** and any other implied construction lines.)

Following **CFLAGS**, the **makefile** defines the **FILES**, **OBJECTS**, and **HEADERS** macros. Each of these macros defines a list of files.

The first dependency line shows that **report** is dependent on the list of files that **OBJECTS** defines. The corresponding construction line loads the **OBJECTS** and creates an executable file named **report**.

The next three dependency lines show that three object files are dependent on the list of files that **HEADERS** defines. There are no construction lines, so when it is necessary, make looks for a source code file corresponding to each of the object files and compiles it. The purpose of these three dependency lines is to ensure that the object files are recompiled if any of the header files is changed.

You can combine several targets on one dependency line, so these three dependency lines could have been combined into one line, as follows.

```
ratio.o process.o tally.o: $(HEADERS)
```

The final three dependency lines send source and header files to the printer. They have nothing to do with compiling the **report** file. Each of these targets (print, printf, and printh) is not dependent on anything. When you call one of these targets from the command line, make executes the construction line following it. As an example, the following command prints all the source files that **FILES** defines.

```
$ make printf
$
```

mesg

Enable/disable reception of messages.

Format

mesg [y/n]

Summary

The mesg utility enables or disables reception of messages sent by someone using the write utility. When you call mesg without an argument, it tells you whether messages are enabled or disabled.

Options

There are no options.

Arguments

The **n** (no) disables reception of messages, and the **y** (yes) enables reception.

Notes

When you first log on, messages are enabled. The nroff and pr utilities automatically disable messages while they are producing output.

Examples

The following example demonstrates how to disable messages.

```
$ mesg n
$
```

The next example calls mesg without an option and verifies that you disabled messages.

```
$ mesg
is n
$
```

mkdir

Make a directory.

Format

mkdir directory-list

Summary

The mkdir utility creates one or more directories.

Options

There are no options.

Arguments

The **directory-list** contains one or more pathnames of directories that mkdir creates.

Notes

You must have write and execute access permission to the parent directory of the directory you are creating. The mkdir utility creates directories that contain the standard invisible entries . (representing the directory itself) and .. (representing the parent directory).

Examples

The following command creates a directory named **accounts** as a subdirectory of the working directory.

```
$ mkdir accounts
$
```

Below, without changing working directories, the same user creates two subdirectories within the **accounts** directory.

```
$ mkdir accounts/prospective accounts/existing
$
```

453

Display a file, one screenful at a time.

Format

more file-list

Summary

The more utility allows you to view a text file at a terminal without missing any of the file. It is similar to cat but pauses each time it fills the screen. In response to the more prompt, you can press the SPACE bar to view another screenful, RETURN to view another line, or DEL to terminate the program. CONTROL-D causes more to display one-half of another screenful of the file; a slash followed by a regular expression causes more to display the next match of the expression near the top of the screen. If you press **v** in response to the prompt, more calls up vi so that you can edit the file—vi displays the portion of the file you were viewing.

The number followed by a percent sign that more displays as part of its prompt represents the portion of the file that it has already displayed.

This utility takes its input from files you specify on the command line or from its standard input.

Options

There are no options.

Arguments

The **file-list** is the list of files that you want to view.

Notes

This utility was developed at Berkeley and is not part of UNIX System V. If your system does not have more, you can use the pg utility. Refer to pg in Part II for more information.

If you enter a question mark in response to the prompt, more displays a complete list of commands that you can use with it.

454

To use vi from more, the **TERM** variable must be set to the proper Terminfo name—see Chapter 2.

Example

The following command line displays the file **letter**. To view more of **letter**, the user presses the SPACE bar in response to the more prompt.

```
$ more letter
.
.
.
—More—(71%)SPACE
.
.
$
```

Move (rename) a file.

Format

mv existing-file new-file-name

mv existing-file-list directory

Summary

The mv utility moves, or renames, one or more files. It has two formats. The first renames a single file with a new filename you supply. The second renames one or more files so that they appear in a specified directory. The mv utility physically moves the file if it is not possible to rename it (that is, if you move it from one physical device to another).

Options

There are no options.

Arguments

In the first form of mv, the **existing-file** is a pathname that specifies the plain file that you want to rename. The **new-file-name** is the new pathname of the file.

In the second form, the **existing-file-list** contains the pathnames of the files that you want to rename, while the **directory** specifies the new parent directory for the files. The files you rename will have the same simple filenames as the simple filenames of each of the files in the **existing-file-list** but new absolute pathnames.

Notes

The UNIX system implements mv as ln and rm. When you execute the mv utility, it first makes a link (ln) to the **new-file** and then deletes (rm) the **existing-file**. If the **new-file** already exists, mv deletes it before creating the link.

As with rm, you must have write and execute access permission to the parent directory of the **existing-file**, but you do not require read or write access permission to the file itself. If you are running mv from a terminal (that is, if mv's standard input comes from a terminal) and you do not have write access permission to the file, mv displays your access permission and waits for a response. If you enter **y** or **yes**, mv renames the file; otherwise it does not. If its standard input is not coming from the terminal, mv renames the file without question.

If the **existing-file** and the **new-file** or **directory** are on different physical devices, the UNIX system implements mv as cp and rm. In this case, mv actually moves the file instead of just renaming it. After a file is moved, the user who moved the file becomes the owner of the file.

The mv utility will not move a file onto itself.

Examples

The first command line renames **letter**, a file in the working directory, as **letter.1201**.

```
$ mv letter letter.1201
$
```

The next command line renames the file so that it appears, with the same simple filename, in the **/usr/archives** directory.

```
$ mv letter.1201 /usr/archives
$
```

The next example renames all the files in the working directory with filenames that begin with memo so they appear in the **/usr/backup** directory.

```
$ mv memo* /usr/backup
$
```

newgrp

Temporarily change the group identification of a user.

Format

newgrp [group]

Summary

The newgrp utility forks a new Shell. While you are using the new Shell, you have the privileges of a member of the group you named on the command line (that is, you can access files a member of the group can access). In order to use newgrp to change your group identification, you must be listed in the **/etc/group** file as a member of the **group**. Refer to page 294 for more information on this file.

Options

There are no options.

Arguments

When you call newgrp without an argument, it changes your group identification back to the group specified in the **/etc/passwd** file. With an argument, it changes your group identification to the **group** you specify.

Notes

If you want to determine which group you are currently associated with, create a file and use ls with the **−l** option to display the group the file is associated with. The file will be associated with the same group as you.

Examples

Following, Alex creates three files, using newgrp first to change to the **pubs** group and then using it without an argument to change back to his login group, **other**. The ls utility displays the different groups he is associated with.

```
$ cat /dev/null > test1

$ newgrp pubs

$ cat /dev/null > test2

$ newgrp

$ cat /dev/null > test3

$ ls -l test?
-rw-r--r-- 1 alex    other       0  Oct   6 21:40  test1
-rw-r--r-- 1 alex    pubs        0  Oct   6 21:40  test2
-rw-r--r-- 1 alex    other       0  Oct   6 21:41  test3
$
```

news

Display news.

Format

news [options]

Summary

The news utility displays news items from the **/usr/news** directory.

Options

Without any options, news displays all files from the **news** directory that were modified more recently than the file **.news_time** in your home directory. Then it updates the modification time of the **.news_time** file. The effect is that, without any options, news displays all news files that you have not seen.

–a   (all) This option displays all news items.

–n   (names) This option displays the names of items that news would print if you were to call it without any options.

–s   This option displays the number of items that news would print if you were to call it without any options.

Arguments

There are no arguments.

Notes

You can press DEL once to stop a news item from printing, or twice to exit from news.

nice

Change the priority of a command.

Format

nice [option] command-line

Summary

The nice utility executes a command line at a lower priority than the command line would otherwise have. You can specify a decrement in the range of 1-19. The Superuser can use nice to increase the priority of a command by using a negative decrement.

Options

Without any options, nice defaults to a decrement of 10 (the absence of an option is equivalent to a **−10** option). You specify a decrement as a number preceded by a hyphen (to give a job the lowest priority possible, use an option of **−19**).

When you log in as the Superuser, you can specify a negative decrement as a number preceded by two hyphens (e.g., **−−12**).

Arguments

The **command-line** is the command line you want to execute at a lower priority.

Example

The following command executes nroff in the background at the lowest possible priority.

```
$ nice −19 nroff —mm chapter1 > chapter1.out &
24135
$
```

nohup

Run a command that will keep running after you log off.

Format

nohup [option] command-line

Summary

The nohup utility executes a command line so that the command will keep running after you log off. Normally when you log off, the system kills all processes you have started.

Options

There are no options.

Arguments

The **command-line** is the command line you want to execute.

Notes

If you do not redirect the output from a process that you execute with nohup, both the standard output *and* error output are sent to the file named **nohup.out** in the working directory. If you do not have write permission to the working directory, nohup opens a **nohup.out** file in your home directory.

Example

The following command executes nroff in the background using nohup.

```
$ nohup nroff —mm memo > memo.out &
14235
$
```

od

Dump the contents of a file.

Format

od [options] file

Summary

The od utility dumps the contents of a file. It is useful for viewing executable (object) files and text files with embedded nonprinting characters. This utility takes its input from the file you specify on the command line or from its standard input.

Options

If you do not specify an option, the dump is in octal.

-c (character) This option produces a character dump. The od utility displays certain nonprinting characters as printing characters preceded by a backslash. It displays any non-printing characters that are not in the following list as three-digit octal numbers.

Symbol	Character
\0	null
\b	BACKSPACE
\f	FORM-FEED
\n	NEWLINE
\r	RETURN
\t	TAB

-d (decimal) This option produces a decimal dump.

-x (hexadecimal) This option produces a hexadecimal dump.

Arguments

The **file** is the pathname of the file that od displays.

Notes

The name od is short for *octal dump.*

Example

The example below shows the **sample** file displayed by cat and od with a **−c** option. The numbers to the left of the characters in the dump are the hexadecimal byte numbers of the first character on each line.

```
$ cat sample
This is a sample file.

It includes TABs:        , and NEWLINEs.
Here's what a dumped number looks like: 755.

$ od −c sample
0000000  T   h   i   s       i   s       a       s   a   m   p   l   e
0000020      f   i   l   e   .  \n  \n   I   t           i   n   c   l   u
0000040  d   e   s       T   A   B   s   :  \t   ,           a   n   d
0000060  N   E   W   L   I   N   E   s   .  \n   H   e   r   e   '       s
0000100      w   h   a   t       a       d   u   m   p   e   d           n
0000120  u   m   b   e   r       l   o   o   k   s       l   i   k   e
0000140  :       7   5   5   .  \n  \0
0000147
```

pg

Display a file, one screenful at a time.

Format

pg [options] file-list

Summary

The pg utility displays a text file on a terminal a screenful at a time. It is similar to cat but pauses each time it fills the screen. In response to the pg prompt, you can press RETURN to view another screenful, press DEL to terminate the program, or give one of the commands discussed below.

    This utility takes its input from files you specify on the command line or from its standard input.

Options

The options allow you to configure pg to your needs and liking.

–c	(cursor) Homes the cursor and clears the screen before displaying each screenful.
–e	(end) Causes pg *not* to pause at the end of each file.
–f	Keeps pg from splitting long lines. It is useful for displaying files that contain lines with nonprinting characters. These characters appear in files to cause the terminal to underline or display characters in reverse video.
+line	Replace **line** with the number of the line you want to start viewing the file at.
–n	(no newline) Causes **pg** commands to take effect as soon as you enter them without waiting for you to press RETURN.
+/pattern/	Replace **pattern** with a string or regular expression

(see the Appendix). The pg utility will start display-ing the file at the first line that contains the string or matches the **pattern**.

−p**prompt**   Replace **prompt** with the prompt you want pg to use in place of its default prompt (:). If you include the string %d in the **prompt**, pg will replace it with the page number it is displaying each time it issues the prompt.

−s   (standout) Causes pg to display all its messages and prompts in standout mode. Standout mode is usually reverse video and is dependent on the Terminfo name you are using to describe your terminal.

−**lines**   Replace **lines** with a number specifying the number of lines you want pg to use as a screen size. If you do not use this option, pg uses one fewer lines than the height of the screen.

Arguments

The **file-list** is the list of files that you want to view.

Notes

Also refer to the more utility described in Part II.

Commands

While you are viewing a file, you can give pg commands that affect what it displays next or how it displays it. Always give a com-mand in response to the pg prompt (a : unless you change it with the −**p** option) and terminate it with a RETURN (unless you use the −**n** option). The pg utility displays a list of available commands when you give the command **h**.

Searching for a Pattern. You can search forward or backward for a pattern using one of the following command formats.

[n]/pattern/[tmb]

[n]?pattern?[tmb]

The **n** is an optional number that searches for the **nth** occurrence of the pattern. If you do not specify **n**, pg searches for the first occurrence. The / delimiter causes pg to search forward and **?** causes it to search backward. [Some terminals cannot handle question marks properly so pg allows you to use carets (^) in place of the question marks.]

The **pattern** is a string or other regular expression that you are searching for. Refer to the Appendix for more information on regular expressions.

The optional character that follows the final delimiter (/ or **?**) indicates where you want pg to position the pattern on the screen. Normally, pg positions the pattern at the top of the screen (**t**). You can select the middle (**m**) or bottom (**b**) of the screen if you prefer. Once you select a position, pg uses that position until you specify a new position.

Displaying Text by Its Position in the File. In response to the pg prompt, you can display a portion of the file based on its location in reference to the beginning of the file or to the portion of the file you are currently viewing.

You can precede each of the following commands with an address. The pg utility interprets an address that you precede with a plus or minus sign as a relative address—an address that is relative to the portion of the file you are currently viewing. A plus indicates forward, toward the end of the file, and a minus indicates backward, toward the beginning of the file. Without a sign, pg assumes the address specifies a distance from the beginning of the file. The address is in units of lines or pages as is appropriate to the command.

SPACE   A SPACE displays the next page. You can enter a number of pages as an address before the SPACE command. (Unless you use the −n option, you must terminate this, and all commands, with a RETURN.)

l   With a relative address, an l scrolls the screen the
        number of lines you specify (the default is one line.)
        With an absolute address, l causes pg to display the line
        you specify at the top of the screen.

d   A **d** or CONTROL-D command scrolls the screen by one-half
        a screenful.

Displaying Other Files.   Use the following commands when
you have specified more than one file on the command line and
you want to view a file other than the one you are currently looking at.

n   Give the command **n** to view the next file. Precede the **n**
      with a number, **i**, to view the **i**th subsequent file.

p   Use the **p** command like the **n** command to view the previ-
      ous file from the **file-list**.

Example

The following example shows pg displaying **memo**. The user just
presses RETURN in response to pg's prompts. In the final prompt,
the EOF stands for *end of file*.

```
$ pg memo
    .
    .
    .
: RETURN
    .
    .
    .
: RETURN
    .
    .
    .
(EOF) : RETURN
$
```

pr

Paginate a file for printing.

Format

pr [options] file-list

Summary

The **pr** utility breaks files into pages, usually in preparation for printing. Each page has a header with the name of the file, date, time, and page number.

The **pr** utility takes its input from files you specify on the command line or from its standard input. The output from **pr** goes to its standard output and is frequently redirected by a pipe to the **lp** utility for printing.

Options

You can embed options within the **file-list**. An embedded option only affects files following it on the command line.

-d   (double-space) This option causes **pr** to double-space its output.

-h   (header) The argument following this option is the page header. The **pr** utility displays this header at the top of each page in place of the filename. If the header contains SPACEs, you must enclose it within quotation marks.

-ln   (length) This option changes the page length from the standard 66 lines to **n** lines. Replace **n** with the number of lines/page you want.

-m   (multiple columns) This option displays all specified files simultaneously in multiple columns.

+n   (page) This option causes **pr** to begin its output with page **n**. You must precede this option with a *plus sign*, not a hyphen. Replace **n** with the page number you want to start with.

469

–n   (columns) This option causes pr to display its output in **n** columns. Precede this option with a hyphen. Replace **n** with the number of columns you want.

–sx (separate) This option separates columns with the single character **x** instead of SPACEs. Replace **x** with the delimiter you want to use. If you do not specify **x**, pr uses TABs as separation characters.

–t   (no header or trailer) This option causes pr not to display its five-line page header and trailer. The header that pr normally displays includes the name of the file, the date, time, and page number. The trailer is five blank lines.

–wn (width) This option changes the page width from its standard 72 columns to **n** columns. Replace **n** with the number of columns you want.

Arguments

The **file-list** contains the pathnames of plain text files you want pr to paginate.

Notes

The write utility can't send messages to your terminal while you are running pr. Disabling messages prevents another user from sending you a message and disrupting pr's output to your screen.

Examples

The first command line shows pr paginating a file named **memo** and sending its output through a pipe to lp for printing.

```
$ pr memo | lp
request id is printer_1-501 (standard input)
$
```

Next, **memo** is sent to the printer again, this time with a special heading at the top of each page. The job is run in the background.

```
$ pr -h ´MEMO RE: BOOK´ memo | lp &
request id is printer_1-502 (standard input)
23456

$
```

Below, pr displays the **memo** file on the terminal, without any header, starting with page 3.

```
$ pr -t +3 memo
  .
  .
  .
$
```

The final command displays the output from ls in six columns on the screen. This command line is useful if your system does not support the –C (column) option of ls.

```
$ ls | pr -6 -t
  .
  .
  .
```

Display process status.

Format

ps [options]

Summary

The ps utility displays status information about active processes.

Options

Without any options, ps displays the status of all active processes that your terminal controls. You will see four columns, each with one of the following headings.

PID   (process ID) This column lists the process ID number of the process.

TTY   (terminal) This column lists the number of the terminal that controls the process.

TIME   This column lists the number of seconds the process has been executing for.

COMMAND This column lists the command name the process was called with. Use the **−f** option to display the entire command line.

−a   (all) This option displays status information for all processes that any terminal controls.

−e   (everything) This option displays status information for all processes.

−f   (full) This option displays a subset of the columns that the **−l** option displays with the addition of the STIME column that lists the time the process started. It displays the full command line in the COMMAND column.

−l   (long) This option displays a complete status report comprising 14 columns, each with one of the following headings.

F	(flags) This column lists the flags associated with the process.
S	(state) This column lists the state of the process.
UID	(user ID) This is the user ID number of the owner of the process.
PID	(see the preceding page)
PPID	(parent PID) This is the process ID number of the parent process.
C	(central processor utilization) The system uses this number for scheduling processes.
PRI	(priority) This is the priority of the process. The higher the number, the lower the priority of the process.
NI	This number is established by the nice utility. It is used in computing the priority of the process.
ADDR	(address) This number is the memory or disk address of the process.
SZ	(size) This number is the size, in blocks, of the core image of the process.
WCHAN	This column is blank for running processes. If the process is waiting or sleeping, this is the event it is waiting for.
TTY	(see the preceding page)
TIME	(see the preceding page)
COMD	(see COMMAND on the preceding page)

–u **name**   This option causes **ps** to display status information about the user **name**. Replace **name** with the login name of the user you want information about.

Arguments

There are no arguments.

Notes

Because of the way **ps** obtains the command line, the COMD column may not be accurate.

Examples

The first example shows the **ps** utility, without any options, displaying the user's active processes. The first process is the Shell (**sh**), while the second is the process executing the **ps** utility.

```
$ ps
    PID   TTY       TIME COMMAND
  24059   tty11    0:05 sh
  24259   tty11    0:02 ps
$
```

With the **–l** (long) option, **ps** displays more information about each of the processes.

```
$ ps –l
F S  UID   PID  PPID  C PRI  NI   ADDR  SZ  WCHAN   TTY      TIME COMD
1 S  108  24059      1  0   30  20    146  16  11502   tty11   0:05 sh
1 R  108  24260  24059 78   54  20    371  24          tty11   0:03 ps
$
```

The next sequence of commands shows how to use **ps** to determine the process number of a process running in the background and how to terminate that process using the **kill** utility. In this case, it is not necessary to use **ps** because the Shell displays the process number of the background processes. The **ps** utility verifies the PID number.

The first command executes **nroff** in the background. The Shell displays the PID number of the process followed by a prompt.

```
$ nroff —mm memo > memo.out &
24264
$
```

Next, ps confirms the PID number of the background task. If you did not already know this number, using ps would be the only way to find it out.

```
$ ps
    PID   TTY        TIME  COMMAND
  24059   tty11      0:05  sh
  24264   tty11      0:05  nroff
  24267   tty11      0:03  ps
$
```

Finally, the kill utility terminates the process. Refer to the kill utility for more information.

```
$ kill 24264

$
```

Delete a file (remove a link).

Format

rm [options] file-list

Summary

The rm utility removes links to one or more files. When you remove the last link, you can no longer access the file and the system releases the space the file occupied on the disk for use by another file (that is, the file is deleted).

To delete a file, you must have execute and write access permission to the parent directory of the file, but you do not need read or write access permission to the file itself. If you are running rm from a terminal (that is, rm's standard input is coming from a terminal) and you do not have write access permission to the file, rm displays your access permission and waits for you to respond. If you enter **y** or **yes**, rm deletes the file; otherwise it does not. If its standard input is not coming from the terminal, rm deletes the file without question.

Options

-f   (force) This option causes rm to remove files for which you do not have write access permission, without asking for your consent.

-i   (interactive) This option causes rm to ask you before removing each file. If you use the **−r** option with this option, rm also asks you before examining each directory. When you use the **−i** option with the * ambiguous file reference, rm can delete files with characters in their filenames that prevent you from deleting the files by other means.

If you are using the C Shell, you can put the command **alias rm rm −i** in your **.login** file to reduce the chances of accidentally deleting a file.

-r   (recursive) This option causes rm to delete the contents of the specified directory and the directory itself. Use this option cautiously.

Arguments

The **file-list** contains the list of files that rm deletes. The list can include ambiguous file references. Because you can remove a large number of files with a single command, use rm with an ambiguous file reference cautiously. If you are in doubt as to the effect of an rm command with an ambiguous file reference, use the echo utility with the same file reference first. The echo utility displays the list of files that rm will delete.

Notes

The sections on the ln utility in Part II and Chapter 4 contain discussions about removing links.

Refer to the rmdir utility in this chapter if you need to remove an empty directory.

Examples

The following command lines delete files, both in the working directory and in another directory.

```
$ rm memo
$ rm letter memo1 memo2
$ rm /usr/jenny/temp
$
```

rmdir

Delete a directory.

Format

rmdir directory-list

Summary

The rmdir utility deletes empty directories from the file system by removing links to those directories.

Options

There are no options.

Arguments

The **directory-list** contains pathnames of empty directories that rmdir removes.

Notes

Refer to the rm utility with the **−r** option if you need to remove directories that are not empty, together with their contents.

Examples

The following command line deletes the empty **literature** directory from the working directory.

```
$ rmdir literature
$
```

The next command line removes the **letters** directory using an absolute pathname.

```
$ rmdir /usr/jenny/letters
$
```

sed

Edit a file (noninteractively).

Format

sed [–n] –f program-file [file-list]

sed [–n] program [file-list]

Summary

The sed utility is a batch (noninteractive) editor. The sed commands are usually stored in a **program-file**, although you can give simple sed commands from the command line. By default, sed copies lines from the **file-list** to its standard output, editing the lines in the process. It selects lines to be edited by position within the file (line number) or context (pattern matching).

The sed utility takes its input from files you specify on the command line or from its standard input. Unless you direct output from a sed program elsewhere, it goes to its standard output.

Options

If you do not use the **–f** option, sed uses the first command line argument as its program.

–f (file) This option causes sed to read its program from the **program** file given as the first command line argument.

–n (no print) sed does not copy lines to its standard output except as specified by the Print (**p**) instruction or flag.

Arguments

The **program-file** is the pathname of a file containing a sed program (see "Description," following).

The **program** is a sed program, included on the command line. This format allows you to write simple, short sed programs without creating a separate program file.

The **file-list** contains pathnames of the plain files that sed processes. These are the input files.

Description

A sed program consists of one or more lines in the following format.

[address[,address]] instruction [argument-list]

The **addresses** are optional. If you omit the **address**, sed processes all lines from the input file. The **addresses** select the line(s) the **instruction** part of the command operates on. The **instruction** is the editing instruction that modifies the text. The number and kinds of arguments in the **argument-list** depend on the instruction.

The sed utility processes an input file as follows.

1. sed reads one line from the input file (**file-list**).
2. sed reads the first command from the **program-file** (or command line), and, if the address selects the input line, sed acts on the input line as the instruction specifies.
3. sed reads the next command from the **program-file**. If the address selects the input line, sed acts on the input line as the new instruction specifies.
4. sed repeats step 3 until it has executed all of the commands in the **program-file**.
5. If there is another line in the input file, sed starts over again with step 1; otherwise it is finished.

Addresses

A line number is an address that selects a line. As a special case, the line number $ represents the last line of the last file in the **file-list**.

A regular expression (refer to the Appendix) is an address that selects the lines that contain a string that the expression matches. Slashes must delimit a regular expression used as an address.

Except as noted, zero, one, or two addresses (either line numbers or regular expressions) can precede an instruction. If you do not use an address, sed selects all lines, causing the instruction to act on every input line. One address causes the instruction to act on each input line that the address selects. Two addresses cause the instruction to act on groups of lines. The first address selects the first line in the first group. The second address selects the next subsequent line that it matches; this line is the last line in the first group. After sed selects the last line in a group, it starts the selection process over again, looking for the next subsequent line that the first address matches. This line is the first line in the next group. The sed utility continues this process until it has finished going through the file.

Instructions

d   (delete) The Delete instruction causes sed not to write out the lines it selects. It also causes sed not to finish processing the lines. When sed executes a Delete instruction, it reads the next input line from the **file-list** and begins over again with the first command in the **program-file**.

n   (next) The Next instruction reads the next input line from the **file-list**. It writes out the currently selected line, if appropriate, and starts processing the new line with the *next* command in the **program-file**.

a   (append) The Append instruction appends one or more lines to the currently selected line. If you do not precede the Append command with an address, it appends to each input line from the **file-list**. You cannot precede an Append instruction with two addresses. An Append command has the following format.

    [address] a
    **text **
    **text **
    .
    .
    .
    text

You must end each line of appended text, except the last, with a backslash. (The backslash quotes the following NEWLINE.) The appended text concludes with a line that does not end with a backslash. The sed utility *always* writes out appended text, regardless of how you set the **−n** flag on the command line. It even writes out the text if you delete the line that you appended the text to.

i   (insert) The Insert instruction is identical to the Append instruction except that it places the new text *before* the selected lines.

c   (change) The Change instruction is similar to Append and Insert except that it changes the selected lines so that they contain the new text. You can use this command with two addresses. If you specify an address range, Change replaces the entire range of lines with a single occurrence of the new text.

s   (substitute) The Substitute instruction is akin to that of vi. It has the following format.

[address[,address]] s/pattern/replacement-string/[g][p][w]

The **pattern** is a regular expression that is delimited by any character (other than a SPACE or NEWLINE). The **replacement-string** starts immediately following the second delimiter and must be terminated by the same delimiter. The final (third) delimiter is required. The replacement string can contain an ampersand (**&**), which sed replaces with the matched **pattern**. Unless you use the **g** flag, the Substitute instruction replaces only the first occurrence of the **pattern** on each selected line.

g   (global flag) This flag causes the Substitute instruction to replace all nonoverlapping occurrences of the **pattern** on the selected lines.

p   (print flag) This flag causes **sed** to send all lines on which it makes substitutions to its standard output. If it makes more than one substitution on a line, the line is sent to its standard output once for each substitution. This flag overrides the **−n** option on the command line.

w (write flag) This flag is similar to the **p** flag, except that it sends the output to a specified file. A single SPACE and the name of a file must follow the Write flag.

p (print) The Print instruction writes the selected lines to the standard output. It writes the lines immediately and does not reflect subsequent changes to the line. This instruction overrides the **−n** option on the command line.

w (write) This instruction is similar to the **p** instruction, except that it sends the output to a specified file. A single SPACE and the name of a file must follow the Write instruction.

r (read) The Read instruction reads the contents of the specified file and appends it to the selected line. You cannot precede a Read instruction with two addresses. A single SPACE and the name of a file must follow a Read instruction.

Control Structures

! (NOT) The NOT structure causes **sed** to apply the following instruction, located on the same line, to each of the lines *not* selected by the address portion of the command.

{ } (group instructions) When you enclose a group of instructions within a pair of braces, a single address (or address pair) selects the lines that the group of instructions operates on.

Examples

The following examples use the input file **new**.

```
$ cat new
Line one.
The second line.
The third.
This is line four.
Five.
This is the sixth sentence.
This is line seven.
Eighth and last.
$
```

Unless you instruct it not to, sed copies all lines, selected or not, to its standard output. When you use the **−n** option on the command line, sed only copies specified lines.

The command line below displays all the lines in the **new** file that contain the word line (all lowercase). The command uses the address /line/, a regular expression. The sed utility selects each of the lines that contain a match for that pattern. The Print (**p**) instruction displays each of the selected lines.

```
$ sed '/line/ p' new
Line one.
The second line.
The second line.
The third.
This is line four.
This is line four.
Five.
This is the sixth sentence.
This is line seven.
This is line seven.
Eighth and last.
$
```

The preceding command does not use the **−n** option, so it displays all the lines in the input file at least once. It displays the selected lines an additional time because of the Print instruction.

The following command uses the **−n** option so that sed only displays the selected lines.

```
$ sed −n '/line/ p' new
The second line.
This is line four.
This is line seven.
$
```

Below, sed copies part of a file based on line numbers. The Print instruction selects and displays lines 3 through 6.

```
$ sed −n '3,6 p' new
The third.
This is line four.
Five.
This is the sixth sentence.
$
```

When you need to give sed more complex or lengthy commands, you can use a program file. The following program file (**pgm**) and command line perform the same function as the command line in the previous example.

```
$ cat pgm
3,6 p

$ sed -n -f pgm new
The third.
This is line four.
Five.
This is the sixth sentence.
$
```

The sed program **prg1** (below) demonstrates the Append instruction. The command in the program file selects line 2 and appends a NEWLINE and the text AFTER. to the selected line. Because the command line does not include the **-n** option, sed copies all the lines from the input file **new**.

```
$ cat prg1
2 a\
AFTER.

$ sed -f prg1 new
Line one.
The second line.
AFTER.
The third.
This is line four.
Five.
This is the sixth sentence.
This is line seven.
Eighth and last.
$
```

The **prg2** program selects all the lines containing the string This and inserts a NEWLINE and the text BEFORE. before the selected lines.

```
$ cat prg2
/This/ i\
BEFORE.
```

```
$ sed -f prg2 new
Line one.
The second line.
The third.
BEFORE.
This is line four.
Five.
BEFORE.
This is the sixth sentence.
BEFORE.
This is line seven.
Eighth and last.
$
```

The next example demonstrates a Change instruction with an address range. When you give a Change instruction a range of lines, it does not change each line within the range but changes the block of text to a single occurrence of the new text.

```
$ cat prg3
2,4 c\
SED WILL INSERT THESE\
THREE LINES IN PLACE\
OF THE SELECTED LINES.

$ sed -f prg3 new
Line one.
SED WILL INSERT THESE
THREE LINES IN PLACE
OF THE SELECTED LINES.
Five.
This is the sixth sentence.
This is line seven.
Eighth and last.
$
```

The next example demonstrates a Substitute command. The sed utility selects all lines because the command has no address. It replaces each occurrence of the string line with sentence and displays the resulting line. The **p** flag displays each line where a substitution occurs. The command line calls sed with the **-n** option so that sed only displays the lines that the program explicitly requests it to display.

```
$ cat prg4
s/line/sentence/p
```

```
$ sed -n -f prg4 new
The second sentence.
This is sentence four.
This is sentence seven.
$
```

The next example is similar to the preceding one, except a **w** flag and filename (**temp**) at the end of the Substitute command cause sed to create the file **temp**. The command line does not include a **-n** option, so it displays all lines, including those sed changes. The cat utility displays the contents of the file **temp**. The word Line (starting with an uppercase L) is not changed.

```
$ cat prg5
s/line/sentence/gw temp

$ sed -f prg5 new
Line one.
The second sentence.
The third.
This is sentence four.
Five.
This is the sixth sentence.
This is sentence seven.
Eighth and last.

$ cat temp
The second sentence.
This is sentence four.
This is sentence seven.
$
```

Below, sed uses the Write command to copy part of a file to another file (**temp2**). The line numbers 2 and 4, separated by a comma, select the range of lines sed is to copy. This program does not alter the lines.

```
$ cat prg6
2,4 w temp2

$ sed -n -f prg6 new

$ cat temp2
The second line.
The third.
This is line four.
$
```

The program **prg7** is very similar to **prg6**, except that it precedes the Write command with the NOT operator (!), causing sed to write the lines *not* selected by the address to the file.

```
$ cat prg7
2,4 !w temp3

$ sed —n —f prg7 new

$ cat temp3
Line one.
Five.
This is the sixth sentence.
This is line seven.
Eighth and last.
$
```

Below, **prg9** demonstrates the Next instruction. When sed processes the selected line (line 3), it immediately starts processing the next line, without printing line 3. Thus, it does not display line 3.

```
$ cat prg9
3 n
p

$ sed —n —f prg9 new
Line one.
The second line.
This is line four.
Five.
This is the sixth sentence.
This is line seven.
Eighth and last.
$
```

The next example uses a textual address. The sixth line contains the string the, so the Next command causes sed not to display it.

```
$ cat prg10
/the/ n
p

$ sed —n —f prg10 new
Line one.
The second line.
The third.
This is line four.
Five.
This is line seven.
Eighth and last.
$
```

The next set of examples uses the file **compound.in** to demonstrate how sed instructions work together.

```
$ cat compound.in
1. The words on this page...
2. The words on this page...
3. The words on this page...
4. The words on this page...
$
```

The first example that uses **compound.in** instructs sed to substitute the string words with text on lines 1, 2, and 3, and the string text with TEXT on lines 2, 3, and 4. It also selects and deletes line 3. The result is text on line 1, TEXT on line 2, no line 3, and words on line 4. The sed utility made two substitutions on lines 2 and 3: it substituted text for words and TEXT for text. Then it deleted line 3.

```
$ cat compound
1,3 s/words/text/
2,4 s/text/TEXT/
3 d

$ sed -f compound compound.in
1. The text on this page...
2. The TEXT on this page...
4. The words on this page...
$
```

The next example shows that the ordering of instructions within a sed program is critical. After line 2 of the program substitutes the string TEXT in place of text, the third line displays all of the lines that contain TEXT. The Print instruction would have displayed no lines, or different lines, if it had been one line before or after its present location.

```
$ cat compound2
1,3 s/words/text/g
2,4 s/text/TEXT/g
/TEXT/ p
3 d

$ sed -f compound2 compound.in
1. The text on this page...
2. The TEXT on this page...
2. The TEXT on this page...
3. The TEXT on this page...
4. The words on this page...
$
```

Below, **compound3** appends two lines to line 2. The sed utility displays all the lines from the file once because no **−n** option
appears on the command line. The Print instruction at the end of
the program file displays line 3 an additional time.

```
$ cat compound3
2 a\
This is line 2a.\
This is line 2b.
3 p

$ sed −f compound3 compound.in
1. The words on this page...
2. The words on this page...
This is line 2a.
This is line 2b.
3. The words on this page...
3. The words on this page...
4. The words on this page...
$
```

The final example shows that sed always displays appended
text. Here line 2 is deleted, but the Append instruction still
displays the two lines that were appended to it. Appended lines
are displayed even if you use the **−n** option on the command line.

```
$ cat compound4
2 a\
This is line 2a.\
This is line 2b.
2 d

$ sed −f compound4 compound.in
1. The words on this page...
This is line 2a.
This is line 2b.
3. The words on this page...
4. The words on this page...
$
```

Invoke the Shell layer manager.

Format

shl

Summary

The Shell layer manager, shl, allows you to control up to seven Shells (layers) from one terminal. Give the command **shl** when you want to start using the Shell layer manager.

Options

There are no options.

Arguments

There are no arguments.

Commands

When you first call the Shell layer manager, you see its prompt. So that you can distinguish it from one of the Shells (layers), the Shell layer manager has its own prompt (>>>). Each of the layers you create using shl uses its name (see below) as a prompt.

At any time, you will be working with the Shell layer manager or a layer that you created (see "create," following). The layer that you are working with interactively is called the *current* layer. Give the command CONTROL-Z when you want to leave the current layer and return to the Shell layer manager. (Refer to the **swtch** argument in the stty section of Part II if you want to use a different character.)

You can abbreviate any of the following commands to as few letters as you wish, as long as it is still unique. In the following list, **name** is the name of a layer and **name-list** is a list of names of one or more layers separated by SPACEs. You can use up to eight characters in a name, but you cannot use the names **(1)** through **(7)** as these are the names shl uses when you create a new layer and do not supply a name.

block [**name-list**]   Suspend execution of a layer in the **name-list** when it attempts to display output on the terminal and it is not the current layer. Resume execution when it becomes the current layer. See "unblock," below. Refer to the **loblk** argument in the stty section of Part II for a description of another method of blocking output.

create [**name**]   Create a new layer (Shell) with the name **name**. If you do not specify a name, shl uses a number from 1-7 enclosed in parentheses as the name. You can refer to a numbered shell with its number alone, without the parentheses.

delete [**name-list**]   Delete all the layers in the **name-list**. Send each process a SIGHUP signal.

help   Display a list of commands.

layers [–l] [**name-list**]   List information about the named layers or all layers if there is not a **name-list**. The **–l** option displays a listing similar to that displayed by **ps**.

quit   Exit from the Shell layer manager.

resume [**name**]   Make the named layer the current layer. If there is no **name**, make the last current layer the new current layer. If you use a name, you can omit the command (e.g., **name** has the same effect as **resume name**).

toggle   Make the layer that was the current layer before the last current layer the new current layer.

unblock [**name-list**]   Reverse the effects of a **block** command.

Example

Refer to Chapter 8 for an example of how to use shl.

sleep

Put the current process to sleep.

Format

sleep time

Summary

The sleep utility causes the process executing it to go to sleep for the time you specify.

Options

There are no options.

Arguments

The **time** is the length of time, in seconds, that the process will sleep.

Notes

The **time** must be less than 65,536 seconds.

Examples

You can use sleep from the command line to execute a command after a period of time. The example below executes a process in the background that reminds you to make a phone call in 20 minutes (1200 seconds).

```
$ (sleep 1200; echo ´Remember to make call.´) &
2145
$
```

You can also use sleep within a Shell script to execute a command at regular intervals. The following **per** Shell script executes a program named **update** every 90 seconds.

```
$ cat per
while (true)
    do
    update
    sleep 90
    done
$
```

If you execute a Shell script such as **per** in the background, you can only terminate it using the kill utility.

sort

Sort and/or merge files.

Format

sort [options] [field-specifier-list] [file-list]

Summary

The sort utility sorts and/or merges one or more text files in sequence. When you use the −n option, sort performs a numeric sort.

The sort utility takes its input from files you specify on the command line or from its standard input. Unless you use the −o option, output from sort goes to its standard output.

Options

If you do not specify an option, sort orders the file in the machine collating (usually ASCII) sequence. You can embed options within the **field-specifier-list** by following a field specifier with an option without a leading hyphen—see "Description," later in this section.

−b   (ignore leading blanks) Blanks (TAB and SPACE characters) are normally field delimiters in the input file. Unless you use this option, sort *also* considers leading blanks to be part of the field they precede. This option causes sort to consider multiple blanks as single field delimiters, with no intrinsic value, so that sort does not consider these characters in sort comparisons.

−c   (check only) This option checks to see that the file is properly sorted. The sort utility does not display anything if everything is in order. It displays a message if the file is not in sorted order.

−d   (dictionary order) This option ignores all characters that are not alphanumeric characters or blanks.

Specifically, sort does not consider punctuation and CONTROL characters.

-f   (fold lowercase into uppercase) This option considers all lowercase letters to be uppercase letters. Use this option when you are sorting a file that contains both uppercase and lowercase text.

-i   (ignore) This option ignores nonprinting characters when you preform a non-numeric sort.

-M   (month) This option compares fields that contain the names of months. It uses the first three nonblank characters in the field, shifts them to uppercase, and sorts in the order JAN, FEB, ..., DEC. It puts invalid entries first in the sorted list.

-m   (merge) This option assumes that multiple input files are in sorted order and merges them without verifying that they are sorted.

-n   (numeric sort) When you use this option, minus signs and decimal points take on their arithmetic meaning and the **-b** option is implied. The sort utility does not order lines or order sort fields in the machine collating sequence but in arithmetic order.

-o **filename** (output filename) The **filename** is the name of the output file. The sort utility sends its output to this file instead of to its standard output. Replace **filename** with a filename of your choice—it can be the same as one of the names in the **file-list**.

-r   (reverse) This option reverses the sense of the sort (e.g., *z* precedes *a*).

-t**x**   (set tab character) When you use this option, replace the **x** with the character that is the field delimiter in the input file. This character replaces SPACEs, which become regular (nondelimiting) characters.

-u   (unique) This option outputs repeated lines only

once. The sort utility outputs lines that are not repeated as it would without this option.

-y**mem**   This option allows you to specify the amount of memory that sort will use, within system limits. Replace **mem** with the number of kilobytes of memory that you want sort to use. If you omit **mem**, sort will use the maximum amount of memory that the system allows. Replace **mem** with 0 to use the minimum amount of memory possible.

-z**rec**   This option allows you to specify the maximum line length when you are merging files. Do not use it if you are sorting files. Replace **rec** with the number of bytes in the longest record you are merging.

Arguments

The **field-specifier-list** specifies one or more sort fields within each line. The sort utility uses the sort fields to sort the lines from the **file-list**. The **file-list** contains pathnames of one or more plain files that contain the text to be sorted. The sort utility sorts and merges the files unless you use the **−m** option, in which case sort only merges the files.

Description

In the following description, a *line field* is a sequence of characters on a line in an input file. These sequences are bounded by blanks and the beginning and end of the line. You use line fields to define a sort field.

A *sort field* is a sequence of characters that sort uses to put lines in order. The description of a sort field is based on line fields. A sort field can contain part or all of one or more line fields. Refer to Figure II-2.

The **field-specifier-list** contains pairs of pointers that define subsections of each line (sort fields) for comparison. If you omit the second pointer from a pair, sort assumes the end of the line. A pointer is in the form ±**f.c**. The first of each pair of pointers begins with a plus sign, while the second begins with a hyphen.

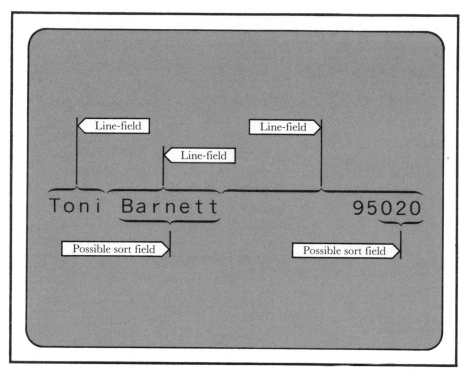

Figure II-2
Line Fields and Sort Fields

You can make a pointer (**f.c**) point to any character on a line. The **f** is the number of line fields you want to skip, counting from the beginning of the line. The **c** is the number of characters you want to skip, counting from the end of the last line field you skipped with **f**.

The **−b** option causes sort to count multiple leading blanks as a *single* line field delimiter character. If you do not use this option, sort considers each leading blank to be a character in the sort field and includes it in the sort comparison.

You can specify options that pertain only to a given sort field by immediately following the field specifier by one of the options **b**, **d**, **f**, **i**, **n**, or **r**. In this case, you must *not* precede the options with a hyphen.

If you specify more than one sort field, sort examines them in the order you specify them on the command line. If the first sort field of two lines is the same, sort examines the second sort field. If these are again the same, sort looks at the third field. This process continues for all the sort fields you specify. If all the sort fields are the same, sort examines the entire line.

If you do not use any options or arguments, the sort is based on entire lines.

Examples

The following examples assume that a file named **list**, shown below, is in the working directory. Each line of the file contains three fields: first name, last name, and ZIP code. All the blanks are SPACEs, not TABs.

```
$ cat list
Tom Winstrom        94201
Janet Dempsey       94111
Alice MacLeod       94114
David Mack          94114
Toni Barnett        95020
Jack Cooper         94072
Richard MacDonald   95510
$
```

The first example demonstrates sort without any options or arguments other than a filename. Below, sort sorts the file on a line-by-line basis. If the first characters on two lines are the same, sort looks at the second characters to determine the proper sorted order. If the second characters are the same, sort looks at the third characters. This process continues until sort finds a character that differs between the lines. If the lines are identical, it doesn't matter which one sort puts first. The **sort** command in this example only needs to examine the first three letters (at most) of each line. The sort utility displays a list that is in alphabetical order by first name.

```
$ sort list
Alice MacLeod       94114
David Mack          94114
Jack Cooper         94072
Janet Dempsey       94111
Richard MacDonald   95510
Tom Winstrom        94201
Toni Barnett        95020
$
```

You can instruct sort to skip any number of line fields and characters on a line before beginning its comparison. Blanks normally separate one line field from another. The next example sorts the same list by last name, the second line field. The **+1** argument indicates that sort is to *skip one line field* before beginning its comparison. It skips the first-name field. Because there is no second pointer, the sort field extends to the end of the line. Now the list is almost in last-name order, but there is a problem with Mac.

```
$ sort +1 list
Toni Barnett           95020
Jack Cooper            94072
Janet Dempsey          94111
Richard MacDonald      95510
Alice MacLeod          94114
David Mack             94114
Tom Winstrom           94201
$
```

In the example above, MacLeod comes before Mack. After finding the sort fields of these two lines the same through the third letter (Mac), sort put L before k because it arranges lines in the order of ASCII character codes. In this ordering, uppercase letters come before lowercase ones and therefore L comes before k.

The **−f** option makes sort treat uppercase and lowercase letters as equals and thus fixes the problem with MacLeod and Mack.

```
$ sort −f +1 list
Toni Barnett           95020
Jack Cooper            94072
Janet Dempsey          94111
Richard MacDonald      95510
David Mack             94114
Alice MacLeod          94114
Tom Winstrom           94201
$
```

The next example attempts to sort **list** on the third line field, the ZIP code. Below, sort does not put the numbers in order but puts the shortest name first in the sorted list and the longest name last. With the argument of **+2**, sort *skips* two line fields and counts the SPACEs after the second line field (last name) as part of the sort field. The ASCII value of a SPACE character is less than that of any other printable character, so sort puts the ZIP code that is preceded by the greatest number of SPACEs first and the ZIP code that is preceded by the fewest SPACEs last.

```
$ sort +2 list
David Mack              94114
Jack Cooper             94072
Tom Winstrom            94201
Toni Barnett            95020
Janet Dempsey           94111
Alice MacLeod           94114
Richard MacDonald       95510
$
```

The **−b** option causes sort to ignore leading SPACEs. With the
−b option, the ZIP codes come out in the proper order (below).
When sort determines that MacLeod and Mack have the same ZIP
codes, it compares the entire lines. The Mack/MacLeod problem
crops up again because there is no **−f** option.

```
$ sort −b +2 list
Jack Cooper             94072
Janet Dempsey           94111
Alice MacLeod           94114
David Mack              94114
Tom Winstrom            94201
Toni Barnett            95020
Richard MacDonald       95510
$
```

The next example shows a **sort** command that not only skips
line fields but skips characters as well. The **+2.3** causes sort to
skip two line fields and then skip three characters before starting
its comparisons. The sort field is, and the following list is sorted
in order of, the last two digits in the ZIP code.

The example takes advantage of the fact that if you use two
options with sort, you can include them both after a single
hyphen. The **−f** option does not fix the MacLeod and Mack problem because sort never compares last names. When it determines
that the last two digits of MacLeod and Mack's ZIP codes are the
same, it compares the entire lines, starting with the first names.
These two lines are in first-name order. The issue of preventing
sort from comparing entire lines is covered shortly.

```
$ sort -fb +2.3 list
Tom Winstrom           94201
Richard MacDonald      95510
Janet Dempsey          94111
Alice MacLeod          94114
David Mack             94114
Toni Barnett           95020
Jack Cooper            94072
$
```

The next set of examples uses the **cars** data file. From left to right, the columns in the file contain each car's make, model, year of manufacture, mileage, and price.

```
$ cat cars
plym      fury      77      73      2500
chevy     nova      79      60      3000
ford      mustang   65      45      10000
volvo     gl        78      102     9850
ford      ltd       83      15      10500
chevy     nova      80      50      3500
fiat      600       65      115     450
honda     accord    81      30      6000
ford      thundbd   84      10      17000
toyota    tercel    82      180     750
chevy     impala    65      85      1550
ford      bronco    83      25      9500
```

Without any options, sort displays a sorted copy of the file.

```
$ sort cars
chevy     impala    65      85      1550
chevy     nova      79      60      3000
chevy     nova      80      50      3500
fiat      600       65      115     450
ford      bronco    83      25      9500
ford      ltd       83      15      10500
ford      mustang   65      45      10000
ford      thundbd   84      10      17000
honda     accord    81      30      6000
plym      fury      77      73      2500
toyota    tercel    82      180     750
volvo     gl        78      102     9850
```

A **+0** sort field specifier indicates a sort from the beginning of the line (skip zero fields). Unless you specify otherwise, a sort field extends to the end of the line.

The following example shows one problem to avoid when you

are using sort. The command line instructs sort to sort on the entire line (+0) and then make a second pass, sorting on the fifth field all lines whose first-pass sort fields were the same (+4). Because no two lines are the same, sort only makes one pass, sorting on each entire line. (If two lines differed only in the fifth field, they would be sorted properly on the first pass anyway, so the second pass would be unnecessary.) Look at the lines with the ltd and mustang. They are sorted by the second field rather than the fifth, demonstrating that sort never made a second pass and never sorted by the fifth field.

```
$ sort +0 +4 cars
chevy    impala   65      85      1550
chevy    nova     79      60      3000
chevy    nova     80      50      3500
fiat     600      65      115     450
ford     bronco   83      25      9500
ford     ltd      83      15      10500
ford     mustang  65      45      10000
ford     thundbd  84      10      17000
honda    accord   81      30      6000
plym     fury     77      73      2500
toyota   tercel   82      180     750
volvo    gl       78      102     9850
```

The next example forces the first-pass sort to stop just before the second field by defining the end of the first sort field (-1). Now the ltd and mustang are properly sorted by price. But look at the bronco. It is less expensive than the other Fords, but sort has it positioned as the most expensive one. The sort utility put the list in ASCII collating sequence order, not numeric order: 9500 comes after 10000 because 9 comes after 1.

```
$ sort +0 -1 +4 cars
chevy     impala   65      85      1550
chevy     nova     79      60      3000
chevy     nova     80      50      3500
fiat      600      65      115     450
ford      mustang  65      45      10000
ford      ltd      83      15      10500
ford      thundbd  84      10      17000
ford      bronco   83      25      9500
honda     accord   81      30      6000
plym      fury     77      73      2500
toyota    tercel   82      180     750
volvo     gl       78      102     9850
```

The **−n** (numeric) option on the second pass puts the list in the proper order.

```
$ sort +0 -1 +4n cars
chevy     impala   65      85      1550
chevy     nova     79      60      3000
chevy     nova     80      50      3500
fiat      600      65      115     450
ford      bronco   83      25      9500
ford      mustang  65      45      10000
ford      ltd      83      15      10500
ford      thundbd  84      10      17000
honda     accord   81      30      6000
plym      fury     77      73      2500
toyota    tercel   82      180     750
volvo     gl       78      102     9850
```

The next example again shows that, unless you instruct it otherwise, **sort** orders a file starting with the field you specify and continuing to the end of the line. It does not make a second pass unless two of the lines appear to be the same. Although this example sorts the cars by years, it does not sort the cars by manufacturer within years.

```
$ sort +2 +0 cars
fiat      600      65      115     450
ford      mustang  65      45      10000
chevy     impala   65      85      1550
plym      fury     77      73      2500
volvo     gl       78      102     9850
chevy     nova     79      60      3000
chevy     nova     80      50      3500
honda     accord   81      30      6000
toyota    tercel   82      180     750
ford      ltd      83      15      10500
ford      bronco   83      25      9500
ford      thundbd  84      10      17000
```

Specifying an end to the sort field for the first pass allows sort to perform its secondary sort properly.

```
$ sort +2 -3 +0 cars
chevy     impala   65      85      1550
fiat      600      65      115     450
ford      mustang  65      45      10000
plym      fury     77      73      2500
volvo     gl       78      102     9850
chevy     nova     79      60      3000
chevy     nova     80      50      3500
honda     accord   81      30      6000
toyota    tercel   82      180     750
ford      bronco   83      25      9500
ford      ltd      83      15      10500
ford      thundbd  84      10      17000
```

The next examples demonstrate an important sorting technique: putting a list in alphabetical order, merging upper- and lowercase entries, and eliminating duplicates.

```
$ cat short
Pear
Pear
apple
pear
Apple
```

A plain sort:

```
$ sort short
Apple
Pear
Pear
apple
pear
```

A folded sort is a good start, but it does not eliminate duplicates.

```
$ sort -f short
Apple
apple
Pear
Pear
pear
```

The **-u** (unique) option eliminates duplicates but causes all the uppercase entries to come first.

```
$ sort -u short
Apple
Pear
apple
pear
```

When you attempt to use both **-u** and **-f**, the lowercase entries get lost.

```
$ sort -uf short
Apple
Pear
```

Two passes are the answer. Both passes are unique sorts, and the first folds uppercase letters onto lowercase ones.

```
$ sort -u +0f +0 short
Apple
apple
Pear
pear
```

Following is a more extensive demonstration of the technique described above.

```
$ cat words
apple
pear
peach
apple
Apple
Pear
prune
Plum
peach
orange
pear
plum
pumpkin


$ sort -u +0f +0 words
Apple
apple
orange
peach
Pear
pear
Plum
plum
prune
pumpkin
```

spell

Check a file for spelling errors.

Format

spell [options] file-list

Summary

The spell utility checks the words in a file against a dictionary file. It displays a list of words that it cannot either find in the dictionary or derive from one of the words in the dictionary. This utility takes its input from files you list on the command line or from its standard input.

Options

-v This option displays all words that are not literally in the dictionary. As the example on the next page shows, it gives a proposed derivation for words spell would normally accept.

-b (British) This option accepts British spellings.

Arguments

The **file-list** is a list of files that spell checks. If you specify more than one file, spell generates one list of words for all the files.

Notes

The spell utility is not a foolproof way of finding spelling errors. It also does not check for misused but properly spelled words (e.g., *read* instead of *red*).

Examples

The following examples use spell to check the spelling in the **check** file. The **−v** option causes spell to display all words that are not actually in its dictionary.

$ cat check
Here's a sampel document that is tobe
used with th Spell utilitey.
It obviously needs proofing quite badly.

$ spell check
sampel
th
tobe
utilitey

$ spell —v check
sampel
th
tobe
utilitey
+ly   badly
+'s   Here's
+s   needs
+ly   obviously
+ing   proofing
+d   used
$

stty

Display or establish terminal parameters.

Format

stty [arguments]

Summary

Without any arguments, stty displays certain parameters affecting the operation of the terminal. For a complete list of these parameters and an explanation of each, see the following "Arguments" section. With arguments, stty establishes or changes the parameter(s) you specify.

Options

Without an option, stty reports only on selected parameters.

-a   (all) This option reports on all parameters.

-g   This option generates a report in a format you can use as arguments to another stty command.

Arguments

The arguments specify which terminal parameters stty is to alter. You can turn on each of the parameters that is preceded by an optional hyphen (indicated in the following list as [-]) by specifying the parameter without the hyphen. You can turn it off by specifying it with the hyphen. Unless specified otherwise, this section describes the parameters in their *on* states.

Modes of Data Transmission.

[-]parenb   Enable parity. When you specify **-parenb**, the system does not use or expect a parity bit when communicating with the terminal.

[-]parodd   Select odd parity. (**-parodd** selects even parity.)

[-]cstopb   Use two stop bits. (**-cstopb** specifies one stop
                   bit.)

[-]raw   The normal state is **-raw**. When the system
                   reads input in its raw form, it does not interpret
                   the following special characters: erase (#), line kill
                   (@), interrupt execution (DEL), and EOF
                   (CONTROL-D). In addition, it does not use parity
                   bits. With typical UNIX system humor, you can
                   specify **-raw** as **cooked**.

Treatment of Characters.

[-]nl   Only accept a NEWLINE character as a line termi-
                   nator. With **-nl** in effect, the system accepts a
                   RETURN character from the terminal as a NEWLINE
                   while it sends a RETURN followed by a LINEFEED to
                   the terminal in place of a NEWLINE.

[-]echo   Echo characters as they are typed (full duplex
                   operation). If a terminal displays two characters
                   for each one it should display, turn the echo
                   parameter off (**-echo**).

[-]lcase   For uppercase only terminals, translate all upper-
                   case characters into lowercase as they are entered.
                   (Also **[-]LCASE**.)

[-]tabs   Transmit each TAB character to the terminal as a
                   TAB character. When **tabs** is turned off (**-tabs**),
                   the system translates each TAB character into the
                   appropriate number of SPACEs and transmits
                   these SPACEs to the terminal. (Also **[-]tab3**.)

Data Line Specifications.

[-]hupcl   Disconnect telephone line when user logs off.
(Also **[−]hup.**)

0   Disconnect telephone line immediately.

50 75 110 134   Set the terminal baud rate to one of these
150 200 300 600   numbers.
1200 1800 2400
4800 9600

shl **Parameters.**   Refer to shl in Part II for more information on
the Shell layer manager (shl) and job control.

swtch **x**   Set the character you use to switch control from a
layer (Shell) to the Shell layer manager. By
default, **x** is null. When **x** is null, stty sets **swtch**
to CONTROL-Z. Replace **x** with the character you
want to use in place of CONTROL-Z. See "erase" in
the following section for conventions you can use
to specify CONTROL characters.

[-]loblk   Block output from the layer that you set this
parameter in. With this parameter set, the sys-
tem will suspend output to the terminal until the
layer is the current (interactive) layer. Setting
loblk is the same as giving the shl **block** command. Use **−loblk** (default) to allow the system
to send output to the terminal even if the layer is
not the current layer.

Special Keys.

ek   Set the erase and line kill keys to their default
values: # and @.

erase **x**   Set the erase key to **x**. To indicate a CONTROL character, precede the **x** with a caret and enclose both characters within single quotation marks (e.g., use ´^H´ for CONTROL-H). Use ´^?´ for DEL and ´^-´ for undefined.

kill **x**   Set the line kill key to **x**. See "erase," above, for conventions.

intr **x**   Set the interrupt key to **x**. See "erase," above, for conventions.

sane   Use this argument to set the terminal parameters to usually acceptable values. The **sane** argument is useful when several stty parameters have changed, making it difficult to use the terminal even to run stty to set things right. If **sane** doesn't appear to work, try entering CONTROL-J **sane** CONTROL-J.

Transmission Delays.   You can specify any one of each of these sets of parameters. Except for 0 (zero), the numbers following the letters do not have special significance but represent a different amount of delay following the transmission of the character. Zero always means no delay.

cr0 cr1
cr2 cr3   Set delay following a RETURN.

nl0 nl1   Set delay following a NEWLINE.

tab0 tab1
tab2 tab3   Set delay following a TAB.

ff0 ff1   Set delay following a FORM-FEED.

bs0 bs1   Set delay following a BACKSPACE.

vt0 vt1   Set delay following a vertical tab.

Notes

The stty utility affects the terminal attached to its standard input. You can view or change the characteristics of a terminal other than the one you are using by redirecting the input to stty. Refer to the following command format.

stty [arguments] </dev/ttyxx

The **ttyxx** is the filename of the target terminal. You can change the characteristics of a terminal only if you own its device file.

Caution. In previous versions of the UNIX system (those released prior to System III), stty reported on or changed the specifications of the terminal attached to its *standard output*. If you are using an earlier version of the operating system, use > in place of < in the preceding command.

Examples

The first example shows stty without any arguments, displaying several terminal operation parameters. (Your system may display more or different parameters.) The character following the erase = is the erase key, and the one following kill = is the line kill key. The stty display always encloses these keys in single quotation marks. A ^ preceding a character indicates a CONTROL key. The example shows the erase key set to CONTROL-H and the line kill key set to CONTROL-U.

If stty does not display the erase character, it is set to its default, #. If you do not see a kill character, it is set to its default, @.

```
$ stty
speed 1200 baud
erase = '^h'; kill = '^u'
—parenb —nl echo
$
```

Next the **ek** argument returns the erase and line kill keys to their default values.

```
$ stty ek
$
```

The next display verifies the change. The stty utility does not display either the erase character or the line kill character, indicating that they are both set to their default values.

```
$ stty
speed 1200 baud
—parenb —nl echo
$
```

The next example sets the erase key to CONTROL-H. A ^ followed by an **h** represents the CONTROL character. You can enter either a lower- or uppercase letter.

```
$ stty erase ´^h´
$ stty
speed 1200 baud
erase = ´^H´; kill = ´@´
—parenb —nl echo
$
```

Below, stty sets the line kill key to CONTROL-X.

```
$ stty kill ´^x´
$ stty
speed 1200 baud
erase = ´^H´; kill = ´^X´
—parenb —nl echo
```

Below, stty turns off TABs so the appropriate number of SPACES are sent to the terminal in place of a TAB. Use this command if a terminal does not automatically expand TABs.

```
$ stty —tabs
$
```

If you log on and everything that appears on the terminal is in uppercase letters, give the following command.

```
$ STTY —LCASE
$
```

Turn on **lcase** if the terminal you are using cannot display lowercase characters.

Display the last part (tail) of a file.

Format

tail [±number][options] [file]

Summary

The tail utility displays the last part of a file. It takes its input from the file you specify on the command line or from its standard input.

Options

Without any options, tail counts by lines. Options must follow immediately after the **number** and not be preceded by a hyphen or a SPACE.

b   (blocks) Count by blocks.

c   (characters) Count by characters.

l   (lines) Count by lines (default).

Arguments

Without a **number**, tail displays the last ten lines of a file.
    If a plus sign precedes the **number**, tail displays blocks, characters, or lines counting from the beginning of the file. If a hyphen precedes the **number**, tail counts from the end of the file.

Examples

The examples are based on the following **lines** file:

```
$ cat lines
line one
line two
line three
line four
line five
line six
line seven
line eight
line nine
line ten
line eleven
$
```

First, tail displays the last ten lines of the **lines** file (no options).

```
$ tail lines
line two
line three
line four
line five
line six
line seven
line eight
line nine
line ten
line eleven
```

The next example displays the last three lines (**−3**, no option) of the file.

```
$ tail −3 lines
line nine
line ten
line eleven
$
```

The example below displays the file, starting at line eight (**+8**, no option).

```
$ tail +8 lines
line eight
line nine
line ten
line eleven
$
```

The final example displays the last six characters in the file (**−6c**). Only five characters are evident (leven); the sixth is a NEW-LINE.

```
$ tail −6c lines
leven
$
```

Create or retrieve files from an archive file.

Format

tar key[options] [file-list]

Summary

The tar utility can create, add to, list, and retrieve files from an archive file. The archive file is usually stored on tape.

Key

Use one (and only one) of the following keys to indicate what type of action you want tar to take. You can modify the action of the key by following it with one or more options. The key and options do not require a leading hyphen.

r   (write) tar writes the **file-list** to the end of the tape. It leaves existing files intact.

x   (extract) tar reads the **file-list** from the tape. Without a **file-list**, it reads all the files from the tape. The tar utility attempts to keep the owner, modification time, and access privileges the same as the original file.

    If tar reads the same file more than once, the last version of the file overwrites previous versions.

t   (table of contents) With a **file-list**, tar displays the name of each of the files in the **file-list** each time it occurs on the tape. Without a **file-list**, tar displays the name of each of the files on the tape.

u   (update) The tar utility adds the files from the **file-list** if they are not already on the tape *or* if they have been modified since they were last written to the tape.

    Because of the checking it does, this option is slow.

c   (create) tar creates a new tape, destroying any files that were previously written to the tape. This key implies the **r** key and, after creating a new tape, functions in the same way as **r**, writing the **file-list** to the tape.

Options

You can specify one or more options following the key. The key and options do not require a leading hyphen.

0-7 Use a number from 0 through 7 to indicate a drive other than the default, which is system dependent (usually 1).

v   (verbose) This option lists each file as tar reads or writes it. With the **t** key, this option displays additional information.

w   (query) This option asks you for confirmation before reading or writing each file. Respond with **y** if you want tar to take the action. Any other response causes tar not to take the action.

f   (file) This option causes tar to write to or read from the next argument instead of the tape drive that the system is set up for tar to use. If you give a hyphen as an argument, tar uses the standard input or output.

b   (block) This option causes tar to use the next argument as a blocking factor for writing a tape. If you do not specify a blocking factor, tar assumes a blocking factor of 1. The largest blocking factor you can use is 20. This option is only effective when you are writing to a raw device. The tar utility automatically determines the blocking factor when it reads a tape.
       Do not use this option if you will want to update the tape or if you are creating a disk file.

l   (links) This option causes tar to display messages if it cannot resolve all the links to files it is copying.

m   (modification time) When you use this option, tar does not maintain the original modification times of files it is extracting. Instead, it sets the modification time to the time of extraction.

Arguments

If you use the **f** and/or **b** options, the first one or two arguments must correspond to the options you use. Following these arguments (if they are present) is the **file-list** that lists the filenames of the files you want to write out or read in.

You can use ambiguous file references when you write files but not when you read them.

The name of a directory file within the **file-list** references all files and subdirectories within that directory.

Notes

The name tar is short for tape archive.

If you write a file using a simple filename, the file will appear in the working directory when you read it back. If you write a file using a relative pathname, it will appear with that relative pathname, starting from the working directory when you read it back. If you use an absolute pathname to write a file, tar reads it back in with the same pathname.

As you read and write files, tar attempts to preserve links between files. Unless you use the **l** option, tar does not inform you when it fails to maintain a link.

Examples

The following example makes a copy of the **/usr/alex** directory, and all files and subdirectories within that directory, on the standard tar tape. The **v** option causes the command to list all the files it writes to the tape as it proceeds. This command erases anything that was already on the tape.

```
$ tar cv /usr/alex
a /usr/alex/letter 5 blocks
a /usr/alex/memo 11 blocks
a /usr/alex/notes 27 blocks
.
.
.
```

In the next example, the same directory is saved on the tape on device **/dev/rmt1** with a blocking factor of 20. Without the **v** option tar does not display the list of files it is writing to tape.

This command runs in the background and displays its only message after the Shell issues a new prompt.

```
$ tar cbf 20 /dev/rmt1 /usr/alex &
3452
$ blocking factor = 20
```

The next command displays the contents of the tape on device **/dev/rmt1**.

```
$ tar tvf /dev/rmt1
Tar: blocksize = 1
rw-rw-rw-201/0    4720   May   7 6:59 1984 /usr/alex/letter
rw-rw-rw-201/0   10420   May   7 6:59 1984 /usr/alex/memo
rw-rw-rw-201/0   27471   May   7 6:59 1984 /usr/alex/notes
.
.
.
```

tee

Copy the standard input to the standard output and one or more files.

Format

> **tee [options] file-list**

Summary

The tee utility copies its standard input to its standard output *and* to one or more files as you specify on the command line.

Options

Without any options, tee overwrites the output files if they exist and responds to interrupts.

–i (no interrupts) With this option, tee does not respond to interrupts.

–a (append) This option causes tee to append output to files (not overwrite them).

Arguments

The **file-list** contains the pathnames of files that receive output from tee.

Examples

In the following example a pipe sends the output from date to tee, which copies it to its standard output and the file **hold.date**. The copy that goes to its standard output appears on the screen. The cat utility displays the copy that was sent to the file.

```
$ date | tee hold.date
Wed Dec 19 09:32:10 PST 1984

$ cat hold.date
Wed Dec 19 09:32:10 PST 1984
$
```

test

Evaluate an expression.

Format

test expression

Summary

The test utility evaluates an expression and returns a condition code indicating that the expression is either true (=0) or false (not =0).

Options

There are no options.

Arguments

The **expression** contains one or more criteria (see the following list) that test evaluates. A **−a** separating two criteria is a logical AND operator: both criteria must be true for test to return a condition code of true. A **−o** is a logical OR operator. When **−o** separates two criteria, one or the other (or both) of the criteria must be true for test to return a condition code of true.

You can negate any criterion by preceding it with an exclamation point (**!**). You can group criteria with parentheses. If there are no parentheses, **−a** takes precedence over **−o** and test valuates operators of equal precedence from left to right.

Within the **expression**, you must quote special characters, such as parentheses, so that the Shell does not interpret them but passes them on to test.

Because each element (such as a criterion, string, or variable) within the **expression** is a separate argument, you must separate each element from other elements with a SPACE.

Following is a list of criteria you can use within the **expression**.

string   This criterion is true if the **string** is not a null string.

–n **string**   This criterion is true if the **string** has a length greater than zero.

–z **string**   This criterion is true if the **string** has a length of zero.

string1 = **string2**   This criterion is true if **string1** is equal to **string2**.

string1 != **string2**   This criterion is true if **string1** is not equal to **string2**.

int1 relop **int2**   This criterion is true if integer **int1** has the specified algebraic relationship to integer **int2**. The **relop** is a relational operator from the following list.

Relop	**Description**
–gt	greater than
–ge	greater than or equal to
–eq	equal to
–ne	not equal to
–le	less than or equal to
–lt	less than

–r **filename**   This criterion is true if the file named **filename** exists and you have read access permission to it.

–w **filename**   This criterion is true if the file named **filename** exists and you have write access permission to it.

–x **filename**   This criterion is true if the file named **filename** exists and you have execute access permission to it.

−f filename	This criterion is true if the file named **filename** exists and is a plain file.
−d filename	This criterion is true if the file named **filename** exists and is a directory.
−c filename	This criterion is true if the file named **filename** exists and is a character special file.
−b filename	This criterion is true if the file named **filename** exists and is a block special file.
−p filename	This criterion is true if the file named **filename** exists and is a named pipe.
−u filename	This criterion is true if the file named **filename** exists and its set user ID bit is set.
−g filename	This criterion is true if the file named **filename** exists and its set group ID bit is set.
−k filename	This criterion is true if the file named **filename** exists and its sticky bit is set.
−s filename	This criterion is true if the file named **filename** exists and contains information (has a size greater than 0 bytes).
−t file-descriptor	This criterion is true if the open file with the file descriptor number **file-descriptor** is associated with a terminal. If you do not specify a **file-descriptor**, test assumes number 1 (standard output).

Notes

The test utility is useful in Bourne Shell scripts. Because the C Shell has the equivalent of test built into it, C Shell scripts do not normally use it.

Examples

The following examples show how to use the **test** utility in Shell scripts. Although **test** will work from a command line, it is more commonly used in Shell scripts to test input or verify access to a file.

The first two examples show incomplete Shell scripts. They are not complete because they do not test for upper- as well as lowercase input or inappropriate responses and do not acknowledge more than one response.

The first example prompts the user, reads a line of input into the user variable **user_input**, and uses **test** to see if the user variable **user_input** matches the quoted string **yes**. Refer to Chapter 8 for more information on variables, Read, and If.

```
$ cat user_in
echo 'Input yes or no: \c'
read user_input
if (test "$user_input" = "yes")
    then echo 'You input yes.'
fi
$
```

The next example prompts the user for a filename and then uses **test** to see if the user has read access permission (**−r**) for the file *and* (**−a**) if the file contains information (**−s**).

```
$ cat validate
echo 'Enter filename: \c'
read filename
if (test −r "$filename" −a −s "$filename")
    then echo 'File' $filename 'exists and
contains information.
You have read access
permission to the file.'
fi
$
```

Without a number, the **−t** criterion assumes a value of 1 for the file descriptor and causes **test** to determine whether the process running **test** is sending output to a terminal. The **test** utility returns a value of true (**0**) if the process is sending its output to a terminal. Following is a listing of the Shell script **term** that runs test.

```
$ cat term
test -t
echo 'This program is (=0) or is not (=1)
sending its output to a terminal:' $?
$
```

First, **term** is run with the output going to the terminal, that is, the output is not redirected to a file. The test utility returns a 0. The Shell stores this value in the Shell variable that records the condition code of the last process, **$?**. The echo utility displays this value.

```
$ term
This program is (=0) or is not (=1)
sending its output to a terminal: 0
$
```

The next example runs **term** and redirects the output to a file. The listing of the file **temp** shows that test returned a 1, indicating that its output was not going to a terminal.

```
$ term > temp
$ cat temp
This program is (=0) or is not (=1)
sending its output to a terminal: 1
$
```

touch

Update a file's modification time.

Format

touch [option] file-list

Summary

The touch utility reads a byte from a file and writes it back to make the time (date) last modified associated with the file current. This utility is frequently used with the make utility.

Options

When you do not specify the **−c** option, touch creates the file if it does not exist.

−c   (no create) Do not create the file if it does not already exist.

Arguments

The **file-list** contains the pathnames of the files touch is to update.

Examples

The following examples demonstrate how touch functions. The first commands show touch updating an existing file. The ls utility with the **−l** option displays the modification time of the file. The last three command lines show touch creating a file.

```
$ ls −l program.c
-rw-r--r-- 1 jenny pubs      136   Nov   7 16:48 program.c

$ touch program.c

$ ls −l program.c
-rw-r--r-- 1 jenny pubs      136   Jun  25 16:33 program.c

$ ls −l read.c
read.c not found

$ touch read.c

$ ls −l read.c
-rw-r--r-- 1 jenny pubs        0   Jun  25 16:35 read.c
$
```

tty

Display the terminal pathname.

Format

tty

Summary

The tty utility displays the pathname of its standard input file if it is a terminal.

Options

There are no options.

Arguments

There are no arguments.

Notes

If its standard input is not a terminal, tty displays not a tty.

Example

The following example illustrates the use of tty.

```
$ tty
/dev/tty11
$
```

umask

Establish file-creation permissions mask.

Format

umask [mask]

Summary

The umask utility specifies a mask that the system uses to set up access permissions when you create a file.

Options

There are no options.

Arguments

The **mask** is a three-digit octal number with each digit corresponding to permissions for the owner of the file, members of the group the file is associated with, and everyone else. When you create a file, the system subtracts these numbers from the numbers corresponding to the access permissions the system would otherwise assign to the file. The result is three octal numbers that specify the access permissions for the file. (Refer to the chmod utility in Part II for a complete description and examples of these numbers.)

Without any arguments, umask displays the file-creation permissions **mask**.

Notes

A **umask** command generally appears in a **.profile** file.

Example

The following command sets the file-creation permissions mask to **066**. The command has the effect of removing read and write permission for members of the group the file is associated with and everyone else. It leaves the owner's permissions as the system

530

specifies. If the system would otherwise create a file with a permission value of **777** (read, write, and execute access for owner, group, and everyone else), it will now create the file with **711** (all permissions for the owner and only execute permission for group and everyone else).

```
$ umask 066
$
```

uniq

Display lines of a file that are unique.

Format

uniq [options] [−fields] [+characters] [input-file] [output-file]

Summary

The uniq utility displays a file, removing all but one copy of successive repeated lines. If the file has been sorted (refer to the sort utility), uniq ensures that no two lines that it displays are the same.

The uniq utility takes its input from a file you specify on the command line or from its standard input. Unless you specify the output file on the command line, uniq sends its output to its standard output.

Options

−c   (count) This option causes uniq to precede each line with the number of occurrences of the line in the input file.

−d   (repeated lines) This option causes uniq to display only lines that are repeated.

−u   (unique lines) This option causes uniq to display only lines that are *not* repeated.

Arguments

In the following description, a *field* is any sequence of characters not containing white space (any combination of SPACEs and TABs). Fields are bounded by white space or the beginning or end of a line.

The **−fields** is a number preceded by a hyphen and causes uniq to ignore the first specified number of fields of each line. When you use this argument, uniq bases its comparison on the remainder of the line.

The **+characters** is a number preceded by a plus sign and causes uniq to ignore the first specified number of characters of each line. If you also use **−fields**, uniq ignores the number of characters you specify after the end of the last field that it ignores. The **+characters** does *not* ignore blanks following the last ignored field. You must take these blanks into account when you specify the number of characters to ignore.

You can specify the **input-file** on the command line. If you do not specify it, uniq uses its standard input.

You can specify the **output-file** on the command line. If you do not specify it, uniq uses its standard output.

Examples

These examples assume the file named **test** in the working directory contains the following text.

```
$ cat test
boy took bat home
boy took bat home
girl took bat home
dog brought hat home
dog brought hat home
dog brought hat home
$
```

Without any options, uniq removes all but one copy of successive repeated lines.

```
$ uniq test
boy took bat home
girl took bat home
dog brought hat home
$
```

The **−c** option displays the number of consecutive occurrences of each line in the file.

```
$ uniq −c test
   2 boy took bat home
   1 girl took bat home
   3 dog brought hat home
$
```

The **−d** option displays only lines that are consecutively repeated in the file.

```
$ uniq -d test
boy took bat home
dog brought hat home
$
```

The **–u** option displays only lines that are *not* consecutively repeated in the file.

```
$ uniq -u test
girl took bat home
$
```

Below, the –fields argument (**–1**) skips the first field in each line, causing the lines that begin with boy and the one that begins with girl to appear to be consecutive repeated lines. The uniq utility only displays one occurrence of these lines.

```
$ uniq -1 test
boy took bat home
dog brought hat home
$
```

The final example uses both the –fields and +characters arguments (**–2** and **+2**) to first skip two fields and then skip two characters. The two characters this command skips include the SPACE that separates the second and third fields and the first character of the third field. Ignoring these characters, all the lines appear to be consecutive repeated lines containing the string at home. The uniq utility only displays the first of these lines.

```
$ uniq -2 +2 test
boy took bat home
$
```

Display the number of lines, words, and characters in a file.

Format

wc [options] file-list

Summary

The wc utility displays the number of lines, words, and characters one or more files contains. If you specify more than one file on the command line, wc displays totals for each file and totals for the group of files.

The wc utility takes its input from files you specify on the command line or from its standard input.

Options

-c   (characters) This option causes wc to display only the number of characters in the file.

-l   (lines) This option causes wc to display only the number of lines in the file.

-w   (words) This option causes wc to display only the number of words in the file.

Arguments

The **file-list** contains the pathnames of one or more text files that wc analyzes.

Notes

A word is a sequence of characters bounded by SPACES, TABS, NEW-LINES, or a combination of these.

Examples

The following command line displays an analysis of the file named **memo**. The numbers represent the number of lines, words, and characters in the file.

```
$ wc memo
        5       31      146 memo
$
```

The next command line shows an analysis of three files. The line at the bottom, with the word total in the right-hand column, contains the sum of each of the columns.

```
$ wc memo1 memo2 memo3
       10       62      292 memo1
       12       74      341 memo2
       12       68      320 memo3
       34      204      953 total
$
```

Display names of users.

Format

who [options]

who am i

Summary

The who utility displays the names of users currently logged on, together with their terminal device numbers, the times they logged on, and other information.

Options

-b   (boot) This option displays the time that the system was last booted.

-H   (header) This option precedes the output from who with a header.

-l   (login) This option lists the lines that are waiting for users to log on.

-q   (quick) This option displays the number of users logged on the system.

-s   (standard) This option displays the same list who displays when you do not use any options.

-t   (time) This option displays the time that the system clock was last changed.

-T   This option is the same as **–u**, but it also includes the **state** field. A + in the **state** field indicates that anyone can write to the terminal, and a – indicates that only the Superuser can write to the terminal. A **?** indicates that the line is bad.

537

-u   (users) This option gives a complete listing of users who are logged on.

Arguments

When given the two arguments am i, who displays the login name of the user giving the command, the terminal device number, and the time the user logged on.

Description

The format of a line that who displays is shown below.

name [state] line time activity PID

The **name** is the login name of the user. The **state** is the state of the terminal (see the **−T** option). The **line** is the device number associated with the line that the user is logged in on. The **time** is the date and time the user logged on. The **activity** is the length of time since the terminal was last used. A period indicates that the terminal was used within the last minute, and an entry of **old** indicates that the terminal has not been used for at least 24 hours. The **PID** is the process ID number of the user's login Shell.

Examples

The following examples demonstrate the use of the who utility.

```
$ who
jenny          tty1      Nov 29 11:01
alex           tty11     Nov 29 18:11

$ who am i
alex           tty11     Nov 29 18:11

$ who -uH
NAME           LINE      TIME              IDLE     PID   COMMENTS
alex           tty11     Nov 29 18:11               1427
$
```

write

Send a message to another user.

Format

write destination-user [tty-name]

Summary

You and another user can use write to establish two-way communication. Both of you must execute the write utility, each specifying the other user's name as the **destination-user**. The write utility then copies text, on a line-by-line basis, from each terminal to the other.

When you execute the write utility, a message appears on the **destination-user**'s terminal indicating that you are about to transmit a message.

When you want to stop communicating with the other user, press CONTROL-D once at the start of a line to return to the Shell. The other user must do the same.

Options

There are no options.

Arguments

The **destination-user** is the login name of the user you are sending a message to. The **tty-name** can be used as a second argument, after the user name, to resolve ambiguities if a user is logged in on more than one terminal.

Notes

It may be helpful to set up a protocol for carrying on communication when you use write. Try ending each message with **o** for "over" and ending the transmission with **oo** for "over and out." This gives each user time to think and enter a complete message without the other user wondering whether the first user is finished.

While you are using write, any line beginning with an exclamation point causes write to pass the line, without the exclamation point, to the Shell for execution.

Each user controls permission to write to that user's terminal. Refer to the mesg utility.

Example

Refer to Chapter 3 for a tutorial example of write.

APPENDIX: REGULAR EXPRESSIONS

A regular expression defines a set of one or more strings of characters. Several of the UNIX utility programs, including ed, vi, grep, awk, and sed, use regular expressions to search for and replace strings.

A simple string of characters is a regular expression that defines one string of characters: itself. A more complex regular expression uses letters, numbers, and special characters to define many different strings of characters. A regular expression is said to *match* any string it defines.

CHARACTERS

As used in this Appendix, a *character* is any character *except* a NEWLINE. Most characters represent themselves within a regular expression. A *special character* is one that does not represent itself. If you need to use a special character to represent itself, see the section of this Appendix on "Quoting Special Characters."

DELIMITERS

A character, called a *delimiter*, usually marks the beginning and end of a regular expression. The delimiter is always a special character for the regular expression it delimits (that is, it does not represent itself but marks the beginning and end of the expression). You can use any character as a delimiter, as long as you use the same character at both ends of the regular expression. For simplicity, all the regular expressions in this Appendix use a forward slash as a delimiter. In some unambiguous cases, the second delimiter is not required. You can usually omit the second delimiter when it would be followed immediately by a RETURN.

SIMPLE STRINGS

The most basic regular expression is a simple string that contains no special characters except the delimiters. A simple string matches only itself.

Regular expression	Meaning	Examples
/ring/	matches ring	ring, spring, ringing, stringing
/Thursday/	matches Thursday	Thursday, Thursday's
/or not/	matches or not	or not, poor nothing

SPECIAL CHARACTERS

You can use special characters within a regular expression to cause it to match more than one string. A regular expression that includes a special character always matches the longest possible string starting as far toward the beginning (left) of the line as possible.

Period

A period matches any character.

Regular expression	Meaning	Examples
/ .alk/	matches all strings that contain a SPACE followed by any character followed by alk	will talk, may balk
/.ing/	matches all strings with any character preceding ing	singing, ping, before inglenook

Square Brackets

Square brackets ([ ]) define a *character class* that matches any single character within the brackets. If the first character following the left square bracket is a caret (^), the square brackets define a character class that matches any single character not within the brackets. You can use a hyphen to indicate a range of characters. Within a character class definition, backslashes, asterisks, and dollar signs (all described in the following sections) lose their special meanings. A right square bracket (appearing as a member of the character class) can only appear as the first character following the left square bracket, and a caret is only special if it is the first character following the left bracket.

Regular expression	Meaning	Examples
/[bB]ill/	defines the character class containing b and B—matches a member of the character class followed by ill	bill, Bill, billed
/t[aeiou].k/	matches t followed by a lowercase vowel, any character, and a k	talkative, took teak, tanker
/number [6-9]/	matches number followed by a SPACE and a member of the character class	number 6 number 8 number 9
/[^a-zA-Z]/	matches any character that is not a letter	1, 7, @, ., }

Asterisk

An asterisk can follow a regular expression that represents a single character. The asterisk represents *zero* or more occurrences of a match of the regular expression. An asterisk following a period matches any string of characters. (A period matches any character, and an asterisk matches zero or more occurrences of the preceding regular expression.) A character class definition followed by an asterisk matches any string of characters that are members of the character class.

Regular expression	Meaning	Examples
/ab*c/	matches a followed by zero or more b's followed by a c	ac, abc, abbc, abbbc
/ab.*c/	matches ab followed by zero or more other characters followed by c	abc, abxc, ab45c, ab 756.345 x cat
/t.*ing/	matches t followed by zero or more characters followed by ing	thing, ting, thought of going
/[a-zA-Z]*	matches a string composed only of letters and SPACES	any string without numbers or punctuation
/(.*)/	matches as long a string as possible between (and)	(this) and (that)
/([^)]*)/	matches the shortest string possible that starts with (and ends with)	(this), (this and that)

Caret and Dollar Sign

A regular expression that begins with a caret (^) can only match a string at the beginning of a line. In a similar manner, a dollar sign at the end of a regular expression matches the end of a line.

Regular expression	Meaning	Examples
/^T/	matches a T at the beginning of a line	This line... That time...
/^+[0-9]/	matches a plus sign followed by a number at the beginning of a line	+5 45.72 +759 Keep this...
/:$/	matches a colon that ends a line	...below:

Quoting Special Characters

You can quote any special character (but not a digit or a paren-thesis) by preceding it with a backslash. Quoting a special charac-ter makes it represent itself.

Regular expression	Meaning	Examples
/end\./	matches all strings that contain end followed by a period	The end., send. pretend.mail
/\/	matches a single backslash	\
/*/	matches an asterisk	*.c, an asterisk (*)
/\[5\]/	matches the string [5]	it was five [5]
/and\/or/	matches and/or	and/or

RULES

The following rules govern the application of regular expressions.

Longest Match Possible

As stated previously, a regular expression always matches the longest possible string starting as far toward the beginning of the line as possible. For example, given the following string:

This (rug) is not what it once was (a long time ago), is it?

The expression: /Th.*is/
matches: This (rug) is not what it once was (a long time ago), is

and: /(.*)/
matches: (rug) is not what it once was (a long time ago)

however: /([^)]*)/
matches: (rug)

One Regular Expression Does Not Exclude Another

If a regular expression is composed of two regular expressions, the first will match as long a string as possible but will not exclude a match of the second. Given the following string:

singing songs, singing more and more

The expression: / s.*ing /
matches: singing songs, singing

and: / s.*ing song /
matches: singing song

Empty Regular Expressions

An empty regular expression always represents the last regular expression that you used. For example, if you give vi the following Substitute command:

s/mike/rober t/

and then you want to make the same substitution again, you can use the command:

s//rober t/

The empty regular expression (//) represents the last regular expression you used (/mike/).

BRACKETING EXPRESSIONS

You can use quoted parentheses, \(and \), to bracket a regular expression. The string that the bracketed regular expression matches can subsequently be used, as explained in "Quoted Digits," page 549. A regular expression does not attempt to match quoted parentheses. Thus, a regular expression enclosed within quoted parentheses matches what the same regular expression without the parentheses would match.

The expression: `/\(rexp\)/`
matches: what `/rexp/` would match

and: `/a\(b*\)c/`
matches: what `/ab*c/` would match

You can nest quoted parentheses. The following expression consists of two bracketed expressions, one within the other.

`/\([a-z]\([A-Z]*\)\)/`

The bracketed expressions are identified only by the opening \('s, so there is no ambiguity in identifying them.

THE REPLACEMENT STRING

The vi and sed editors use regular expressions as Search Strings within Substitute commands. You can use two special characters, ampersands (**&**) and quoted digits (**n**), to represent the matched strings within the corresponding Replacement String.

Ampersands

Within a Replacement String, an ampersand (**&**) takes on the value of the string that the Search String (regular expression) matched.

For example, the following Substitute command surrounds a string of one or more numbers with **NN**. The ampersand in the Replacement String matches whatever string of numbers the regular expression (Search String) matched. Two character class definitions are required because the regular expression $[0-9]*$ matches *zero* or more occurrences of a digit, and *any* character string is zero or more occurrences of a digit.

`s/[0-9][0-9]*/NN&NN/`

Quoted Digits

Within the regular expression itself, a quoted digit (\n) takes on the value of the string that the bracketed regular expression beginning with the nth \(matched.

Within a Replacement String, a quoted digit represents the string that the bracketed regular expression (portion of the Search String) beginning with the nth \(matched.

For example, you can take a list of people in the form

```
last—name, first—name initial
```

and put it in the following format

```
first—name initial last—name
```

with the following vi command.

```
1,$s/\([^,]*\), \(.*\)/\2 \1/
```

This command addresses all the lines in the file (1,$). The Substitute command (**s**) uses a Search String and a Replacement String delimited by forward slashes. The first bracketed regular expression within the Search String, \([^,]*\) , matches what the same unbracketed regular expression, [^,]*, would match. This regular expression matches a string of zero or more characters not containing a comma (the **last-name**). Following the first bracketed regular expression is a comma and a SPACE that match themselves. The second bracketed expression \(.*\) matches any string of characters (the **first-name** and **initial**).

The Replacement String consists of what the second bracketed regular expression matched (\2) followed by a SPACE and what the first bracketed regular expression matched (\1).

SUMMARY

A regular expression defines a set of one or more strings of characters. A regular expression is said to match any string it defines.

The following characters are special within a regular expression.

Special character	Function
.	matches any single character
$[xyz]$	defines a character class that matches x, y, or z
$[\char94 xyz]$	defines a character class that matches any character except x, y, or z
$[x-z]$	defines a character class that matches any character x through z inclusive
*	matches zero or more occurrences of a match of the preceding character
^	forces a match to the beginning of a line
$	forces a match to the end of a line
\	used to quote special characters
$\backslash(xyz\backslash)$	matches what xyz matches (a bracketed regular expression)

The following characters are special within a Replacement String.

Character	Function
&	represents what the regular expression (Search String) matched
$\backslash n$	a quoted number, n, represents the nth bracketed regular expression in the Search String

GLOSSARY

Absolute pathname. A pathname that starts with the root directory (/). An absolute pathname locates a file without regard to the working directory.

Access. In computer jargon, this word is frequently used as a verb to mean use, read from, or write to. To access a file means to read from or write to the file.

Access permission. Permission to read from, write to, or execute a file. If you have "write access permission to a file," it means that you can write to the file. Also, *access privilege.*

Alphanumeric character. One of the characters, either uppercase or lowercase, from A to Z and 0 to 9, inclusive.

Ambiguous file reference. A reference to a file that does not necessarily specify any one file but can be used to specify a group of files. The Shell expands an ambiguous file reference into a list of filenames. Special characters represent single characters (?), strings of zero or more characters (*), and character classes ([ ]) within an ambiguous file reference.

Angle bracket. There is a left angle bracket (<) and a right angle bracket (>).

Append. To add something to the end of something else. To append text to a file means to add the text to the end of the file.

Argument. A number, letter, or word that gives some information to a program and is passed to the program at the time it is called. A command line argument is anything on a command line following the command itself.

Arithmetic expression. A group of numbers, operators, and parentheses that can be evaluated. When you evaluate an arithmetic expression, you end up with a number.

Array. An arrangement of elements (numbers or strings of characters) in one or more dimensions. The C Shell and awk can store and process arrays.

ASCII. This acronym stands for the American National Standard Code for Information Interchange. It is a code that uses seven bits to represent both graphic (letters, numbers, and punctuation) and CONTROL characters. You can represent any textual information, including program source code and English text, in ASCII code. Because it is a standard, it is frequently used when exchanging information between computers.

There are extensions of the ASCII character set that make use of eight bits. The seven-bit set is common; the eight-bit extensions are still coming into popular use.

Asynchronous event. An event that does not occur regularly or synchronously with another event. UNIX system signals are asynchronous; they can occur at any time because they can be initiated by any number of irregular events.

Background process. A process that is not run in the foreground. Also called a *detached process,* a background process is initiated by a command line that ends with an ampersand (**&**). You do not have to wait for a background process to run to completion before giving the Shell additional commands.

Baud rate. Transmission speed. Usually used to measure terminal or modem speed. Common baud rates range from 110 to 19,200 baud. You can roughly convert baud to characters per second by dividing by ten (e.g., 300 baud equals approximately 30 characters per second).

Bit. The smallest piece of information a computer can handle. A bit is either a 1 or 0 (on or off).

Blank character. Either a SPACE or a TAB character, also called *white space.*

Block. A disk or tape is divided into sections (usually 1024 bytes long, but shorter on some systems) that are written at one time. Each of these sections is a block.

Block device. A disk or tape drive. A block device stores information in blocks of characters. A block device is represented by a block device (block special) file. See *Character device.*

Block number. Disk and tape blocks (see *Block*) are numbered so that the UNIX system can keep track of the data on the device. These numbers are block numbers.

Braces. There is a left brace ({) and a right brace (}).

Bracket. Either a square or angle bracket.

Branch. In a tree structure, a branch connects nodes, leaves, and the root.

Buffer. An area of memory that stores data until it can be used. When you write information to a file on a disk, the UNIX system stores the information in a disk buffer until there is enough to write to the disk or until the disk is ready to receive the information.

Byte. Eight bits of information. A byte can store one character.

Calling environment. A list of variables and their values that is made available to a called program. See "Environment and Exporting Variables" in Chapter 8 and "Variable Substitution" in Chapter 9.

Case-sensitive. Able to distinguish between uppercase and lowercase characters. Unless you set the **ignorecase** parameter, vi performs case-sensitive searches.

Catenate. To join sequentially, or end to end. Also *concatenate*. The UNIX cat utility catenates files—it displays them one after the other.

Character class. A group of characters that defines which characters can occupy a single character position. A character class definition is usually surrounded by square brackets. The character class defined by [abcr] represents a character position that can be occupied by *a*, *b*, *c*, or *r*.

Character device. A terminal, printer, or modem. A character device stores or displays characters one at a time. A character device is represented by a character device (character special) file. See *Block device*.

Command line. A line of instructions and arguments that executes a command. This term usually refers to a line that you enter in response to a Shell prompt.

Concatenate. See *Catenate*.

Condition code. See *Exit status.*

Console terminal. Also, *console.* The main system terminal, usually the one that receives system error messages. In releases of the UNIX system prior to System V, one specific terminal was always the console terminal. With System V, any terminal that is being used for system administration can become the console terminal.

CONTROL character. A character that is not a graphic character such as a letter, number, or punctuation mark. They are called CONTROL characters because they frequently act to control a peripheral device. RETURN and FORM-FEED are CONTROL characters that control a terminal or printer.

   The word CONTROL is printed in uppercase letters in this book because it is a key that appears on most terminal keyboards. It may be labeled CNTRL or CTRL on your terminal. CONTROL characters, frequently called nonprinting characters, are represented by ASCII codes less than 32 (decimal).

Current (process, line, character, directory, event, etc.). The item that is immediately available, working, or being used. The current process is the process that is controlling the program you are running; the current line or character is the one the cursor is on; the current directory is the working directory.

Cursor. A small lighted rectangle or underscore that appears on the terminal screen and indicates where the next character is going to appear.

Daemon. A process that runs in the background, independent of a terminal, and performs a function. An example is the printer daemon, which controls the job queue for the printer.

Debug. To correct a program.

Default. Something that is selected without being explicitly specified. When used without an argument, ls displays a short list of the files in the working directory by default.

Detached process. See *Background process.*

Device. See *Peripheral device.*

Device driver. The program that controls a device such as a terminal, disk drive, or printer.

Device file.   Also called a *special file*. A file that represents a device. There are five kinds of UNIX system files: plain, directory, fifo, block device, and character device files.

Device filename.   The pathname of a device file. Most device files are located in the **/dev** directory.

Device number.   See *Major device number* and *Minor device number*.

Directory.   Short for *directory file*. A file that contains a list of other files.

Disk slice.   A portion of a disk. A disk slice can hold a file system or another structure, such as the swap area.

Element.   One thing, usually a basic part of a group of things. An element of a numeric array is one of the numbers that is stored in the array.

Environment.   See *Calling environment.*

EOF.   An acronym for **End Of File**.

Error output.   A file that a program can send output to. Usually, this file is reserved for error messages. Unless you instruct the Shell otherwise, it directs this output to the terminal.

Exit status.   The status returned by a process; either successful (usually 0) or unsuccessful (1).

Expression.   See *Logical expression* and *Arithmetic expression.*

File.   A collection of related information, referred to by a filename. The UNIX system views peripheral devices as files, allowing a program to read from or write to a device, just as it would read from or write to a file.

Filename.   The name of a file. You use a filename to refer to a file.

Filename extension.   The part of a filename following a period.

Footer.   The part of a format that goes at the bottom (or foot) of a page.

Foreground process.   When a program is run in the foreground, it is attached to the terminal. You must wait for a foreground process to run to completion before you can give the Shell another command. See *Background process.*

Fork. To create a process. When one process creates another process, it forks a process.

Header. The part of a format that goes at the top (or head) or a page.

Hexadecimal number. A base 16 number. Hexadecimal numbers are composed of the hexadecimal digits 0-9 and A-F. Refer to the following table.

Decimal	Hex	Decimal	Hex
1	1	14	E
2	2	15	F
3	3	16	10
4	4	17	11
5	5	20	14
6	6	31	1F
7	7	32	20
8	8	33	21
9	9	64	40
10	A	96	60
11	B	100	64
12	C	128	80
13	D	256	100

Home directory. The directory that is the working directory when you first log on. The pathname of this directory is stored in the **PATH** (Bourne Shell) or **path** (C Shell) variable.

Indention. When speaking of text, the blank space between the margin and the beginning of a line that is set in from the margin.

Inode. A part of the directory structure that contains information about a file.

Input. Information that is fed to a program from a terminal or other file.

Installation. A computer at a specific location. Some aspects of the UNIX system are installation dependent.

Invisible file. A file whose filename starts with a period. These files are called invisible because the ls utility does not normally list them. Use the **−a** option of ls to list all files, including invisible ones.

I/O device. Short for *input/output device*. See *Peripheral device.*

Justify. To expand a line of type to the right margin. A line is justified by increasing the space between words and sometimes between letters on the line.

Kernel. The heart of the UNIX operating system. The kernel is the part of the operating system that allocates resources and controls processes. The design strategy has been to keep the kernel as small as possible and to put the rest of the UNIX operating system into separately compiled and executed programs.

Leaf. In a tree structure, the end of a branch that cannot support other branches. See *Node.*

Log off. To stop using a terminal on a UNIX system so that another user can log on.

Log on. To gain access to a UNIX system by responding correctly to the login: and password: prompts.

Logical expression. A collection of strings separated by logical operators (>, >=, =, <=, and <) that can be evaluated as true or false.

Login name. The name you enter in response to the login: prompt. Other users use your login name when they send you mail or write to you.

Login Shell. The Shell that you are using when you first log on. The login Shell can fork other processes that can run other Shells.

Machine collating sequence. The sequence that the computer orders characters in. The machine collating sequence affects the outcome of sorts and other procedures that put lists in alphabetical order. Many computers use ASCII.

Macro. A single instruction that a program replaces by several (usually more complex) instructions. A C Shell Alias is a macro.

Main memory. Random access memory that is an integral part of the computer. As contrasted with disk storage. Although disk storage is sometimes referred to as memory, it is never referred to as main memory.

Major device number. A number assigned to a class of devices, such as terminals, printers, or disk drives. Using the ls utility with the −l option to list the contents of the /dev directory displays the major and minor device numbers of many devices (as major:minor).

Merge.   To combine two ordered lists so that the resulting list is still in order.

Minor device number.   A number assigned to a specific device within a class of devices. See *Major device number.*

Mount.   To mount a file system is to make it accessible to system users. When a file system is not mounted, you cannot read from it or write to it.

Node.   In a tree structure, the end of a branch that can support other branches. See *Leaf.*

Nonprintable character.   See CONTROL *character.* Also, *nonprinting character.*

Null string.   A string that could contain characters but doesn't.

Octal number.   A base 8 number. Octal numbers are composed of the digits 0-7 inclusive.

Output.   Information that a program sends to the terminal or other file.

Partition.   See *Disk slice.*

Pathname.   A list of directories, separated by slashes (/). A pathname is used to trace a path through the file structure to locate or identify a file.

Pathname element.   One of the filenames that form a pathname.

Pathname, last element of a.   The part of a pathname following the final / or the whole filename if there is no /. A simple filename.

Peripheral device.   A disk drive, printer, terminal, plotter, or other input/output unit that can be attached to the computer.

Physical device.   A device, such as a disk drive, that is physically—as well as logically—separate from other similar devices.

PID.   This acronym stands for **P**rocess **ID**entification and is usually followed by the word *number.* The UNIX system assigns a unique PID number to each process when it is initiated.

Pipe. A connection between two programs such that the standard output of one is connected to the standard input of the other. Also, *pipeline.*

Plain file. A file that is used to store a program, text, or other user data. See *Directory file* and *Device file.*

Printable character. One of the graphics characters: a letter, number, or punctuation mark. As contrasted with a nonprintable or CONTROL character. Also, *printing character.*

Process. The UNIX system execution of a program.

Prompt. A cue from a program, usually displayed on the terminal, indicating that it is waiting for input.

Quote. When you quote a character, you take away any special meaning that it has. You can quote a character by preceding it with a backslash or surrounding it with single quotation marks. For example, the Shell expands * into a list of the files in the working directory. The command **echo *** displays a list of these files. The command **echo *** or **echo '*'** displays *.

Recursive routine. A program or subroutine that calls itself, either directly or indirectly.

Redirection. The process of directing the standard input for a program to come from a file other than the terminal or directing the standard output to go to a file other than the terminal.

Regular character. A character that always represents itself. See *Special character.*

Regular expression. A string—composed of letters, numbers, and special symbols—that defines one or more strings. See the Appendix.

Relative pathname. A pathname that starts from the working directory. See *Absolute pathname.*

Restricted Shell. A Shell that provides a controlled environment for a user. The environment does not allow a user to change directories with cd, change the value of the **PATH** Shell variable, specify pathnames other than simple pathnames, or redirect output.

Return code. See *Exit status.*

Root directory.   The ancestor of all directories and the start of all absolute pathnames.

Root file system.   The file system that is always available when the system is brought up in single-user mode. The name of this file system is always /. You cannot unmount or mount the root file system.

Run level.   The run level describes the state of the operating system. A run level of 2 usually indicates the system is running multiuser, while 1 (or sometimes 6) indicates single-user mode.

Scroll.   To move lines on a terminal up or down one line at a time.

Session.   As used in this book, the sequence of events between when you start using a program such as an editor and when you finish, or between when you log on and the next time you log off.

Shell.   The UNIX system command processor.

Shell script.   A program composed of Shell commands. Also, *Shell program.*

Signal.   A very brief message that the UNIX system can send to a process, apart from the process' standard input.

Simple filename.   A single filename, containing no slashes (/). A simple filename is the simplest form of a pathname. Also, the last element of a pathname.

Sort.   To put in a specified order, usually alphabetic or numeric.

SPACE character.   A character that appears as the absence of a visible character. Even though you cannot see it, a SPACE is a printable character. It is represented by the ASCII code 32 (decimal).

Spawn.   See *Fork.*

Special character.   A character that does not represent itself unless it is quoted. Special characters for the Shell include the * and ? ambiguous file references.

Special file.   See *Device file.*

Spool.   To place items in a queue, each waiting its turn for some action. Often used when speaking about the lp utility and the printer: lp spools files for the printer.

Square bracket. There is a left square bracket ([ ) and a right square bracket ( ]).

Standard input. A file that a program can receive input from. Unless you instruct the Shell otherwise, it directs this input so that it comes from the terminal. See Chapter 4.

Standard output. A file to which a program can send output. Unless you instruct the Shell otherwise, it directs this output to the terminal. See Chapter 4.

Status line. The bottom (usually the 24th) line of the terminal.

Sticky bit. An access permission bit that causes an executable program to remain on the swap area of the disk. It takes less time to load a program that has its sticky bit set than one that doesn't.

String. A sequence of characters.

Subdirectory. A directory that is located within another directory.

Superuser. A privileged user who has access to anything any other system user has access to and more. The system administrator must be able to become a Superuser in order to establish new accounts, change passwords, and perform other administrative tasks.

Swap. To move a process from memory to a disk or vice versa. Swapping a process to the disk allows another process to begin or continue execution.

System administrator. The person who is responsible for the upkeep of the system.

System console. See *Console terminal.*

Termcap. An abbreviation of **term**inal **cap**ability. The **termcap** file contains a list of various types of terminals and their characteristics. System V replaced the function of this file with the Terminfo directory.

Terminfo. An abbreviation of **term**inal **info**rmation. The **/usr/lib/terminfo** directory contains many subdirectories, each containing several files. Each of these files is named for, and contains a summary of the functional characteristics of, a particular terminal. Visually oriented programs, such as vi, make use of these files.

Tty.   A terminal. Tty is an abbreviation of **teletypewriter**.

User ID.   A number that the **/etc/passwd** file associates with a login name.

Variable.   A name and an associated value used in a program such as a Shell script.

White space.   A collective name for SPACEs and/or TABs.

Work Buffer.   A location where ed and vi store text while it is being edited.

Working directory.   The directory that you are associated with at any given time. The relative pathnames you use are built on the working directory.

INDEX

Nonalphabetic Characters

. command 212
. directory entry 60, 304
.. directory entry 60, 304
.cshrc file 246, 247, 268, 289
.exrc file 125
.login file 28, 58, 268, 289, 299
.logout file 269
.profile file 27, 58, 268, 284, 285, 289, 298

\ character 35
[ ] character class 95
* ambiguous file reference 94
| pipe symbol 87, 90, 217
< redirect input symbol 84
> redirect output symbol 81
` command substitution symbol 213
~ character 267

key 18, 26, 30
#argv variable 263
$ prompt 20, 22
$, use with variables 196
$! variable 208
$# variable 199
$$ variable 207, 214, 265
$0 variable 214, 298
$? variable 209
$* variable 198

% prompt 20, 22
& background process 91, 207, 217
>> append output 87
? ambiguous file reference 92
@ command 256, 277
@ key 19, 26, 30

/ directory 55, 64
/.profile file 284
/bin directory 65
/dev directory
  about 65, 79, 304
  null file 299
  syscon device file 287, 290
/etc directory
  about 65, 283
  checklist file 287, 292
  gettydefs file 284, 288, 292
  group file 294
  inittab file 284, 286, 288, 290, 295, 315
  mnttab file 296, 309
  motd file 289, 296, 321
  passwd file 246, 284, 289, 296
  profile file 284, 285, 289, 298
  rc file 286, 288, 292, 299
  shutdown file 290, 299
/lost+found directory 292, 300
/tmp directory 65, 319
/unix file 286, 300
/usr directory
  /usr/lib/spell/spellhist file 319
  about 64
  adm directory 319
  mail directory 319
  news directory 300, 319
  spool directory 319
  tmp directory 319
/usr/bin directory 65

A

Aborting execution 26
Absolute pathname 56, 551
Access 551

563

V